Restorative Justice and
Violence Against Women

INTERPERSONAL$\mathcal{V}$IOLENCE

Series Editors

Claire Renzetti, Ph.D.

Jeffrey L. Edleson, Ph.D.

RESTORATIVE JUSTICE AND VIOLENCE AGAINST WOMEN

Edited by
James Ptacek

OXFORD
UNIVERSITY PRESS

2010

OXFORD
UNIVERSITY PRESS

Oxford University Press, Inc., publishes works that further
Oxford University's objective of excellence
in research, scholarship, and education.

Oxford   New York
Auckland   Cape Town   Dar es Salaam   Hong Kong   Karachi
Kuala Lumpur   Madrid   Melbourne   Mexico City   Nairobi
New Delhi   Shanghai   Taipei   Toronto

With offices in
Argentina   Austria   Brazil   Chile   Czech Republic   France   Greece
Guatemala   Hungary   Italy   Japan   Poland   Portugal   Singapore
South Korea   Switzerland   Thailand   Turkey   Ukraine   Vietnam

Published by Oxford University Press, Inc.
198 Madison Avenue, New York, New York 10016

www.oup.com

Library of Congress Cataloging-in-Publication Data
Restorative justice and violence against women / edited by James Ptacek.
p.   cm. — (Interpersonal violence)
Includes bibliographical references and index.
ISBN 978-0-19-533548-4
1. Women—Violence against.   2. Abused women.   3. Restorative justice.
I. Ptacek, James.
HV6250.4.W65R465 2010
364.6′8—dc22
2009016950

1   3   5   7   9   8   6   4   2

Printed in the United States of America
on acid-free paper

To my son,
Alex Ptacek Zimmer

CONTENTS

EDITOR'S INTRODUCTION

James Ptacek

We need to create new ways for abused women to find justice. Despite significant accomplishments by the feminist antiviolence movement over the past 35 years, community activists know well that justice is out of reach for most victims. Seeking ways to expand options for women and increase accountability for violent men, the contributors to this book have examined both the dangers and potential benefits of using restorative justice to address crimes against women. Feminism and restorative justice are both strong, global social movements that see violence against women as a problem; each movement, however, has a unique view on how this problem can be best resolved.

The informal mediation practices referred to as "restorative justice" (RJ) seek to decrease the role of the state in responding to crime and increase the involvement of personal, familial, and community networks in repairing the harm caused by crime. In the many parts of the world where it is practiced, RJ is most commonly applied to youth crimes. However, in many areas, RJ is prohibited from being used for crimes against women. Nevertheless, there is increasing use of these practices to address intimate violence, rape, and child sexual abuse. This has created deep concerns among feminist antiviolence activists, especially because very little research supports using RJ in these cases. Conflicts have occurred between the feminist and RJ movements over this topic in Canada, New Zealand, Australia, the United States, and many other countries.

Restorative Justice and Violence Against Women faces this growing controversy by gathering together feminist scholars and activists who offer a range of different perspectives on RJ. The contributors to this book have done extensive work on the problem of violence against women. Some are strongly in favor of using restorative practices in cases of violence against women, some are strongly opposed, and the opinions of many lie somewhere in between.

This book poses challenges both for the RJ movement and for feminism. Restorative practitioners have much to learn from feminists about the consequences of victimization and the dangers of "one size fits all" interventions. At the same time, feminist activists—who understand too well the limitations of the criminal legal system—have much to learn from restorative practitioners. Restorative justice proposes powerful ideas about expanding the options for victims of violence. This book is designed to advance a dialogue between these two social movements, and to convince people working in each that they have much to learn from one another.

ABOUT THE BOOK

This collection offers perspectives from scholars and community activists in the United States, Australia, Canada, and New Zealand. The topics address woman battering, rape, the physical and sexual abuse of children, and youth violence against mothers. A number of the chapters address how racism poses problems for addressing violence, both for feminists and RJ practitioners.

Overview: Restorative Justice and Feminist Activism

Chapter 1 outlines the central arguments in the book. In this chapter, I describe how the U.S. criminal legal system "co-opts" or undermines feminist activism, and how feminists are responding. Feminist-designed restorative practices represent one way that activists are resisting this co-optation. This introductory chapter places restorative approaches within the context of other feminist innovations in community organizing, including work concerning violence against women of color.

Critical Perspectives on Restorative Justice in Cases of Violence Against Women

This section identifies a number of feminist concerns about RJ. In Chapter 2, Loretta Frederick and Kristine C. Lizdas offer a thoughtful critique of restorative justice that nonetheless finds its basic principles laudable. The authors draw parallels between the goals of RJ and the battered women's movement. They conclude with a discussion of the shortcomings of not just restorative justice, but of the criminal legal system and feminist antiviolence organizing as well. Frederick and Lizdas are attorneys with the Battered Women's Justice Project in the United States.

In Chapter 3, Canadian legal scholar Rashmi Goel examines how sentencing circles in Canada are failing to meet the needs of Aboriginal women. Sentencing circles are a type of restorative practice used in Canada and in Native American communities in the United States. Goel traces how dynamics of race and gender operate at cross purposes to complicate the ability of these practices to deliver safety and justice to Aboriginal victims of domestic violence.

Pamela Rubin gives a rich description of a conflict between feminists and the Canadian government in Chapter 4. Faced with a new initiative by the Nova Scotia Department of Justice to apply RJ to cases of sexual assault and intimate partner violence, women's groups mobilized to secure a moratorium on this initiative and to establish a more inclusive process for developing justice policies on crimes against women. Rubin is the coordinator of the Women's Innovative Justice Initiative in Nova Scotia.

Julie Stubbs, an Australian law professor, has been a critic of restorative practices as they have been implemented in Australia and New Zealand. In Chapter 5, Stubbs reviews the current research on restorative practices and what they offer to victims of gendered violence. Her chapter includes a discussion of Indigenous justice and Indigenous views of restorative justice.

Heather Nancarrow interviewed members of two Australian task forces on violence against women that came up with conflicting perspectives on the usefulness of RJ. One was an Indigenous women's task force; the other was made up largely of non-Indigenous women. The Indigenous women's task force issued a report stating that restorative processes empower Indigenous peoples and facilitate community involvement in preventing crime. In contrast, the non-Indigenous women's task force recommended that restorative practices should never replace criminal prosecution for violence against women. Nancarrow's research in Chapter 6 seeks to make sense of these competing positions. Nancarrow is the Director of the Queensland Centre for Domestic and Family Violence Research.

In Chapter 7, Kathleen Daly and Heather Nancarrow present an examination of youth violence against mothers in Australia. This kind of violence has barely been named, let alone researched in the United States. Daly and Nancarrow offer an in-depth analysis of three cases of violence against mothers that were processed through youth conferences, a kind of RJ commonly used in Australia and New Zealand. They analyze the experience of victims, the dynamics of the offenses, and how conference coordinators viewed the cases before, during, and after the conference. Since the dynamics in these youth-offender cases are similar to those for adult offenders, they illustrate the strengths and limitations of restorative practices in cases of gendered violence. Kathleen Daly is the Director of the Gender, Race, and Justice Research Program at Griffith University in Australia.

From Critique to New Possibilities: Innovative Feminist Projects

This section contains descriptions of new antiviolence interventions that either explicitly use RJ or that use similar kinds of methods for achieving justice.

Joan Pennell is a professor of social work who founded the first shelter for battered women and their children in Newfoundland, Canada. Working with her colleague Gale Burford, she developed the Family Group Decision Making project to deal with battering and child abuse in Newfoundland and Labrador. Now living in North Carolina, Pennell has developed a new restorative approach to domestic violence called "safety conferencing." Chapter 8 is co-written by Joan Pennell and Mimi Kim. Kim is a social worker with 15 years of experience working on domestic violence and sexual assault, including work with the Asian and Pacific Islander Institute in the United States. Their chapter is a dialogue about their two different approaches to stopping violence against women and children.

In Chapter 9, Mimi Kim presents her innovative project, Creative Interventions. This project seeks to create community-level antiviolence interventions that mobilize women's immediate social networks. This chapter locates this project within the context of RJ and other new antiviolence projects being developed by radical organizations such as Incite! Women of Color Against Violence and Critical Resistance. Kim will discuss how these radical organizations have created a growing political space in which antiviolence and anti–prison-industrial-complex activists are challenging both state-sponsored and interpersonal forms of gender-based violence.

Psychologist Mary Koss is the author of more than 200 publications on sexual assault. She developed a pilot RJ project for sexual assault cases in Arizona called RESTORE: Justice that Heals. In Chapter 10, Koss describes this innovative, feminist-designed restorative approach to rape. She explains, in rich detail, how this program was designed to meet the needs of survivors, needs largely neglected by the existing criminal legal system.

Shirley Jülich, a researcher at the Auckland University of Technology, has studied child sexual abuse in New Zealand. Drawing from her research on survivors' views of justice, in Chapter 11 Jülich examines a new restorative project in New Zealand, Project Restore. This project, inspired by Mary Koss' program, was initiated by adult survivors of child sexual abuse. Project Restore-NZ seeks to overcome the shortcomings of the traditional legal system and provide survivors with a sense of justice.

Andrea Smith is a Cherokee feminist, human rights activist, and Assistant Professor of Media and Cultural Studies at the University of California, Riverside. She coordinated the 2000 Color of Violence: Violence Against Women of Color conference in Santa Cruz, California, and co-founded the national organization that arose from this conference, Incite! Women of Color Against Violence. In Chapter 12, Smith examines the politics of RJ and outlines a number of new antiviolence strategies developed by women of color.

Conclusion

In the final chapter, I draw out common themes and questions raised by the contributors and offer recommendations for future antiviolence work.

This book contains passionate arguments, insightful criticism, innovative approaches, and messy, practical details about what justice practices really look like. It is my hope that this animated collection will spark new conversations about how to meet the needs of survivors.

ACKNOWLEDGMENTS

I want to thank the contributors to the book for their inspirational work and their generous spirit. This book grew out of lively conversations over many years with activists, scholars, and practitioners. In addition to the contributors, I must acknowledge Donna Coker, Kay Pranis, Gale Burford, Quince Hopkins, Ted German, Fernando Mederos, Michele Bograd, Tom Denton, Kersti Yllö, Madeline Adelman, Sally Engle Merry, Sharene Razack, and Mindie Lazarus-Black. I had rich exchanges with Mary Lauby, Debra Robbin, and Craig Norberg-Bohm at the Massachusetts Coalition Against Sexual Assault and Domestic Violence; with Lisa Hartwick and Peggy Barrett at the Boston Area Rape Crisis Center; and with Juan Carlos Areán and Lonna Davis at the Family Violence Prevention Fund.

I am further grateful for the encouragement of my colleagues at Suffolk University, especially Carolyn Boyes-Watson, Lynda Field, Michèle Plott, Amy Agigian, Susan Sered, Felicia Wiltz, Erika Gebo, and the late Sharon Kurtz. Maura Roessner and Mallory Jensen at Oxford University Press were wonderful to work with at every stage of the process.

Special thanks go to Judith Herman, Kathleen Ferraro, Raquel Kennedy Bergen, Walter DeKeseredy, Jeff Edleson, Kim Cook, Susan Ostrander, and Kendall Dudley for their support of this project. Claire Renzetti has been so good to me I don't know where to begin!

My greatest thanks go to my life partner Bonnie Zimmer, who founded and directed a domestic violence advocacy program. I draw tremendous inspiration from her. I have also learned much from her remarkable advocates, and from the women her program has served.

BIOGRAPHICAL NOTES

ABOUT THE EDITOR

James Ptacek has been working on issues of violence against women in the United States since 1981. He has been a batterers' counselor and has conducted training on domestic violence intervention for hospital, mental health, and criminal justice professionals. He has done research on men who batter; on rape and battering on college campuses, and on battered women's experience with the courts. His new research focuses on the social class dimensions of intimate violence. Jim was guest editor of a special issue of *Violence Against Women* on "Feminism, Restorative Justice, and Violence Against Women" (May 2005;11[5]). He is an Associate Professor of Sociology at Suffolk University in Boston, where he is also on the faculty of the Master's Program in Crime and Justice Studies and the Master's Program in Women's Health.

ABOUT THE CONTRIBUTORS

Kathleen Daly is Professor of Criminology and Criminal Justice, Griffith University (Brisbane). She writes on gender, race, crime, and justice; and on restorative and Indigenous justice. From 1998 to 2006, she received three Australian Research Council (ARC) grants to direct a program of research on the race and gender politics of "new justice" practices. She has launched an international project on innovative responses to sexual violence, also funded by the ARC (2008–2011). In addition to six books or edited collections, she has published over 60 articles in journals, edited collections, and law reviews. She was president of the Australian and New Zealand Society of Criminology from 2005–2009, and is a fellow of the Academy of the Social Sciences in Australia.

Loretta Frederick, J.D., is senior legal and policy advisor of the Battered Women's Justice Project, a national resource center in the United States on domestic violence criminal and civil legal issues. Since 1978 she has done training and consultation on domestic violence legal issues with judges, advocates, attorneys, prosecutors, and law enforcement officers in the United States and internationally. Loretta serves as faculty for the National Judicial Institutes on Domestic Violence and was a consultant for the U.S. Marine Corps on the development of its Coordinated Community Response to domestic violence. Her work with the Minnesota State Bar Association has included her current role as chair of the Domestic Abuse Committee as well as a past term as chair of the Family Law Section.

Rashmi Goel was born and raised in Canada. She is currently an assistant professor in the Sturm College of Law at the University of Denver in Colorado, where she teaches criminal law, comparative law, and a seminar entitled Multiculturalism, Race and the Law. Her research focuses on culturally specific adjudication and its manifestations in a number of legal arenas, including family law, international and comparative law, and criminal law. Professor Goel's work addresses the cultural constraints surrounding domestic violence and RJ, and examines the political context for Aboriginal peoples in which these reforms must operate or fail. Outside the law school, Professor Goel puts her knowledge in these areas to work in Colorado and California, helping to establish dispute-resolution mechanisms for high school students.

Shirley Jülich is a senior lecturer in the Centre for Business Interdisciplinary Studies and the program leader for restorative justice at AUT University, Auckland, New Zealand. Her Ph.D. investigated the complex relationship between the criminal justice system, RJ, and child sexual abuse from the perspective of adult survivors of child sexual abuse. Shirley is a founding member of Project Restore, a program that aims to address gendered violence by using RJ processes. Her research interests focus on the intersection of gendered violence, recovery, and justice, including the economic consequences of this relationship for victims, offenders, their families, and the broader society.

Mimi Kim is a long-time antiviolence advocate who has worked primarily in Asian communities. She is a steering committee member of the Asian and Pacific Islander Domestic Violence Institute, a national resource center in the United States. Mimi is also a founding member of Incite! Women of Color Against Violence, where she has been working collectively with women of color nationally and internationally to create community-based solutions to violence. Mimi continues her domestic violence advocacy as the founder and executive director of Creative Interventions, an Oakland, California-based resource center supporting community-based interventions to domestic violence and other forms of intimate violence. She is also a program consultant for Shimtuh: Korean Domestic Violence Program, an Oakland-based program that she co-founded in 2000. Mimi is currently a Ph.D. candidate in the Department of Social Welfare at University of California, Berkeley.

Mary P. Koss is a Regents' Professor in the Mel and Enid Zuckerman Arizona College of Public Health in Tucson, Arizona and founder of the RESTORE and the Safety Connections programs. Professor Koss has worked in the field of violence against women for more than 30 years. She served on the National Academy of Sciences Panel on Violence Against Women and currently co-chairs the American Psychological Association Presidential Initiative on Violence Against Women and Children. She has twice testified before the U.S. Senate on matters relating to sexual violence surveillance and sexual assault in the military. She is past co-chair and current member of the Coordinating Committee of the Sexual Violence Research Initiative, funded by the Global Forum and the Ford Foundation and based in Pretoria, South Africa. She coordinates the Sexual Violence Applied Research Group of VAWnet.org, the Centers for Disease Control (CDC)-funded national online research resource on sexual and physical violence.

Kristine C. Lizdas serves as staff attorney for the Battered Women's Justice Project (BWJP), a national resource center on domestic violence legal issues in the United States. Kristine researches and monitors legal and policy development in the field of domestic violence. She specializes in such areas as law enforcement policy and practice, firearms, dedicated domestic violence courts, interagency data-sharing, custody law, and RJ. Prior to joining BWJP in 1999, Kristine spent several years with the Duluth Domestic Abuse Intervention Project (DAIP) as a community organizer, co-writing the Duluth Domestic Violence Safety and Offender Accountability Audit manual, and piloting the Safety Audit through several projects. Kristine has trained for and provided consultation to a variety of local, state, and national organizations, governmental agencies, and academic institutions.

Heather Nancarrow, MA (Hons) is the director of the Queensland Centre for Domestic and Family Violence Research, Central Queensland University, Australia. She has more than 25 years of experience in the field of domestic violence prevention, including roles in community-based women's refuges and government policy and legislative administration. Heather's research interests include justice responses to Indigenous family violence, the utility of RJ for cases of domestic and family violence, dating violence, and the associations between spousal domestic violence and child abuse.

Joan Pennell, MSW, Ph.D., is professor and head, Department of Social Work, North Carolina State University. She is the principal investigator of the North Carolina Family-Centered Meetings Project, which receives funding for work in child welfare and schools. Through the American Humane Association, she is serving on an international team reviewing research on family group decision making. She previously directed the North Carolina Family Group Conferencing Project. Before her return to the United States, she was a principal investigator (with Gale Burford) for a Newfoundland and Labrador, Canada, demonstration of family group conferencing in situations of child maltreatment and domestic violence. She helped to found the first shelter for abused women and their children in Newfoundland. She has co-facilitated support groups for abused women of European and Aboriginal descent.

Pamela Rubin, LL.B., is based in Halifax, Nova Scotia, where she coordinates research and policy initiatives focusing on women's safety and equality. Ms. Rubin leads collaborative, community-based research in Nova Scotia to support more effective responses to violence against women. Her work has emphasized the prevention of revictimization in the justice and social service systems. She also contributes to the field of gender-impact analysis and has designed and conducted innovative, narrative evaluations of family mediation programs for Justice Canada and the governments of Nunavut, Newfoundland, and Labrador. Ms. Rubin has taught women's studies and criminology at Saint Mary's University and Mount Saint Vincent University in Halifax. Ms. Rubin is the coordinator of the Women's Innovative Justice Initiative, a research and policy group comprised of Nova Scotia equality-seeking women's organizations, and partners in the Family Law Information Project for Abused Women, a project of Status of Women Canada.

Andrea Smith (Cherokee) is a long-time antiviolence and Native American activist and scholar. She is co-founder of Incite! Women of Color Against Violence, a national grassroots organization that utilizes direct action and critical dialogue. Andrea began her advocacy work as a rape crisis counselor with Chicago Women of All Red Nations. She coordinated the Native Women and Sexual Assault Research project for Amnesty International, and is the author of *Conquest: Sexual Violence And American Indian Genocide* (South End Press, 2005). She holds a B.A. from Harvard University in comparative study of religion, a Masters of Divinity from the Union Theological Institute, and a Ph.D. from the University of California, Santa Cruz, in the history of consciousness. She is currently an Assistant Professor of Media and Cultural Studies at the University of California, Riverside.

Julie Stubbs is Professor of Criminology in the Faculty of Law, University of Sydney. Her research focuses on violence against women, including domestic violence law reforms, battered women's syndrome, women as victims and offenders in homicide matters, post-separation violence, sexual assault, and RJ. She has worked with the New South Wales (NSW) Bureau of Crime Statistics and Research as senior research officer and was for a time acting deputy director. She has worked as a consultant to Legal Aid, the Office of the Status of Women, the NSW Police Service, the NSW Bureau of Crime Statistics and Research, the Australian Law Reform Commission, the Royal Commission into the NSW Police Service, and the Australian Institute of Judicial Administration.

Restorative Justice and
Violence Against Women

I

OVERVIEW
Restorative Justice and
Feminist Activism

1

RESISTING CO-OPTATION
Three Feminist Challenges to Antiviolence Work

JAMES PTACEK

According to research reports from around the world, violence against women is horribly common and profoundly consequential. Together, physical and sexual abuse contribute to poor physical and reproductive health in women, suicidality, drug and alcohol abuse, depression, posttraumatic stress, poverty and hunger, and mortality both in women and their children. Intimate violence undermines women's economic livelihood, women's participation in public life, and women's involvement in politics. Violence against women and girls is a major dimension of gender inequality worldwide (UN Secretary-General 2006; Walby 2005). In the United States, feminist organizing has produced dramatic changes in how abused women are treated by the law, hospitals, mental health professionals, and organized religion.

Decreases in the rates of violence against women in the United States have occurred in recent years (Bureau of Justice Statistics 2006; Catalano 2006). But since this trend has been part of a broad decrease in all types of crime (Finkelhor and Jones 2008; Zimring 2007), it is difficult to assess the impact made by these institutional changes. What is clear is that the majority of women victimized by rape and intimate partner violence in the United States will not contact the police (Tjaden and Thoennes 2000). Attempts to increase prosecution and conviction rates for rape over several decades are generally regarded as failures (Seidman and Vickers 2005; Spohn and Horney 1992, 1996). And responses to domestic violence by the criminal legal system are increasingly being criticized as inflexible and unresponsive to the needs of the most vulnerable women (Dasgupta 2003; Goodman and Epstein 2008).

Violence that specifically targets women of color and immigrant women in the United States, such as "enforcement violence" committed by the police, correction officials, and immigration officers, is rarely given public attention (Bhattacharjee 2001; Richie 2006). Further, at a time when the United States is at war, many forms of abuse are kept out of the public spotlight, such as the violence suffered by Iraqi and Afghani women, the victimization of women within the U.S. military, and militarized prostitution.

Going back as far as the late nineteenth century in the United States and Great Britain, feminists have confronted state indifference to crimes against women. But alongside the history of how feminism has transformed state responses is the story of how the state has sought to co-opt feminist activism. "Co-opt" is a rich word. Dictionaries offer a number of synonyms for co-opt: absorb, assimilate, take over, appropriate. How is feminist antiviolence activism being absorbed, assimilated, taken over, and appropriated by the state? I would add other synonyms, as well: neutralize, depoliticize, distort, displace, dominate, transform, undermine, subvert. How is feminism affected by conservative state agendas in these ways? In recent years, there has been much reflection about whether feminism is relying too heavily on the criminal legal system to stop violence; about how, in the process, the state is blurring feminist visions of justice; and about what new forms of social action must be developed.

A number of feminists working against violence have been examining the conflict-resolution approaches loosely grouped under the rubric of "restorative justice" (RJ). Arising from a variety of different sites around the world, RJ is a social movement that seeks to transform how communities respond to crime. Most restorative practices are concerned with youth crimes. But is it possible that within these informal practices there are new ideas for feminists about supporting victims, holding offenders accountable, and addressing the harm that violence does to communities?

This book focuses on feminist perspectives on RJ. But RJ is not the only new idea about antiviolence work explored here; to make sense of the controversy surrounding RJ among feminists, I contrast RJ with other recent feminist innovations. This exploration reveals points of controversy as well as points of convergence between feminism and RJ.

My observations are informed by over 25 years of work on the problem of violence against women. This includes work as a batterers' counselor and as a researcher, teacher, and trainer of heathcare, social service, and legal professionals. But while I have been an active participant in the feminist movement against violence, I nonetheless have profound limitations as an observer of feminist organizing. Some are obvious: I'm a straight, white, professional-managerial-class man (with U.S. citizenship). Among the many ways that this social location affects my insights, however, is one perhaps less obvious: I have no personal experience of terror.

I take these limitations seriously, as should the reader. And yet, because feminist visions of justice have inspired such profound social change over the past 30 years, I am moved to explore these innovations in antiviolence work. Each one challenges activists to rethink what justice might look like for abused women and how this can be accomplished. My goal is to facilitate the cross-fertilization of these community-organizing strategies, in the hope they will inspire new visions of justice.

WHAT IS RESTORATIVE JUSTICE?

Historical Background

The recent development of what is now called "restorative justice" is a consequence of social movements for civil rights and women's rights. According to Daly and Immarigeon (1998), during the 1960s and 1970s challenges were made to racist practices in policing, in the courts, and in prisons in the United States. This organizing, which included campaigns for prisoners' rights and Native American rights, was mirrored by anti-colonial movements in New Zealand, Australia, Canada, and South Africa. In the 1970s, feminist campaigns countering violence against women highlighted how the legal system mistreated victims. In the wake of these social movements, new thinking arose around alternatives to prisons, methods of conflict resolution, and victim advocacy. Legal scholars began writing about "informal justice" and "community justice." Some have traced the roots of this "new thinking" about dispute resolution to ancient methods of justice found in the traditions of Judaism, Christianity, and Islam (Barrett and Barrett 2004).

Several different forms of mediation evolved in the 1970s and 1980s, not all of which are currently classified as RJ. In *community mediation* (also called alternative dispute resolution), trained mediators address community conflicts between landlords and tenants, businesses and consumers, management and labor, and even universities and students. Interpersonal conflicts, including cases of intimate partner violence, are also dealt with in community mediation centers. Feminist legal scholars and activists have criticized the use of community mediation in cases of intimate violence (Lerman 1984; Lerman, Keuhl, and Brygger 1989; Rowe 1985). But community mediation, which continues to operate in the United States, Canada, and elsewhere is not generally viewed as RJ. Proponents of RJ argue that community mediation deals largely with civil as opposed to criminal matters, and is settlement-driven, meaning that it prioritizes reaching an agreement—often too quickly—over discussing the broader impact of the conflict on the people involved. In contrast, those forms of mediation that have come to be called RJ are seen as "dialogue-driven" (Umbreit and Greenwood 2000:2).

Faith-based victim–offender reconciliation programs were the first to use the term "restorative justice." In this form of mediation, the focus is on repairing the harm caused by crime and a bringing about reconciliation between victims and offenders through face-to-face interaction. The first program was created by Mark Yantzi in Kitchener, Ontario in 1974. Yantzi was a probation officer working with the Mennonite Central Committee, a Christian organization with a tradition of working on peace and justice issues. Confronted with two teenagers who had vandalized a number of homes, two churches, and a business during a night of drinking, Yantzi had a suggestion: "Wouldn't it be neat for these offenders to meet the victims?" (Peachey 2003:178). The young offenders met with the victims of their crimes and took responsibility for their actions. They were fined, placed on probation, and ordered to make restitution to all they had harmed. The Mennonite Central Committee, encouraged by this case, created victim–offender reconciliation programs in Canada and the United States. The major principles of restorative justice were developed out of these programs (Zehr 1990). But in the 1990s, victim advocates criticized the focus on reconciliation and forgiveness. Others resisted the religious elements of this approach (McCold 2006).

Victim–Offender Mediation, Conferences, and Circles

A number of different models are housed within the concept of RJ. But all of them promote dialogue as a way to meet the needs of victims, offenders, and communities affected by crime. Currently, the three most commonly identified practices of RJ are victim–offender mediation, family group conferencing, and peacemaking circles.

Victim–offender mediation arose as a more secular version of earlier faith-based victim–offender reconciliation programs (McCold 2006). Victim–offender mediation prioritizes face-to-face interactions between victims and offenders, under the guidance of trained mediators. Umbreit and Greenwood describe its unique features:

> Victim–offender mediation is primarily "dialogue-driven," with emphasis upon victim empowerment, offender accountability, and restoration of losses. Most VOM sessions (more than 90%) result in a signed restitution agreement. This agreement, however, is secondary to the importance of the initial dialogue between the parties. This dialogue addresses emotional and informational needs of victims that are central to both the empowerment of the victims and the development of victim empathy in the offenders, which can help to prevent criminal behavior in the future. (Umbreit and Greenwood 2000:2)

The logic of focusing the encounter only on the victim and the offender, with only minimal involvement by the mediator, is that a one-on-one interaction will enable offenders to accept responsibility for the harm. In this view, having police officers, parents, or other authority figures present would interfere with this process. Beginning in the United States and Canada in the early 1970s, victim–offender mediation programs have spread dramatically. According to the Victim Offender Mediation

Association (VOMA), there are 1200 programs around the world (VOMA 2005).

In the 1990s, *family group conferencing* became popular. Sometimes called *community conferencing* or simply *conferencing*, this began as a way to reduce the number of young Maori offenders held by the New Zealand legal system. Inspired by Maori traditions, family group conferencing involves a wider kind of meeting between victims, offenders, family members, and supporters under the guidance of a coordinator. Like victim–offender mediation, the goals are to hold offenders accountable, empower victims, and reach an agreement. But the logic of conferencing is that victims and offenders cannot do this alone. A police officer may present information on the offense. Those supporting the victim are invited to say how they were affected by the crime. Those supporting the offender, generally family members or friends, can help ensure the agreement is carried out.

Since 1991, all youth crimes in New Zealand except homicide are dealt with through family group conferences. Conferencing spread to Australia and North America in the 1990s and is being used 150 communities in the United States (Mirsky 2003).

Within many Indigenous communities in Canada and the United States *peacemaking circles* are used as forums for addressing crime and other community problems. Peacemaker Courts were formed by the Navajo Nation in the United States in 1982 to reassert a traditional form of problem solving within the Anglo justice system (Coker 1999). Circles became well-known in Canada after Barry Stuart, a white Yukon judge, recognized the circle as a legitimate sentencing practice in a 1992 legal decision (Goel, Chapter 3 in this volume; Stuart 1992). There are numerous variations on circles. Stuart, who has developed a model loosely drawn from Indigenous practices, describes circles for healing, circles for sentencing, and circles that are open to the entire community (Stuart 1997).

Applied most commonly to cases of youth crime, these approaches can be used to prevent a criminal case from going to trial, as part of sentencing or probation, as a form of dialogue while offenders are incarcerated, and as a planning forum after offenders are released. Restorative practices have become popular as a way to respond to crime and other harms that take place in schools (Braithwaite 2006).

Restorative approaches to crime have spread rapidly over the past two decades. Currently over 80 countries use restorative practices to address crime (Porter 2005). The United Nations (UN) has adopted the basic principles of RJ, and it encourages countries to implement them (Van Ness 2002). In 2006, the UN published a handbook on RJ programs around the world (Parker 2007).

Although restorative practices were not created to deal with crimes of violence against women, and are expressly prohibited from being used in such cases in many legal jurisdictions, they are nonetheless being applied to cases of violence between intimate partners (Edwards and Sharpe 2004; Goel 2000;, see Goel, Chapter 3 in this volume), youth violence against mothers (Daly and Nancarrow, Chapter 7 in this volume), rape (Daly 2002), and child sexual abuse (Bushie 1999; Yantzi 1998). Although extensive research has been done on restorative approaches to youth crime, there have been surprisingly few evaluations of restorative applications to crimes against women (Cheon and Regehr 2006; Edwards and Sharpe 2004; Stubbs, Chapter 5 in this volume). One review of research on the use of victim–offender mediation, conferencing, and circles in cases of violence against women was able to find only eight studies (Edwards and Sharpe 2004).

This has raised many concerns among feminists, as these crimes require different responses than do property crimes by young people. Conferences on RJ and violence against women have been held in Canada and Australia to address these issues (Coward 2000; Strang and Braithwaite 2002).

For some feminists, informal approaches to confronting violence hold great appeal, particularly in light of the limitations of the criminal legal system and the ways in which it has co-opted feminist visions of justice. However, whether restorative approaches, as they are currently configured, represent viable alternatives to the criminal legal system is a hotly contested topic among feminists.

Feminist interest in RJ arises in part out of resistance to co-optation. To underscore the different and even conflicting approaches to antiviolence work, I compare three different kinds of feminist organizing around violence: the Duluth Model of institutional advocacy; recent organizing across communities of color; and feminist projects that incorporate restorative practices. Each of these different approaches presents new challenges to previous ways of working against violence.

THE CO-OPTATION OF FEMINIST ANTIVIOLENCE ACTIVISM

Feminists have raised many concerns in recent years about the limitations of the criminal legal system as a means of stopping violence against women. And a rich and growing feminist literature details how the state has co-opted antiviolence efforts (Coker 2000, 2001; Crenshaw 1991; Daniels 1997; Danner 2000; Ferraro 1996; Gottschalk 2006; Incite! 2006, 2007a; McMahon and Pence 2003; Miccio 2005; Pence 2001). A two-day round-table discussion that gathered feminists from across the United States framed the questions in this manner:

> It is clear that the criminal legal system has been, and continues to be, a lifesaver for many battered women, including women of color. . . .
>
> Unfortunately, when state power intervenes, it often takes over. Many people who call for assistance end up having no say in the intervention once the legal system has entered into their lives. Heavy

investment in the criminal legal system has had a disproportionate negative impact on the lives of people of color, further decimating poor communities and communities of color.

What, then, is the appropriate role of the state and, in particular, the criminal legal system in preventing violence against women? Are we over-relying on the criminal legal system? Have we gone too far or not far enough in developing and utilizing legal strategies for addressing violence against women? Would a questioning of legal intervention turn back the clock to the "old days" when the state would not intervene at all in abuse of women within families and on the streets? (Dasgupta 2003:1–2)

The report of this roundtable discussion, hosted by the Ms. Foundation, identified a number of limitations in the criminal processing system. First, the report cited the research, mentioned earlier, that indicates most victims of intimate violence and sexual assault do not seek help from the police (Tjaden and Thoennes 2000, cited in Dasgupta 2003:1). Second, the report stated that crime policies addressing violence affect women from different groups in different ways, particularly with respect to racism, poverty, and immigration status. Whether the issue is mandatory arrest, legal advocacy, or domestic violence restraining orders, "the benefits and burdens of these policies are distributed unequally" (Dasgupta 2003:9). Third, the report argued that the criminal legal system is itself racist. "Racial bias permeates the legal and other state systems, with dispropor-tionately devastating effects on communities of color, poor, and immigrant peoples" (Dasgupta 2003:12). The report went so far as to reject the term "criminal justice system" entirely: "We use the term criminal legal system rather than criminal justice system in recognition that the system dispro-portionately singles out people of color for punishment and is therefore not a system of 'justice'" (Dasgupta 2003:6).[1]

The participants at this roundtable discussion highlighted the social costs of investing in the criminal legal system. They maintained that, at a time of massive incarceration of young men of color, poor men, African American men, and Latinos are disproportionately arrested for domestic violence. Further, they noted that incarceration rates for poor women and women of color have also increased dramatically, and that many of these women have histories of child sexual abuse and intimate violence. They stated that poor children and children of color are being institutionalized in increasing numbers. And while recent legal reforms have addressed the needs of abused immigrant women, many women are increasingly fearful of any contact with federal immigration officials in the current political climate.

If the roundtable conference was clear on outlining the costs of working with the criminal processing system, the report was less clear on possible alternatives. But RJ was briefly mentioned, along with reparation, community education, community-based safety groups, and community squads to intervene with abusive partners.

Differing feminist perspectives on the role of the state were raised in this report, ranging from working to transform the criminal processing system, to divesting from any reliance on the state, to developing new forms of community justice. It will be useful to examine these conflicting feminist perspectives more fully.

RESISTING CO-OPTATION: INSTITUTIONAL ADVOCACY TO STOP VIOLENCE

The Coordinated Community Response Model

Aware of the failures of state responses to women, some activists continue to invest their energies in making the legal system more responsive to victims and in transforming its gender, racial, class, and heterosexist biases. This is one strategy of the Domestic Abuse Intervention Project (DAIP), and Praxis International, a related organization, both based in Duluth, Minnesota. The DAIP created the *Duluth Model*, perhaps the most widely known feminist antiviolence approach in the United States and in many parts of the world. This program has long advocated the development of a "coordinated community response" to domestic violence that includes the monitoring of these responses by battered women's groups. The coordinated community response model emphasizes that the community, not the victims, is responsible for addressing violence. Key elements in this model include the police, courts, advocates for abused women, and social service agencies that work with victims and offenders. A batterers' intervention program was developed as part of the Duluth Model, and the curriculum for this program has been adapted for use in many different communities. The widely used "Power and Control Wheel" that is part of this curriculum has been translated into over a dozen languages (Pence and Paymar 1993:2). The goal of a coordinated community response is "to modify, coordinate, and monitor the response of community agencies" that work with victims and offenders (Pence and Shepard 1999:3). Training sessions on the Duluth Model have been conducted across the United States and in Europe, Latin America, New Zealand, and Australia (Shepard and Pence 1999:291–292).

The premise of the coordinated community response is that the state perpetuates intimate violence through policies and practices that fail to protect women and fail to hold abusive men accountable. In this view, the state is already involved in the lives of abused women; the most important priority is to change what the state is doing: "The criminal justice system has always been a 'player' in domestic violence, visible or invisible. Activists pursued an agenda of criminalization because many believed that men would not stop battering women until the community thought of it as a crime and treated it as such" (McMahon and Pence 2003:62).

The Safety and Accountability Audit

But, even in Duluth, the DAIP found that despite a citywide mandatory-arrest policy, legal advocacy for abused women, a carefully designed educational program for batterers, and coordination with the courts, the police, and social service agencies, the policies and practices of these agencies still failed to deliver safety and accountability in many cases each year.

Ellen Pence, one of the founders of the DAIP, was further concerned that the criminal legal system was pulling advocates away from solidarity with abused women and toward the agendas of the state. As the coordinated community response model became widely used, "The agenda for change focused more on increased efficiency, arrests, and convictions than on critiquing the impact of institutional responses on the safety, autonomy, and integrity of battered women" (Pence 2001:339). Pence pointed out that much of the federal money raised under the Violence Against Women Act was funneled through prosecutors and the police, who sought to manage advocates working with women.

In response to these problems, Pence, along with the Domestic Abuse Intervention Project, developed a new framework for monitoring community responses to domestic violence. The *safety and accountability audit* is a way to democratize evaluation research and make the experiences of abused women central to this process:

> [A] successful community response to domestic violence needs to
> establish the means to evaluate state and community interventions
> from the standpoint of women seeking protection. This standpoint
> must be contrasted with the standpoint of effective case management
> or a "law-and-order" perspective that measures success in terms of
> arrests, conviction rates, and incarcerations. (Pence 1996:59)

According to Pence, a participant at the Ms. Foundation roundtable, "Many of the [domestic violence] laws and regulations passed were either ignored or cynically turned against battered women or against men in marginal positions in society" (Pence 1996:27–28). Pence seeks to hold criminal justice institutions accountable to the communities they supposedly serve.

The safety and accountability audit was developed by Pence through a study of how battered women were processed through the Duluth criminal legal system. The audit was designed as a tool to both investigate the treatment of battered women within criminal justice institutions and, at the same time, to mobilize change in these institutions. Pence proposes that the audit be conducted by an interdisciplinary team made up not of outside consultants, but rather of battered women's advocates and criminal legal practitioners from the very institutions being evaluated. This positions advocates within a position of authority in the investigation, guaranteeing that their experience, observations, and insights will guide the evaluation. By enlisting criminal justice practitioners as part of the audit team, this furthers the ability of the audit to facilitate institutional coordination as a part of the investigation itself, and makes the recommendations that follow from the audit more powerful and more credible than if outsiders delivered them. "It is almost as if we are saying that this whole system was set up before we started to think about the unique aspects of domestic violence. Our job is to redesign every step in the process with domestic violence cases in mind" (Pence and Lizdas 1998:56).

An important goal of the safety audits is to assess institutional bias based on gender, race, ethnicity, age, immigration status, language, and sexual orientation. Pence wants to change the ways such biases shape the responses of the criminal legal system and the consequences of intervention:

> Even when police uniformly apply their arrest powers to men of
> different or ethnic backgrounds, arrest does not mean the same thing
> to a Latin man and an Anglo man, to a poor man and a middle-class
> man, or to a gay man and a straight man; nor does it have the same
> impact on their partners. (Pence 1996: 31)

One safety audit examined how U.S. legal responses to domestic violence harm Indigenous women and their children. This audit was developed by Mending the Sacred Hoop, a Native American domestic violence advocacy program allied with the DAIP. The research was conducted by team of Indigenous scholars, elders, community members, and consultants. Framed from the standpoint of Indigenous women, the audit examined the case processing of battered women by the legal system. This required ride-alongs with the police, observations of court hearings, analysis of court files, interviews with practitioners, and focus groups with Indigenous women. Here is how the audit describes the problems with the U.S. case processing of Indigenous women:

> We had expected we might uncover individual bias and cultural
> insensitivity, women-blaming, or lack of cultural competency that
> lead to poor protection of Indigenous women and their children in
> the U.S. legal system. Instead, we found an all-pervasive way of
> knowing and thinking about and acting on cases involving violence
> against Indigenous women [that] produces a false account of
> Indigenous women's experiences and promotes a course of state
> intervention in women's lives that not only often fails to protect
> women under the stated goal of the U.S. system to ensure public
> safety, but actually draws Indigenous women into state forms of social
> regulation that further endanger them . . .
>
> While the damage rendered by the United States upon Indian
> women through the process of colonization can never be fully
> remedied, certain measures can be taken to stem the current epidemic
> level of violence confronting Indian women. Such efforts must link
> the restoration of the right of Indian women to live free of violence
> within their homes and society to the restoration of the rights of their

respective nations to protect Indian women legally, socially, and spiritually. (George and Wilson 2002:61, 338)

The safety and accountability audit represents a new model of institutional advocacy. It offers a guide to community organizing that evaluates how state institutions fail abused women. It addresses the mechanics of state responses, the institutional processing of women who report abuse. It challenges activists to transform and monitor community institutions, based on the knowledge of women within these communities. By centralizing survivors in this process and making it locally accountable, this method seeks to realize new visions of justice for women.

Pence sees this as a tool that could be used to examine many different problems, including institutional responses to sexual harassment or racialized policing practices (Pence 1996:5, 196). Praxis International, an organization that grew out of the DAIP, has published a workbook on conducting safety and accountability audits, and offers consultation to community groups on this process (Pence and Lizdas 1998).

The Duluth Model is being used in places where RJ is popular, including Australia, where this model is operating in six different sites (Holder 1999). In New Zealand, where family group conferencing originated, a project to adapt the Duluth Model was developed with the support of both Maori and Pakeha (European) women (Balzer 1999).

The DAIP is critical of RJ, seeing it as "potentially dangerous" for domestic violence cases (Pence and Lizdas 1998:151). But the Battered Women's Justice Project (BWJP), a coalition that includes the DAIP, has produced a report that examines RJ in considerable depth. Although the BWJP opposes RJ in cases of intimate violence, the report identifies common principles that are held by both RJ and the battered women's movement: both seek to restore victims of crime, both promote the involvement of the community in responding to crime, and both place crime within a broader social context. Although they are critical of the RJ movement, the authors of the BWJP report seek a dialogue with RJ practitioners about violence against women (Frederick and Lizdas, Chapter 2 in this volume).

RESISTING CO-OPTATION: ANTIVIOLENCE ORGANIZING IN COMMUNITIES OF COLOR

In response to co-optation and the limitations of state responses, other feminists are developing new, community-specific ways of stopping violence against women (Fullwood 2002; Mitchell-Clark and Autry 2004; Rosewater and Goodmark 2007). Black feminist organizing around crimes against women has a long history. In the late 1800s, the black women's club movement mobilized against the terrors of lynching and the rape of black women by white men. In the 1890s, Ida Wells-Barnett published pamphlets analyzing lynching and rape in the context of race, gender, and economic oppression. In "Lynch Law in America," written in 1900, Wells-Barnett challenged white Americans to see the lie behind the justifications of lynching as a means of protecting white women from rape (Carby 1985).

In the second wave of feminism in the United States, new organizing arose around violence against women of color. In 1980, two years after the founding of the National Coalition Against Domestic Violence (NCADV), the Washington, D.C. Rape Crisis Center hosted the First National Conference on Third World Women and Violence. In 1981, a Women of Color Task Force was instituted within the NCADV (Davis 2000:5).

These efforts challenged the idea that feminists were united around a single antiviolence strategy; in particular, many feminists of color questioned whether arrests and prosecution are the most effective ways to stop violence against women. In Massachusetts in the 1980s, many white feminists recommended mandatory arrest as a means of stopping battering; but women of color in several shelters expressed opposition to giving the police even more authority in their communities.[2] Similarly, in Minnesota, women of color opposed mandatory arrests (Hudon 2000). Neither state currently has statewide mandatory arrest policies.

Addressing Violence Against Women Within Communities of Color

In the 1980s and 1990s, a number of local and national antiviolence organizations were created within communities of color. Programs for Asian women arose across the country. The New York Asian Women's Center (2006) was founded in 1982 to create resources for battered Asian immigrant women. Manavi (2007) was founded in New Jersey in 1985 to respond to the victimization of South Asian women. The Asian Women's Shelter (2008) in San Francisco opened in 1988.

A group of African American activists and scholars came together in 1993 to develop the Institute on Domestic Violence in the African American Community (IDVAAC). According to the Institute, existing interventions have failed African Americans:

> IDVAAC was first formed in 1993, when a group of scholars and practitioners informally met to discuss the plight of the African American community in the area of domestic violence. The group ultimately agreed that the "one-size-fits-all" approach to domestic violence services being provided in mainstream communities would not suffice for African Americans, who disproportionately experience stressors that can create conditions that lead to violence in the home. (IDVAAC 2007)

The Institute publishes materials on domestic violence and prisoner re-entry, and on culturally competent child visitation centers. IDVAAC hosts national conferences on violence in African American families and serves as a clearinghouse for research.

In 1997, the first national Latino conference on domestic violence was held in Washington, D.C., which led to the founding of Alianza: The National Latino Alliance for the Elimination of Domestic Violence. Alianza's mission is to "promote understanding, initiate and sustain dialogue, and generate solutions that move toward the elimination of domestic violence affecting Latino communities, with an understanding of the sacredness of all relations and communities" (Alianza 2007). The organization is developing culturally specific approaches to working with both survivors and with abusive men.

New Feminist Organizing Across Communities of Color

In 2000, a feminist conference in Santa Cruz, California broke new ground. Called The Color of Violence: Violence Against Women of Color, this conference sought new ways to mobilize feminist activists. Over 1000 women attended, and another 2000 had to be turned away for lack of space. According to Andrea Smith (Cherokee), the coordinator of the conference:

> Sexual/domestic violence within communities of color cannot be addressed seriously without dealing with the larger structures of violence, such as militarism, attacks on immigrants and Indian treaty rights, police brutality, the proliferation of prisons, economic neo-colonialism, and institutional racism. . . .
>
> [M]any organizations address violence directed at communities of color—police brutality, racism, economic exploitation, colonialism. Many other organizations address violence against women within communities. But very few organizations address violence on both fronts simultaneously. . . . The challenge women of color face is to combat both personal and state violence. We must develop strategies that assure safety for survivors of sexual/domestic violence without strengthening the oppressive criminal justice apparatus. (Smith 2000:15)

Smith was also a participant at the Ms. Foundation roundtable. Among the presenters at the conference were women with long histories as leaders within anti-rape and anti–domestic violence organizations, including women from Mending the Sacred Hoop, Manavi, the IDVAAC, and Alianza. But there were also advocates for immigrant women, as well as activists working in the areas of Native rights, prisoner's rights, and inter-national human rights. Workshop titles included "Colonialism and Violence," "Racism and Heterosexism," "Violence and the Global Economy," and "Challenging the Depoliticization of the Anti-Violence Movement." Angela Davis gave the keynote address and raised the issue of co-optation directly:

> Given the racist and patriarchal patterns of the state, it is difficult to envision the state as the holder of solutions to the problem of violence

against women of color. However, as the antiviolence movement has been institutionalized and professionalized, the state plays an increasingly dominant role in how we conceptualize and create strategies to minimize violence against women. . . . The state can assimilate our opposition to gender domination into projects of racial—which also means gender—domination. (Davis 2000:4, 6)

A new organization was founded as a result of this conference, Incite: Women of Color Against Violence. National conferences were held in Chicago in 2002 and in New Orleans in 2005. The organization also hosts regional meetings of women of color, produces a newsletter, has local chapters, and operates a website that includes a community organizing kit. Incite is active internationally and has sent delegations to meetings of the World Social Forum (Incite! 2003a).

In their "Principles of Unity" Incite identifies the state as the "central organizer of violence" that oppresses women of color and their communities. In order to resist co-optation, Incite further states that they "Discourage any solicitation of federal or state funding for Incite activities" (Incite! 2007b). Incite promotes ideas for "direct action, critical dialogue, and grassroots organizing" (Smith 2000:15) that address violence against women in its many forms, including hate crimes, trafficking, forced sterilization, and "state violence" by police officers, prison guards, immigration officials, and the military.

Two books drawn from conferences organized by Incite have been published (Incite! 2006, 2007b). These works discuss co-optation by the state and co-optation by the "nonprofit industrial complex"—the web of foundations operating under state management that Incite views as having a detrimental impact on social justice activism.

Both restorative practitioners and Incite activists are critical of the criminal processing system. Both emphasize the importance of community-based strategies in responding to crimes. Both seek to mobilize the power of informal sanctions rather than formal legal measures. And yet many feminists of color involved with Incite are critical of RJ. The Aboriginal Women's Action Network in Vancouver, British Columbia is opposed to RJ in cases of violence against women and children. They argue that Aboriginal women do not feel safe using these practices, and despite the racism of the legal system, they want access to formal interventions (Polios 2002). Incite itself has criticized RJ for inadequate safety measures for survivors, and for placing pressure on Native women to reconcile with their offenders (see Smith, Chapter 12 in this volume).

Incite has a working document that addresses the principles of community accountability and contains descriptions of specific community models that address race-based violence against women (Incite! 2003b). Incite challenges feminists to address state violence and the racial politics of the state and, given the importance of these issues, the reliance of feminist projects upon the state.

RESISTING CO-OPTATION: FEMINIST/RESTORATIVE ANTIVIOLENCE PROJECTS

Concerned that efforts to change the criminal processing system have monopolized the energies of activists—and with too meager a result on stopping violence—some feminists are examining restorative practices, searching for new ways to create justice for abused women. But as indicated earlier, there is intense controversy about RJ among feminists. To appreciate the potential of feminist/restorative projects, it will help to lay out the criticisms feminists have raised more fully.

Feminist Criticisms of Restorative Justice

Feminists have made many criticisms of RJ (Coker 1999, 2002; Coward 2000; Stubbs, 2002, 2004; Daly and Stubbs 2006, 2007). Their concerns center around three main themes: women's safety, offender accountability, and the broader politics of gender and race.

There is deep skepticism that existing RJ practices can respond to the risks women face from violence. The bad experiences that feminists have had with older forms of court-sponsored mediation create distrust of newer forms. A report on abused women in family mediation by the Transition House Association of Nova Scotia offers vivid support for such skepticism: Based on interviews with 34 abused women who had gone through court-connected mediation to resolve family law matters, the study found that most would not recommend mediation to other abused women:

> Abused women reported intimidation and revictimization in mediation regardless of the form of abuse: physical, sexual, emotional, psychological, or financial. Women reported that their mediator or conciliator minimized emotional, psychological, or financial abuse, or simply did not recognize certain behaviours as abusive. When women brought up the fact that their ex-partner was harassing, stalking, or otherwise continuing to abuse them during the mediation, their mediators did not terminate mediation. (Rubin 2000:8)

Mediators appeared indifferent to women's complaints of threats, stalking, and harassment during the process. Many of the abused women reported coercive pressures to accept mediation by court mediators. If a court system can so badly botch old-fashioned mediation, many feminists ask, what would it do with RJ?

Feminists have argued that the current literature on restorative practices lacks an understanding of the dynamics of violence against women and the context of gender inequality that shapes these dynamics (Coward 2000). This is the same criticism feminists have made of traditional legal practices (see Rubin, Chapter 4 in this volume). Without an understanding of women's risks and the context of gender inequality, interventions that prioritize face-to-face meetings between abused women and their offenders could easily pressure abused women to take responsibility for changing their partners, thus making women's safety a secondary concern.

Further skepticism exists about whether offenders can truly be held accountable in the informal practices of RJ. The danger here is of "cheap justice," as Donna Coker (1999) puts it, meaning that these processes could be too easy on offenders—or too easy to manipulate—and thus both ineffective and unjust. Further concern exists that informal processes might not be able to successfully denounce violence against women within the broader community.

More broadly political matters have also been identified by feminists. Many worry that by pushing cases of violence against women out of the criminal legal system and into restorative practices, the gains of feminists in getting these crimes publicized and denounced would be rolled back. Racial politics are also at issue. The president of the United Native Nations in Canada stated that she believed the government asked for their input and then ignored the concerns of Native women about using circles (Coward 2000; see Stubbs, Chapter 5 in this volume).

Is Restorative Justice Truly Victim-Centered?

Along with these concerns, there is also the question of whether RJ is actually victim-centered. This is often the claim of leading supporters. According to John Braithwaite (2003:86), "Restorative justice means restoring victims, a more victim-centered criminal justice system, as well as restoring offenders and restoring community." Howard Zehr (2002:32–33) calls RJ a "victim-oriented approach."

But, as has been shown, the most commonly used restorative practices, as innovative as they are, were all developed with a focus on offenders. Mark Yantzi's creative approach to probation in Kitchener, Ontario was an attempt to influence two teenaged youth (Peachey 2003). Family group conferencing was adapted by the New Zealand government from Maori traditions as a way to reduce the number of Maori youth behind bars and to respond to charges of racism (Love 2000). In the legal opinion that made sentencing circles an option in Canada, Yukon judge Barry Stuart was concerned with how the justice system failed to meet the needs of offenders, and thus contributed to recidivism (Stuart 1992).

These important developments are transforming legal systems in progressive ways. Although existing research is largely based on restorative practices concerning youth crime, studies show that victims are more satisfied with these practices than with traditional legal processes (Green 2007; Umbreit, Vos, and Coates 2006). But it is something else to say these restorative practices are victim-centered.

A major guiding principle in RJ worldwide is John Braithwaite's concept of *reintegrative shaming*. This is a form of shame that condemns the action of the offender, but welcomes the offender back into the community if he or she is remorseful. This stands in contrast to stigmatizing or *disintegrative shaming*, which condemns, isolates, and exiles the criminal actor (Braithwaite 1989). Although this is an important critique of traditional legal practices, this concept is all about the offender's shame, not the victims' shame; it concerns the need to reintegrate offenders, not the need to reintegrate victims who have lost social connections through their own feelings of shame. As Judith Herman (2005:598) argues, "In crimes of sexual and domestic violence . . . the person who needs to be welcomed back into the community, first and foremost, is the victim."

Most RJ programs in the United States do not offer any assistance to victims unless the victims are interested in working with their offenders; however, many programs will work with offenders, even when victims are not involved (Achilles and Zehr 2001). The claim, then, that RJ is "victim-centered" is misleading.

However, trends exist within and around RJ that are responding to this. A number of leading figures within the RJ movement worked together with victim advocates on a "Listening Project" (Mika et al. 2004). This project sent teams with both RJ proponents and victim advocates to seven states to gather information on victim needs, justice from the perspectives of victims, and victims' views of RJ. The goal was "to collaboratively propose an action plan to create more responsive restorative justice programs and beneficial outcomes for victims" (p. 32).

Another recent idea is that of *parallel justice*. Susan Herman proposes parallel justice as a new set of obligations that the state should adopt toward crime victims, obligations not directly connected to offenders. Although she sees benefits for victims using RJ, Herman finds that RJ reproduces many of the same problems victims have identified with the existing legal system: Both meet the needs of very few victims, both are offender-centered, and both neglect many of the needs victims have for rebuilding their lives. Parallel justice seeks a path to justice for victims that parallels what RJ offers to offenders. Herman wants greater efforts by the legal system to make victims safe following crimes; greater victim support, compensation, and assistance; a forum for victims to share their experience of crime; and case managers to coordinate resources for victims (Herman 2004).

The Question of Offender Recidivism

Given its focus on offenders, it may be surprising that reducing recidivism is not viewed as a central goal of RJ (Hayes 2007; McCold 2003; Morris 2003; Zehr 2002). Paul McCold (2003:95) puts it this way: "Restorative justice offers advantages for victims, offenders, their families and communities, even if the practice is eventually shown to have no direct effect on offender recidivism." Allison Morris (2003:466) says that "It could reasonably be argued that reducing offending is not really an objective of restorative justice; its focus is holding offenders accountable and making amends to victims." And according to Howard Zehr (2002:9), "Restorative justice is not primarily designed to reduce recidivism or repeating offenses," even though he acknowledges that RJ has been promoted as reducing crime.

There have nonetheless been many attempts to determine whether RJ reduces reoffending. Of course, many different practices (with numerous variations) are included under the concept of RJ, but in general the research on whether RJ reduces recidivism is mixed (Bonta et al. 2006; Hayes 2007; Umbreit, Vos, and Coates 2006). A review of 39 studies using comparison groups by Bonta and colleagues came to four conclusions: RJ interventions are generally associated with small, but significant reductions in recidivism; court-ordered programs do not appear to reduce recidivism; effects are more pronounced for low-risk offenders; and "for high-risk offenders, restorative justice may be insufficient to decrease recidivism" (Bonta et al. 2006:117).

Again, this research is largely based on youth crime; few evaluations have been made of restorative practices in cases of violence against women (Edwards and Sharpe 2004; Stubbs 2004; see Stubbs, Chapter 5 in this volume). But since repeated offending is a common characteristic of crimes against women, new efforts to create justice for these victims must address revictimization.

Anger and Forgiveness

I further believe that an underlying conflict exists about anger, forgiveness, and their place in recovery from violence. A stated goal of RJ is to reduce not only victims' fear of offenders, but victims' anger toward offenders (Curtis-Fawley and Daly 2005:606). It is as if a central problem with victimization is the anger it creates in victims, and forgiveness, through a restorative process, is the solution. In RJ training conferences and events that I have attended in the United States, there have been tables filled with books about forgiveness on display. Forgiveness, then, seems to be a powerful emotional process that RJ harnesses.

Clearly, there are many problems for survivors in the aftermath of violence, and women struggle with feelings of hatred or anger toward those who abused them. As Judith Herman points out, it is toxic for a survivor to feel as though she harbors the same hatred that her offender has (Herman 1992:188–190). But many survivors struggle with the *absence* of anger, often for long periods after being abused, especially in cases of child sexual abuse and intimate violence. For many feminists, anger is a powerful process that facilitates insights about injustice and galvanizes action against it. Allowing space for survivors to feel anger can be liberating. When forgiveness is rushed, it does harm to survivors of violence. Sharon Lamb (1996:161), who has much to say about victimization and justice, claims "Victims tend to show premature forgiveness just as readily as they blame themselves."

I think these two theories-in-practice run in opposing directions. It is as if restorative practitioners see victims' anger as an obstacle to justice and forgiveness as transformative, whereas feminist antiviolence activists see forgiveness as an obstacle to justice and victims' anger as transformative. Admittedly, this is an oversimplification. But fear of victims' outrage leads people to silence survivors. And there are gendered dimensions to this silencing, with particular fears attached to women's anger. I think these fears are present within the field of RJ, just as they are present everywhere else, and that fears of women's anger motivate pressures on victims to forgive.

Feminist Convergence with Restorative Principles

Despite these criticisms, many tendencies within feminist activism are converging with aspects of RJ. The work of Incite to develop interventions that don't rely on the criminal legal system is one parallel, but many others also exist. There is a language of healing within RJ: healing for victims, for communities, and, more controversially for some, for offenders. This language resonates with profeminist antiviolence work with men of color. This can be seen even in the title of the book, *Family Violence and Men of Color: Healing the Wounded Male Spirit*, edited by Ricardo Carrillo and Jerry Tello (1998). This language is also visible in the approach to batterers' counseling by Alianza (2001). The "Fathering After Violence Project" of the Family Violence Prevention Fund uses an explicit reparative framework in its curriculum for abusive men who are fathers. This goal of this program is to increase safety for abused women and their children by encouraging abusive men to become better fathers and co-parents. Working with men who have completed batterers' counseling, and who renounce violence, this project helps to heal the relationships between abusive men and their children (Fleck-Henderson and Areán 2004). The Family Violence Prevention Fund has also created two monographs to guide family conferences in cases of child abuse where there is evidence of intimate violence (Carrillo and Carter 2001; Carter 2003). Another longstanding feminist organization, the Domestic Abuse Project in Minneapolis, has a Restorative Parenting program, aimed at repairing relationships between abusive men and their children (Mathews [n.d.]).

Theologian Marie Fortune, who has written extensively about violence against women and children, uses language that resonates with RJ. She speaks of justice in terms of restoration and right relation (Fortune 1987). Fortune offers a guide to what she calls "justice-making," or ways in which community members can help survivors find justice (Fortune 2005). The process of justice-making includes offender accountability, restitution, and vindication of the victim or survivor. However, Fortune (1995) sees mediation in cases of violence against women and children as inappropriate.

The use of circles as a strategic method is not unique to RJ. In her social justice approach to family therapy, Rhea Almeida uses separate "culture circles" for women and men to facilitate support for survivors and accountability for abusers. The term "culture circles" comes from

Paulo Freire's methods for developing a critical consciousness of oppression. Almeida's Cultural Context Model frames intimate violence against the background of multiple forms of inequality and uses cultural circles to promote change (Almeida and Lockard 2005; Almeida and Durkin 1999).

Activists working to end intimate violence in lesbian, gay, bisexual, and transgender relationships are also, like restorative practitioners, critical of those who would demonize offenders. Ann Russo raises this in relation to lesbian relationships. "In a society quick to criminalize lesbians and the violent behavior of anyone associated with the 'underclass,'" Russo (1999:93) argues, "it is important that we not contribute to the demonization of lesbians or envision criminalization as the primary solution to battering." Russo urges antiviolence activists to work for broader social and political change.

Feminist/Restorative Hybrid Projects: The Work of Joan Pennell

Feminists working within the RJ movement are turning the concerns about safety and offender accountability upside down. They argue that existing legal responses fail victims of battering, rape, and child abuse in terms of safety and accountability. To keep people safe, it is necessary to widen the circle of responsibility, and this is what restorative practices can accomplish.

Joan Pennell founded the first shelter for abused women and their children in Newfoundland. A social worker by training, her community activism addresses the overlap between child abuse and battering. According to Pennell, state responses to these forms of abuse have been problematic. In the United States, an increasing reliance on punitive legal approaches to child abuse has led to mother-blaming and the removal of the children of battered women on the grounds that these children are being exposed to violence. Furthermore, legal interventions in cases of battering often backfire against poor women and women of color, in the form of discriminatory policing practices and mutual arrests. Pennell asks:

> Can women and children advocates collaborate with state institutions
> without becoming co-opted to goals contrary to their own beliefs? In
> answer, some women's advocates are calling for divestment from state
> intervention and proposing community solutions, including
> restorative practices. (Pennell 2006:289)

Pennell seeks to expand antiviolence work to include informal networks and community institutions beyond the legal system. In this way, she sees her work as extending the coordinated community response model of the Duluth program. Even supporters of the Duluth Model acknowledge that work on the criminal legal system displaced work on other community institutions (Holder 1999, Pence 1999). Pennell seeks to empower abused women and their children by mobilizing informal supports and developing partnerships between families and community institutions:

Family group conferencing brings together the family of concern with their relatives, friends, and other close supports—that is, their informal network—to develop a plan to safeguard children and other family members. Before these plans go into effect, they must be authorized by the involved protective agencies. Repeated studies have documented the benefits of this partnership-building model in democratizing decision making, respecting family and community cultures, and promoting the safety and well-being of children and women. (Pennell and Francis 2005:668)

Together with Gale Burford, Pennell designed and evaluated a restorative approach to child abuse and battering in Canada. They see their work as influenced by the feminist and Aboriginal movements, as well as by RJ (Pennell and Burford 2002). In developing their version of Maori family group conferencing, Pennell and Burford worked collaboratively with women's organizations, advocates for children and youth, offenders' programs, state officials, and academic researchers (Pennell and Burford 1994).

Pennell states that their version of a conference, called a "family group decision-making conference," is designed as a planning forum and is not intended as mediation or therapy. Family group decision-making conferences are meant to mobilize both formal and informal resources for abused women and abused children, including legal measures, advocacy for abused women, batterers' counseling, drug and alcohol assistance, and the support of families and friends. Using this approach, victims attend a conference with their abusers, and both victims and offenders have supporters. There is a formal role for the police, probation officers, social service workers, and women's advocates in the conference, and trained facilitators prepare all participants for these encounters. The outcome of the conference is an agreement, reached by all family members, on a plan of action to stop abuse. The facilitator, in consultation with legal officials, must approve the plan.

Stopping chronic and severe violence requires intervention, according to Pennell. She sees the responsibility to intervene as both individual and collective; the goal of conferencing is to "widen the circle" of support for victims. Pennell believes that conferencing breaks the conspiracy of silence surrounding abuse and taps into the strengths of the community. The involvement of family members and friends provides more "eyes" to guard against reoffending (Pennell 1999).

Pennell and Burford prioritize the safety of women and children, and they are therefore concerned with offender recidivism. Their follow-up research on the 32 families that participated in conferences found that abuse and neglect declined by half following the conferences (Pennell and Burford 2000:145–46). No violence occurred during these meetings or as a result of these meetings (Pennell 2005:167).

In North Carolina, Pennell developed another hybrid project: Instead of simply following her Canadian design, she developed a new feminist/restorative approach incorporating the involvement of women's shelters, batterer's counseling programs, children's services, child welfare workers, the domestic violence court, police, and the North Carolina Coalition Against Domestic Violence. Focus groups were conducted with shelter staff and with a multiracial group of abused women (Pennell and Francis 2005:676–678). Because the safety of family members should be the central priority in any antiviolence intervention, she called it "safety conferencing."

Pennell (2005) has published an extensive examination of safety issues in family group conferencing that have wide application to any restorative approach to violence against women. She discusses how conferences can be productive even without the participation of offenders, whether they are excluded for safety reasons or are otherwise unavailable (see Pennell and Kim, Chapter 8 in this volume).

Feminist/Restorative Hybrid Projects: Mary Koss and RESTORE

During the course of the 30 years that psychologist Mary Koss has been working on the problem of rape, she has published over 200 articles, including ground-breaking research on rape on college campuses. In 2000, she received an award from the American Psychological Association for Distinguished Contributions to Research in Public Policy. In accepting this award, Koss challenged both her colleagues and feminist activists to focus their energies in a direction different from that of the criminal processing system:

> Currently, a large amount of money is spent on justice responses to violence against women that are not rooted in historical approaches to problem solving among many of the groups that constitute U.S. society, ill-serve victims, and are not very effective in reducing the prevalence of violence by perpetrators. . . .
>
> [V]ictim advocates . . . have poured energy into advocating for incremental reforms in retributive justice processing that, if the past 20 years are any indication, will fail to substantially influence either the processes or outcomes of criminal and civil justice. We, as practitioners of psychological science and practice, can no longer passively support justice responses that the tools of our profession have revealed to be psychologically damaging and ineffective. Further, we cannot expect the law to compete with norms that encourage and condone violence against women. We must disseminate information on alternatives like communitarian justice that are better grounded in psychological theory, advocate for demonstration projects using new methodologies such as community conferences, and sustain primary prevention initiatives aimed at decreasing the social policy and cultural supports for violence against women. (Koss 2000:10)

According to Koss, existing criminal legal responses fail victims of violence against women in terms of safety. Under the present adversarial justice system, women who go through the courts to adjudicate battering and rape pay a "psychic price" (p. 1335) in stress, humiliation, and fear of the loss of their children. In her view, RJ models are designed to operate alongside the current criminal justice system, and thus do not require a reversal of feminist gains or safety measures. Furthermore, community conferences could address not only the physical and sexual violence in such cases, but also the accompanying psychological abuse and other controlling behaviors. And since community conferences are nonadversarial, there is greater room for an active role by advocates in these processes.

The existing system also fails victims in terms of offender accountability. Conferences, on the other hand, could expand the social control resources within the community acting upon abusive men. Since they are not designed to be adversarial, conferences lessen the offender's need to minimize or deny the violence. And conferences could potentially invite the community to denounce violence against women.

More broadly political concerns could also be addressed by restorative practices. Koss states that both women and men of color have been discriminated against by the criminal justice system. According to Koss, "with its nonincarceration focus, and being a process that is shaped by the participation of other members of the victim's and offender's cultural groups, communitarian justice has the potential to mitigate the racism that is perceived to permeate criminal justice" (Koss 2000:1339).

Koss established a feminist/restorative approach to address sexual assault called RESTORE (Responsibility and Equity for Sexual Transgressions Offering a Restorative Experience). The mission of RESTORE is "To facilitate a victim-centered, community-driven resolution of selected individual sex crimes that creates and carries out a plan for accountability, healing, and public safety" (Koss, Bachar, Hopkins, and Carlson 2004:1448). The RESTORE project combines feminist and restorative elements. The community networking undertaken to design the project is not unlike a coordinated community response. Mary Koss first began developing the RESTORE project in 1999 in Arizona, and in 2000 created collaborative relationships with rape crisis advocates, prosecutors, the police, probation officers, legal counsel, and university evaluators (Koss et al. 2004). This kind of collaboration is essential, according to Koss, to fulfill the mission of RESTORE. Koss outlines the RESTORE process in Chapter 10.

These feminist/restorative hybrid projects address many of the criticisms raised about RJ. Joan Pennell and Mary Koss designed their projects with extensive consultation from local feminist organizations. As a result, the needs of survivors are central to their interventions. Both Pennell and Koss are also committed to evaluation research on their projects, with a goal of changing or ending those practices found to be harmful.

Inspired by RESTORE, a new project is under development in New Zealand to meet the needs of adult survivors of child sexual abuse (see Jülich, Chapter 11 in this volume). This initiative is being created by advocates for victims and counselors working with offenders.

There are also new feminist innovations aligned with *transformative justice*, which is a critique and extension of restorative justice. According to Ruth Morris, who popularized the term, "even restorative justice does not go far enough. It still accepts the idea that one event now defines all that matters of right and wrong—it leaves out the past, and the social causes of all events" (Morris, cited in Harris 2006:557). From this perspective, the point is not to "restore" individuals to the conditions in which they found themselves before the crime. Rather, transformative justice seeks to change both the consequences of crime *and* the larger context of social inequality in which the crime occurred. Creative Interventions, a San Francisco–based organization aligned with transformative justice, is developing a method for mobilizing communities to intervene against intimate and interpersonal violence without using the criminal legal system (see Kim, Chapter 9 in this volume).

CONCLUSION

These three forms of feminist activism challenge previous ways of doing antiviolence work. The Duluth institutional advocacy model challenges activists to transform legal institutions and audit their responsiveness to the needs of victims. Incite challenges activists to address violence against women and violence against communities of color at the same time. With their feminist/restorative hybrid models, Joan Pennell and Mary Koss challenge activists to "widen the circle" of resources that can support victims, hold offenders accountable, and create new community justice practices.

There are many ideas here about how to resist co-optation. There are also strategies for developing community accountability in the safety audit, in the work of Incite, and in the guidelines developed by Joan Pennell.

Combining these three approaches could spark new antiviolence initiatives and new ways to investigate injustice. What would be revealed by a gender- and racial-impact audit of how an entire criminal processing system responds to crimes against women, one that examined the practices from policing, to the courts, to the treatment of men and women in jails and prisons, and to probation and parole? What would a safety and accountability audit reveal about the operation of existing and untested restorative approaches to intimate violence? What can antiviolence activists learn from RJ about mobilizing neighborhood networks for the majority of rape survivors who will not contact the legal system? How might activists mobilize around against the scandal of militarized prostitution involving the U.S. armed forces? What are the goals around which the global human rights movements of feminism and RJ can find common ground?

Restorative practitioners can learn a lot from feminists. When peacemaking circles and family group conferences create spaces for painful stories, people often share things beyond what is anticipated. When recountings of child sexual abuse and rape and intimate violence appear unexpectedly in these stories, are restorative practitioners prepared to respond? Are they familiar with the local community resources for survivors and offenders? If these two movements for social justice are to fulfill their goals, greater efforts must be made to keep them from working against one other.

Judith Herman (2005) writes of justice from "the victim's perspective," making an argument for a feminist vision of justice that is distinct from both the right-wing "get tough on crime" approach, and from the offender orientation of many restorative programs. Many feminist visions are depicted in this chapter; yet, as much as they differ from one another, collectively they illustrate what Herman is saying: All the activists described here resist co-optation by the state and all strive to create woman-centered forms of justice. Different as they are, the activists who are transforming legal systems, organizing in communities of color, and developing hybrid projects all embody visions of justice that renew the meaning of feminism. These developments offer inspiration at a time of increasing social injustice in the United States and around the world, at the beginning of a new century that is already terribly violent.

NOTES

1. In a parallel vein, Joanne Belknap (2007:1) replaces the term "criminal justice system" with *crime processing, criminal processing,* or *criminal legal system,* due to the lack of justice for many victims and offenders. My writing here follows the language of Belknap and the Ms. Foundation Report.
2. Personal experience as a member of the Battered Women's Working Group, a subcommittee of the Massachusetts Governor's Anti-Crime Council, 1987–89.

REFERENCES

Achilles, Mary and Howard Zehr. 2001. "Restorative Justice for Crime Victims: The Promise and the Challenge." Pp. 87–99 in *Restorative Community Justice: Repairing Harm and Transforming Communities,* edited by Gordon Bazemore and Mara Schiff. Cincinnati, OH: Anderson.

Alianza: The National Latino Alliance for the Elimination of Domestic Violence. 2001. "Forum on Latinos Who Batter: Hope for Those Who Hurt Others." April. Retrieved December 21, 2007 (http://www.dvalianza.org/resor/reports.htm).

———. 2007. "Mission." Revised February 8; retrieved December 16, 2007 (http://www.dvalianza.org/about/mission.htm).

Almeida, Rhea V. and Tracy Durkin, 1999. "The Cultural Context Model: Therapy for Couples with Domestic Violence." *Journal of Marital and Family Therapy* 25:313–324.

Almeida, Rhea V. and Judith Lockard. 2005. "The Cultural Context Model: A New Paradigm for Accountability, Empowerment, and the Development of Critical Consciousness Against Domestic Violence." Pp. 301–320 in *Domestic Violence at the Margins: Readings on Race, Class, Gender, and Culture,* edited by Natalie J. Sokoloff. New Brunswick, NJ: Rutgers University Press.

Asian Women's Shelter. 2008. "About Us/History." San Francisco: Asian Women's Shelter. Retrieved January 8, 2008 (http://www.sfaws.org/ 3_about/abo_history.html).

Balzer, Roma. 1999. "Hamilton Abuse Intervention Project: The Aotearoa Experience." Pp. 239–254 in *Coordinating Community Responses to Domestic Violence: Lessons from Duluth and Beyond,* edited by Melanie F. Shepard and Ellen Pence. Thousand Oaks, CA: Sage, 1999.

Barrett, Jerome T. and Joseph P. Barrett. 2004. *A History of Alternative Dispute Resolution: The Story of a Political, Cultural, and Social Movement.* San Francisco: Jossey-Bass.

Belknap, Joanne. 2007. *The Invisible Woman: Gender, Crime, and Justice (3e).* Belmont, CA: Thompson Wadsworth.

Bhattacharjee, Anannya. 2001. *Whose Safety? Women of Color and the Violence of Law Enforcement.* Philadelphia: American Friends Service Committee and the Committee on Women, Population, and the Environment.

Bonta, James, Tanya A. Rugge, Robert B. Cormier, and Rebecca Jesseman. 2006. "Restorative Justice and Recidivism: Promises Made, Promises Kept?" Pp. 108–118 in *Handbook of Restorative Justice: A Global Perspective,* edited by Dennis Sullivan and Larry Tifft. London: Routledge.

Braithwaite, John. 1989. *Crime, Shame, and Reintegration.* Cambridge, UK: Cambridge University Press.

———. 2003. "Restorative Justice and a Better Future." Pp. 83–97 in *A Restorative Justice Reader: Texts, Sources, Context,* edited by Gerry Johnstone. Portland, OR: Willan Publishing.

———. 2006. "Narrative and 'Compulsory Compassion.'" *Law & Social Inquiry* 31:425–446.

Bureau of Justice Statistics. 2006. *Rape Trends.* Washington, DC: Bureau of Justice Statistics Web Site. Revised September 10, 2006; retrieved January 7, 2008 (http://www.ojp.usdoj.gov/bjs/glance/rape.htm).

Bushie, Burma. (1999). "Community Holistic Circle Healing: A Community Approach." Paper presented at the Building Strong Partnerships for Restorative Practices conference, Burlington, Vermont, August 5–7.

Carby, Hazel V. 1985. "'On the Threshold of Woman's Era': Lynching, Empire, and Sexuality in Black Feminist Theory." *Critical Inquiry* 12:262–277.

Carrillo, Ricardo and Janet Carter. 2001. *Guidelines for Conducting Family Team Conferences When There Is a History of Domestic Violence.* San Francisco: Family Violence Prevention Fund.

Carrillo, Ricardo and Jerry Tello, eds. 1998. *Violence and Men of Color: Healing the Wounded Male Spirit.* New York: Springer.

Carter, Lucy Salcido. 2003. *Family Team Conferences in Domestic Violence Cases: Guidelines for Practice.* San Francisco: Family Violence Prevention Fund.

Catalano, Shannan. 2006. *Intimate Partner Violence in the United States.* Washington, DC: Bureau of Justice Statistics Web Site. Revised December 20, 2006. Retrieved November 16, 2007 (http//www.ojp.usdoj.gov/bjs/intimate/ipv.htm).

Cheon, Aileen and Cheryl Regehr. 2006. "Restorative Models in Cases of Intimate Partner Violence: Reviewing the Evidence." *Victims and Offenders* 1:369–394.

Coker, Donna. 1999. "Enhancing Autonomy for Battered Women: Lessons from Navajo Peacemaking." *UCLA Law Review* 47:1–111.

———. 2000. "Shifting Power for Battered Women: Law, Material Resources, and Poor Women of Color." *U.C. Davis Law Review:*33:1006–1053.

———. 2001. "Crime Control and Feminist Law Reform in Domestic Violence Law: A Critical Review." *Buffalo Criminal Law Review* 4:801–860.

———. 2002. "Transformative Justice: Anti-Subordination Processes in Cases of Domestic Violence." Pp. 128–152 in *Restorative Justice and Family Violence,* edited by Heather Strang and John Braithwaite. Cambridge, UK: Cambridge University Press.

Coward, Stephanie. 2000. "Restorative Justice in Cases of Domestic and Sexual Violence: Healing Justice?" *AiR: Abuse Information & Resources for Survivors.* Retrieved January 7, 2008 (http://www.hotpeachpages.net/canada/air/rj_domestic_violence.html).

Crenshaw, Kimberlé Williams. 1991. "Mapping the Margins: Intersectionality, Identity Politics, and Violence Against Women of Color." *Stanford Law Review* 43:1241–1299.

Curtis-Fawley, Sarah and Kathleen Daly. 2005. "Gendered Violence and Restorative Justice: The Views of Victim Advocates." *Violence Against Women* 11:603–638.

Daly, Kathleen. 2002. "Sexual Assault and Restorative Justice." Pp. 62–88 in *Restorative Justice and Family Violence,* edited by Heather Strang and John Braithwaite. Cambridge, UK: Cambridge University Press.

Daly, Kathleen and Russ Immarigeon. 1998. "The Past, Present, and Future of Restorative Justice: Some Critical Reflections." *Contemporary Justice Review* 1:21–45.

Daly, Kathleen and Julie Stubbs. 2006. "Feminist Engagement with Restorative Justice." *Theoretical Criminology* 10:9–28.

———. 2007. "Feminist Theory, Feminist and Anti-Racist Politics, and Restorative Justice." Pp. 149–170 in *Handbook of Restorative Justice,* edited by Gerry Johnstone and Daniel W. Van Ness. Cullompton, Devon, UK: Willan Publishing.

Daniels, Cynthia, ed. 1997. *Feminists Negotiate the State: The Politics of Domestic Violence.* Lanham, MD: University Press of America.

Danner, Mona J.E. 2000. "Three Strikes and It's Women Who Are Out: The Hidden Consequences for Women of Criminal Justice Policy Reforms." Pp. 215–224 in *It's a Crime: Women and Justice,* edited by Roslyn Muraskin. Upper Saddle River, NJ: Prentice-Hall.

Dasgupta, Shamita Das. 2003. *Safety and Justice for All: Examining the Relationship Between the Women's Anti-Violence Movement and the Criminal Legal System.* New York: Ms. Foundation. Retrieved February 26, 2009 (www.ms.foundation.org/user-assets/PDF/Program/safety_justice.pdf).

Davis, Angela. 2000. "The Color of Violence Against Women." *Color Lines* Fall: 4–8.

Edwards, Alan and Susan Sharpe. 2004. *Restorative Justice in the Context of Domestic Violence: A Literature Review.* Edmonton, AB: Mediation and Restorative Justice Centre.

Ferraro, Kathleen J. 1996. "The Dance of Dependency: A Genealogy of Domestic Violence Discourse." *Hypatia* 11:77–91.

Finkelhor, David and Lisa Jones. 2008. "Good News: Child Victimization Has Been Declining. Why?" Pp. 122–147 in *Childhood Victimization: Violence, Crime, and Abuse in the Lives of Young People,* by David Finkelhor with contributors. New York: Oxford University Press.

Fleck-Henderson, Ann and Juan Carlos Areán. 2004. *Breaking the Cycle: Fathering After Violence: Curriculum Guidelines and Tolls for Batterer Intervention Programs.* San Francisco: Family Violence Prevention Fund.

Fortune, Marie M. 1987. "Justice-Making in the Aftermath of Woman-Battering." Pp. 237–248 in *Domestic Violence on Trial: Psychological and Legal Dimensions of Family Violence,* edited by Daniel Jay Sonkin. New York: Springer.

———. 1995. "Forgiveness: The Last Step." Pp. 201–206 in *Violence Against Women and Children: A Christian Theological Sourcebook,* edited by Carol J. Adams and Marie M. Fortune. New York: Continuum.

———. 2005. *Sexual Violence: The Sin Revisited.* Cleveland, OH: Pilgrim Press.

Fullwood, P. Caitlin. 2002. *Preventing Family Violence: Community Engagement Makes the Difference.* San Francisco: Family Violence Prevention Fund.

George, Lila and Alex Wilson. 2002. *Community Based Analysis of the U.S. Legal System's Interventions in Domestic Abuse Cases Involving Indigenous Women.* Washington, DC: National Institute of Justice (Available from MPDI Inc., 202 East Superior Street, Duluth MN 55806).

Goel, Rashmi. 2000. "No Women at the Center: The Use of the Canadian Sentencing Circle in Domestic Violence Cases." *Wisconsin Women's Law Journal* 15:293–334.

Goodman, Lisa A. and Deborah Epstein. 2008. *Listening to Battered Women: A Survivor-Centered Approach to Advocacy, Mental Health, and Justice.* Washington, DC: American Psychological Association.

Gottschalk, Marie. 2006. *The Prison and the Gallows: The Politics of Mass Incarceration in America.* Cambridge, UK: Cambridge University Press.

Green, Simon. 2007. " 'The Victims' Movement' and Restorative Justice." Pp. 171–191 in *Handbook of Restorative Justice,* edited by Gerry Johnstone and Daniel W. Van Ness. Cullompton, Devon, UK: Willan Publishing.

Harris, M. Kay. 2006. "Transformative Justice: The Transformation of Restorative Justice." Pp. 555–566 in *Handbook of Restorative Justice: A Global Perspective,* edited by Dennis Sullivan and Larry Tifft. London: Routledge.

Hayes, Hennessey. 2007. "Reoffending and Restorative Justice." Pp. 426–444 in *Handbook of Restorative Justice,* edited by Gerry Johnstone and Daniel W. Van Ness. Cullompton, Devon, UK: Willan Publishing.

Herman, Judith L. 1992. *Trauma and Recovery.* New York: Basic Books.

———. 2005. "Justice from the Victim's Perspective." *Violence Against Women* 11:571–602.

Herman, Susan. 2004. "Is Restorative Justice Possible Without a Parallel System for Victims?" Pp. 75–83 in *Critical Issues in Restorative Justice,* edited by Howard Zehr and Barb Toews. Monsey, NY and Cullompton, Devon, UK: Criminal Justice Press and Willan Publishing.

Holder, Robyn. 1999. "Pick 'n Mix or Replication: The Politics and Process of Adaptation." Pp. 255–271 in *Coordinating Community Responses to Domestic Violence: Lessons from Duluth and Beyond,* edited by Melanie F. Shepard and Ellen Pence. Thousand Oaks, CA: Sage.

Hudon, Eileen. 2000. "Organizing Against Violence in Communities of Color." Pp. 91–92 in *Color of Violence: Violence Against Women of Color Conference Summary*. Minneapolis, MN: Incite! Women of Color Against Violence.

Incite! Women of Color Against Violence. 2003a. "Incite! World Social Forum Delegation Report Back." *Incite! Women of Color Against Violence Newsletter* March 18:8–15. Minneapolis, MN: Incite!

————. 2003b. *Incite! Women of Color Against Violence Community Accountability Principles/Concerns/Strategies/Models Working Document*. March 5. Retrieved February 26, 2009 (http://www.incite-national.org/index.php?s=93).

————, ed. 2006. *Color of Violence: The Incite! Anthology*. Cambridge, MA: South End Press.

————, ed. 2007a. *The Revolution Will Not Be Funded: Beyond the Non-Profit Industrial Complex*. Cambridge, MA: South End Press.

————. 2007b. "Principles of Unity." Minneapolis, MN: Incite! Retrieved March 5, 2007 (http://www.incite-national.org/about/unity.html).

Institute on Domestic Violence in the African American Community (IDVAAC). 2007. "About Us: Overview." Minneapolis, MN: IDVAAC. Retrieved December 16, 2007 (http://www.dvinstitute.org/about/overview.htm).

Koss, Mary P. 2000. "Blame, Shame, and Community: Justice Responses to Violence Against Women." *American Psychologist* 55:1332–1343.

————, Karen J. Bachar, C. Quince Hopkins, and Carolyn Carlson. 2004. "Expanding a Community's Justice Response to Sex Crimes Through Advocacy, Prosecutorial, and Public Health Collaboration: Introducing the RESTORE Program." *Journal of Interpersonal Violence* 19:1435–1463.

Lamb, Sharon. 1996. *The Trouble with Blame: Victims, Perpetrators, and Responsibility*. Cambridge, MA: Harvard University Press.

Lerman, Lisa. G. 1984. "Mediation of Wife Abuse Cases: The Adverse Impact of Informal Dispute Resolution on Women." *Harvard Women's Law Journal* 7:57–113.

Lerman, Lisa G., Sheila J. Kuehl and Mary Pat Brygger. 1989. *Domestic Abuse and Mediation: Guidelines for Mediators and Policy Makers*. Report to the U.S. Department of Justice.

Love, Catherine. 2000. "Family Group Conferencing: Cultural Origins, Sharing, and Appropriation—A Maori Reflection." Pp. 13–30 in *Family Group Conferencing: New Directions in Community-Centered Child and Family Practice*, edited by Gale Burford and Joe Hudson. New York: Aldine de Gruyter.

Manavi. 2007. "Herstory." New Brunswick, NJ: Manavi. Retrieved January 8, 2008 (http://www.manavi.org/about-herstory.php).

Mathews, David. (n.d.) "Restorative Parenting: A Strategy for Working with Men Who Batter and Are Fathers." San Francisco: Family Violence Prevention Fund. Retrieved February 19, 2009 (http://toolkit.endabuse.org/Resources/Restorative/FVPFResource_viewccb4.html).

McCold, Paul. 2003. "A Survey of Assessment Research on Mediation and Conferencing." Pp. 67–117 in *Repositioning Restorative Justice*, edited by Lode Walgrave. Cullompton, Devon UK: Willan Publishing.

————. 2006. "The Recent History of Restorative Justice: Mediation, Circles, and Conferencing." Pp. 23–51 in *Handbook of Restorative Justice: A Global Perspective*, edited by Dennis Sullivan and Larry Tifft. London: Routledge.

McMahon, Martha and Ellen Pence. 2003. "Making Social Change: Reflections on Individual and Institutional Advocacy with Women Arrested for Domestic Violence." *Violence Against Women* 9:47–74.

Miccio, G. Kristian. 2005. "A House Divided: Mandatory Arrest, Domestic Violence, and the Conservatization of the Battered Women's Movement." *Houston Law Review* 42:237–323.

Mika, Harry, Mary Achilles, Ellen Halbert, Howard Zehr, and Lorraine Stutzman Amstutz, 2004. "Listening to Victims—A Critique of Restorative Justice Policy and Practice in the United States." *Federal Probation* 68:32–38.

Mirsky, Laura. 2003. "Family Group Conferencing Worldwide: Part One in a Series." *Restorative Practices eForum*, February 20. Retrieved January 7, 2008 (http://www.restorativepractices.org/library/fgcseries01.html).

Mitchell-Clark, Kelly and Angela Autry. 2004. *Preventing Family Violence: Lessons from the Community Engagement Initiative.* San Francisco: Family Violence Prevention Fund.

Morris, Allison. 2003. "Critiquing the Critics: A Brief Response to Critics of Restorative Justice." Pp. 461–476 in *A Restorative Justice Reader: Texts, Sources, Context,* edited by Gerry Johnstone. Portland, OR: Willan Publishing.

New York Asian Women's Center. 2006. *History of NYAWC.* Retrieved January 8, 2008 (http://www.nyawc.org/about/history.html).

Parker, Lynette. 2007. "United Nations Publishes Handbook on Restorative Justice." *Restorative Justice Online*, February. Retrieved January 7, 2008 (http://www.restorativejustice.org/editions/2007/feb07/unhandbook).

Peachey, Dean E. 2003. "The Kitchener Experiment." Pp. 178–186 in *A Restorative Justice Reader: Texts, Sources, Context,* edited by Gerry Johnstone. Portland, OR: Willan Publishing.

Pence, Ellen L. 1996. *Safety for Battered Women in a Textually Mediated Legal System.* Unpublished doctoral dissertation in the Sociology of Education, University of Toronto, Ontario, Canada.

———. 1999. "Some Thoughts on Philosophy." Pp. 25–40 in *Coordinating Community Responses to Domestic Violence: Lessons from Duluth and Beyond,* edited by Melanie F. Shepard and Ellen Pence. Thousand Oaks, CA: Sage.

———. 2001. "Advocacy on Behalf of Battered Women." Pp. 329–343 in *Sourcebook on Violence Against Women,* edited by Claire M. Renzetti, Jeffrey L. Edleson, and Raquel Kennedy Bergen. Thousand Oaks, CA: Sage.

Pence, Ellen and Kristine Lizdas. 1998. *The Duluth Safety and Accountability Audit.* Duluth, MN: Minnesota Program Development, Inc.

Pence, Ellen and Michael Paymar, eds. 1993. *Education Groups for Men Who Batter: The Duluth Model.* New York: Springer.

Pence, Ellen and Melanie F. Shepard. 1999. "An Introduction: Developing a Coordinated Community Response." Pp. 3–23 in *Coordinating Community Responses to Domestic Violence: Lessons from Duluth and Beyond,* edited by Melanie F. Shepard and Ellen Pence. Thousand Oaks, CA: Sage.

Pennell, Joan. 1999. "Using Restorative Justice Practices in Situations of Family Violence." Presentation at Building Strong Partnerships for Restorative Practices Conference, Burlington, Vermont, August 5–7, 1999.

———. 2005. "Safety for Mothers and Their Children." Pp. 163–181 in *Widening the Circle: The Practice and Evaluation of Family Group Conferencing with Children, Youths, and Their Families,* edited by Joan Pennell and Gary Anderson. Washington, DC: NASW Press.

———. 2006. "Stopping Domestic Violence or Protecting Children? Contributions from Restorative Justice." Pp. 296–298 in *Handbook of Restorative Justice: A Global Perspective,* edited by Dennis Sullivan and Larry Tifft. London: Routledge.

Pennell, Joan and Gale Burford. 1994. "Widening the Circle: The Family Group Decision Making Project." *Journal of Child & Youth Care* 9:1–12.

———. 2000. "Family Group Decision Making: Protecting Children and Women." *Child Welfare* 79:131–158.

———. 2002. "Feminist Praxis: Making Family Group Conferencing Work." Pp. 108–127 in *Restorative Justice and Family Violence,* edited by Heather Strang and John Braithwaite. Cambridge, UK: Cambridge University Press.

Pennell, Joan and Stephanie Francis. 2005. "Safety Conferencing: Toward a Coordinated and Inclusive Response to Safeguard Women and Children." *Violence Against Women* 11:666–692.

Polios, Vicki. 2002. "An Inside Look at the Aboriginal Women's Action Network." *Indigezine: A First Nation Studies Program Magazine* Summer. Vancouver: University of British Columbia. Retrieved January 8, 2008 (http:// research2.csci.educ.ubc.ca/indigenation/vicki.htm).

Porter, Abbey J. 2005. "Restorative Justice Takes the World Stage at United Nations Crime Congress." *Restorative Practices eForum,* June 14. Retrieved December 20, 2007 (http://www.realjustice.org/library/uncrimecongress.html).

Richie, Andrea J. 2006. "Law Enforcement Violence Against Women of Color." Pp. 138–156 in *Color of Violence: The Incite! Anthology,* edited by Incite! Women of Color Against Violence. Cambridge, MA: South End Press.

Rosewater, Ann and Leigh Goodmark, 2007. *Steps Toward Safety: Improving Systemic and Community Responses for Families Experiencing Domestic Violence.* San Francisco: Family Violence Prevention Fund.

Rowe, Kelly. 1985. "The Limits of the Neighborhood Justice Center: Why Domestic Violence Cases Should Not Be Mediated." *Emory Law Journal* 34:855–910.

Rubin, Pamela. 2000. *Abused Women in Family Mediation: A Nova Scotia Snapshot. A Report Prepared by The Transition House Association of Nova Scotia* (THANS). Halifax, NS: THANS. Retrieved January 31, 2009 (http://www.thans.ca/file/30).

Russo, Ann. 1999. "Lesbians Organizing Lesbians Against Battering." Pp. 83–96 in *Same-Sex Domestic Violence: Strategies for Change,* edited by Beth Leventhal and Sandra E. Lundy. Thousand Oaks, CA: Sage.

Seidman, Ilene and Susan Vickers. 2005. "The Second Wave: An Agenda for the Next Thirty Years of Rape Law Reform." *Suffolk University Law Review* 38:467–491.

Shepard, Melanie F. and Ellen Pence, eds. 1999. *Coordinating Community Responses to Domestic Violence: Lessons from Duluth and Beyond.* Thousand Oaks, CA: Sage, 1999.

Smith, Andrea. 2000. "The Color of Violence." *Color Lines* Winter:14–15.

Spohn, Cassia and Julie Horney. 1992. *Rape Law Reform: A Grassroots Revolution and Its Impact.* New York: Plenum Press.

———. 1996. "The Impact of Rape Law Reform on the Processing of Simple and Aggravated Rape Cases." *Journal of Criminal Law & Criminology* 86:861–884.

Strang, Heather and John Braithwaite, eds. 2002. *Restorative Justice and Family Violence.* Cambridge, UK: Cambridge University Press.

Stuart, Barry. 1992. *Reasons for Sentencing, Regina versus Philip Moses.* Yukon Territory: Territorial Court, CanLII 2814.

———. 1997. *Building Community Partnerships: Community Peacemaking Circles.* Ottawa, Ontario: Department of Justice Canada.

Stubbs, Julie. 2002. "Domestic Violence and Women's Safety: Feminist Challenges to Restorative Justice." Pp. 42–61 in *Restorative Justice and Family Violence,* edited by Heather Strang and John Braithwaite. Cambridge, UK: Cambridge University Press.

———. 2004. "Restorative Justice, Domestic Violence, and Family Violence." *Australian Domestic & Family Violence Clearinghouse* Issues Paper 9:1–23.

Tjaden, Patricia and Nancy Thoennes. 2000. *Extent, Nature, and Consequences of Intimate Partner Violence: Findings from the National Violence Against Women Survey* (NCJ 181867). Washington, DC: U.S. Department of Justice.

Umbreit, Mark S. and Jean Greenwood. 2000. *Guidelines for Victim-Sensitive Victim-Offender Mediation: Restorative Justice Through Dialogue* (NCJ 176346). Washington, DC: U.S. Dept. of Justice, Office of Justice Programs, Office for Victims of Crime.

Umbreit, Mark S., Betty Vos, and Robert Coates. 2006. *Restorative Justice Dialogue: Evidence-Based Practice.* Center for Restorative Justice & Peacemaking, January 1. Retrieved June 9, 2007 (rjp.umn.edu/img/assets/13522/RJ_Dialogue_Evidence-based_Practice_1–06.pdf).

UN Secretary-General. 2006. *In-Depth Study on All Forms of Violence Against Women: Report of the Secretary-General.* New York: United Nations General Assembly. Retrieved November 15, 2007 (http://www.un.org/womenwatch/daw/vaw/SGstudyvaw.htm).

Van Ness, Daniel. 2002. "UN Economic and Social Council Endorses Basic Principles on Restorative Justice." *Restorative Justice Online, August.* Retrieved January 7, 2008 (www.restorativejustice.org/editions/2002/August02/ECOSOC%20Acts).

Victim Offender Mediation Association (VOMA). 2005. "Learn About VOMA." *Victim Offender Mediation Web Site.* Last modified April 6. Retrieved December 14, 2007 (http://www.voma.org/abtvoma.shtml).

Walby, Sylvia. 2005. *Violence Against Women and the Millennium Development Goals.* New York: United Nations, Division for the Advancement of Women. Retrieved November 15, 2007 (http://www.un.org/womenwatch/daw/vaw/consultation_galvanizing.htm).

Yantzi, Mark. 1998. *Sexual Offending and Restoration.* Scottsdale, PA: Herald Press.

Zehr, Howard. 1990. *Changing Lenses: A New Focus for Crime and Justice.* Scottsdale, PA: Herald Press.

———. 2002. *The Little Book of Restorative Justice.* Intercourse, PA: Good Books.

Zimring, Franklin E. 2007. *The Great American Crime Decline.* New York: Oxford University Press.

II

CRITICAL PERSPECTIVES ON RESTORATIVE JUSTICE IN CASES OF VIOLENCE AGAINST WOMEN

2

THE ROLE OF
RESTORATIVE JUSTICE
IN THE BATTERED
WOMEN'S MOVEMENT

Loretta Frederick & Kristine C. Lizdas

The twentieth century saw the birth of two reform movements, both directed, in whole or part, to challenging the Western criminal justice system. In its nascence, the battered women's movement, a multifaceted reform movement, directed a portion of its energies to challenging the non-Indigenous Western criminal justice system's ambivalence toward and unresponsiveness to domestic violence. To this day, this movement continues to push the system's responsiveness to domestic violence. The battered women's movement has never promoted the naïve hope that the criminal justice system can reliably keep all battered women safe or definitively establish a shared intolerance for domestic violence, but this movement does promote the criminal justice system's potential to advance both goals.

On the other hand, the second of these reform movements, the restorative justice (RJ) movement, challenges the foundational concepts of the modern criminal justice apparatus. It critiques the retributive and punitive nature of the criminal justice system and favors the fostering of healing relationships among offenders, victims, and communities.

Both movements employ practices that hold the promise of being truly effective responses to domestic violence. But both movements also engage in practices that are ineffective in different ways for very different reasons. The critique of each is unique because each movement's need for improvement arises from its orientation to the issue of violence against women.

The term "restorative" as used in this chapter has a specific meaning to the authors, who take the position that practices which are truly "restorative" of the victim, the offender, and the community must be effective, redemptive, and liberating. For the purposes of this chapter, the "effectiveness" of the practice will be measured against the goal of creating safety and stopping violence in the lives of the involved parties and in the community as a whole. Practices that are "redemptive" are those which offer offenders an opportunity to change. Finally, "liberation" of victims from the tyranny of violence, coercion, and control is necessary to right the wrongs done by domestic violence perpetrators.

As disparate as the battered women's and restorative justice movements are, it was not unforeseeable that they would cross paths. And it is at this crossroads that both movements have the opportunity to engage in some introspection as well as dialogue. Although these movements evolved in response to different social issues and have very distinct agendas, they do share several fundamental principles.

FOUR PRINCIPLES COMMON TO THE RESTORATIVE JUSTICE AND BATTERED WOMEN'S MOVEMENTS

Analyses of the principles underlying the RJ and battered women's movements reveal at least four strong points of commonality. These are the movements' interests in (1) restoring victims of crime, (2) preventing individual offenders from reoffending, (3) promoting the role of the community in responding to crime, and (4) addressing the social context in which crime is committed. Each movement, however, implements these principles in vastly different ways and through disparate practices. As outlined later, these differences are the result of each movement having arisen from a unique political standpoint and in response to different social problems.

Principle One: Restoring Victims of Crime

Restorative justice proponents and battered women's advocates both seek to improve the condition of the victim. However, it is not clear whether the notion of "restoration" as applied to domestic violence cases is limited to returning to a victim those things (rights, resources, security, autonomy) that she once possessed but lost as a result of the crime, or whether "restoration" should mean providing to a victim those things to which she was entitled but that she may have never possessed by virtue of her class, race, gender, or other circumstances. In many instances, domestic violence victims have never had the tangible and intangible necessities for being safe, whole, and vested with full human rights. Certainly, both movements would promote the safety and security of victims.

RJ proponents criticize the traditional criminal justice system's response for focusing on holding the offender accountable to the state for violations of codified norms (criminal laws), while ignoring the need to repair the harm done to victims. RJ is seen as offering a mechanism through which an offender, the offender's family, friends, and/or the community at large can provide those things lost to the victim as a result of the crime, whether they be they tangible (money, property, medical expenses) or intangible (sense of worth, safety, closure). RJ proponents take the position that crime damages the balance and equilibrium between victim and offender; the traditional ("retributive") response damages both victim and offender; and RJ restores equilibrium.

Whether RJ *practices,* especially as administered by correctional or prosecutorial arms of government, truly promote victim restoration in domestic violence cases depends on the community, the program, and the participants; how much each of them is invested in this aspect of restorative justice; whether they fully understand the problem presented by the crime; and whether they respect the victim's autonomy.

The language of victim "restoration" has not often been used by the battered women's movement, although the primacy of battered women's interests and needs have been advocated quite strongly by its activists. This movement has its roots in the work of battered women themselves to shelter and support each other, aided by other activists. Central to its philosophy is the notion that an intervention is not effective, redemptive, and liberating ("restorative") unless it accounts for the fact that battering deprives women of their safety, autonomy, liberty and, too often, their very lives. Because the stakes are so high, and because women's needs are clear, the battered women's movement has spent much of its political capital encouraging and cajoling communities into providing battered women with the services and assistance (including safe housing and civil and criminal justice system responses) required to fully restore their safety, freedom, and autonomy. This work, often called *systems advocacy* or *institutional advocacy,* is paralleled and informed by *individual advocacy,* which is founded on the principle that battered women should determine the direction of their lives. Although the two kinds of advocacy inform each other, they can conflict. For example, advocates doing criminal justice system reform work can find themselves in the awkward but necessary position of advocating on Monday for a pro-prosecution policy and on Tuesday that charges against an individual defendant be dropped because her battered partner desires that outcome.

Principle Two: Preventing Individual Offenders from Reoffending

Both movements are motivated to change the behavior of individuals who have already committed antisocial acts such as domestic violence. But what is considered by each movement to be *effective* in changing men's violence against women reflects differing views about what causes domestic violence. These differences can mean that the movements' approaches to accomplishing this goal differ, sometimes dramatically.

A primary goal of many RJ practices is to improve the likelihood that an offender will choose not to violate society's norms when presented with the option to do so. RJ proponents argue that the goal of offender reformation and rehabilitation is not well addressed by the standard criminal justice system's response. In fact, the promise of reducing recidivism and easing docket pressures through the use of RJ practices has contributed to the growing popularity of this movement and the increasing interest of criminal justice system practitioners in creating RJ programs.

RJ emphasizes the engagement of the community in the rehabilitation of the offender because crime is seen as being rooted in economic, racial, and other types of oppressions that result in disenfranchisement. In fact, the RJ movement stands for the proposition that many individual offenders are not irredeemable but are capable, especially with the help of the community, of transformation into law-abiding and responsible members of the community.

It is interesting to note that the original focus of RJ on the rehabilitation of the offender proved to run contrary to popular sentiment, which favored the most retributive aspects of the criminal justice system. In response to this political reality, RJ programs began emphasizing the restoration of victims and the healing of the community, thereby making RJ more palatable to the public (Marshall 1998).

The battered women's movement's approach reducing recidivism is based upon its understanding of why women are battered by their partners. The movement believes, first, that culture and laws have long reflected the belief that intimate partner violence against women is acceptable and that, therefore, to deter abusers from further violence, communities must convey a strong message of intolerance for domestic abuse. Second, the movement contends that an individual's life experience may teach him or her that violence is an effective and appropriate means to achieving the goal of controlling a partner (control to which he/she is entitled) and that, therefore, individual abusers must be taught different values and skills. Third, the movement believes that when batterers use violence against their partners they are responsible for making that decision and must be provided with a range of disincentives (including formal ones such as those provided by the legal system) and also opportunities to learn new ways of thinking about their families.

Principle Three: Engaging the Community in Mending Harms Caused by Crime

Both social movements share a goal of involving the community more meaningfully in addressing social problems. But how each engages the community on domestic violence reflects differing beliefs about what will be effective in addressing the damage to victims and their communities.

The philosophy of RJ largely focuses on mending the harm caused by crime through utilizing the resources available within the parties' communities. The community becomes involved in exploring all aspects of the crime, as well as in understanding its role or responsibility in the crime. The word "communities" is used very broadly in the RJ context. It can mean family, friends, and neighbors, or representatives from various aspects of the community—e.g., spiritual institutions, criminal justice institutions, social services, or businesses. One core value of RJ is the centrality of community in addressing crime. Instead of addressing crime by treating an offender as an isolated object in the criminal justice process, it deals with an offender relationally—as a member of a community whose actions affect the entire community.

RJ places less emphasis on the use of a legal hierarchy and more emphasis on the role of the community in responding to criminals. It employs a relational model that its proponents believe is most adept at creating real personal change. Mark Umbreit describes the role of the community as follows:

> Restorative justice is a victim-centered response to crime that provides opportunities for those most directly affected by crime—the victim, offender, their families, and representatives of the community—to be directly involved in responding to the harm caused by the crime. Restorative justice is based upon values that emphasize the importance of providing opportunities for more active involvement in the process of: offering support and assistance to crime victims; holding offenders directly accountable to the people and communities they have violated; restoring the emotional and material losses of victims (to the degree possible); providing a range of opportunities for dialogue and problem-solving among interested crime victims, offenders, families, and other support persons; offering offenders opportunities for competency development and reintegration into productive community life; and strengthening public safety through community building. (Umbreit 1999)

It is this collective, relational process that most distinguishes RJ from the standard criminal justice system response. "Restorative justice is a process whereby the parties with a stake in a particular offense resolve collectively how to deal with the aftermath of the offense and its implications for the future" (Umbreit 1999).

Many in the RJ movement stand strongly on the principle that crime affects everyone in the community and can best be mended by that same community in concerted action with the offender. However, the RJ movement's understanding of the harm that is caused by domestic violence (as well as the proper role of the community in addressing it) differs from that of the battered women's movement.

Changing the community climate of tolerance toward domestic violence has always been a primary goal of the battered women's movement. In pursuing these goals, advocates and battered women have turned to the community, recognizing that individual women alone, advocates alone, police alone, batterers' intervention services alone, or the courts alone are unlikely to be successful at stopping individual batterers or keeping individual women safe. The movement contends that as communities become more engaged in providing victims with safety and in holding offenders accountable, they make progress in reducing their own tolerance for violence within their communities.

Accordingly, the battered women's movement strongly encourages a community-wide response to this social issue. One prominent model of community intervention in domestic violence evolved from an experiment in Duluth, Minnesota, in the early 1980s that evolved into what is now referred to as the Coordinated Community Response (CCR) model. Most CCR efforts have focused on various criminal justice system strategies—whether they consist of linking police and prosecution more closely, developing stronger communication between probation departments and offender programs, or increasing courts' accountability to victims.

Advocates have long worked directly with battered women, as well, to help them identify those in their own communities who might support them. Since the beginning, battered women, assisted in many cases by their advocates, have tried to enlist their allies (friends, family, and community members) in stopping the violence and persuading their batterers to play a more positive role in the family. Advocates in communities of color have employed and refined this approach in ways that mainstream advocates have not, and the programs serving more isolated and disempowered communities have a lot to teach others about the benefits of helping a woman to organize her community.

Principle Four: Addressing the Context of Crime

Both movements share a social analysis that criminal incidents must be examined in the context in which they occur. Historically, the work of the battered women's movement worldwide has been based on the knowledge that violence against women in intimate relationships is simply one form of the nearly universal gender-based discrimination that operates to keep women in subservient roles. The RJ movement has articulated and even centralized the role that other biases, notably classism and racism, play in the creation of conditions that lead to crime. For example, within some juvenile justice circles, RJ proponents seek to address the "social and economic conditions in a community that significantly affect the inclusion or exclusion of young people with respect to society," and promote the concept of a "restorative community justice model of intervention" (White 2001). Theory and practice, however, have not evolved to reflect an understanding of some of the other aspects of social identity, such as gender.

Like RJ proponents, advocates in the battered women's movement have long strived to assert the relevance of social context in domestic violence crime. But although many advocates encourage the community to understand domestic violence within the larger context of sexism, they do not often address the role of race or class bias in the problem or the solutions. Battered women's advocates articulate the position that gender-based oppression takes many forms including rape, economic discrimination against women, and, of course, domestic violence. They have joined their voices with those of other feminist thinkers to expose the extent to which cultural institutions such as the legal system (as shown by the case law of many past years) have perpetuated female subordination to men. It is clear that, wherever it originated and however it is maintained, domestic violence is a worldwide phenomenon affecting women in every nation. The battered women's movement sees this violence as arising directly from social and historical contexts.

Women of color have attempted to lead the battered women's movement to a more nuanced understanding of the context of crime, including the interrelatedness of various forms of oppression. Seeing sexism as inextricably linked to racism, classism, homophobia, and ageism is fundamental to much feminist thought and literature, including that on battering (Schechter 1982). This awareness shapes much of the analysis and strategy of many battered women's advocates. This analysis has not, however, been reflected in the criminal justice system reform work of the many advocates who have largely neglected to address class, race, and other biases in that system's response to domestic violence.

It is no coincidence that RJ proponents look to the field of domestic violence as a fitting forum for the application of RJ practices. And it is no coincidence that some battered women advocates are more than a little curious about the burgeoning RJ movement. Many of the principles and much of the language of each movement resonate for the other. While each takes a different approach to each the four principles listed, the areas of overlap are still clear. Where the movements substantially diverge is in the application of those principles to actual practice. The following section details areas of conflict between the practices of the RJ movement and the battered women's movement and makes recommendations for each.

TOWARD MORE EFFECTIVE, REDEMPTIVE, AND LIBERATING RESPONSES TO BATTERED WOMEN

Each of these movements has charted its own course in its attempt to restore victims, stop violent behavior, involve communities, and incorporate the social context of crime. And each movement has seen its successes and failures. Fortunately, an examination of each movement's efforts in pursuit of its own goals can provide important lessons in the strengths, weaknesses, and limitations of their philosophies and practices. Such an examination can be made by analyzing the movements in light of the four goals that the authors submit should drive all interventions in domestic violence cases: (1) restoring battered women's safety, autonomy, and agency; (2) preventing further violence by batterers against their intimate partners; (3) making egalitarianism and peace the community standards for conduct in intimate relationships; and (4) addressing solutions to the social context of crime.

Goal One: Restoring Battered Women's Safety, Autonomy, and Agency

A primary facet of battering is the abuser's restriction of his partner's liberty—controlling how she spends her time, whom she sees, where she goes. Consequently, a successful intervention is one that focuses on respecting a battered woman's freedom to make choices for herself and restoring to her the control over her own life.

Interventions that promote battered women's safety will also be those tailored to the context in which their abusers have committed the violence. Most intimate relationship violence against women is committed in the context of the offender's use of power and control tactics, including intimidation and threats. Such battered women are subject both to batterer-generated risks and life-generated risks (Davies, Lyon, and Monti-Catania 1998). Risks that are batterer-generated are not only those of further violence, but of other negative outcomes that stem from attempts to resist controls or separate from the abuser: eviction, loss of housing or employment, inability to find decent child care, being reported to child protection by their abusers, or loss of child custody to their abusers. Life-generated risks are those arising from those circumstances in a woman's life over which she has little or no control, such as economics, education/training, discrimination, language, gender, immigration status, housing, physical and mental health, access to services, legal status, history, social circumstances and status, and socio-cultural practices. A batterer can and often does manipulate these life-generated risks to punish or control his or her victim.

Therefore, battered women's safety and autonomy is promoted when the offender is not only stopped from committing other violent and intimidating acts, but the woman's life-generated risks are minimized and the social, legal, and moral climate in the community supports the cessation of the violence.

The Battered Women's Movement

The battered women's movement has a history of centralizing the needs and autonomy of individual women, embracing "women-centered advocacy" and refusing to join in the chorus of voices (of social workers, criminal legal system practitioners, and others) telling these women what they should do. The work of reforming the criminal legal system, which was driven by battered women's need for safety after an incident, has had mixed results in advancing victim safety and autonomy. In fact, the movement's focus on victim autonomy and safety has to some extent been eroded in the recent past.

Since its origins, the battered women's movement has focused heavily on victim safety by pushing communities to fund shelters, create civil restraining order remedies, offer services such as support groups and advocacy, and reform institutional responses to victims and perpetrators.

To the extent that the practical services that the battered women's movement provides—such as shelter, support, and individual "women-directed" or "women-centered" advocacy—actually help women become safer and more autonomous, they are doing very "restorative" work. Domestic violence programs undertake, and must continue to undertake, both systems and individual advocacy that create real life options (and increase autonomy), especially because the battered women's movement is alone in having this as its chief work. Advocating for women's autonomy would certainly be the most effective, redemptive, and liberating of all activities.

Difficulties in advancing women's safety and autonomy have arisen in three areas.

First, ample evidence suggests that the same biases that have infected other institutional responses to domestic violence are present in the programming decisions of many battered women's programs. Many communities of color and those consisting of people with limited English capacity as well as some lesbian, gay, disabled, and other victims of domestic violence have made it clear that they are not being adequately served by existing programs. As a result, some have created their own options for safety without engaging mainstream services.

Inaccessibility must be addressed if programs are to deal with the life-generated risks these women face. Programs must begin offering to assist and partner with communities, to help organize around the issues *chosen by the women in the community*. These efforts will serve to cement relations, improve mainstream services, and inform later organizing to stop battering in those communities.

Second, a trend is noted in some programs, especially some shelters, toward the treatment of battered women as primarily in need of mental health or psychological therapy. This is truly not restorative; rather, it merely substitutes one view of what women should do (that of the abusive partner) for another (the program's). This trend toward depoliticizing violence against women will substantially weaken advocates' ability to address the life-generated risks faced by women every day. Women who are poor, disabled, discriminated against, undereducated, or immigrant—and because of their gender are at increased risk of being assaulted by their partners—have real problems *of a political nature* that seriously compromise their safety and that of their children. Engagement with the community to address these and related risks, not just to raise the funds necessary to shelter and counsel women, is a critical component of the movement to end violence against women.

Third, the battered women's movement has worked from early on to reform the criminal justice system's response to victims, and many are safer as a result. But many programs that focus heavily on criminal justice reform work have not done enough to address those other needs that women repeatedly identify. These include safe and affordable housing, child care, true autonomy, and community support for staying in a relationship while staying safe.

Finally, the criminal justice system, one of the chief tools of the movement, has not seen itself as having the function of identifying or addressing crime victims' life-generated risks until very recently. The criminal system must become more accessible to battered women whose life-generated conditions might otherwise exclude them from help or meaningful participation. For example, interpreters must be available to assist law enforcement, prosecutors, defense counsel, and victim witness staff and advocates to respond properly to cases involving non–English-speaking parties, including hearing impaired persons. Criminal court sentences and conditions of release pending trial should reflect consideration of the life-generated risks that may be complicating the lives of battered women. Child care should be available in courthouses so that parents with few resources can participate in civil and criminal hearings. Legal proceedings must take into account the fact that working-class or poor battered woman might lose their jobs if they must repeatedly take time off for court appearances. Immigration issues and other collateral consequences of legal proceedings must be considered by practitioners at every level.

The reality is that most battered women do not want their partners prosecuted. Although it is crucial to promote battered women's autonomy, interjecting this autonomy into the criminal justice system's batterer accountability activities is very complicated. Because women who summon the police hope that they will not have to direct the removal of their partners in order to obtain protection, police should continue to make warrantless arrests of predominant aggressors where they have probable cause to believe that a crime has been committed. But beyond the arrest stage, the role of women's autonomy should increase in importance and they should be consulted by prosecutors who attend to their safety concerns and life-generated risks.

Battered women's advocates must avoid relying too heavily on the criminal justice system as the means to victim safety, recognizing that the criminal courts are not an option for many women. Because many battered women would choose civil legal remedies such as child custody and civil protection orders over criminal proceedings, advocates must redouble their efforts to ensure that women have access to competent legal advocates and attorneys.

Advocates must also supplement their criminal justice system reform work with a more holistic approach that not only seeks to reform institutions but to organize communities to protect women. CCR models must be retooled to include healthcare providers, faith communities, and community organizations, as well as families, friends, employers, and others with a personal connection to victims or offenders. Advocates must engage with women to look beyond the civil and criminal justice systems to their (or their abusers') families, friends, employers, faith communities, and neighbors to build support for these women, increase their safety, and encourage the batterers to cease their violence. It must be recognized, however, that the community to which a woman and her advocate might go for support and protection may disagree that she is entitled to it or may blame her for the violence. Accordingly, the community education that the movement has been promoting for years should be tailored to the message that *all* women deserve to live free of violence and intimidation and that the immediate community of each battered woman and each batterer must take steps to make this safety and freedom a reality.

Critical to women's safety is the confidentiality of her communications with her advocate. Domestic violence programs must ensure that any collaboration with the criminal justice or child welfare systems does not jeopardize the fundamental right of women to a confidential relationship with an advocate.

The Restorative Justice Movement

The RJ movement, too, has evolved practices that are designed to advance the safety and autonomy of crime victims. Victim–offender mediation, for example, has placed the emphasis upon victim healing, offender accountability, and restoration of losses (Marshall 1998). In family group or community conferencing, "the victim has the opportunity to express feelings and ask questions about the offense. After a thorough discussion of the impact of the offense on those present, the victim is asked to identify desired outcomes from the conference and thus helps to shape the obligations that will be placed on the offender" (Umbreit 2000). In sentencing circles, victims have the choice whether to be present and what "community" should be present on their behalf.

Applied properly, the principles of the RJ movement might lead its practitioners to identify and address victim safety, including life-generated risks, and autonomy. But because current RJ practices suffer from other flaws that inhibit their effectiveness in domestic violence cases, the utility of meeting this goal through RJ practices has not been borne out.

For example, although sentencing (as with sentencing circles) in a domestic violence case might be better informed if it involved members of the parties' communities, these RJ practices are far more private in nature than are the more formal adjudicatory legal system's procedures. The criminal justice system's response to domestic violence (which serves as the chief method whereby the offenders are held publicly accountable) is designed, in part, to cut through the secrecy surrounding the abuse and to undermine the communities' tacit acceptance of violence against women. There is a strong likelihood that RJ sentencing practices simply undercut the public accountability function of the justice system; the more private, less-public sentencing process could actually leave many women unprotected and could inadvertently slow the progress toward ending domestic violence. Therefore, domestic violence cases should not be diverted (avoiding conviction, for example) into RJ programs that allow the batterer to evade public accountability. Engagement with the community should increase, not decrease, accountability.

The engagement of community is, itself, one aspect of RJ practices that might have the most potential for restoring battered women's safety, autonomy, and agency. However, the risks associated with this are many and have not, to date, been satisfactorily resolved. This is an area ripe for open and creative discussions between the two movements.

Of course, one issue raised by the involvement of community in domestic violence sentencing, is the question of what persons or group constitutes "community." Arguably, "community" should not mean "white, middle-class, able-bodied, heterosexual" for the purposes of responding to the needs of batterers or to battered women who do not have those characteristics.

But the most confounding and problematic aspect of community involvement in domestic violence cases is the prevalence in the community of norms that support violence against women, excusing such violence as private or as deserved by the victim. For the past several decades, battered women's activists have documented society's proclivity for blaming victims of domestic violence for the abuse they suffer, as people ask not "why did he hurt her?" but instead, "why didn't she leave him?" and even assert that his violence against her was understandable, considering her behavior. In this social context, employing the community to keep the victim safe might be quite risky. Therefore, the only "community" that should be asked to address a particular offense or offender should be one that deeply understands four things: (1) the dynamics of domestic violence; (2) the harm done to a victim in the past and the likelihood of harm in the future; (3) the likely response of the offender to any proposed resolution; and (4) the dynamics, both political and personal, that might affect the process or the result.

Other RJ practices that involve mediation-like activities can fail to address battered women's safety because of the relationship power imbalances that result from the coercive controls exercised over victims by their perpetrators. In battering cases, the perpetrator of domestic abuse has often wrested power from the victim/survivor; the abuser believes himself to be entitled to control her actions, words, and beliefs. As a result of this and other tactics of power and control, the victim/survivor is often reluctant to voice any disagreement with the batterer and may fear retaliation for objecting to or even revealing the fact of the abuse (Belzer 2003). This power imbalance has many implications for battered women's autonomy, their ability to fully participate, and the voluntary nature of their agreement to engage in such a practice.

For example, a victim may not feel (or be) free to state her views on the sentencing of her abusive partner, especially in a process that specifically values each participant's voice (and "truth") equally. Accordingly, any use of such facilitated processes in domestic violence cases must be only at the request of the victim and in the manner she desires. A battered woman should never be asked to sit in a group with her abuser and his support system. If she requests to participate in such a meeting, she must be well prepared and provided adequate support, assistance, and protection during and in the months following the process. If she is asked for her input in any manner other than in a meeting with her abuser, she must be fully informed about who will have access to the information she provides. She must also be assisted in assessing the risks and benefits of participating, even in this less-intrusive process. In the last analysis, if RJ's goal of victim safety and autonomy is to be advanced in domestic violence cases, any facilitated process must account for the fact that the abuser intended (and may still intend) to create and maintain power over the victim.

A relationship power imbalance caused by battering also has implications for the process for inviting victims to participate. Most RJ practitioners assert that participation in any process must be voluntary. The choice to participate is a very complex one for battered women; autonomy as applied to this choice is often difficult to ensure. A battered woman may be pressured—especially if invited by a system that focuses more on the reform of the perpetrator than the needs of the victim—to participate in a process that is uncomfortable or even dangerous for her. Or, she may want to participate because she thinks she will obtain an illusory benefit from participation, such as the abuser's reasons for making her life so miserable.

Because of the power balance implications of battering, it is critical that all *current* facilitative RJ practices include screening for and exclusion of cases involving domestic violence. Any process that places the battered woman in a negotiating relationship with the source of her fears offers her a false promise of hope and might, therefore, place her in danger. To date, the RJ movement has failed to adequately address these concerns.

Restitution is a last example of the difficulties RJ proponents have had in applying the movement's principles to domestic violence cases. Restitution holds the promise of helping battered women recover from the financial devastation frequently wrought by their abusive partners. Restitution's usefulness, however, is limited in that it depends heavily on (1) the availability of advocates, attorneys, or prosecutors to assist the victim in assessing the financial costs associated with the crime; (2) the ability of the victim and her advocate to articulate the need for recompense and to advocate for it; (3) the willingness of the court to entertain the request and to rule appropriately; and (4) the ability of the defendant to pay restitution (in addition, perhaps to child support, batterer's intervention program fees, and costs associated with defense). A restitution practice that was meaningful and accessible for victims would address at least the first three of these concerns.

The extent to which any RJ practice that could be developed is effective and liberating for battered women depends on whether: (1) the definition of what is effective and liberating to any individual woman is determined by her, in a process which involves, at her discretion, working with an advocate from a program outside the criminal justice system; (2) any agreements that would bind either the community or the offender to taking specific steps are enforceable and enforced; (3) the process itself does not make her uncomfortable or endanger her; and (4) she is provided, as part of the process, with the resources necessary to her restoration. The extent to which any practice could be redemptive for the abuser is addressed in the next section.

Goal Two: Preventing Further Violence by Batterers

Because batterers are themselves responsible for the choice to use violence (regardless of their histories and of the existence of factors that place them at greater risk of choosing violence), interventions designed to stop battering must be directed at batterers and not at their victims. Furthermore, no intervention can ignore the reality that the batterer's violence serves a purpose and that the batterer believes significant benefits are to be gained through the use of intimate partner violence. Finally, because violence often escalates when the batterer's control is being challenged, any intervention must take into account the real possibility that the violence will be repeated and may even worsen.

The Battered Women's Movement

The work of the battered women's movement to stop individual abusers from committing further acts of abuse has focused largely on reforms of the criminal and civil legal systems and on creating and providing batterer intervention programs.

Many activists were encouraged by the growing evidence that a well-designed criminal justice system response to domestic violence could actually deter batterers (Stark 1996). Advocates viewed reform of the criminal justice system as best accomplished through training and other advocacy activities designed to change police, prosecution, probation, and court practices. The resulting collaborations became some of the most important work of many domestic violence programs. To this day, the battered women's movement's attempts to reform the criminal justice system in partnership with its professionals continue to flourish.

Although the effectiveness of the criminal justice system response to domestic violence has improved dramatically in the last 30 years, to be most effective, prosecutors and courts must improve their ability to gather sufficient information, including victim preferences and risk or danger assessments in order to distinguish among cases. Closer scrutiny would allow criminal justice system practitioners to better tailor their responses to the needs of each offender (to treatment or education programs, sanctions, and limits on freedom where appropriate) and to increase the likelihood that the offender's treatment of his partner will change.

Practices that offer more effective interventions include the kind of law enforcement methods now being promoted in many U.S. communities: prioritization of domestic violence calls for immediate response; separate interviews with all parties and witnesses in a manner reflective of the potential seriousness of the incident; sensitive and competent approaches to victims on the scene and afterward; careful collection of evidence and assessment of probable cause to believe a crime has been committed, including whether the violence was motivated by self-defense; follow-up investigations and contacts with victims; and competent testimony at trial.

Prosecutorial practices that can assist in conveying to the abuser the message that his actions are not acceptable are: recognition and respect for the ongoing risks and other concerns that the victim may be facing; charging decisions that take into account the history behind and context of the incident; and ensuring that the victim is not placed in a central role in the case against her partner.

The courts' messages to and treatment of those accused of domestic violence crimes may be the most critical. Practices that convey the clearest message to abusers include control of the offender's behavior toward the victim in the courtroom; the issuance of clear court orders that are unequivocal in their message that repeated violence will not be tolerated; the insistence on complete information on the offender, the incident, and any history of abuse; and the adoption of consistency and fairness in response to violations of court orders. The role of incarceration in the criminal justice system's response to domestic violence, which has been minimal to date, should be limited to situations in which it is likely to improve public or victim safety or to convey the message of society's concern to a serial or serious abuser.

Many of these interventions are based upon the belief that the abuser alone has the ability to stop his violence, and that the victim will usually be unable or unwilling in leading the charge to hold her abuser accountable. Thus the criminal justice system essentially circumvents the victim and instead deals directly with the abuser. Warrantless misdemeanor arrests (made in the absence of the victim's express request or even assent) and evidence-based prosecution (wherein the case is brought forward based upon the available evidence, including the victim's out-of-court statements, such as excited utterances) are both directed at the abuser and increasingly minimize the role of the victim in holding the offender accountable or confronting him in order to stop his violence.

It should be noted that most of the criminal justice system interventions that discourage future violence, such as close supervision and appropriate treatment or batterer's intervention programs, may be utilized in some cases even in the absence of a conviction. In light of the severe collateral consequences of even a misdemeanor conviction (such as deportation of a legal immigrant, ineligibility for government benefits or public housing, prohibition from certain jobs such as child care), the criminal justice system must assess in each case whether conviction is necessary to obtain the kind of relief that will ensure victim safety.

One of the serious unintended consequences of criminal justice system intervention has been the arrest and prosecution of battered women who fight back, whether legally or illegally. These practices undermine the community's ability to prevent the batterer's future violence.

Batterer's intervention programs (BIPs) were developed beginning in the 1980s by men and women in the battered women's movement who understood that abusive men should not just be held accountable by the criminal justice system but should also be offered an opportunity to learn to relate to their partners in a more egalitarian and nonviolent manner. In fact, the goal of interventions is equality and mutual respect in intimate relationships. The Power and Control Wheel, developed by the Duluth Domestic Abuse Intervention Project for use with offenders, has a companion, the Equality Wheel, which is used as a representation of healthy, equal partnerships. It is this vision of relationships that many BIPs seek to share with abusive men.

BIPs are essentially redemptive in character in that they are rooted in the belief that men can change and that communities should assist in that process. The original groups used psycho-social models combining education and supportive confrontation, a practice that is continued today by most groups, although other models have been created since. Their efficacy in stopping batterers has been the subject of much controversy and research, although the most credible and longitudinal work is that of Gondolf, who found that the success of the groups in reducing levels of violence was tied directly to whether they were embedded in a community, especially in its legal system, which held the batterer accountable in many ways (Gondolf 2002).

The challenge now is to ensure that (1) these programs are truly accountable to the women whose partners are served by them, (2) they meet commonly accepted standards, and (3) the community creates options for intervention that are truly accessible to all abusers, regardless of their language, economic status, and culture.

The Restorative Justice Movement

As indicated earlier, many RJ practices are directed at reducing recidivism, as through victim–offender mediation (designed in part to educate the offender about the impact of his crime on the victim and community) and family group conferencing or circle sentencing (to engage the community in working with the offender to change his behavior). Although these practices have been shown to be effective in many juvenile crime cases, their efficacy beyond those circumstances is a subject of disagreement.

RJ practices that could best prevent repeat *domestic* violence are those that convey to the abuser the clear expectation that the violence must stop (and provide the tools to do so) while also providing the kind of protective support the woman desires. Some current RJ practices do have potential in this regard, but some can actually increase the danger to the victim in several ways.

First, practices that engage the victim and abuser together in discussion create an environment that easily confuses the messages carried to both, and further imply that both parties have a role in creating the problem and in finding a solution. Domestic violence cases are particularly vulnerable to misinterpretation and victim-blaming. The only hope for change in a batterer can come from his realization that what he has done is wrong and that he, and not his partner, is fully responsible for the act and for making changes. Practices that result in confusion about responsibility for the violence and its effects are dangerous.

Second, because experience shows that a batterer represents a real threat of future violence to his victim, practices that do not assume, in the absence of information to the contrary, that such a danger exists will further endanger her. The chief weakness in the RJ movement's practices as applied to domestic violence cases is that, although they attempt to focus on restoration of victims, they have not accounted for one of the chief characteristics of most domestic violence cases: the existence of ongoing danger occasioned by the victim's resistance to the batterers' authority and control.

Third, practices that presume that domestic violence offenders are not aware of the consequences of their violent acts provides batterers with the opportunity to manipulate intervenors and sabotage the process. A much safer presumption is that a domestic violence offender uses violence in his relationship because he is aware that violence creates the desired effect of maintaining authority and control in a relationship.

The RJ movement should start to centralize victim safety by committing to work directly with battered women and their advocates to examine and critique the current practices with the goal of ensuring that women's safety is central to the process. For example, mediation-based practices must not be applied to domestic violence cases in the absence of clear and convincing evidence that the victim is, in a truly informed manner, affirmatively seeking to participate with her abuser in such a process.

RJ practitioners must not engage a community in domestic violence cases unless and until the battered women's movement is satisfied that the norms of the engaged community include opposition to gender-based violence and an understanding of the dynamics of battering and other systems of oppression. In the last analysis, the extent to which any practice would be truly redemptive for batterers depends on whether it offers a realistic hope for change: it must address the deep-seated and community-supported beliefs of the abuser about the roles of women and relationships.

Goal Three: Making Egalitarianism and Peace the Community Standards for Conduct in Intimate Relationships

Any intervention, even one primarily focused on responding to an individual perpetrator or victim of domestic violence, must account for its impact on the larger community's views about such violence. No public intervention (or failure to intervene) is neutral in its effect on community norms: for centuries the victim-blaming and inaction of all social institutions both reflected and encouraged the prevailing view of domestic violence as a private matter of little consequence. Both the RJ and battered women's movements must work to ensure that their practices have a positive impact on community norms. "Community," however defined, must be transformed in order to stop the violence.

The Battered Women's Movement

Many aspects of feminist work reflect a commitment to this goal of changing the climate in which people decide what conduct is appropriate with their intimate partners. Community education and media campaigns are a long-standing part of the work. Criminal justice system reform was instituted in part to change norms in the community.

Such work raises at least two issues. First, the degree to which the movement has relied on the criminal justice system to change a community's thinking about violence against women must be reviewed and rethought. The criminal justice system has not directly engaged in activities addressing this goal, except to the extent that it communicates to offenders (actual or potential) that they do not have the right to control their partners through violence. Those messages are not overt in most cases, at least regarding behaviors such as coercive controls that are not criminal but are otherwise harmful to the victim. Research is mixed on the deterrent effect of domestic violence prosecutions, but it does appear that, at least for felony assailants, conviction and jail time reduce recidivism. In any event, it is questionable whether the criminal justice system could or should undertake activity that would advance the goal of changing community norms, considering that social change of this kind is not within its core mission.

Second, to the extent that domestic violence services and discourse become gender neutralized, the ability of the movement to directly address the causes of power imbalances in relationships (gender role distinctions and patriarchal notions about family) and thereby erode the support for such violence against women will be weakened. As a result, the goal of establishing egalitarianism and nonviolence as a community standard for intimate relationships will be not be met.

The Restorative Justice Movement

This idea of a community standard has not been explicitly promoted by the RJ movement, at least in the context of intimate partner violence. To the extent that its practices (such as sentencing circles or community conferencing) could be designed to make violent partners less so, the goal of changing the community norms would be advanced only secondarily. If, however, the engagement of community members, which is the hallmark of RJ theory, were done for the purpose of creating a world (or at least a neighborhood) in which men and women were equally safe and free of coercive controls in their relationships, and if that work were done in concert with a movement already engaged in sending that message, serious progress in meeting this goal would be possible. Clearly, individuals who do engage with others to right the wrongs in their communities are more likely to be law-abiding and responsible. Theoretically, therefore, community members who are informed about and engaged in ending violence against individual women by holding individual men more accountable are more likely to convey their intolerance for such violence generally. This could have a dramatic impact on community norms; hence, joint work on this issue by both movements should be pursued.

Goal Four: Addressing Solutions to the Social Context of Crime

Both movements and the criminal justice system must reassess the extent to which they are engaging in the work without accounting for and addressing the prevailing norms of the culture, which include sexism, racism, and other forms of oppression.

The Battered Women's Movement

The battered women's movement does and should resist institutional responses that do not account for the social context within which domestic violence occurs. This is especially critical when the responses are directed only at the couple's relationship or only at the batterer's behavior as individual pathology or deviance. Recently, advocates have been asking the criminal justice system to consider the social context of an incident by adopting predominant aggressor laws or police procedures. These provisions require officers confronted with violence by each party against the other to analyze the historical context in which the incident occurred. A history of battering of one party by the other might, for example, lead to the conclusion that one party acted in self-defense or that arrest should be reserved for the battering partner, who is the more dangerous, primary/predominant aggressor. Such contextualization assists the criminal and civil courts to respond more effectively to each incident and offender.

Despite the fact that race, class, and ethnicity (and other characteristics that convey privilege) influence the needs of domestic violence victims and the efficacy of remedies, the battered women's movement does not focus enough attention on ensuring that its services are tailored to the distinct needs of women of all cultures, classes, and races. In addition, despite a long-documented history of racism and other bias in the legal and social services systems, advocates doing institutional reform work have not centralized the effort to eliminate bias in these systems or its own. Women of color, lesbians, the disabled, and other activists have long criticized the movement's failure to accept, much less seek, leadership from those who could guide these efforts, and this criticism is valid. (Sokoloff 2005). Perhaps advocates who want to address internal movement biases by, among other things, engaging the members of dis-enfranchised communities, should seek a dialogue with RJ practitioners who have a history of community engagement.

The Restorative Justice Movement

Practitioners of RJ seek to engage the community in the process of restoring peace to the community, and they have been explicit about the role that race, class, and ethnicity can play in creating the conditions for crime. However, little in the existing literature on RJ and domestic violence indicates that restorative practices have been developed to adequately address the significance of gender in the incidence, function, and impact of battering and in the potential problems associated with engaging a gender-biased or ill-informed community in solutions to domestic violence (Strang 2002).

The RJ movement should engage in this discussion with the battered women's movement, must learn to intersect the social context of battering (including gender) into its analysis, and must figure out how to prioritize victim safety while transforming community response to crime.

CONCLUSION

Given the overlap of principles and values in the battered women's and RJ movements, it is fitting that they provide to each other opportunities for learning and growth. The RJ movement offers the battered women's movement the opportunity to contemplate and respond to its own histor-ical overreliance on the criminal justice system. The concepts of restoration and making people "whole" reminds battered women's advocates to define and pursue an agenda focused on providing battered women what they need to keep themselves and their children safe—to focus even more strongly on empowering battered women and restoring their autonomy and agency—and of the centrality of women and children's experiences to its work. RJ also provides a much-needed reminder to the mainstream battered women's movement to expand its analysis, work, and network of partners so as to be a relevant and empowering movement for battered women from all communities.

Similarly, the battered women's movement offers the RJ movement the opportunity to critically contemplate whether its practices, when applied in the very different field of domestic violence, actually accomplish the goals that they do in nondomestic violence cases. The battered women's movement challenges RJ proponents' analysis of the reasons individuals use power and violence. The RJ movement has the opportunity to expand its definition of "restoration" by listening to battered women themselves regarding what is truly necessary for them to feel whole and empowered. Additionally, battered women's advocates invite RJ propo-nents to explore the conundrum that restorative practices, as currently and narrowly conceived, don't fit all social problems—that common and straight-forward issues such as fear and power imbalances confound otherwise well-intentioned practices. This crossroads offers the opportunity for growth and change to both movements, and both would be wise to seize upon it.

ACKNOWLEDGMENTS

This chapter is an adaptation of an unpublished manuscript by the same authors of the same title. This manuscript is available through the Battered Women's Justice Project (www.bwjp.org).

REFERENCES

Belzer, Lydia. 2003. *Domestic Abuse and Divorce Mediation: Suggestions for a Safer Process. Loyola Journal of Public Interest Law* 5 Loy.J.Pub.Int.L 37.

Davies, Jill, Eleanor Lyon and Diane Monti-Catania. 1998. *Safety Planning with Battered Women: Complex Lives, Difficult Choices.* Thousand Oaks, CA: Sage.

Gondolf, Edward S. 2002. *Batterer Intervention Systems: Issues, Outcomes and Recommendations.* Thousand Oaks, CA: Sage.

Marshall, Tony F. 1998. *Restorative Justice: An Overview.* St. Paul, MN: Center for Restorative Justice and Peacemaking, University of Minnesota.

Schechter, Susan. 1982. *Women and Male Violence: The Visions and Struggles of the Battered Women's Movement.* Boston, MA: South End Press.

Sokoloff, Natalie, ed. 2005. *Domestic Violence at the Margins: Readings on Race, Class, Gender, and Culture.* New Brunswick, NJ: Rutgers University Press.

Stark, Evan. 1996. "Mandatory Arrest of Batterers: A Reply to Its Critics." Pp. 115–49 in *Do Arrests and Restraining Orders Work?*, edited by Eve S. Buzawa and Carl G. Buzawa. Thousand Oaks, CA: Sage.

Strang, Heather and John Braithwaite, eds. 2002. *Restorative Justice and Family Violence.* Cambridge, UK: Cambridge University Press.

Umbreit, Mark S. 1999. *What Is Restorative Justice?* St. Paul, MN: Center for Restorative Justice and Peacemaking.

———. 2000. *Family Group Conferencing: Implications for Crime Victims.* Washington, DC: U.S. Department of Justice.

White, Rob. 2001. "Restorative Community Justice: Community Building Approaches in Juvenile Justice." Paper presented at the Fourth National Outlook Symposium on Crime in Australia, Canberra, Australia, June 21–22.

3

ABORIGINAL WOMEN AND POLITICAL PURSUIT IN CANADIAN SENTENCING CIRCLES

At Cross Roads or Cross Purposes?

RASHMI GOEL

This book seeks to survey restorative justice (RJ) practices used in the effort to quell domestic violence and other crimes against women.[1] Such an examination would be incomplete without considering the Canadian experience: Canada has a long tradition of RJ practices, beginning with Mennonite initiatives in the 1970s (Yantzi 1998). In the 1980s and 1990s, with interest in RJ growing around the globe, Canada appeared to the lead the way, with formal recognition of sentencing circles and the implementation of community conferencing for young offenders (Law Commission of Canada 2003). Today, the Canadian government continues to endorse RJ practices at both the federal and provincial levels (Dickson-Gillmore and LaPrairie 2005). Even the Canadian Criminal Code lists "alternative measures" as a priority and advises all alternatives to incarceration be considered (Canadian Criminal Code [1985], section 718). RJ has been formally embraced as part of the Canadian criminal justice blueprint.

Enticed by the promise of RJ, groups have applied the practices to all kinds of offences, even homicide (*R. v. Kahpeaysewat*, cited in Adam 2006). Indeed, the only limitation placed on the use of alternative measures in the Canadian Criminal Code (CCC) is that such use must be consistent with the protection of the public (CCC [1985], subsection 718 (e)). Therefore, Canadian use of RJ in domestic violence cases is hardly surprising.

The range of RJ *practices* has also been wide. Family group conferencing, diversion, and peace bonds,[2] all used in other countries, are also widely used in Canada (Law Commission of Canada 2003; Dickson-Gillmore and LaPrairie 2005). The sentencing circle, however, has been unique[3] to the Canadian landscape. First introduced in 1992 (*R. v. Moses* 1992), the sentencing circle is an RJ method grounded in Aboriginal/First Nations[4] traditions. Since Aboriginal people are disproportionately incarcerated in Canada (CBC News 2008; Jackson 1989; Royal Commission on Aboriginal Peoples [RCAP] 1995), any practice based in Aboriginal customs understandably merits attention.

As with all RJ initiatives, the stated goal is to fashion a sentence that balances offender rehabilitation, community security, and reparation for the victim (Van Ness and Strong 2002). But the unstated goals and implications cannot be overlooked. Tied from the outset to Aboriginal customs, the sentencing circle has been used almost exclusively with Aboriginal defendants (but see *R. v. Sellon* 1996). Sentencing circles are thus tied to "the Indian problem," and sentencing circle success carries with it all the hopes and rewards of solving that problem. Consequently, sentencing circle goals extend beyond the relationship between the offender and his community (both broadly and narrowly defined) to the relationship between Aboriginal communities and the majority/mainstream community. Thus, modern sentencing circles encompass both political and RJ aims. Canadian sentencing circles have been used in domestic violence cases with Aboriginal defendants for almost 15 years. Unfortunately, despite the money, time, and effort invested, one cannot herald sentencing circles as an unqualified success (Acorn 2004). Domestic violence in Aboriginal communities has not been markedly decreased. To understand why, we must examine the relationship between the diverse objectives that permeate the process.

This chapter argues that the sentencing circle's political and RJ objectives are not entirely congruent, but instead work against each other to the detriment of Aboriginal victims. To illustrate this, I first provide the statistics on domestic violence in Aboriginal communities and an overview of sentencing circles and their use to date. I then delineate the varying goals of sentencing circles before turning to examine how political goals hamper the realization of restorative justice goals. Finally, to illustrate these effects, I look to one account of a sentencing circle held in a domestic violence case. Ultimately, I argue that Aboriginal victims of domestic violence are caught at the crossroads of these objectives, unable to find justice for themselves or their communities.

DOMESTIC VIOLENCE RATES IN
ABORIGINAL COMMUNITIES

As already noted, sentencing circles are generally applied to Canadian Aboriginal peoples. This alone brings unique challenges to the process. Aboriginal peoples currently experience the worst social conditions of any persons in Canada (Jackson 1989, RCAP 1996). The unemployment rates are devastating; based on the 2001 Census, 23.3% of registered Indians were unemployed (Statistics Canada 2001). Social ills involving alcohol and violence abound (RCAP 1996), and the suicide rate is three times that of other Canadians (RCAP 1995). Domestic violence rates are no less disturbing. A 1999 Statistics Canada survey found that one in four Aboriginal women reported abuse by her partner, compared to one in eight for other Canadian women (Canadian Centre for Justice Statistics 2001; and see Statistics Canada, General Social Survey 2004, which shows little change). A report by the Ontario Native Women's Association stated that 80% of Aboriginal women surveyed had experienced family violence (Ontario Native Women's Association 1989:6). In British Columbia, a study by the Helping Spirit Lodge pilot project cited that 86% of respondents experienced or witnessed family violence (British Columbia 1992). These studies clearly indicate an enormous problem. Aboriginal women are being abused by their partners with distressing frequency, and the number of family members exposed to the violence is shocking. Mainstream adversarial justice methods have proven ineffective in combating this crisis (CBC News 2005). For every sentencing circle, this is the backdrop.

SENTENCING CIRCLES: AN OVERVIEW

The first sentencing circle held in the Canadian justice system was in *R. v. Moses* (1992), in the Yukon Territorial Court of Judge Barry Stuart. Phillip Moses was a member of the Na-cho Nyàk Dun First Nation who had been convicted of carrying a weapon for the purpose of committing an assault. Moses was only 26 years old, but already had a long history of violent crime spanning 43 convictions.

As with any sentencing, four basic principles were in play: protection of the public, deterrence (general and specific), rehabilitation, and denunciation or retribution (CCC subsection 718 (e)). However, Judge Stuart sought to better connect this sentencing with the values of the resident population. He chose this case to depart from mainstream sentencing practices and turned instead to a community-based restorative model. In keeping with the area's predominantly Aboriginal population, Judge Stuart used the circle as the vehicle of reform. In Aboriginal culture, the circle is a sacred symbol; all life is said to exist in a circle, demonstrating the equality and connectedness of all things (Dickson-Gillmore and LaPrairie 2005). Every member of the circle, including ones' self, is to be respected.

Judge Stewart rearranged the courtroom physically, dispensing with tables, creating a circle of simple chairs (*R. v. Moses* 1992:366–372). He then called on community members, the prosecutor and defence counsel, the victim and the offender and their families, to participate in the lengthy and emotional experience of determining Mr. Moses' sentence. One by one, they each presented their role in the process, their perspective on the problem, and their suggestion for a solution. When the circle reached a consensus, Mr. Moses was given a suspended sentence with a two-year probation that incorporated community reintegration, alcoholism treatment, and job placement.

Since *Moses,* sentencing circles have been conducted in numerous communities across the country (Dickson-Gillmore and LaPrairie 2005). The presence of sentencing circles in the Canadian justice system demonstrates an acceptance of RJ principles in policy and in practice. As sentencing circle sentences have operated as suspended and conditional sentences, they may be fairly said to fall under the "alternative measures" provisions of the Criminal Code in either form (CCC section 718). Unfortunately, statistics identifying how many circles have been conducted are unavailable (Dickson-Gillmore and LaPrairie 2005), but Judge Stuart stated that an estimated 400 were conducted in the Yukon alone between 1991 and 1995 (Roberts and LaPrairie 1996).

Although the sentencing circle is drawn from Aboriginal customs, it is *not* a complete return to traditional Aboriginal dispute-resolution techniques (Lowe and Davidson 2004). Several authors have opined that sentencing circles are an example of *inventing* tradition, not *returning* to tradition (Cameron 2006a, 2006b; Dickson-Gillmore 1992; Green 1998; McIvor 1996; Orchard 1998; Spiteri 2002). This makes sense. First, the modern sentencing circle cannot replicate a traditional pre-contact healing or sentencing circle because modern circles operate under the authority of the colonial power—the Canadian criminal justice system; pre-contact circles involved Aboriginal community members only, without *any* involvement from the white justice system. Second, even if circles involved only Aboriginal community members, it is difficult to determine pre-contact responses to antisocial activity in general, and spousal abuse in particular, so what is truly traditional may never be known. Although today's sentencing circle may be, in some respects, consistent with Aboriginal values and ideals, it is impossible to know to what degree (LeBaron 2004). Third, there is no one set of Aboriginal values that can be applied across the board; the Aboriginal community in Canada is diverse and culturally complex, and thus "traditional" may mean several different things.

Instead, modern sentencing circles should be considered a fusion of two judicial cultures. Tim Quigley is a University of Saskatchewan law professor and sentencing expert. Early on, Prof. Quigley articulated the definitive features of the sentencing circle:

> Although there is, as might be expected, some variation from place to place, there are common features to these types of modern Sentencing

Circles. First of all, they are really a *hybrid* of the traditional form of Aboriginal community justice and our criminal justice system. The judge retains the final authority to impose a sentence. What changes is the process by which that sentencing is arrived at. In principle at least, Sentencing Circles are a variation in procedure, not necessarily a change in the substance of sentencing. (Quigley 1994:288)

The hybrid nature to which Quigley refers is evident in three areas: the participants, the authority, and the parameters of use. For instance, regarding participants, a judge ordinarily sentences with the benefit of a pre-sentence report (usually prepared by a psychologist), arguments by the Crown prosecutor and the defence attorneys, the guidance of case law, and the limitations of the Criminal Code. A sentencing circle expands these resources to include elders, community members, and the offender's and victim's families. Often, the social worker or case worker, the probation officer, and other rehabilitation experts such as the psychologist will attend (*R. v. Moses* 1992). Without the barriers of podiums or witness boxes, participants face each other as community members and persons, not titles and positions. In his decision, Judge Stuart wrote:

> Currently the search for improving sentencing champions a greater role for victims of crime, reconciliation, restraint in the use of incarceration, and a broadening of sentencing alternatives that calls upon less government expenditure and more community participation. As many studies expose the imprudence of excessive reliance upon punishment as the central objective in sentencing, rehabilitation and reconciliation are properly accorded greater emphasis. All these changes call upon communities to become more actively involved and to assume more responsibility for resolving conflict. To engage meaningful community participation, the sentence decision-making process must be altered to share power with the community, and where appropriate, communities must be empowered to resolve many conflicts now processed through criminal courts. (*R. v. Moses* 1992:360)

The sentencing circle is thus an example of sentencing reform at the community level, forging a new partnership between mainstream justice and community members and invoking common responsibility for the offender's rehabilitation.

The authority is also hybrid (Yazzie 2004). Although some circle sentences have been unusual, even including banishment (*R. v. W.B.T.* 1997), ultimately the judge is bound to the minimum and maximum sentences prescribed in the Criminal Code (*R. v. Morin* 1995). While other participants may suggest and even agree on a particular sentence, the sentence cannot be imposed without the judge's approval, the Code's authority, and the sentencing maximums and minimums identified therein. That being said, in practice, judges accord great deference to the circle's consensus. To date, I have heard of only one judge rejecting the sentence proposed by the circle. This illustrates a willingness among the judiciary to embrace Aboriginal value systems and cultural practices. Clearly, the circle's consensus carries its own authority too.

Finally, case law has established some limitations and parameters on sentencing circle use. These parameters reference the needs of the justice system and the fundamentals for RJ success. In *R. v. Joseyounen* (1995), Judge Fafard of the Saskatchewan Provincial Court outlined seven criteria for sentencing circle use: (1) the accused must agree to the sentencing circle; (2) the accused must have deep roots in the community from which the circle is drawn; (3) there must be elders willing to participate; (4) the victim must be a willing participant in the circle; (5) it should be determined whether the victim suffered from battered women's syndrome and, if so, additional counselling and support should be made available to her; (6) disputed facts are to be resolved in advance; and (7) the case must be one in which the court was willing to take a calculated risk and depart from the usual sentencing range.

In *R. v. Morin* (1995), the Saskatchewan Court of Appeal considered the *Joseyounen* criteria. Although the court was unanimous that sentencing circles were, by then, an established component of the Canadian justice system and that RJ principles and Aboriginal identity played vital roles in assessing whether to hold a circle, the majority held that, where an offender had a long history of violent offences, a calculated risk was not appropriate.

In *R. v. Gladue* (1999), the Supreme Court of Canada considered the kind of community necessary for a sentencing circle. In affirming the entitlement of Aboriginal offenders to special consideration in sentence determination, the Court found that, while some sort of community was required, it need not be limited to rural or reserve communities. Rather, even the loose network of support possessed by some urban Aboriginals was sufficient to invoke the RJ requirement and initiate a sentencing circle.

The use of judicial discretion and precedent to determine *when* a sentencing circle may be held, while not determining the circle's outcome, is clearly another example of the hybrid nature of the modern sentencing circle.

SENTENCING CIRCLE OBJECTIVES

As a merger of two judicial cultures, sentencing circles have particular objectives. Some of these are common to any restorative justice measure, but others are goals unique to the political ambitions of the Aboriginal community.

Restorative Justice Goals

Sentencing circle goals consistent with restorative justice can be summarized as follows:

- *Rehabilitation.* The sentencing circle aims to discern what is best for this individual offender and those things necessary to his rehabilitative success. As such, it focuses more on the offender's needs than on the sentencing practices of the past.
- *Accountability.* The circle assumes that when all members affected communicate openly, each will urge and assist the offender to take responsibility for his actions.
- *Reconnection.* RJ sees criminal behavior as damaging relations between the offender, the victim, and the community at large. Thus, RJ proceedings should restore those connections, and the connection between the community and the justice process, by eliciting community input (Green 1998; Dickson-Gilmore and LaPrairie 2005; *R. v. Moses* 1992; *R. v. Naapaluk* 1995).
- *Victim healing.* The circle should promote victim safety, security, and healing by providing the victim an opportunity to voice her needs and by responding to her interests.

These four goals are traditional RJ goals. They are common to family group conferencing, victim–offender mediation, community healing circles, and sentencing circles (Lilles 2002). However, Canadian sentencing circles are subject to other goals. According to RJ principles, the sentencing circle—judge, prosecutor, defence counsel, elders, offender, victim, and family members—form one community. Problems arise, however, because sentencing circles are applied exclusively to Aboriginal peoples.[5] This creates an overlapping set of group dynamics—that of Aboriginal (or minority interests) versus mainstream (or majority interests). Although the mainstream adversarial process may be subject to divisions of offender versus state, and offender versus victim, the sentencing circle process is subject to another division—Aboriginal versus white man.

Political Goals

Because Aboriginal peoples in Canada are a racial and ethnic minority with a history of subjugation (Miller 1989), they come to the judicial process with specific political goals. These political goals may be summarized as follows:

- *Expression and education.* Aboriginal communities view the sentencing circle as an opportunity to express and bring attention to the historical causes of societal problems in Aboriginal communities—causes like colonialism, racism within and outside of the justice system, residential school experiences, and intergenerational abuses. In other words, the circle serves as an opportunity to highlight the victimization of Aboriginal peoples at the hands of the majority community.

- *Autonomy and self-governance.* The circle represents the involvement of Aboriginal people in controlling the future of their own people. It provides a culturally grounded and community-based method of working with Aboriginal people and, as such, signifies a step toward greater cultural and judicial autonomy for Aboriginal peoples (Lilles 2002; Dickson-Gillmore and LaPrairie 2005).
- *Integration.* Finally, the circle is a way of reasserting traditional Aboriginal methods of dispute resolution. It may help to bridge the gap between Aboriginal spiritual notions and the Western justice system (*R. v. Webb* 1993:153), integrate one into the other, and contribute the Aboriginal perspective to the general fight against criminal behavior in Canada.

Although both sets of goals are indeed laudable, RJ goals and political goals may not be compatible at this stage. When we examine sentencing circles in domestic violence cases, we find that one set of goals hinders the achievement of the other. Thus, we find that goals external to RJ processes have a significant effect on the achievement of RJ goals. Aboriginal victims of domestic violence are caught at the crossroads of these objectives, unable to find justice for themselves or their communities. To examine this phenomenon, it is useful to examine how the political goals of Aboriginal peoples affect the process and RJ goals in the circle.

HOW POLITICAL GOALS AFFECT THE SENTENCING CIRCLE'S RESTORATIVE GOALS

Rehabilitation

According to Judge Stuart, "Healing—not punishment—is the central, but not exclusive focus of the Circle" (Stuart 1997:9). In the context of criminal justice, healing the offender inevitably means rehabilitation.

Initial statistics on the use of sentencing circles were very promising (*R. v. Alaku* 1993). Recidivism rates dropped, dramatically in some places (Stuart 1997). Many, including myself, thought this was the magic bullet to end the high rates of Aboriginal incarceration (Acorn 2004; Goel 2000). Even today, there are some compelling successes. For instance, the northern Manitoba Ojibway community of Hollow Water instituted healing and sentencing circles as part of their Community Holistic Circle Healing Program in 1987 to deal with the plague of sexual abuse in their community. Their structure is a unique blend of mainstream and community justice involving four circles of healing and accountability. Although sexual abuse is at least as complicated a problem as domestic violence, with similar cautions, the Hollow Water community was not deterred. By their 1997 report, they could boast a recidivist rate of only 4–5% as compared to the average sexual offender recidivist rate of 14–19%. Hollow Water continues to receive acclaim as an Aboriginal and RJ triumph (Aboriginal Peoples Collection of Canada 1997).

Despite such accounts, broader figures challenge this picture of success. Today, Aboriginal offenders continue to occupy a disproportionate number of prison cells. Rates of domestic abuse have not dropped significantly (Statistics Canada 1999, 2004). In fact, more and more Aboriginal women are making use of social services due to abuse (Statistics Canada 2006). Although recidivism rates for sentencing circle participants in particular are not available, recidivism rates in general have not dropped significantly (Babcock, Green, and Robie 2004).

To further rehabilitation, the circle must assess the needs of the offender, determine how those needs can best be met, and provide the necessary resources, physical and emotional, for that change. In fact, political goals undermine the effective function of the circle here. Some circle time is always spent recounting the offender's history and acknowledging the factors that contributed to his criminal conduct, but because the circle is an outlet to express the history of Aboriginal victimization, this can lead to undue attention being placed on these historical factors, discounting personal responsibility. Because other members of the circle will likely have had some similar experiences (to say otherwise would belie the high rates of social problems in Aboriginal communities), recounting these factors and their effect on the entire community may partially excuse the offender's behavior, or at a minimum, shift some focus away from the offender's responsibility.

The self-governance goal also influences the circle. Although motivation might not be lacking, the support necessary to effect change may be. A frequent circle solution is to take the offender back into the community and set him up with community support systems, whereby he can learn anger management and alternative ways of expressing his frustration (Wilson, Hucaluk, and McWhinnie 2003). Influenced by the desire for self-governance, communities may overestimate their ability to control the offender and underestimate the resources required to do so (Lilles 2002). Aboriginal communities suffer disproportionately from cuts in social programs due to isolation and lack of providers who might speak the language and understand the culture. Although the circle itself may include a social worker, probation officer, and psychologist, remote communities often do not have regular access to these professionals (McIvor 1996). Conversely, urban communities with access to these professionals often lack the cohesiveness necessary for social sanctions.

Furthermore, the problems First Nations communities face are myriad, ranging from poverty and isolation, to severe alcohol abuse and violence (RCAP 1995). The enormity of the problems may simply weaken the community and lead rapidly to frustration and fatigue. As a result, even good intentions are thwarted by poor resources.

Finally, the desire to demonstrate the uniqueness of the Aboriginal approach may compel communities to choose noncustodial sanctions even when incarceration is the most appropriate. Some have opined that offenders seek sentencing circles largely because they are reputedly an easy out—sentences are less severe, rarely resulting in incarceration (Wilson et al. 2003:366). This brings into question not only the ability of the community to provide the necessary rehabilitative support (Green 1998; Orchard 1998), but also the offender's desire to change. If the offender lacks close ties to his community, the emotional and social community sanction may not motivate him enough to change, and habitual offenders likewise may not be swayed by community pressure even when strong ties are present.

Accountability

RJ practices have been touted for their personal manner of providing accountability. Sentencing circle offenders are forced to face their own families and community members, whose censure likely means much more than that of the impersonal justice system. This can work very well where community members are physically and emotionally close.

However, this dynamic is complicated when community members also see themselves as victims of the mainstream system. The us–them dynamic associated with victim–offender interactions might simply shift to one in which the community and the offender stand as victims of the state. Community elders may feel hypocritical judging a community member for crimes they themselves have committed. This could work to excuse the offender or to blame the victim for bringing punishment on a fellow member. This dynamic may be exacerbated by the rampant domestic violence present in all Aboriginal communities. The sheer pervasiveness of the violence may serve to normalize it for the offender and the community, lessening the stigma of community censure (Ross 1994).

Outside the community, sentencing circles can provide accountability as conditional sentences; if the offender fails to comply with the terms of the sentencing circle, a custodial sentence can ensue. Current figures do not clearly indicate how often offenders breach sentencing circle dispositions and revert to custodial sentences. If the primary recourse available for sentencing circle violations is removal from the community however, this too poses problems; enforcement of sentencing circle terms actually vests in non-Aboriginal authorities—not the community members committed to the offender's rehabilitation. This places community members in a painful predicament. While they want the offender to take responsibility for his actions, including any violation of sentencing circle terms, they also want to ensure that the program is viewed as successful. Community members may be reticent to report the offender's violations because these violations would be viewed as failures. Furthermore, the prospect of sending the offender to prison only emphasizes the longstanding victimization of Aboriginal peoples by the Canadian mainstream. If one goal of the sentencing circle is to extricate the offender from this system, it stands to reason that sending him back feels like a personal and community failure.

Reconnection

Alienation is a root cause of crime in Aboriginal communities. Scott Clark states:

> [T]hese processes [colonization, modernization and their recent agent, mass communication], sometimes insidious and almost always negative, result in the breakdown or weakening of informal structures and traditional institutions that once existed to reinforce communal values and maintain social integrity. The forces that drive apart community members, and more particularly family members, leave in their wake a cadre of alienated individuals who are prone to committing offenses. (Clark 1992:514)

In response, reports have emphasized the need for community input and involvement in the justice system to combat this disaffection. In 1992, the Saskatchewan Indian Justice Review Committee made a series of specific recommendations on sentencing alternatives. Recommendation 4.3 is especially noteworthy:

> WE RECOMMEND THAT:
> subject to community support, community justice committees be established for adult aboriginal offenders to parallel the activities of youth justice committees. Committee responsibilities might include advising on presentence reports and sentencing, providing crime prevention and public legal education programming, and administering alternative measures. (Linn 1992:41)

Community justice committees were subsequently established in some provinces but specifically exempt family violence cases. For such cases, the sentencing circle may be the only vehicle for community input.

Community input may however be compromised by political goals. In particular, the desire for self-government may force a unified front, especially vis-a-vis the state. Some participants may concede with the positions enunciated by elders, even when at heart they disagree, so that the views expressed in the sentencing circle may not always be the real views of community members. This poses specific dangers when the offender is expected to return to the community: neighbors and friends might say they have forgiven the offender even if hard feelings remain; members might promise support they can't really deliver (Green 1998). Or, worst of all, members may choose a nonincarceratory resolution when incarceration is the only way to guarantee safety. In the end, this can create problems when the offender is released into their care.

Victim Healing

In the conventional justice system, victims' opinions are regularly discounted (Galaway 1985). In a domestic violence case, this disregard is exacerbated by the lingering view that spousal abuse is a private crime.

Some still suspect judicial involvement in domestic violence cases is unnecessary interference. Furthermore, the adversarial system focuses much of its attention on the offender, and his rights against the power of the state (Galaway 1985). In disregarding the victim at the same time it purports to represent her, the system actually supports the offender by privileging his side of the story. Even in domestic violence cases, where often the victim knows the offender best, her view is sometimes discounted in the presentence report. Courts sometimes release even a habitual batterer because it is his first criminal charge (*R. v. Naapaluk* 1994:5).

Such disregard is akin to willful blindness. If anyone is deserving of having a voice in the sentence, surely it is the abused spouse. This is a particularly powerful argument for RJ in domestic violence cases, where the victim lives with the threat of assault on a daily basis. A sentencing circle has the potential to rectify the imbalance. The victim can make sentencing suggestions directly to the judge. Even if the victim has no specific suggestions, her in-person testimony, without the constraining rules of court, should provide a more accurate picture of the home situation and thus a more appropriate sentence. The victim can relate previous battering events to establish a *history* of assault for circle members. Informed, the community can come together to punish and/or rehabilitate the offender and support the victim (*R. v. Moses* 1992:73–74). However, these goals cannot be achieved without a supportive atmosphere in which the victim can honestly express her feelings without fear.

In practice, the community's political goals can frustrate a safe and supportive environment, both ignoring and silencing the victim. Such dynamics may begin prior to any charge. For instance, women may be reluctant to charge abusers because of the treatment the men receive at the hands of the white justice system.

The hybrid nature of the sentencing circle compounds this problem. Because the state retains authority, the sentencing circle does not shift focus from the offender to the victim (as other RJ practices might); it merely shifts focus from the offender to the offender's sanction. Coupled with the desire to expose Aboriginal victimization, continued focus on the offender makes his suffering at the hands of the state even more prominent than the victim's suffering at the hands of the offender. The victim may feel her own problems are not ones she should complain about.

Self-government likewise impairs the victim's ability to advocate for herself. In the Aboriginal way, it is important to put the community before herself. To go along with the community view of the correct sentence, when in fact she feels differently, may be her way of putting the community before herself.

Finally, the importance of supporting a uniquely Aboriginal response to the problem is also voiced by community leaders, only increasing the pressure on victims to toe the line. The victim is not only the victim but probably the batterer's greatest well wisher. Often, he is the father of their children and despite his violence, she desires to keep the marriage together and still loves him. Incarceration can be the last straw to an already weakened marriage, and can plunge the woman and her children into poverty due the loss of the family income. Many see an inherent contradiction in using incarceration, a violent means, to teach the inappropriateness of violence (Berzins 1991). These considerations make traditional Aboriginal noncustodial sanctions highly attractive.

Some traditional methods used by Aboriginal people to prevent antisocial behavior include: (1) teaching by elders, (2) warning and counseling by elders, (3) ridicule or ostracism (shaming), (4) mediation and negotiations, or (5) compensation and restitution (Coyle 1986). For the most severe crimes, traditional methods also include public punishment, physical punishment, execution, or banishment (Coyle 1986), but domestic violence sentencing circles have not issued such sanctions.

Although some studies have found incarceration a wake-up call to batterers and a first step toward rehabilitation, the few cases available do not suggest a preponderance of requests for incarceration by Aboriginal victims of domestic violence (Galaway 1985; Monture-Okanee 1993; Razack 1999; R. v. Naapaluk 1995). Since, per Joseyounen and Morin, courts may only authorize a sentencing circle when a calculated risk is warranted, the victim may hide the full extent of the abuse and her true desires for sentencing to retain more Aboriginal options for sentencing. Although she might prefer the batterer's incarceration, the victim could be pressured into accepting a noncustodial punishment.

THE CASE OF *R. V. NAAPALUK*

Because most sentencing circles are not reported in full, and because transcripts are not easily available, it is difficult to be sure that women are in fact being silenced in circles. We do however have two separate perspectives on a 1993 sentencing circle in a domestic violence case. The defendant, Jusipi Naapaluk, had plead guilty to assaulting his wife, Kullutu Naapaluk. This was Jusipi's fourth formal charge but he freely admitted to the court that he had "probably beaten [his] wife more than fifty times" (*R. v. Naapaluk* 1995:225). Jusipi had already served several prison terms. Judge Dutil elected to hold a "consultation circle" prior to sentencing. Prior to the circle, he emphasized that he would be the final authority on any sentence plan "advice" from the circle members. The circle participants were the judge, the interpreter, the chairman of the Inuit Working Group on Justice, the victim, the accused, defence counsel, the probation officer, two social workers, the mayor, the Crown prosecutor, the sister and mother of the accused, the sister and a friend of the victim, and an elder (Pp. 229–230).

Consider Judge Dutil's version of the *Naapaluk* sentencing circle. He states in his judgement:

Discussion was continuous. All the participants expressed themselves amply; some spoke several times. There were no formalities, and participation took various forms ... The accused himself spoke several times, as did the victim, his wife. (*R. v. Naapaluk* 1995:11)

In her work as a cross-cultural researcher, feminist author and former in-house legal counsel to Tungavik Federation of Nunavut, Mary Crnkovich was able to observe this circle personally. Her report on the case was commissioned by the Department of Justice Canada (Crnkovich 1994). Although this case was early in the implementation of sentencing circles, Crnkovich's observations have been widely quoted (Levis 1998; Cameron 2006a, 2006b) and accepted as an honest indicator of what occurs in such cases. Her account is in sharp contrast to Judge Dutil's.

At no time during the circle discussion did the offender or others hear from the victim, in her own words, what the impact of the accused's actions had been on her or her family. The victim appeared to be very nervous in the circle and would only briefly speak when asked a question by the judge. (Crnkovich 1995:117)

To summarize her account, Crnkovich found the victim was outnumbered (i.e., she had very few supporters), responded only to direct questions of the judge and then only to acknowledge the concerns and wishes of the community leaders, spoke only three times, and was very nervous throughout. The greatest focus was placed on the offender and how to help him—not on the impact the abuse had on the victim and her children. The victim's clear discomfort was compounded by the fact that no one really explained what her role was to be or even that she need not participate if she would rather not. Crnkovich ponders the victim's quandary in the following passage:

[T]he Sentencing Circle may have imposed an even greater silence. This circle was the first of its kind, being supported by the Judge and Inuit leaders. If she spoke out about further abuses or her dislike of this sentence, what would she be saying about this process everyone supported? Now, in addition to fearing her husband's retribution, she may fear by speaking out she would be speaking out against the community. The sentence created in this circle is one endorsed not only by the mayor and other participants but by the judge and a highly respected Inuit politician. The pressure to not speak out against a sentencing alternative supported by so many is great. The victim may be afraid to admit she is being beaten [in later counselling sessions] because such an admission, she may fear, may be interpreted as a failure of this process. She may hold herself to blame and once again continue to suffer in silence. (Crnkovich 1996:172–173)

Despite the opportunities the sentencing circle represents, it is likely that even today, 15 years later, victims are not speaking freely. The

Joseyounen criteria, suggesting battered women have support groups in circles, has not been promulgated as a threshold requirement: Circles take place without this safeguard. Nor would a support group necessarily counteract the views of other circle participants who share the political motivations that undermine the circle's RJ goals. The persistence of rampant domestic violence in Aboriginal communities suggests rather that women are unable to harness the benefits of the sentencing circle for their own safety and security.

CONCLUSION

Ultimately, the diverse goals at issue in sentencing circles operate at cross-purposes in domestic violence cases. Because they are applied exclusively to Aboriginal people, sentencing circles represent an opportunity for political empowerment as much as they represent RJ. For Aboriginal women, empowerment as Aboriginal peoples requires that they suppress their own interests as victims. They are once again caught at the crossroads. Both mainstreamers and Aboriginal people are asking the circles to do too much; mainstreamers want sentencing circles to eliminate the Indian problem (Aboriginal crime and social ills) by achieving perfect RJ, and Aboriginal people want the circles to achieve self-government. But the goals are incongruent and, as a result, the circles have had little impact at all. Perhaps the only answer to this problem is to reduce expectations and expand options. Both mainstreamers and Aboriginal peoples need to explore and acknowledge the limitations of sentencing circles, especially in their modern manifestation.

For instance, the sentencing circle is a narrow instrument for education about Aboriginal victimization; only the circle's few participants are exposed. Although these individuals are certainly powerful, as judges and prosecutors, the sphere of influence should be broadened to include other judicial actors (who do not participate in sentencing circles) and the common populace (who have little involvement with the justice system). Although the Royal Commission on Aboriginal Peoples did go some way to achieving this, more grassroots education would be useful. Such efforts might reduce the pressure on the circle as a vehicle for education by increasing external opportunities for education.

Also, sentencing circles should not be painted as pure, traditional Aboriginal dispute resolution when they derive their authority and power from the Canadian criminal justice system. This misrepresentation obscures the pursuit of self-governance and cultural integration that is so much a part of current functioning. As with education, expanding the opportunities for self-governance and cultural integration would at least relieve some of this pressure.

In addition, expanding the opportunities and options within RJ for Aboriginal and other participants would likely be useful. Within Nova

Scotia alone, a population of only 935,000, seven separate RJ programs exist within the Alternative Measures Network.

The *Report of the Aboriginal Justice Inquiry of Manitoba* states:

> While the role of Aboriginal women in Aboriginal society is not well understood in non-Aboriginal circles, we have been told, and accept, that a resumption of their traditional roles is the key to putting an end to Aboriginal female mistreatment. The immediate need is to begin to heal from the decades of denigration they have experienced. But the ultimate objective is to encourage and assist Aboriginal women to regain and occupy their rightful place as equal partners in Aboriginal Society. (As cited in Razack 1999:912–13)

This proposal has its difficulties (for example, determining the role of women in traditional Aboriginal society, and accepting or adjusting the role of women in patriarchal Aboriginal societies). Nevertheless, it may be the best solution for the current circles' problems. The challenge for Aboriginal women today is to find power and voice within modern Aboriginal society, whether that is through a return to traditional values or the adoption of new ones. Perhaps with women at the helm, the needs of victims will no longer be frustrated by the needs of their communities.

NOTES

1. Others may prefer the terms "interpersonal violence," "spousal abuse," or "intimate violence."
2. A *peace bond* is a court order designed to prevent an assault. A peace bond orders a person to be of good behavior and obey conditions the judge orders. A bond may last for up to 12 months and is provided for under section 810 of the Canadian Criminal Code. In the context of domestic violence, it is the Canadian corollary of a restraining order.
3. Also seen in Minnesota, but there are differences between this practice and that in Canada. Further, both of these practices are markedly different from Navajo peacemaking circles.
4. While First Nations is the preferred term, it does not include all populations of Aboriginal ancestry, such as the Inuit and the Metis. Therefore, I use the broader term *Aboriginal* to refer to all communities who identify as such.
5. There has been only one documented case of the sentencing circle being applied to a non-Aboriginal offender—see *R. v. Sellon* (1996).

REFERENCES

Aboriginal Peoples Collection of Canada. 1997. *The Four Circles of Hollow Water.* Ottawa: Public Works and Government Services Canada.

Acorn, Analise. 2004. *Compulsory Compassion: A Critique of Restorative Justice.* Vancouver: University of British Columbia Press.

Adam, Betty Ann. 2006. "Conditional Sentence in Stabbing Case Believed to the First Use of Sentencing Circle in a Homicide." *The StarPhoenix,* August 25, 2006. Retrieved January 9, 2008 (http://www.lead-alda.ca/news.aro).

Babcock, Julia C., Charles E. Green, and Chet Robie. 2004. "Does Batterers' Treatment Work? A Meta-Analytic Review of Domestic Violence Treatment." *Clinical Psychology Review* 23:1023–1053.

Berzins, Lorraine. 1991. "Is Legal Punishment Right?" Presentation at the National Association of Criminal Justice Conference, October 9, Victoria, British Columbia.

British Columbia. 1992. *Is Anyone Listening?: Report of the British Columbia Task Force on Family Violence.* Ministry of Women's Equality. Victoria, BC: Queen's Printer.

Cameron, Angela. 2006a. "Stopping the Violence: Canadian Feminist Debates on Restorative Justice and Intimate Violence." *Theoretical Criminology* 10:49–66.

———. 2006b. "Sentencing Circles and Intimate Violence: A Canadian Feminist Perspective." *Canadian Journal of Women and the Law* 18 n0.2:479–512.

Canadian Centre for Justice Statistics. 2001. Family violence in Canada: A Statistical Profile 2001. Ottawa: Statistics Canada.

Canadian Criminal Code. 1985. Revised Statutes of Canada, Chapter C-46, Section 718.

CBC (Canadian Broadcasting Centre) News. 2005. "Domestic Violence Rate Unchanged, Statistics Canada Finds." July 14. Retrieved January 10, 2008 (http://www.cbc.ca/canada/story/2005/07/14/domestic-violence-050714.html).

———. 2008. "Rise in Female, Aboriginal Inmates Alters Prison Population: StatsCan." December 15. Retrieved February 19, 2009 (http://www.cbc.ca/canada/story/2008/12/15/statscan-prisons.html).

Clark, Scott. 1992. "Crime and Community: Issues and Directions in Aboriginal Justice." *Canadian Journal of Criminology* 513:514.

Coyle, Michael. 1986. "Traditional Indian Justice in Ontario: A Role for the Present?" *Osgoode Hall Law Journal* 24:605–33.

Crnkovich, Mary. 1994. *Report on a Sentencing Circle in Nunavik.* Inuit Women and Justice, Progress Report Number One. Ottawa: Paktuutit Inuit Women's Association of Canada.

———. 1995. "The Role of the Victim in the Criminal Justice System—Circle Sentencing in Inuit Communities." *Public Perceptions of the Administration of Justice* 442D: 97–129. Retrieved February 27, 2009 (http://ciaj-icaj.ca/francais/publications/1995.html).

———. 1996. "A Sentencing Circle." *Journal of Legal Pluralism* 36:159–181.

Dickson-Gilmore, E. Jane. 1992. "Resurrecting the Peace: Traditionalist Approaches to Separate Justice in the Kahnawake Mohawk Nation." Pp. 259–277 in *Aboriginal Peoples and Canadian Criminal Justice,* edited by Robert A. Silverman and Marianne O. Nielsen. Toronto: Butterworths.

Dickson-Gilmore, E. Jane and Carol LaPrairie. 2005. *Will the Circle Be Unbroken: Aboriginal Communities, Restorative Justice and the Challenges of Conflict and Change.* Toronto: University of Toronto Press.

Galaway, Burt. 1985. "Victim Participation in the Penal Corrective Process." *Victimology: An International Journal* 10: 617–630.

Goel, Rashmi. 2000. "No Women at the Center: The Use of the Canadian Sentencing Circles in Domestic Violence Cases." *Wisconsin Women's Law Journal* 15: 293–334.

Green, Ross Gordon. 1998. *Justice in Aboriginal Communities: Sentencing Alternatives.* Saskatoon, SK: Purich Publishing.

Jackson, Michael. 1989. "Locking Up Natives in Canada: Report of the Canadian Bar Association Committee on Imprisonment and Release." *University of British Columbia Law Review* 23:215–300.

Law Commission of Canada. 2003. *What Is a Crime? Challenges and Alternatives: A Discussion Paper*. Ottawa: Law Commission of Canada.

LeBaron, Michelle. 2004. "Learning New Dances: Finding Effective Ways to Address Intercultural Disputes." Pp. 11–27 in *Intercultural Dispute Resolution in Aboriginal Contexts*, edited by Catherine Bell and David Joshua Kahane. Vancouver: University of British Columbia Press.

Levis, Charlene. 1998. "Circle Sentencing: The Silence Speaks Loudly: Considering Whether the Victims' Needs Can Be Met Through Circle Sentencing." Thesis: University of Northern British Columbia. Available at http://www.hotpeachpages.net/canada/air/rjCharlene.html.

Lilles, Heino. 2002. "Circle Sentencing: Part of the Restorative Justice Continuum." Paper presented to Dreaming of a New Reality, The Third International Conference on Conferencing, Circles, and Other Restorative Practices, Minneapolis, Minnesota, August 8–10.

Linn, Patricia. 1992. *Report of the Saskatchewan Indian Justice Review Committee*. Regina, SK: Government of Saskatchewan.

Lowe, Diana and Jonathan H. Davidson. 2004. "What Is Old Is New Again." Pp. 280–297 in *Intercultural Dispute Resolution in Aboriginal Contexts*, edited by Catherine Bell David Joshua Kahane. Vancouver: University of British Columbia Press.

McIvor, Sharon. 1996. *Contemporary Aboriginal Justice Models: Completing the Circle*. Kahnawake, QC: Canadian Bar Association.

Miller, James Roger. 1989. *Skyscrapers Hide the Heavens: A History of Indian–White Relations in Canada*. Toronto: University of Toronto Press.

Monture-Okanee, Patricia. 1993. "Reclaiming Justice: Aboriginal Women and Justice Initiatives in the 1990s." In *Royal Commission on Aboriginal Peoples, Aboriginal Peoples and the Justice System: Report of the Round Table on Aboriginal Justice Issues*. Ottawa: Minister of Supply and Services Canada.

Ontario Native Women's Association. 1989. *Breaking Free: A Proposal for Change to Aboriginal Family Violence*. Thunder Bay: Ontario Native Women's Association.

Orchard, Bonnie. 1998. "Sentencing Circles in Saskatchewan." Masters of Law thesis, College of Law. University of Saskatchewan, Saskatoon, Saskatchewan.

Quigley, Tim. 1994. "Some Issues in Sentencing of Aboriginal Offenders." Pp. 269–300 in *Continuing Poundmaker and Riel's Quest: Presentations Made at a Conference on Aboriginal Peoples and Justice*, edited by Richard Gosse, James Youngblood Henderson, and Roger Carter. Saskatoon, SK: Purich Publishing.

R. v. Alaku, 112 D.L.R. (4d) 732 (1993).

R. v. Gladue, 133 C.C.C. (3d) 385 (1999).

R. v. Joseyounen, 1 C.N.L.R. 182 (1995).

R. v. Morin, 1 S.C.R. 771 (1993).

R. v. Moses, 71 C.C.C. (3d) 347 (1992).

R. v. Naapaluk, 2 C.N.L.R. 143 (1994).

R. v. Sellon, 172 Newfoundland Supreme Court Trial Division (unreported) (April 4, 1996).

R. v. W.B.T., 2 C.N.L.R. 140 (1997).

R. v. Webb, 1 C.N.L.R. 148 (1993).

Razack, Sherene. 1999. *Looking White People in the Eye: Gender, Race and Culture in the Courtrooms and Classrooms.* Toronto: University of Toronto Press.

Roberts, Julian V. and Carol LaPrairie. 1996. "Sentencing Circles: Some Unanswered Questions." *Criminal Law Quarterly* 39:69–83.

Ross, Rupert. 1994. "Duelling Paradigms? Western Criminal Justice Versus Aboriginal Community Healing." Pp. 241–268 in *Continuing Poundmaker and Riel's Quest: Presentations Made at a Conference on Aboriginal Peoples and Justice,* edited by Richard Gosse, James Youngblood Henderson, and Roger Carter. Saskatoon, SK: Purich Publishing.

Royal Commission on Aboriginal Peoples (RCAP). 1995. *Choosing Life: Special Report on Suicide Among Aboriginal Peoples.* Ottawa: Canadian Government Publishing.

———. 1996. *Bridging the Cultural Divide: A Report on Aboriginal People and Criminal Justice in Canada.* Ottawa: Commission on Aboriginal Peoples.

Spiteri, Melani. 2002. "Sentencing Circles for Aboriginal Offenders in Canada: Furthering the Idea of Aboriginal Justice Within a Western Justice Framework." Paper presented at the Third International Conference on Conferencing, Circles, and other Restorative Practices, August 8–10, Minneapolis, Minnesota.

Statistics Canada. 1999. *General Social Survey.* Ottawa: Statistics Canada.

——— 2001. *Census Report.* Ottawa: Statistics Canada.

——— 2004. *General Social Survey.* Ottawa: Statistics Canada.

——— 2006. *Measuring Violence Against Women: Statistical Trends 2006.* Ottawa: Statistics Canada.

Stuart, Barry. 1997. *Building Community Justice Partnerships: Community Peacemaking Circles.* Ottawa: Department of Justice.

Van Ness, Daniel W., and Karen Heetderks Strong. 2002. *Restoring Justice (2e).* Cincinnati, OH: Anderson Publishing.

Wilson, Robin J., Bria Huculak and Andrew McWhinnie. 2003. "Restorative Justice Innovations in Canada." *Behavioral Sciences and the Law* 20:363–380.

Yantzi, M. 1998. *Sexual Offending and Restoration.* Waterloo, ON: Herald Press.

Yazzie, Robert. 2004. "Navajo Peacemaking and Intercultural Dispute Resolution." Pp. 107–115 in *Intercultural Dispute Resolution in Aboriginal Contexts,* edited by Catherine Bell and David Joshua Kahane. Vancouver: University of British Columbia Press.

4

A COMMUNITY OF
ONE'S OWN?

When Women Speak to Power About
Restorative Justice

PAMELA RUBIN

In 1998, the Nova Scotia Department of Justice issued *Restorative Justice: A Proposal for Nova Scotia,* outlining its plans for the most ambitious institutionalization of restorative justice (RJ) anywhere in Canada, the Nova Scotia Restorative Justice Initiative (NSRJI). Included among eligible offences were to be both sex offences and partner assaults. In rooms in churches and meeting halls and community justice offices, a facilitated interaction involving a victim, a violent man, and a support person for the violent man would be used to create sentencing recommendations. That the cases were only to be referred for sentencing reflected the province's previous disastrous experience with pre-trial diversion for sexual assault.[1] Diversionary RJ for these crimes would be considered later, the initiative's vision document promised.

Virtually all offences would be categorized as level one, two, three, or four, and be eligible for cautioning, diversion, and pre-sentence and post-sentence RJ processes depending on their category. "Community justice for all" would be delivered across Nova Scotia by existing alternative measures groups that were swiftly renaming themselves "community justice" groups. These groups, although nominally community-based, would rely almost completely on contracts with the provincial justice system to exist. Their staff was generally among the lowest paid of justice professionals, with no expertise in partner or sexual violence, nor were survivor organizations generally represented on the boards of these "community" agencies. A four-part phase-in would see a larger and larger swath of offences handled first for youth, then for adults.

How did an initiative that would go so far so fast emerge fully grown from the Nova Scotia Department of Justice? Since women's organizations (or any other community organizations serving survivors of violence) and the public were not involved in the development of the initiative, it is hard to say. The picture we have pieced together is that of a small group of personally ambitious and visionary justice policy makers who created the initial plan, then presented it to colleagues and decision makers who found it attractive. One of the reasons for the attraction was likely that, for a cost-conscious government that was handing out bonuses to deputy ministers for reducing their budgets, the new process held out the prospect of substantial savings in court processing time and staff resources by down-loading cases to lower-cost, community-based groups. Caseloads for legal aid and prosecutors were and continue to be unmanageable—violence against women cases, often seen as low priority, illegitimate, or unwinnable—could be removed at a stroke, reducing the burdens on these professionals by 20–30%. In addition to that motivation, this generation of justice system managers had been educated in local universities that challenged retributive justice and the sanctity of adversarialism. Unfortunately, feminist analysis of crime and law was mostly left out of this reformist trend. The research interests of individual academic criminologists and legal scholars fanned the flames, with prominent Dalhousie professors who spoke of "getting to victims" and "breaching the wall" into interpersonal violence very early on. With support from the managerial establishment, the opportunity beckoned to academics. What could be a better laboratory for experimenting with RJ theories than the somewhat isolated and poverty-stricken communities of Nova Scotia? Who would object?

In 1999, a phone call was received at a sexual assault center from the Nova Scotia Department of Justice: "Would you be able to provide training to our volunteer facilitators?" This was the first time the sexual assault center had heard anything about the initiative. After reminding the government that the sexual assault center received very limited funding and could not provide free training for Department of Justice initiatives, the center director quickly notified women's equality-seeking organizations across the province. Nobody else knew anything about this major shift in how the criminal justice system would handle misogynist violence.

Shelters, women's centers, and sexual assault centers responded to the Department of Justice with great concern that input from survivors of sexual assault or woman abuse was not solicited or considered in the design of the program to determine appropriate practices or goals. It was unclear how the proposed initiative would achieve its goal of addressing the underlying causes of crime insofar as they involve systemic discrimination and violence against women. No Nova Scotia research had taken place to support the Department's claim that the RJ program would increase the satisfaction of women survivors of male violence with the justice process, and the Department could provide no clear evidence of this anywhere else. The proposed initiative did not take into account the safety, power, and control issues specific to sexual assault and woman abuse, or contemplate necessary security measures before, during, and after conferences. Organizations serving women in communities across the province also had experienced increased expectations for services, with no commensurate increases in funding, over many years: plans for "community ownership" of RJ measures could mean in practice the downloading of government responsibilities onto community organizations without supplying added resources.

The Department of Justice agreed to a meeting with organizations serving women who had survived these crimes to discuss the new approach, at which bureaucrats claimed they had consulted with the busiest shelter in the province. The director of that shelter could only remember a brief conversation in the hallway when at Justice's offices on another matter— was that the "consultation?" After a number of tense communications, the Department of Justice agreed to a moratorium on referrals to RJ for crimes of sexual violence or partner violence, while women's organizations conducted independent research with Nova Scotia women on their view of the initiative. The Department refused to fund the research, however. Support from the now-gutted federal Status of Women Women's Program was obtained to hear directly from Nova Scotia women and girls who (or whose assailant) participated in RJ. Did it restore their harm? What was it like sitting in that room? Would they do it again? I would coordinate this effort.

A new RJ coordinator for the province was brought in around this time. Pat Gorham was previously the community justice coordinator in a hardscrabble part of Nova Scotia who was doing wonderful things building bridges for criminalized youth back to their communities and families. I had been the evaluator for one of her federally funded initiatives, and had given rave reviews to the down-to-earth, tireless support her staff gave to youth coming back from jail. We liked and respected each other. Although Pat had no formal background of feminist analysis of violence against women, she deeply valued the principles of respectful communication of the sort that were used in community justice in her previous work. Because she incorporated these principles into her work with all persons, not just clients, we were soon able to work together in a collaborative way that had never been possible before with departmental RJ proponents.

She was the first "establishment" person willing to have a thorough look at the literature concerning RJ and social inequality, and specifically women's concerns about the replication of oppression through informal means such as community justice. Soon, we were talking about how the Nova Scotia research could go forward with her help, because she cared deeply about hearing from people, in this case Nova Scotia women. She cared deeply about truly serving men and women in a way that was not going to endanger their physical or psychological safety, and she understood how easy it was for centralized authorities to disconnect from actual community experiences and needs. For her, it was important to keep talking together, and that started to give me a better view of RJ and its practitioners. She was talking straight with me, instead of sending down writs from an office cubicle on high.

We got to work designing a way to reach female participants in RJ that would protect their anonymity (many of them would have been under 18 at the time of participation) and came up with a pretty clever system. Meanwhile, our coalition of women's groups worked on the overall research plan and instruments. Because we anticipated attacks from the government based on methodology, our plans were subject to two independent reviews by professors at Mount Saint Vincent University,[2] and shaped in accord with their recommendations.

When the reply came to our carefully crafted research plan we were disappointed. The Department of Justice's senior researcher ridiculed our narrative approach, which he could not even consider "research." He suggested a long series of changes, which we tried to navigate for a while. After endless stalling and committee reviews, it became clear that the Department wasn't going to assist us in letting women speak out about their RJ experience.

In the absence of the Nova Scotia Department of Justice's timely support for reaching RJ participants, the women's organizations on the project committee chose to use focus groups and interviews with women to gather a *prospective* reaction to RJ. Women were made of aware of the research by newspaper ads and features in local newspapers, and were referred by service providers at transition houses, women's centers, the Avalon Sexual Assault Centres, and the Elizabeth Fry Societies.

A research plan was collaboratively designed by abused women and the organizations seeking their equality, and sought to gather two key per-spectives from women most likely to be directly affected (survivors of male violence and criminalized women). What were women's responses to NSRJI goals, objectives, and protocols? And further, women were enlisted to share their vision for RJ; what did women see as restorative of the harms they had experienced?[3]

WOMEN'S RESPONSES TO THE RESTORATIVE JUSTICE INITIATIVE

One hundred-and-twenty-five women participated in focus groups in the various regions of the province and in the Aboriginal, African Nova Scotian and immigrant communities. Two focus groups were also held for women prisoners. An additional group was held for nonoffending mothers of sexually abused children. We specifically sought women who had not only experienced misogynist violence but had some experience of the criminal justice system, either as victim/survivors, witnesses, or as criminalized persons. The failure of the current justice system to address misogynist violence was often cited as a reason by proponents for introducing RJ: it could do no more harm than the current system. We wanted women to be able to evaluate the RJ proposal based on their experiences of the current justice system. Having been through it, were they so desperate for an alternative that anything could be tried with nothing to lose?

Replicating Old Patterns of Discrimination

One of the first points made by women was that the same professionals would be referring, participating in, and using the RJ processes and outcomes: police, prosecutors, judges, social workers, etc. Many women identified significant problems in the existing criminal justice system as arising from systemic patterns of discrimination or direct discrimination by some of these professionals. There was nothing in place to prevent the carry-over of these problems into RJ. NSRJI was not a true alternative system, but rather was highly intermeshed with the conventional justice system. The ability of RJ to achieve its stated goals would be limited by the extent to which the justice context in which it is operating continues to perpetuate discrimination.

Women identified significant problems in the existing system, which they feared would be made worse under NSRJI, by giving actors from these same problem systems more discretion and less scrutiny by abandoning the public nature and record keeping of courts. Under the existing system, women said that abuse was trivialized, that there was a pervasive attitude of victim-blaming, and that referral practices were discriminatory, both in racist and heterosexist ways, which affected access to programming. Women said that there was a systemic failure to provide safety for abused women, and a lack of community awareness and understanding. There were reports of community hostility to abused women. Comments included:

> I think that by taking it out of the courtroom, [it's saying] it's not a crime, let's deal with it in a nice way so that everyone is "happy." And it is a crime.
>
> The last time I was at the police station, the officer said to me that my husband feels right bad, because the neighbors are going to know that the police were involved. That's too bad isn't it? I should have asked them how embarrassed they think he'll feel when the neighbors see the police come for the last time [referring to her death].
>
> One more time, all they are doing is setting the man free, to walk the streets, to wait for the [forum], in a little corner room, where his lawyer ... maybe my mother and maybe his step-father are going to meet up and decide what should be done with him because he beat his wife and kids? That doesn't sound even humane to me.

Safety Concerns

Women also identified new problems that they feared could be caused by NSRJI directly. The primary concern was safety and security, for themselves, their children, and survivor-supportive participants. This is what women spent the majority of the time discussing, in every focus group examining survivors' perspectives on restorative justice and woman abuse:

> I actually think the town cops are afraid of him.
>
> I wouldn't feel safe in a circle. I'd need security, two bodyguards, a fence, Plexiglas . . .
>
> When somebody finally said [to us], "This has got to stop, you have got to tell him, 'this is what you've done, you've broken my nose, you've broken my collar bone,' he just looked at me and said, 'You're dead when we're out of here. I'll get you when we're alone.' "
>
> I had a hard time standing in a courtroom with my husband, [even] knowing there were police everywhere. Because police don't mean anything to him. There was a judge, a bail bondsman, there were tons of people there. I was scared to death. .It doesn't matter how much they smile and wave while they are there. It's what he's going to do afterwards. I felt fear in a courtroom, never mind going into a room where I've got nobody to look out for me.

Safety fears involved the periods before, during, and after community justice fora, and in some cases were very long term (for example, abusers' attitudes toward women involved in sentencing, upon their release).

Some women emphasized the important role the formality of the courtroom and the power of the judge and other court personnel played in their and the abuser's experience. One transition house staff person spoke about an abuser threatening his victim with gestures in the courtroom, making the motion of holding a gun to her head and pulling the trigger:

> I saw it, and one of the sheriffs saw it and she said, "Did you see that?" The judge was still in the courtroom, he hadn't left yet, he turned around. It was caught. If the sheriff hadn't seen that, we would have had the woman crushed.

Because we were aware that the use of victim surrogates was a solution proposed by some RJ proponents in difficult cases such as misogynistic violence and sexual violence, we asked women if this would meet their needs. Women did not feel that victim surrogates were an appropriate response to their concerns. They felt that no surrogate could or should speak for them. Concerns also existed that the presence of a surrogate could communicate a survivor's intimidation to her abuser/assailant, and thus encourage his abusiveness.

Women described grave safety concerns about any meeting with their abusers:

Participant: A lot of them, even if they were convicted, if they went to that forum, would be going with a lot of anger.

Facilitator: What does that anger mean for you?

Participant: Possible death.

There is no way [restorative justice] is going to protect me. I don't feel protected unless he is in jail. One way or another, he is going to come and get me. I feel this every day of my life.

I would fear for my safety. It seems to trigger his physically abusive behavior when he sees me.

[A community justice forum] is not going to change their mind. When I walk out of the building and they see me walking down the street, after I just said what he had done, in front of . . . I'm history, I'd be dead.

Safety concerns extended to children, and supportive family or community members:

We had two cops . . . who met us there at my home. There was a person there from [transition house] with me. He went crazy. "There is the one that took my wife away," he said.

The trial part and all that, it just happened fast enough for me. I didn't have to be there, my kids didn't have to do anything. The video statements worked fine.

I wouldn't take another soul, helper, or friend with me to help me . . . why would you bring a good person into it, a person he can retaliate against?

Neighbors are terrified that he will retaliate.

Elders may be afraid of him. One elder already had this; there can be a backlash. . . . How is the abuser going to be monitored?

Women were adamant that community forum participation with an abuser would be psychologically negative for them, endangering hard-won recovery from abuse. Many women stated that fears for their and others' physical safety, and the triggering of patterns of fear and intimidation that had been programmed into them by the abuser would prevent them from participating at all or participating genuinely in anything like a community justice forum for sentencing purposes:

How could you think straight when the person who had instilled so much fear in you . . . for years and years and years, I can't do it. All of that would come back. Even if just little bits and pieces come out, it would be so unnerving, that you couldn't think straight. They know us, they know the triggers . . . it would be that look, the look, the dead cold look. I would just have to see that and think, "I'm in trouble." I would want to run out of the room . . . they have their looks or their hand motions, you know?

> I would be terrified. I would not speak my mind or speak the truth.
>
> I'm thinking of my personal experience, I could not have gone through that process [community justice forum]. Anyone outside . . . could not have known what those triggers were inside me.
>
> Facilitator: Triggers?
>
> A look you see, prior to being victimized.
>
> My daughter says, "I never have to see him again, right? I never have to see him?" She is always saying that to me.

Many women stated that for their and others' safety and healing, what was most needed was a period of custody for the abuser, but this was exactly the recommendation they felt they could never make in a community justice forum, because of danger and intimidation. They felt that custodial sentencing should be the responsibility of judges. Women felt that as long as sentencing was coming from women survivors, it would be discounted and any message to the abuser would be lost:

> I would rather have the court send a message to my partner that his behavior was unsociable, unacceptable, than to sit in a small room and try . . . because then it's me . . . and I don't want to be there. I don't even want to be in court. But to be there in a small room and being responsible for helping to determine the outcome, to me, is about the worst place I could possibly imagine.
>
> That's the very reason why the police took it out of your hands to arrest your husband on domestic violence because women weren't doing it . . . Because too many women say, "Oh, I changed my mind." . . . They are too scared. Now the police say, "Fine, we are going to take that over." You go and put a woman next to her husband and say, "Now you tell me dear, what would you like for him?" After 20 years of being beat?
>
> Instead of me having to fight to keep him off me, let the law say he can't be there . . . it's much easier when it's the judge who's the one telling him he has to go to jail.
>
> It's another way for them not to take responsibility. He would say, "I wouldn't have gotten that if it wasn't for her" . . . like, "She did this," not like, "I did something wrong so the law made me do this because it was wrong behavior." No, he would say, "That's my wife."

Confidentiality

Confidentiality was a prime concern of women who had survived abuse crimes. Women, particularly those from smaller communities, had no confidence that they would emerge from restorative justice processes with confidentiality, which they viewed as a key component of their dignity and both physical and psychological security. Women's needs for confidentiality in discussing their experience may not fit well with restorative processes as contemplated in RJ. These needs could include anonymity, limited exposure of family members, or restricting their sharing of experience to other women who had also been through abuse. Confidentiality issues were also linked to issues around women's healing needs. Women also were concerned about abusers learning personal information about them through RJ sessions once they had fled the relationship.

Pressuring Women to Participate

Women questioned the genuineness of the voluntary nature of their participation. In focus groups on RJ, Native women who had experienced abuse identified pressures to "drop charges" and felt analogous pressures would be placed on them to participate in RJ regarding crimes by abusers. These pressures were identified as coming from both prosecutors and Royal Canadian Mounted Police (RCMP). Black women identified pressures from their community leaders and other community members to use non–justice-system approaches to deal with abuse. They also anticipated likely pressures from spouses' family members to deal with abuse in a way perceived as less likely to result in incarceration (such as RJ). One focus group participant felt family members would be able to use children to pressure abused women into participating in RJ. Focus groups dealing with criminalized women's issues identified potentially coercive pressures related to RJ, such as a woman's responsibility to her children to get out of the system as quickly as possible (and avoid any risk of incarceration through pleading not guilty), even if it means being unjustly "accountable" for crimes against her abuser and facing him in a forum.

Women's Caretaking Responsibilities

Women still are usually the primary caregivers for children, and often the sole caregiver. Women also shoulder an unequal burden for other "caring" responsibilities such as elder-care or caring for the health needs of the family. Justice measures that impact differently on caregivers necessarily impact differently on women as a group. In interviews and focus groups, women identified many issues arising in their justice experience related to their caregiver roles, and raised implications regarding NSRJI. Many women were concerned that the same ignorance regarding children and abuse that they faced with justice and social services personnel in the past would be replicated in the RJ context. They also saw the resolution of "family" law matters as integral to overall justice. Women were also concerned that RJ might not consider their children as "official victims" of the woman abuse or relate to their needs.

A special focus group was held in Halifax for women who were non-offending parents of sexually abused children. These women emphasized the problems associated with the simultaneity of criminal processes and family processes, two systems that often operate in isolation and sometimes with highly different approaches to the abuser, leaving the women to navigate a convoluted system in which they felt their safety, their children's safety, and their parental status may be jeopardized at any time. Community fora were seen as just another minefield—how would they be expected to act here to show they were good parents? These women were also concerned that the breadth of impact on their entire family would not be met in community justice fora that focused on the abuser and the survivor only, and didn't consider healing needs of nonoffending mothers and siblings.

Just as further contact in a community justice forum may not meet the healing needs of women who have experienced abuse, so also did women identify that further contact with abusers was not among the healing needs of children. In fact, women indicated that children's healing was dependent on feeling safe from further contact. Women were also concerned about children's perception of their mother's involvement in the sentencing of abusive partners. Women in conflict with the law made clear the primacy of their relationships with their children, and how the impact of incarceration on families was not currently considered in the justice system. These women and their service providers also identified women's caregiving responsibilities as potential obstacles to fulfilling conditions agreed to in RJ fora.

Difficulties in Defining "Community"

The definition of "community" for RJ purposes is a crucial question that may determine the course of justice in these processes, and one that many women felt was problematic. Women were asked what community means to them, and who was part of their community. Most said their community was those to whom they could turn for support. Many reported feelings of isolation from community when this was defined as all people in a certain geographic area. For many women, community shrank and changed radically after criminalization and/or after surviving abuse:

> My community is my faculty advisor, the women's groups that
> I am involved with, and my family. My home community is
> very judgemental. . . . Some people are very unforgiving.
>
> When sex abuse is disclosed, you are up against the whole
> community by yourself. And everyone is related to you!
>
> I was devastated when [my religious community] supported the
> abuser. They blamed me for reporting my child's disclosures to
> Children's Aid. They believed his story about my being crazy. I was
> suddenly alone and abandoned during the investigation. I no longer
> felt welcome among what was my community of over 20 years.

Survivors of male violence reported widespread victim-blaming. They described their shock and despair when trusted community members directed this at them and supported the abuser or assailant. Women reported feeling that, after becoming involved in criminalized ways of living, their real community was made up of only those closest to them, often other people on the street or other criminalized persons. Women also indicated that transition houses, sexual assault centers, and women's centers became an essential part of community for them. Some felt dislocated and unsure of what community really meant. Some were also concerned about defining community in such a way, for the purposes of community justice, that only privileged members of the larger community would be invited to participate, and that women with the most experience of women's access to justice would be excluded.

> My family? I haven't spoken to my family in five years.
>
> What does the participation of ordinary community lay members mean? Community services says they have ordinary community lay members who sit on the Appeals Board. These people have never known a day of poverty. They are usually in high-ranking positions and they have no idea ... but they are "ordinary lay community people." I think that what [government] is actually saying ... is don't bring in the women's community because they are too radical, don't bring in the poverty rights people ... because they are advocates.

Community Indifference

Many women were extremely concerned about community attitudes, a lack of understanding of woman abuse and women's criminalization, and a paucity of community competence to administer justice for women. In their view, this could take the form of simple ignorance of and indifference to abuse; victim-blaming; partiality toward the abuser; stereotyping based on race, mental disability, sexual orientation, or other personal characteristics; and reflexive condemnation of women in conflict with the law. Many of the aspects of systemic discrimination women described as existing within the justice system were seen as writ large in the broader community. Women spoke about how little change had taken place in community attitudes toward abuse in various areas or communities of Nova Scotia and how local communities had demonstrated indifference to abuse education and to women and their families:

> They may not be totally up to speed here with the rest of the world ... domestic violence is an accepted form of life. It is something the community doesn't look down upon ... it is just part of normal everyday life in a lot of communities.
>
> [Regarding sex roles of men and women] When I first came here to Nova Scotia with my husband 14 years ago, I, really, in my lifetime I thought I had been taken back 50 years.

Ten years of the [Aboriginal] Family Treatment Centre but the community doesn't respond. The elders are set in their ways.

Women talked about the judging and blaming they experienced from the community in general. They also spoke about their doubts that anyone who had not been through criminalization or abuse could truly understand their situations:

They don't understand what the problem is. They are not being abused. You know how really difficult it is to get the community all together and talk about woman abuse. . . . The community I live in . . . they look at me, and they think I'm a nice person but they think, "Oh, she's the one who made him do that."

They reported how abusers would involve family and community in continuing the abuse:

Community support? They are all just as bad as he is. He doesn't get at me through himself. I have to worry [here]. We've been physically attacked in public by his friends. . . . He has others do his dirty work for him. . . . He had my phone cut off, my power cut off. He called people on me. I can get my phone and power hooked back up . . . but when I am walking down the street and my children are being called names. . . . And my mother-in-law is going around saying I am spending all this money. I'm on Social Assistance, and she is threatening to call and to have all my money cut off. These are her grandkids.

The gentlemen, the husbands, the boyfriends . . . they are very influential. They can go out and tell their buddies, "She did this, she deserved that, do you know what she did to me? She was sleeping with so and so." That's what they can do. They've done it to you all their lives. They have manipulated you, they have brainwashed you . . . and they can do it to other people as well.

Women also emphasized the fact that abusers may be influential, well-connected community members, and that this was a factor that could impact justice, especially in smaller communities:

One time out of ten, it is going to be a man who has influence in this town, or has money or has connections in this town. Then he gets convicted of beating his wife. Then they go to this restorative thing, and they look at him for his full life. . . . Most [abusers] are . . . charismatic people. They have good friends and that's the way it is.

Criminalized women said the restorative process would require them to repair the harm they did, and fulfill a set of conditions imposed by the community. But these women wondered, what could they could expect from their communities in return? Many women saw their experiences of child abuse, woman abuse, disability, and poverty as significant to their involvement in crime. They pointed to the lack of community caring or resources available to help them deal with these experiences. Many women felt that living on the street and being subject to criminalization were linked with general community indifference. As survivors rather than "offenders," many raised the possibility of community justice as a reciprocal commitment between community and a criminalized woman.

To take on a role of reciprocal commitment, of being a "community of care" in a larger sense than just a woman's immediate existing supports, communities must have the resources to do so. Women reported their experience of not being able to access enough resources relevant to breaking the cycle of criminalization unless they went outside the province or were imprisoned. Women's equality-seeking organizations are an obvious linkage for RJ-related community involvement in support for woman survivors of abuse and/or criminalization. But women's service providers were very leery of new expectations that would be placed on them because of RJ, and these organizations anticipated an under-resourcing of RJ responsibilities on top of their already under-resourced situation.

Police as Facilitators

Women addressing the possibility of justice forums facilitated by RCMP officers were uniformly critical of the idea. This was due to their disappointment regarding the trivialization of abuse by officers, officers' willingness to charge victimized women with assault of the abusive partner, and a misogynistic attitude that women described concerning certain individual officers.

The role of a police officer as referrer/facilitator of restorative justice involving women has potential to greatly reinforce existing systemic discrimination against women at the time of ordinary police action and to reinforce power imbalances between men and women in the context of abuse. Women's response to the possibility of police officers as facilitators was uniformly and strongly negative.

Negative Legal Consequences

Women identified potential negative legal consequences of participating in RJ fora. They were concerned about adverse consequences of not fulfilling the conditions imposed through fora, through no fault of their own. Federally sentenced women decried this possibility and cited the imposition of pre-parole requirements that they were kept from meeting in a timely way, or from fulfilling at all. Women were also not confident that statements in community justice fora would not be used as admissions or as sources of information for other proceedings. Service providers raised caution about the loss of evidence if discussions in community justice fora or reabuse occurring in these fora are to be removed from the evidence pool. They were also concerned that abuse survivors who chose not to participate would be seen as unforgiving or uncooperative and that this might affect family law determinations around their parenting.

WOMEN'S VISIONS OF RESTORATION

In focus groups and in individual interviews, women were asked what was needed to restore the harm they had experienced due to abuse or criminalization. Putting aside reaction to NSRJI or to other alternative measures, women were asked to share their vision of what a RJ program serving women's needs would look like.

A Woman-centered Approach with a Focus on Systemic Discrimination

The involvement of women most directly affected in planning and development was viewed as basic to any program that was to be truly restorative. Many women saw room for improvement regarding inclusiveness. Survivors of male violence called for a shift of focus from the abuser to the abuse survivors' needs, including criminalized survivors. Women also felt it was crucial to address systemic discrimination in the justice system and in society generally. Education on abuse and women's equality issues was needed, in these women's view, for all justice system professionals. Women cited outdated and insensitive remarks, actions, and attitudes of police, lawyers, judges, and other justice system professionals throughout discussions. They felt that mandatory education on abuse, women's equality, and cultural sensitivity was needed, in particular for judges who, women felt, would not educate themselves on these issues unless compelled.

Some women called for greater female representation among police, lawyers, and especially judges. Some wished to explore the idea of specialized family violence courts in which justice professionals involved would have had substantial training on abuse issues. Criminalized women also expressed how excellent it would be if women who had been in similar situations of criminalization were the facilitators of RJ. They regarded this approach as a straightforward way to make processes women-centered, and to have people with real expertise in women's experience involved.

Expanded Community Resources for Women

When asked what a RJ program of their own design would include, women uniformly included increased women's services in community. Many women's ideas were as simple as a self-help group that could meet regularly, but women did not have the available resources to do even this without support in many instances. Criminalized women emphasized the availability of help for addictions in the community as absolutely key to ending their cycle of criminalization.

Economic Assistance

Women spoke about how abuse was linked to economic obstacles of many sorts. Most women exiting abusive relationships suffer economic loss in extricating themselves and must face substantial hurdles to a stable livelihood. Criminalized women also face substantial obstacles to stable livelihoods. It is not surprising that many women identified economic help as primary to restoring the harm they have experienced. Women talked about how inadequate resources were in women's prisons for job training and education. In particular, they decried being told to work on jobs ostensibly for job training but that involved the acquisition of no real-world job skills, and of being cut off from using computers and other equipment that they understood would help them with job readiness. Women also described how a lack of income did not allow them to access services or programs because they did not have transportation or childcare.

Measures to Prevent Further Abuse

A crucial prerequisite to restoring harm is to establish women's safety. Women recommended a number of possible measures to prevent further woman abuse. These included custodial sentencing for crimes involving violence against women; stricter and better-enforced no-contact provisions for abusive men, including no contact involved with child visitation (women should not be criminalized for contact with the abuser subject to such orders, however). Other measures included a forced change of residence for abusers, follow-up with survivors to monitor their fears, a greater availability of silent alarms for survivors, and presumption against bail in cases of abuse or stalking. It is important for RJ proponents not to dismiss these types of safety measures as "retributive" or morally unworthy of victims.

Community Education and Activism

Women agreed that community education was part of restoring the harm caused by abuse and/or criminalization. This would not only be restorative in relation to particular women, but would be transformative for the community altogether. Other women extended the wish for community education to community activism. Some criminalized women discussed community openness toward federally sentenced women, which was thwarted by prison administration. They felt communities should have a greater ability to extend resources to prisoners if communities chose to do so.

THE LISTENING DAY

In the past, when women's organizations collected women's accounts of justice policies that were having a negative impact, the Nova Scotia Department of Justice had ignored or attempted to discredit such research.

In response, women's organizations had used the news media to publicize the research and create political pressure that bureaucrats would respond to and finally move on creating safer and fairer approaches. This had been the case in 2000, for example, around the issue of expecting abuse survivors to negotiate family law issues in mediation with their assailants (Rubin 2000). The government, which had been turning a blind eye to some outrageous risks, was forced to put in place a screening tool to eliminate some of these dangers, owing to negative publicity created when women's stories of terror and injustice were released.

In dealing with NSRJI however, women's organizations did not move immediately to public pressure after concluding the research. Because we trusted the RJ coordinator, we released some initial findings to her. We also discussed women's responses with Jennifer Llewellyn, a local law professor who had background in both RJ and feminist analysis of the law. Jennifer had been active with the government and other academics in bringing forward feminist concerns, while still being a proponent of RJ. She had the ear and respect of politicians on these issues.

Planning the Listening Day

Both Jennifer and Pat suggested that there be a day set aside for dialogue between government and women's organizations prior to the public release of our research. My suggestion was that instead of dialogue, we have a "Listening Day." Since the government had plowed so far ahead into this without any consultation with women or women's organizations, some pure listening was needed to catch up and balance the process so far. To our delight, both Pat and Jennifer readily agreed that was appropriate. Jennifer indicated to her connections that if they wanted to see NSRJI go forward with community buy-in, they needed to do this. Pat also championed the idea to her superiors at the Department of Justice. When she got favorable signals, Pat worked together with me to craft a day that would meet both our needs: to have women's concerns heard and to respect the community justice agencies' work and dedication so far. Our aim was to start off on a new path of inclusive development of innovative justice approaches.

Our Listening Day took place in October 2002. The government footed the bill, allowing research participants and women's organizations to attend from across the province. Funding was a new form of respect, which made women feel they weren't shouting into the wind.

Very importantly, because of the departmental sponsorship, participation was strongly encouraged among targeted justice employees. They came not only from community justice, but from corrections, court services, and victim services, and attendance was very high.

Recommendations from the Listening Day

On the morning of Listening Day, women's organizations presented various aspects of their research on RJ to the assembled audience. For the two days prior, women from everywhere in the province met to discuss the research and recommendations. We wanted only to present those themes and recommendations on which there was unanimous consensus among women's equality-seeking groups. In the end, all of the research themes were presented, and women's organizations made three key recommendations:

1. While not rejecting RJ principles, the Nova Scotia Restorative Justice Initiative and the RCMP Restorative Justice Program, as currently configured, are unacceptable for the handling of partner violence and sex crime.
2. We recommend that the RCMP, the Nova Scotia Department of Justice, and its contracting agencies participate with us in a long-term inclusive policy development process regarding RJ and women's access to justice.
3. As that goes forward, we recommend that the moratorium on the referral of sex offenses and spousal and partner violence continue, and further that compliance with the moratorium be monitored through this period through more effective mechanisms, and that the establishment of more effective monitoring mechanisms for the moratorium be part of our first inclusive work together.

During the afternoon of our Listening Day, participants split into groups for an "inclusiveness exercise." Each group had a mix of professions present, representing women's organizations and the various justice system officials, including community justice staff. Each group was to brainstorm around the question of how to move forward and be inclusive of women on RJ policy planning and implementation, and in particular, how to include women of diverse communities. Suggestions were simply listed and discussion on their merits was deferred. This exercise had great value for working relationships in the long term: A morning of government and justice professionals listening to women's organizations helped dispel the feeling of "stuckness" over previous exclusion of women's voices; a collaborative exercise following in the afternoon was the first occasion for justice professionals and feminist activists to work together on RJ in mutual openness. And it addressed the major recommendation of women's organizations: that an inclusive policy process be established.

THE JOINT WORKING GROUP

The main idea emerging from the inclusiveness exercise was that we should form a feminist/government Joint Working Group (JWG). Pat and I got to work on this, with the goal of examining women's stories from the research more closely and then moving into a dialogue mode. Because of the Department's sponsorship, representatives from police, corrections, the prosecutors' office, the sex offender treatment program, and community justice were committed to participate. To have our best chance at success Pat and I created and observed the following protocols with the group:

- Working groups and other initiatives should be co-chaired, with one chair from the justice system and one chair from a women's organization.
- A critical number of women's advocates should participate in the group that is at least equal to the number of justice system professionals participating.
- Women's community organizations should choose their own representatives to the Joint Working Group.
- A consensus model should be followed for decision making and the creation of reports.
- Meetings should be planned well in advance and should only proceed if critical numbers from both the justice system and women's organizations can attend.
- In recognition of the limited resources of women's community organizations, honoraria and travel costs should be provided for participation.
- Meeting locations should alternate between justice system facilities and women's organizations' facilities.
- Decision making should not be rushed on complex issues affecting women; it must be recognized that this is an education process that requires the building of working relationships for the long haul.

The joint working group met for almost two years. During that time, the group took an unhurried look at women's concerns. Many of the justice professionals expressed how important this learning process was for them. They appreciated hearing in a detailed way about women's physical and psychological safety issues, and about the unintended consequences that might impact families, communities, and other legal proceedings. There was also a discussion of justice innovations that might fit better with women's own ideas of restoration.

It emerged over our time together that, in fact, many justice professionals themselves were uncomfortable with the NSRJI scheme for handling partner violence and sex crimes. Community justice providers felt that their staffs and volunteers did not have the expertise or security measures in place to handle these very difficult cases. Psychologists managing the province's sex offender treatment program were concerned about how assessments and treatment could be mandated without convictions. They were also concerned that communities lacked the expertise to understand sex crimes, recidivism, and prevention. For example, there was concern that community members may not understand the need for no-contact orders for fathers who had assaulted children, or how behaviors that laypersons associate with ordinary parenting can be twisted into grooming the child for further sexual abuse. Another example was the common presumption that sexually aggressive youth behavior was less dangerous or less entrenched and therefore more amenable to RJ processes; psychologists expert in working with such youth indicated that few differences exist between adults and youth in the degree of seriousness or entrenchment of the behaviors.

Prioritizing Safety for Abused Women and Their Children

By far, the issue area of greatest concern to the JWG was safety, both physical and psychological, for women who had experienced partner violence and/or sex offences. This parallels the 2003 research, in which participating women also identified safety for themselves, their children, and survivor-supportive participants as their greatest concern about NSRJI. The processes used under the NSRJI were not created in specific contemplation of crimes of violence against women. That these crimes are different from others was accepted explicitly for the first time by government through the JWG.

Some differences affecting safety of participants in processes under NSRJI were acknowledged specifically. It was established that, unlike assaults between strangers, the typical pattern of intimate violence is one in which an abuser controls and intimidates a woman through a pattern of emotional, financial, and physical abuse over a period of time. This poses unique risks for intervention because the abuser and victim may continue to reside together, have contact related to children, or have ongoing contact for other reasons. The very discussion of accountability for partner violence, or the mere presence of the abuser's habitual target, may incite the abuser's anger and trigger further abuse. Further, evidence indicates that lethality and recidivism risks associated with partner violence escalate after separation, and this period of elevated risk may overlap with justice processes. In cases of sexual offending, the group accepted that under-standing the risks associated with sexual abuse requires expert knowledge that is often counterintuitive to lay community members.

A highlighted theme was that, with regard to safety, "we need to go forward from the assumption that practices will have to change" if NSRJI were ever to handle these cases. The JWG consensus was that the current protocols and processes associated with the NSRJI could precipitate further abuse and were not adequate to ensure the safety of participants in cases involving woman abuse or sexual offences.

The JWG highlighted a number of points to address *before* modeling any safety response. "Move a couple steps back and define . . . what the first principles of RJ are, and ensure that these inform the structures that develop." This could mean expanding on vision statements, identifying what benefits we are seeking for the individuals affected by these particular crimes, defining "community" and what its restorative responsibility is in cases of violence against women, and stating how shifting justice from court to community agency in these cases would better serve women as a class. An associated theme states it pithily: "We need to be clear as to whose needs are the starting point. Is it the victim's needs or the system's?"

It must be made clear, in an evidence-based way, what RJ can and cannot accomplish in these cases. This will help protect both the safety of potential participants and the reputation of the RJ program. The JWG pointed out that we may need to shift focus to another model specifically built to serve women, one flexible enough to respond to unique needs.

"There is a need to explore . . . the congruence of restorative justice processes (particularly any that were to be pre-court) with the current response to family violence" (such as the provincial government's Framework for Action Against Family Violence) (Russell and Ginn 2001). Are there shared goals? Are there competing goals?

Safety and issues of voluntary participation go beyond the informed decision to participate. Safety planning would be needed before, during, and immediately subsequent to the RJ process, as well as for longer-term follow-up. In what is typically an ongoing pattern of control and intimidation, occurring within a social context of family and community pressures on the woman targeted for abuse, participants' safety and voluntary participation are much more serious challenges. They will require a much more expert and intensive assessment and preparation to ascertain or provide. JWG members emphasized that such considerations will need to come well before the referral and the option to RJ is offered.

Last, we need a broader awareness of endangerment, including prior incidents and other victims—we can't take a narrow, incident-specific approach. This has implications for model development: RJ already has a difficult fit with the court system, in which the focus is on the specific event rather than on the ongoing dynamic of control and domination.

Thinking Through the Meaning of Community

The role of community was identified in the 2003 report as an area of question and concern for abused and assaulted women and their front-line service providers. These included questions regarding how to define community, given the dislocation and community rejection women experience after reporting a crime; community issues for women from diverse cultural groups; community attitudes and awareness levels regarding violence against women; and community resources for women.

The JWG highlighted three priorities from among themes discussed in this area. First, we need to think in the direction of a broader social development model, one that more explicitly links crimes with issues of mental health, shelter, economic disparities, and gender and other discrimination. Second, the lack of community awareness and understanding of violence against women has the potential to result in harm from well-meaning but uninformed interventions. And third, we need a collaborative and inclusive process to define who is "community" in these processes.

Modeling a Collaborative Dialogue

In addition to sharing our expertise on violence against women, the JWG process allowed us to learn about and model collaborative dialogue between government and the feminist community. At the end of our time together, the JWG decided to document key learning points about dialogue in this situation:

1. The co-management of the process by the Nova Scotia Department of Justice and the women's community was an important building block of mutual trust and respect among different participants, and facilitated consensus-based progress. Continuing this co-management model for future development would likely result in sensitive work that would be more readily accepted by both justice professionals and the community. Continuing the balance between feminists providing front-line services and those primarily involved in policy development would be important too.

2. It is crucial that any future planning group be of a representative nature, similar to that of the JWG. Also, further consultation with justice professionals, women's equality-seeking organizations, and other community is needed to determine if other voices should also be present in such a development group. For example, some felt that representatives from various justice sectors should be involved. Other missing voices identified by JWG members include Child and Family Services and "consumers."

3. The issues or crimes being addressed must be clearly distinguished prior to any policy or program development. They should be "unbundled," in order to assess the particular challenges they represent. For example, areas that may require different approaches and expertise include partner violence, different types of sex offenses and, as well, possibly differing youth and adult approaches.

4. The sizeable body of knowledge required to consider these issues properly was apparent through the JWG process. Any further process of development of policy and programming requires the commitment of all involved to integrate current research on RJ, sex offending, and other forms of violence against women, and on systemic challenges to women's access to justice.

5. It was apparent that JWG members came to the discussion with some shared and some differing goals. Being explicit from the beginning about goals arising out of professional or personal experience would be useful in focusing the work. For example, if reducing caseload is an issue for justice professionals, that should be explicit from the beginning, as these issues will

tend to shape discussion and planning toward solving problems that may be beyond RJ's mandate.

6. Prior to beginning a development process, there should also be discussion of priority among shared goals, such as reducing recidivism, community change that will reduce crime, and/or better meeting survivors' needs.

7. Program and policy design will require research that identifies the needs of Nova Scotians more clearly. This should include an examination of police records and child protection complaints. Efforts should be made in this research to bring forward women's voices.

Because we were able to finance our own research and advocacy, because women's organizations refused to back down in the face of government ridicule, because a few RJ proponents felt morally responsible to hear women's voices, and because RJ proponents didn't want to bring down their whole project on this point, a moratorium was placed on dealing with partner and sexual violence through the NSRJI, and it remains in place as of this writing. The Listening Day and the JWG were the first feminist community/government co-managed events ever to take place in Nova Scotia to determine justice policy.

CONCLUSION

Have the lessons learned about gender analysis and the value of collaborative work been internalized by the academics and system players involved? Subsequent developments have initially been disappointing in this regard. In a recent community/government committee called by the government to review domestic violence, the community was neither financed to participate nor allowed to choose its own representatives. Quarterly meetings established with women's organizations subsequent to the JWG were eventually abandoned by the Department of Justice's research, policy, and planning division.

Most troubling was that, despite the stated commitment to communication and collaboration on further initiatives arising from the JWG, Dalhousie University recruited only justice system partners for governance of a major new RJ research initiative. Even more alarming, a project on intimate partner violence was funded, outlined, and academic researchers based in Ontario hired, all without our prior knowledge. Had we been working in communication and collaboration, it is likely that the women's community would have offered their own proposal in this large initiative, but because we weren't informed, it was too late. Both the exclusion from any representation in governance as well as the development of a specific intimate partner violence project without the involvement of the women's community were major disappointments. We in the women's community ended up scratching our heads, wondering if we had been part of the same process all along, and if Dalhousie University professors could see no problem with this. For her part, Jennifer Llewellyn adamantly defended her intention to honor and involve the women's community at a time in the planning she felt was more appropriate. The women's community was experiencing the power imbalance between ourselves and the university, and we felt betrayed.

To address the situation, I worked again with Pat to develop a communication process. I suggested that since the women's community felt there had been a harm, could we use any of her RJ techniques to address this? We made a plan for a circle involving the academics and the women's community, to be facilitated by a trusted third party, Gola Taraschi, an analyst at the Department of Justice with a commitment to both the space of talking circles and equality values.

In the circle, no changes were committed to immediately. Nothing changed in the fundamental power imbalance between the university and women's equality-seeking community. But I can say that the experience created a space in which to move forward with less bitterness and discouragement. It affirmed for me again that the safety and equality concerns around particular RJ techniques and institutionalizations do not mean that the women's community is opposed to some of the underlying principles of RJ. In fact, some of these are decidedly mutual: respect for human experience, confidence that change can occur, and the elimination of force as the primary means to achieve aims. Nova Scotia will be an interesting bellwether in the coming years, as sectors with different claims to power and authenticity address how justice innovation can help end misogynist violence. Whether these sectors can work together will be very telling with regard to the RJ movement's claim to the ability to effect positive change and increase human dignity.

Perhaps the most fundamental question to address for its proponents will be the role of "community" in community justice, while the status quo in the mainstream "community" includes gender oppression enforced by violence. Are RJ proponents willing to view the community of women who have lived through gendered violence, whose lives are dedicated to ending it, to supporting each other and transforming our society, as valued leaders in the search for justice for misogynist violence?

NOTES

1. A very serious sexual assault, originally to be prosecuted as an indictable offence, was reduced to a summary offence, very likely in order to qualify for adult diversion, which was only available for cases prosecuted on a summary basis. The perception arose that this was done at the behest of influentials who were part of the community establishment, of which the accused was a previous pillar. The diversion went ahead, resulting in the assailant being required to write an essay on trust (he had been in a position of trust and authority vis-à-vis the victim at the time of the assault), and he remained free of criminal record. Women's equality-seeking organizations complained to the provincial Minister of Justice.

The assailant in this case, because of an absence of a conviction, was able to pass criminal background checks and was hired to work in a setting in which he would have access to children, which was discovered later by justice officials. In response to this case, at least in part, the Nova Scotia government ended the inclusion of sexual offenses in diversion.

2. Drs. Meredith Ralston and Cynthia Matheson.

3. Two women who had been through restorative justice processes also came forward after hearing about our project, and their stories, which rejected the process, were included too.

REFERENCES

Rubin, Pamela. 2000. *Abused Women in Family Mediation: A Nova Scotia Snapshot. A Report Prepared by The Transition House Association of Nova Scotia* (THANS). Halifax, NS: THANS. Retrieved January 31, 2009 (http://www.thans.ca/file/30).

Russell, Dawn and Diana Ginn. 2001. *Framework for Action Against Family Violence: 2001 Review.* Halifax, NS: Department of Justice.

5

RESTORATIVE JUSTICE, GENDERED VIOLENCE, AND INDIGENOUS WOMEN

Julie Stubbs

The application of restorative justice (RJ) for offences such as domestic violence and sexual assault continues to be highly contested, but the debate has become more complex and nuanced. I begin this chapter with a consideration of theoretical constraints on the capacity of RJ to promote victim interests, and then provide an overview of the debate with respect to offences of gendered violence. I use the term "gendered violence" to reflect the range of behaviors referred to in the relevant literature. Much of this research is specific to domestic violence or sexual assault, but I also draw from research concerning Indigenous communities that commonly refers to a wider range of violent practices and includes a more expansive notion of family than is common in the domestic violence literature. In the second part of the chapter, I examine literature concerning RJ responses to gendered violence in Indigenous communities. Research and commentary on Indigenous communities often fails to engage with the intersection of gender and race (or other social relations), and thus Indigenous women's needs and interests within RJ processes are still commonly obscured. The discursive character of RJ requires that participants tell their stories and that reasoned discussion will occur, resulting in an agreed upon outcome.[1] The capacity of parties to participate effectively is rarely questioned, yet victims in particular may face real obstacles to full participation. I argue that the opportunities and risks afforded by the discursiveness of RJ can be magnified by the impact of colonization on Indigenous women. I conclude by urging the consideration of hybrid developments that move beyond the oppositional contrast between RJ and criminal justice and adopt antisubordination as a principle in working toward safe and just outcomes.

THE BENEFITS OF RESTORATIVE JUSTICE
FOR VICTIMS OF CRIME

The benefits of RJ claimed for victims of crime include a wide range of symbolic, material, therapeutic, and moral outcomes (Stubbs 2007). International reviews have highlighted wide diversity between and within jurisdictions and some uncertainty about the prevailing RJ models, practices, and policies in use (Miers 2007). This diversity may be celebrated by some RJ proponents who emphasize restorative values rather than any one model (Pranis 2007), but the details of given schemes matter profoundly when assessing the merits and safety of RJ for victims, offenders, and the community. Much of the extant evidence has been derived from evaluations of programs for juvenile offenders, with less detail available regarding adult schemes.

Studies have found wide variations in victim participation rates in different schemes (from 7% to 85%, Dignan 2003:137). A growing body of evidence suggests that victims and other participants report high levels of satisfaction with RJ (Strang 2002; Sherman and Strang 2007) although satisfaction has been conceptualized and measured inconsistently (Van Ness and Schiff 2001; Wemmers and Canuto 2002). Daly found high levels of satisfaction and perceived procedural fairness among participants, but less evidence for "restorativeness"; "these findings suggest that although it is possible to have a process perceived as fair, it can be harder for victims and offenders to resolve their conflict completely or to find common ground" (2001:76). Victims have reported reduced levels of fear, anxiety, and anger and show less interest in seeking vengeance (Strang 2002), and emerging research suggests a reduction in symptoms of posttraumatic stress after participating in RJ (Strang et al. 2006; but see Cheon and Regehr 2006). However, Daly has found that RJ "may do little to assist victims who have been deeply affected by crime" (2005:164); she noted "the variable nature of restorative processes, which can be contingent on the offence, the . . . victim and the subjective impact of victimisation" (2005:167). Many other claims have not been tested empirically, and few studies have specifically examined gender relations within RJ (but see Cook 2006; Daly 2002b). Claims of benefits for the community also may have a positive impact for victims and offenders, but Kurki's observation that "community level outcomes are yet to be defined and measured" (2003:294) continues to be apt.

The aspirations of the RJ movement to deliver such a range of benefits to victims of crime are laudable. However, the capacity of RJ to advance victims' interests remains limited by several factors. First, it does not have

"its own concept of either victim or victimization" and thus lacks a foundation for challenging opposing claims (Green 2007:184–5). Second, a
theoretical basis for how and why RJ might benefit victims is rarely articulated (Acorn 2004; Strang et al. 2006). Third, despite emerging evidence
that experiences of RJ might vary according to victim, offender, and
offence characteristics and to the subjective experience of victimization,
little theoretical or empirical work guides practice in responding to these
issues. Fourth, the tendency of much RJ literature to theorize crime as a
discrete incident is at odds with research demonstrating that domestic
violence is commonly recurrent and escalating and that the threat of
violence may be ongoing and not reducible to discrete incidents (Coker
2002; Stubbs 2002). These are very salient concerns when dealing with
offences such as domestic violence or sexual assault, which are not
universally denounced nor well understood and where victim blaming is
common (Coker 2002).

Debating the Merits of Restorative Justice for Gendered Violence

The use of RJ for cases of domestic violence, or other gendered violence,
continues to be controversial. The debate has been summarized by Daly
and Stubbs (2006; see also Curtis-Fawley and Daly 2005; Edwards and
Sharpe 2004). Proponents typically point to the opportunity for victims to
participate and have a voice and receive validation, and for offenders to take
responsibility, for a communicative and flexible environment and relationship repair (if that is a goal; Daly and Stubbs 2006). Those who oppose the
use of RJ or urge caution point to risks such as victim safety being compromised in the process, possible manipulation of the process by offenders,
pressure on victims to participate and/or agree to an outcome, communities that are under-resourced to support the parties, the lack of a community consensus condemning the violence, mixed loyalties among
possible supporters, poor prospects for changing the offender's behavior,
and the possibility that RJ may be seen to symbolize a lenient approach
(Daly and Stubbs 2006). A more nuanced debate has begun to emerge
as commentators recognize the diversity of victims' experiences and engage
with empirical findings that suggest that outcomes may be more contingent than indicated by earlier accounts. Achilles and Zehr acknowledge
that some RJ programs have been naïve in "attempting to apply restorative
approaches in highly problematic areas (such as domestic violence) without
adequate attention to complexities and safeguards" (2001:93). Commentary is beginning to differentiate between types of gendered violence and
their prospects for the safe use of RJ or similar processes (Curtis-Fawley and
Daly 2005). For instance, Hopkins, Koss and Bachar (2004; Hopkins and
Koss 2005) see merit in adapting RJ for responding to date rape, but urge
caution with respect to using RJ for ongoing intimate violence without
further evidence that it can be pursued safely.

The literature commonly emphasizes the opportunities afforded to participants by the discursive character of RJ, such as the ability to tell their stories and participate in determining an agreement about how to redress the harm. Pranis says that "personal narratives are the primary source of information and wisdom [in RJ] but...the critical element is to use [them] to understand the harms, the needs, the pains and the capacities of all participants so that *an appropriate new story* can be constructed" (emphasis added, 2002:31). Barbara Hudson summarizes what is appealing about RJ as "the openness of story telling and exploration of possibilities for constructive and creative responses to offences" (2003:192). RJ offers the victim of domestic violence "the opportunity to choose how to present herself...[to express] *her* feelings, her understanding of events, her wishes and demands for the future..." (Hudson 2003:183, emphasis in the original). However, Hudson recognizes that the discursiveness of RJ is not without problems, such as the risk of domination and the reproduction of power relations (2006), and she emphasizes the need for "strong procedural safeguards" (2003:183). As Daly (2002a) has pointed out, RJ offers both opportunities and risks in freeform discussion. We know little about how meaning is constructed in RJ processes and whose stories might prevail (Stubbs 2007). Few empirical studies have examined how social relations such as gender, race, class, or age are expressed in RJ (Daly and Stubbs 2007; but see Cook 2006). There is no reason for confidence that a "new story" derived in the RJ process will necessary reflect a progressive understanding of victimization or gendered violence (Coker 2002; Stubbs 2007). As Roche has argued, the informality of a restorative process may permit a range of possible outcomes, including tyranny (2003). Without an explicit commitment to challenging subordination, older, limited understandings of gendered violence may prevail (Busch 2002). Questions remain about the extent to which the values orientation of RJ is adequate to ensure victim's interests are met in the absence of an explicit normative commitment to challenging subordination (Coker 2006; Hudson 2006).

Although it is common for RJ guidelines to indicate that victim safety is a key principle, Wemmers notes that no study in her review had asked "whether restorative measures respond to victims' need for security and to their fear of crime" (2002:53). A related concern is the finding by Presser and Lowencamp that offender-screening criteria on RJ encounters were not "victim oriented, research-driven, nor consistently applied" (1999:335).

Consultations with Victims and Victim Advocates

Advocacy groups in several jurisdictions, particularly Canada, have undertaken consultations relating to RJ responses to gendered violence. Somewhat belatedly, governments or other key agencies have begun to consult communities concerning the future development of RJ. The findings have varied in detail but the prevailing view urges caution; consultation reports commonly emphasize concerns about victim safety, offender accountability, fears about the possible re-privatization of gendered violence, and questions about whether women's organizations and communities have the resources to take on the demands that might arise from RJ.

Stephanie Coward found that professionals and practitioners in the women's movement in Canada did not oppose RJ per se, but were concerned about its use for domestic violence. They pointed to a lack of consultation with women's and victims' groups, the likely effects of power imbalances between the parties, a lack of training and evaluation standards, and questions such as: would domestic and sexual violence be denounced sufficiently in such processes?; would women's groups' attempts to have the criminal justice system take the offences seriously be undermined?; would victims be given an informed choice about participating?; and would resources be made available to the community to deal with such issues? (Coward 2000). Similar findings have been reported across Canada (Lund and Devon Dodd 2002; Provincial Association of Transition Houses Saskatchewan 2000; Rubin 2003; see also Rubin, Chapter 4 in this volume).

The Canadian Aboriginal Women's Action Network (AWAN) is "strongly opposed to the application of restorative justice measures in cases of violence against Aboriginal women and children" and has urged a moratorium on new developments, in part because "there has been no emphasis in case law or in current restorative justice models on the legacy of colonialism for Aboriginal women and children: racism, sexism, poverty, and violence" (AWAN 2001: para 2; Cameron 2006). That position was reached after extensive research and consultations with Aboriginal women and communities (Stewart, Huntley, and Blaney 2001). Participants identified potential in RJ but "women expressed fear that restorative justice reforms would fail to address the underlying power inequity rife in communities from years of oppression" (Stewart et al. 2001:39). They noted that alternative justice approaches operate on a "premise that presupposes a healed community," existing models had "a lack of accountability and structure," and "a failure to do follow-up with offenders and enforce sentences would further add to their victimization" (Stewart et al. 2001:40). They were also concerned about the use of diversion, resources predominantly going to offenders, victim-blaming, and risks to the safety of women and children in communities and in restorative processes. McGillivray and Comaskey reached similar findings in their study with Aboriginal women in Manitoba. The women saw community-based dispute resolution for dealing with intimate violence "as partisan and subject to political manipulation" (1999:143) and worried that offenders might stack the process with their supporters and avoid responsibility for their actions, and that diversion may meet offenders' needs but not victims' needs for safety. Respondents expressed dissatisfaction with aspects of

conventional criminal justice but did not reject the Anglo-Canadian criminal justice system on cultural grounds. In a somewhat similar vein, The
Native Women's Association of Canada has offered conditional support to
RJ, recommending that funding be provided for 'restorative, "alternative"
and Indigenous justice initiatives' but 'only when it is clear that Aboriginal
women and their needs have been fully included' (2008:11).

Outcomes in Canada have been uneven. A federal/provincial/
territorial working party on spousal abuse recommended *against* the use
alternative justice processes such as RJ in spousal violence cases *except*
where nine specified conditions were met, supported by training and
resources (Ministry of Justice [Canada] 2003). In Prince Edward Island,
the Justice Options for Women project considered RJ in limited circumstances in which RJ was victim-initiated and post-charge only (Lund and
Devon Dodd 2002), but ultimately RJ was not adopted (Justice Options
for Women 2006). The province of Nova Scotia has a moratorium on RJ
for spousal/partner violence and sexual assaults (Rubin 2003). However,
RJ is used for offences including violence against women in British
Columbia (Cameron 2006) and Alberta (Edwards and Haslett 2003),
and circle sentencing and other community-based programs used for
Indigenous offenders in several jurisdictions include gendered violence.

In Australia, Curtis-Fawley and Daly (2005) sought the views of
advocates from sexual assault, child sexual assault, and domestic violence
services in two states. Respondents saw possible benefits in RJ for gendered
violence, such as giving victims a chance to speak in a way that courts did
not provide, redressing power imbalances by giving emphasis to the victim,
and the possibility of avoiding criminal justice altogether. However, they
feared that victims could be revictimized, that RJ might be seen as a "soft"
option, or that RJ practice may fall short of its ideals. Some rejected the idea
that RJ should be a complete alternative to criminal justice (see also
Nancarrow, Chapter 6 on the views of Indigenous and non-Indigenous
Australian women).

A New Zealand study of adult victims of child sexual assault found
some support for a RJ-like process but some diffidence on the part of
respondents about what that might mean in practice; the respondents
worried about the power of the offender to manipulate the process and
whether the process would be victim-centered (Jülich 2006; see also Jülich,
Chapter 11 in this volume). The majority of submissions to a New Zealand
government inquiry on the use of RJ for family violence supported RJ, but
the strongest support was from RJ practitioners. Those opposed thought
that RJ was inappropriate or dangerous due to power imbalances, a lack of
specialist training and expertise among RJ practitioners, and the need for
"strong state sanction" (Parker 2004). However, proponents also urged
caution and emphasized the need for "careful assessment and screening of
cases and the paramount importance of victim safety" (Parker 2004:5) and
the need for extra time and resources for such matters. A model of best
practice developed subsequently by the New Zealand Ministry of Justice

recommends that RJ is used only in "appropriate cases" and states that "[t]he use of restorative justice processes in cases of family violence and sexual violence must be very carefully considered ... and will not always be appropriate" (2004: Principle 8, no page numbers).

Consultations by the U.K. government attracted opposition from some women's advocacy organizations: Refuge (2003) and Women's Aid (2003) were open to the use of RJ for other offences but voiced strong opposition to RJ being used for sexual offences and domestic violence. In South Africa, the Commission on Gender Equality also has recommended against the use of RJ for sex offences or domestic violence due to concerns about victim safety (Commission on Gender Equality 2004).

Experience with Restorative Justice Programs

Offences of gendered violence are often excluded from contemporary RJ programs, but historically, models now labeled restorative often included such offences within generic schemes. For instance, gendered violence has been included by victim–offender reconciliation programs (Umbreit 1990) and victim–offender dialogue meetings from the 1980s (Genesee County n.d.). Umbreit and colleagues reported that a "surprising number" (2000:7) of victim–offender mediation programs in the United States include domestic violence (1%), familial sexual assault (9%), and stranger sexual assault (7%) (2000:8). However, no evaluations of responses by these programs to gendered violence have been identified. Prisons departments in several countries operate RJ programs post-conviction; these are typically not limited by offence type and in some cases may involve direct encounters between the victim and offender, in which all parties consent (Van Ness 2007). From 1991 to 1994, nearly half of the victim–offender mediations undertaken in a Langley, British Columbia project with inmates were for sexual assault matters (Roberts 1995:39). An evaluation reported few differences by offence type, but noted that adult survivors of child sex offences judged offenders to "lack authenticity" (Roberts 1995:111) and recommended longer-term follow-up with all victims.

The youth justice conferencing models in South Australia (SAJJ) and New Zealand are atypical in that they are state-funded programs that respond to the full range of offending by young people and thus routinely include sexual offences and family violence (Parker 2004). Daly has reported findings of several studies of sexual offences by young people in SAJJ; she finds that conferences were a better option for victims than courts, because offenders admit responsibility and an outcome is achieved, whereas a large proportion of court cases are dismissed or withdrawn (Daly 2005). New Zealand also uses Family Group Conferences (FGC) for child protection matters, in which sexual and/or physical abuse issues may be raised (Parker 2004). In addition to funding pre-sentence, court-referred RJ schemes that exclude domestic or family violence, the New Zealand Government also funds community-based schemes. The latter schemes vary—some are diversionary and others are post-conviction schemes—and some include domestic violence, family violence, and sexual offences. Community schemes are also funded by other sources. A review of five government-funded community schemes that include family violence is underway,[2] but little is currently known about the processes, safeguards, or outcomes used in those schemes (Parker 2004).

Recently the Australian Capital Territory has taken a distinctive approach by legislating for RJ to be used for both young offenders and adults across a wide range of offences. Domestic violence offences, which may include some sexual offences, are to be included in a future stage II once a policy platform for managing those matters has been developed,[3] but will be referred to the scheme only after a guilty plea or conviction. The *Crimes (Restorative Justice) Act (2004)* requires that a chief executive determine the suitability of a matter for RJ after considering factors such as any power imbalance between the parties and the physical and psychological safety of parties (s.33); it remains unclear how that assessment will be undertaken.

In addition to generic programs that include some offences of gendered violence, a small number of adult RJ programs deal specifically with domestic violence, sexual violence, and/or other forms of gendered violence; some of those were reviewed by Stubbs (2004). Few programs have been subject to evaluation and most available documentation is purely descriptive, thus there is little available evidence on which to assess the claims made.

The work of Joan Pennell and colleagues is particularly influential in debates over the potential for RJ to respond effectively to gendered violence. The Family Group Decision Making Project in Newfoundland and Labrador focused on child welfare but commonly involved various forms of family violence (Pennell and Burford 2002). It is widely seen as a very promising model based in feminist praxis, planned in conjunction with government and nongovernment agencies, women's advocates and Indigenous organizations, and with the capacity to generate resources to assist the parties in redressing the harm caused. Evaluations were positive, but the project was discontinued contrary to the wishes of the local Inuit community because the federal funding was time-limited.[4] The North Carolina Family Group Conferencing Project is a similar project focused on child welfare also undertaken by Pennell and others. Building on this experience with child welfare, Pennell and Francis (2005) document the process they used to engage battered women, advocates, and other stakeholders in planning a coordinated approach to safety planning for women and children under the auspices of a domestic violence program, drawing on formal and informal services and supports. It seems that offenders may be included in the process in some circumstances (see Pennell and Kim, Chapter 8 in this volume).

The DOVE program in the U.K. traces its roots to FGC in Newfoundland, Labrador, and New Zealand; victims/survivors of domestic violence, their children, and supporters attend a FGC with the objective of preparing a plan to enhance their safety. Perpetrators sometimes attend. A formative evaluation of the program (Social Services Research and Information Unit 2003) documents 30 referrals; nine cases proceeded to a FGC but parties agreed to participate in the research in only six cases. Outcomes were mixed: fewer children were on the child protection register, and only one family had further incidents recorded by police in the immediate follow-up period, but several stakeholders offered less support for the program at the 1-year point than they had initially. Four victims rated FGC as very good as a tool for dealing with domestic violence, but two had mixed feelings (Social Services Research and Information Unit 2003).

RESTORE was an innovative RJ program developed by Mary Koss and colleagues at the University of Arizona together with criminal justice personnel and community advocates. It responded to early feminist criticisms of RJ by careful design: cases of "ongoing intimate violence" were excluded, consistent with their preference for a cautious approach centered on victim safety (Hopkins et al. 2004; see Koss, Chapter 10 in this volume). It was limited to first-time offenders who pleaded guilty to misdemeanor sex offenses, where victims and offenders were aged at least 18 years, relied on consent by victim and offender, and was court-ordered. A similar program is being established in New Zealand, which seems to contemplate the inclusion of a wider range of sexual offences, including adult survivors of child sexual assault (Jülich 2006; see Jülich, Chapter 11 in this volume).

Restorative Justice and Indigenous Peoples

RJ may offer opportunities for community engagement in new justice forms that benefit Indigenous communities. However, the aspirations of Indigenous groups often embrace wider visions of justice, including self-determination (Cunneen 2003; Nancarrow 2006; Smith 2005), and the alternative justice initiatives pursued in Indigenous communities are not confined to RJ (Cameron 2006; Cunneen 2007; Marchetti and Daly 2004; Memmott et al. 2006). There are problems in conflating Indigenous justice with RJ, but no agreement on how to differentiate between the two. Circle sentencing is commonly designated as an example of RJ but Marchetti and Daly (2004) disagree and classify it as an Indigenous justice practice; the Hollow Water Community Holistic Circle healing program (Couture et al. 2001) is often claimed as RJ but is more expansive and multilayered than typical models of RJ. Research needs to analyze the specific features of different models and to consider the level of control or ownership Indigenous people have in any scheme. Few Indigenous schemes have been evaluated, and Dickson-Gilmore and LaPrairie lament that continued assertions of success in the absence of evaluative data actually hinder future developments (2005). The fact that some Indigenous people are participants in mainstream models of RJ also is often overlooked.

It is commonly assumed that RJ will be beneficial for Indigenous people (and peoples) in contrast to conventional criminal justice, which has been so damaging. However, debates that pit RJ against criminal justice obscure the fact that many extant RJ practices are not alternatives but are grafted onto criminal justice and may deflect attention from other possibilities more aligned with Indigenous aspirations. Claims that RJ is derived from Indigenous modes of dispute resolution are overgeneralized and have attracted strong criticism because they ignore important differences between Indigenous peoples and their practices and because the claims have sometimes substituted for consultation with Indigenous peoples about the development or imposition of RJ programs (Cunneen 2003; Daly 2002a; Dickson-Gilmore and LaPrairie 2005; Tauri 1999).

One key dimension on which programs differ is the legal and political framework in which they operate. For instance, the Navajo Nation has the authority "to exercise jurisdiction over tribal matters" (Cunneen 2007:124; see also Coker 2006); by contrast, Indigenous Australians have no recognized basis to "develop their own jurisdiction over legal matters . . . except . . . where the state permits them to do so as a matter of policy or practice" (Cunneen 2007:124). In Canada, sentencing circles developed from judicial sentencing discretion (McNamara 2000). So, whereas Navajo peacemaking functions within Navajo law, developments in Australia and Canada typically "fit within the broader criminal justice framework" (Cunneen 2007:124). However, some Indigenous commentators object strongly to RJ or Indigenous justice practices that rely on the state. For instance, Smith decries developments that add to the power of the criminal justice system, and she promotes political organizing to "challenge state violence and build communities" (2005:729; Incite! 2003; see Smith, Chapter 12 in this volume). She notes that gendered violence is not separable from state violence, as the former has been an integral tactic of colonization.

Dickson-Gilmore and LaPrairie argue that claims that sentencing circles[5] in Canada offer self-governance or empowerment are overstated since, although participants may have a role in shaping the sentence, the power typically remains with the judge (Dickson-Gilmore and LaPrairie 2005). However, the politics of such developments are complex and vary by jurisdiction (Daly and Stubbs 2007). Circle sentencing has begun to be introduced in some parts of Australia. These developments have adapted Canadian practices, often with support by Australian Indigenous organizations such as the Aboriginal Justice Advisory Council in New South Wales or by Indigenous communities (Marchetti and Daly 2004). Cunneen provides both optimistic and pessimistic readings of RJ and its relationship to Indigenous justice ideals. His pessimistic account sees RJ as coinciding with criminal justice practices emphasizing individual responsibility and more punitive measures, in a bifurcated system in which Indigenous people are denied the benefits associated with RJ ideals and are "channelled into more punitive processes"

(2007:119). His more optimistic reading sees hybrid developments of RJ with criminal justice, such as in sentencing circles and Indigenous courts, as offering opportunities for the pursuit of social justice and for Indigenous communities to develop "organically connected restorative justice processes that resonate with Indigenous cultures" to replace "state-imposed forms of restorative justice" (2007: 120).

RJ is often promoted as community-based and as a mechanism for transforming communities, but insufficient attention has been paid to the capacity of communities to develop and sustain RJ processes (Blagg 2002; Crawford and Clear 2001). Dickson-Gilmore and LaPrairie (2005) have drawn renewed attention to questions about the resources available to Indigenous communities to take on responsibilities arising from RJ. For instance, they stress the costs of circle sentencing on under-resourced communities that may be held responsible for monitoring and supporting offenders without additional resources to fund that work. AWAN's (2001) statement opposing RJ for violence against Indigenous women and children in Canada demonstrates the significance of this concern; they emphasize the lack of necessary services to support victims on reserves and the contraction of state funding for off-reserve services.

RESTORATIVE JUSTICE, GENDERED VIOLENCE, AND INDIGENOUS WOMEN[6]

Indigenous women's responses to RJ have emphasized concerns about violence to women and children. As noted in the consultations described earlier, respondents were typically open to the principles of RJ, often in conjunction with self-determination, but they differed in their assessment of whether RJ ideals could be realized in their community or context. There is strong agreement in the literature that responses to violence against women and children in Indigenous communities need to be community-driven, crafted with the full involvement of Indigenous people and these responses must reflect the needs and capacities of particular communities (Behrendt 2002; Blagg 2002; Kelly 2002; Memmott et al. 2006). However, they also must recognize that "women are part of that community too" (Stewart et al. 2001:57). Nonetheless, significant debates continue among Indigenous women about the way forward. Cameron has described the different approaches adopted by Indigenous women in Canada: some have a focus on culture, with self-determination as their primary goal, whereas others focus on both culture and gender and see "the gendered nature of intimate violence in their communities and the failures of both conventional and Aboriginal justice systems to address it" (2006:55). Similarly, within Australia, some Indigenous women stress the need for inclusive community-wide healing (Atkinson 2002; Lawrie and Matthews 2002), while others see an urgent task in pursuing safety for women and children (Greer 1994).

Some Indigenous women's advocates and scholars are concerned that the community focus of RJ may obscure or trump the interests of women and children. The risks and opportunities afforded by the discursive character of RJ described earlier may be magnified by the impact of colonization. As Cunneen has observed, "gendered patterns of knowledge and culture" have been distorted by colonization; it cannot be assumed that RJ "will privilege or indeed give a voice to minority women" (2003:187). Some accounts of Indigenous programs commonly cited by RJ scholars as successful have been challenged, especially by Indigenous women, as failing to address women's interests (LaRoque 1997; Nahanee 1992; Nightingale 1994). Critical accounts of circle sentencing in some Canadian Indigenous communities demonstrate how well-intended attempts to respond to cultural differences may have silenced some women and put their safety at risk (Crnkovich 1996; Goel 2000). This problem is not confined to RJ but may occur in other justice practices when attempts to accommodate culture fail to recognize the different interests within communities; intersecting social relations including but not limited to sexism and racism, may subject women to multiple disadvantage (Crenshaw 1991; Razack 1994; see Goel, Chapter 3 in this volume).

Circle sentencing was recently piloted in one New South Wales Indigenous community and has been extended to other communities. The preliminary evaluation report is based on the first 13 cases; eight of these are documented as case studies. It is very positive, citing a high level of satisfaction among participants and finds that participants were able to discuss the effect of the offence on the victim(s) openly. The Aboriginal elders were seen as the greatest strength of the program, instilling morals and values, and lending authority and legitimacy to the process (Potas et al. 2003). However, the findings also suggest a need for closer attention to the interests of victims of gendered violence. At least two case studies included domestic violence but with no mention of any safety planning or follow-up with victims. Most victims reported that they had been unclear about what to expect and were unprepared for the "emotional intensity" of the process (2003:40). Some participants wanted more women involved "to ensure that participants are particularly sensitive to the feelings of victims and offenders, and that they have an adequate awareness of the dynamics of domestic violence" (2003:41). A separate women's panel for domestic violence was also suggested.

Coker (1999, 2006) has offered qualified support for the use of Navajo peacemaking in response to domestic violence. She distinguishes peacemaking from typical RJ on three dimensions: Peacemaking was designed and is run by the Navajo Nation, whereas most RJ used for Indigenous persons is controlled by non-Indigenous agencies; peacemaking uses "concepts of gender harmony," which provide "a powerful cultural resource for addressing domestic violence"; and individuals may choose to initiate the process independently of any legal process (2006:69). However, she remains concerned that participation may be coerced, that too little attention is focused on victim safety, and that there is little engagement between peacemaking and battered women's advocates (see also concerns with peacemaking raised by Smith, Chapter 12 in this volume).

CONCLUSION

The literature reviewed in this chapter indicates that some openness to RJ principles exists, but that a prevailing skepticism remains about what that might mean in practice. This skepticism is well-founded for both theoretical and empirical reasons. Without a strong normative commitment to antisubordination and a clear theoretical framework for understanding victimization, *generic* models of RJ cannot be relied on to promote victim interests in cases of gendered violence, nor to challenge racism or other forms of prejudice. New responses to gendered violence are more likely to be effective, safe, and responsive to difference when the design and practice is guided by the principle of antisubordination and draws on the expertise of women's advocates in the communities that they serve. Commentators have long urged RJ practitioners and women's advocates to learn from each other (Coker 2002; see Frederick and Lizdas, Chapter 2 in this volume). The oppositional contrast of RJ to conventional criminal justice so common in the literature is not helpful in advancing future developments. New approaches are likely to require state and non-state resources and coercive back-up to ensure safety and compliance, and thus are apt to be hybrid models that draw from both RJ and conventional criminal justice (Hudson 2002). For instance, RESTORE could be characterized in this way. Although there is strong resistance to the diversion of offenders who commit gendered violence (Curtis-Fawley and Daly 2005; Hudson 2002; McGillivray and Comaskey 1999), RESTORE seemed to meet such concerns in the use of diversion *from* court *into* therapeutic programs with regular monitoring and follow-up of offenders (see Koss, Chapter 10 in this volume).

Future developments would be aided by a greater recognition of the distinctions between Indigenous justice and RJ. Indigenous women often desire community control of justice initiatives but also recognize obstacles to safe and just outcomes in their communities, especially when proposals fail to recognize the impact of colonization and of violence on women and children. Not all communities are well-placed to take this on, and debates would do well to avoid the presumption of "a healed community" (Stewart et al. 2001:30) or the idealization of community. The preconditions for sustainable and effective new justice models must be identified. These are likely to include mechanisms to facilitate women's engagement in the planning and delivery of new initiatives and the provision of resources to allow women to be genuine participants in any justice process, to support victims of gendered violence within the community, and to develop and sustain the community infrastructure that underpins community-based justice initiatives where they are appropriate.

ACKNOWLEDGMENTS

I wish to acknowledge the research assistance of Dr. Kelly Richards.

NOTES

1. In addition to its reliance on oral discourse, RJ is also discursive in another sense; it invokes a set of underlying concerns and themes about what it means to be restorative and what processes and outcomes are expected.
2. Crime Research Centre, University of Victoria Wellington. Retrieved March 30, 2007 (http://www.vuw.ac.nz/cjrc/research-projects/current-projects/Five Sites.aspx).
3. J. Hinchey, personal communication, November 10, 2006.
4. J. Pennell, personal communication, June 28, 2007.
5. They distinguish sentencing circles from healing circles and see the latter as being more community-based (Dickson-Gilmore and LaPrairie 2005).
6. Some Indigenous women within Australia prefer the term "family violence" rather than "domestic violence" (or other alternatives) to reflect the wider range of relationships and contexts within which violence occurs in Indigenous communities. However, it is acknowledged that patterns of family violence within Indigenous communities are highly gendered (Memmott et al. 2006). This chapter draws on a range of international sources that use different terminology to refer to violence against women and children within Indigenous communities. The various terms used in this section reflect those used in the literature from which it was derived and, unless otherwise stated, are used interchangeably.

REFERENCES

Aboriginal Women's Action Network (AWAN). 2001. *Aboriginal Women's Action Network (AWAN Policy): The Implications of Restorative Justice in Cases of Violence Against Aboriginal Women and Children.* Retrieved March 30, 2007 (http://www.casac.ca/english/awan.htm).

Achilles, Mary and Howard Zehr. 2001. "Restorative Justice for Crime Victims: The Promise and the Challenge." Pp. 87–99 in *Restorative Community Justice: Repairing Harm and Transforming Communities,* edited by Gordon Bazemore and Mara Schiff. Cincinnati, OH: Anderson Publishing.

Acorn, Annalise. 2004. *Compulsory Compassion: A Critique of Restorative Justice.* Vancouver: University of British Columbia Press.

Atkinson, Judy. 2002. "Voices in the Wilderness: Restoring Justice to Traumatised Peoples." *The University of New South Wales Law Journal* 25:233–41.

Behrendt, Larissa. 2002. "Lessons from the Mediation Obsession: Ensuring That Sentencing Alternatives Focus on Indigenous Self-Determination." Pp. 178–190 in *Restorative Justice and Family Violence,* edited by Heather Strang and John Braithwaite. Melbourne: Cambridge University Press.

Blagg, Harry. 2002. "Restorative Justice and Aboriginal Family Violence: Opening a Space for Healing." Pp. 191–205 in *Restorative Justice and Family Violence,* edited by Heather Strang and John Braithwaite. Melbourne: Cambridge University Press.

Busch, Ruth. 2002. "Domestic Violence and Restorative Justice Initiatives: Who Pays If We Get It Wrong?" Pp. 223–248 in *Restorative Justice and Family Violence,* edited by Heather Strang and John Braithwaite. Melbourne: Cambridge University Press.

Cameron, Angela. 2006. "Stopping the Violence: Canadian Feminist Debates on Restorative Justice." *Theoretical Criminology* 10:49–66.

Cheon, Aileen and Cheryl Regehr. 2006. "Restorative Justice Models in Cases of Intimate Partner Violence: Reviewing the Evidence." *Victims and Offenders* 1:369–394.

Coker, Donna. 2002. "Transformative Justice: Anti-Subordination Processes in Cases of Domestic Violence." Pp. 128–152 in *Restorative Justice and Family Violence,* edited by Heather Strang and John Braithwaite. Melbourne: Cambridge University Press.

———. 2006. "Restorative Justice, Navajo Peacemaking and Domestic Violence." *Theoretical Criminology* 10:67–86.

Commission on Gender Equality (South Africa). 2004. *Submission to the Portfolio Committee on Correctional Services Draft White Paper on Corrections in South Africa.* Retrieved March 30, 2007 (http://www.cge.org.za/userfiles/documents/submission4feb04final.doc).

Cook, Kimberly. 2006. "Doing Difference and Accountability in Restorative Justice Conferences." *Theoretical Criminology* 10:107–124.

Couture, Joe Ted Parker, Ruth Couture, and Patti Laboucane. 2001. *A Cost-Benefit of Hollow Water's Community Holistic Circle Healing Process.* Ottawa: Solicitor General.

Coward, Stephanie. 2000. "Restorative Justice in Cases of Domestic and Sexual Violence: Healing Justice?" *AiR: Abuse Information & Resources for Survivors.* Retrieved March 30, 2007 (http://www.hotpeachpages.net/canada/air/rj_domestic_violence.html).

Crawford, Adam and Todd Clear. 2001. "Community Justice: Transforming Communities Through Restorative Justice? Pp. 127–49 in *Restorative Community Justice,* edited by Gordon Bazemore and Mara Schiff. Cincinnati, OH: Anderson Publishing.

Crenshaw, Kimberle. 1991. "Mapping the Margins: Intersectionality, Identity Politics and Violence Against Women of Color." *Stanford Law Review* 43:1241–1300.

Crnkovich, Mary. 1996. "A Sentencing Circle." *Journal of Legal Pluralism* 36:159–181.

Cunneen, Chris. 2003. "Thinking Critically About Restorative Justice." Pp. 182–194 in *Restorative Justice: Critical Issues,* edited Eugene McLaughlin, Ross Fergusson, Gordon Hughes, and Louise Westmarland. London: Sage, in association with The Open University.

———. 2007. "Reviving Restorative Justice Traditions?" Pp. 113–131 in *Handbook of Restorative Justice,* edited by Gerry Johnstone and Daniel W. Van Ness. Cullompton, Devon, UK: Willan.

Curtis-Fawley, Sarah, and Kathleen Daly. 2005. "Gendered Violence and Restorative Justice: The Views of Victim Advocates." *Violence Against Women* 11:603–638.

Daly, Kathleen. 2001. "Conferencing in Australia and New Zealand: Variations, Research Findings and Prospects." Pp. 59–84 in *Restorative Justice for Juveniles: Conferencing, Mediation and Circles,* edited by Allison Morris and Gabrielle Maxwell. Oxford, UK: Hart Publishing.

———. 2002a. "Restorative Justice: The Real Story." *Punishment & Society* 4: 55–79.

———. 2002b. "Sexual Assault and Restorative Justice." Pp. 62–88 in *Restorative Justice and Family Violence,* edited by Heather Strang and John Braithwaite. Melbourne: Cambridge University Press.

———. 2005. "A Tale of Two Studies: Restorative Justice from a Victim's Perspective." Pp. 153–174 in *New Directions in Restorative Justice: Issues, Practice and Evaluation,* edited by Elizabeth Elliott and Robert Gordon. Cullompton, Devon, UK: Willan.

Daly, Kathleen and Julie Stubbs. 2006. "Feminist Engagement with Restorative Justice." *Theoretical Criminology* 10:9–28.

———. 2007. "Feminist Theory, Feminist and Anti-Racist Politics, and Restorative Justice." Pp. 149–170 in *Handbook of Restorative Justice,* edited by Gerry Johnstone and Daniel W. Van Ness. Cullompton, Devon, UK: Willan.

Dickson-Gilmore, Jane and Carol LaPrairie. 2005. *Will the Circle Be Unbroken: Aboriginal Communities, Restorative Justice and the Challenges of Conflict and Change.* Toronto: University of Toronto Press.

Dignan, Jim. 2003. "Towards a Systematic Model of Restorative Justice." Pp. 135–156 in *Restorative Justice and Criminal Justice: Competing or Reconcilable Paradigms?* edited by Andrew von Hirsch, Julian Roberts, and Anthony Bottoms. Oxford, UK: Hart Publishing.

Edwards, Alan and Jennifer Haslett. 2003. *Domestic Violence and Restorative Justice: Advancing the Dialogue.* Paper presented to 6th International Conference on Restorative Justice, June 1–4, Vancouver, British Columbia, Canada. Retrieved March 30, 2007 (http://www.sfu.ca/cfrj/fulltext/haslett.pdf).

Edwards, Alan and Susan Sharpe. 2004. *Restorative Justice in the Context of Domestic Violence: A Literature Review.* Edmonton, Canada: Mediation and Restorative Justice Centre. Retrieved March 30, 2007 (http://www.mrjc.ca/forms/CM%20Documents/RJ-DV%20Lit%20Review%20PDF.pdf).

Genesee County. n.d. *Victim-Offender Dialogue Meetings and Community Conciliation Cases.* Retrieved March 30, 2007 (www.co.genesee.ny.us/dpt/communityservices/conccases.html).

Goel, Rashmi. 2000. "No Women at the Center: The Use of the Canadian Sentencing Circle in Domestic Violence Cases." *Wisconsin Women's Law Journal* 15:293–334.

Green, Simon. 2007. "The Victims' Movement and Restorative Justice." Pp. 171–191 in *Handbook of Restorative Justice,* edited by Gerry Johnstone and Daniel W. Van Ness. Cullompton, Devon, UK: Willan.

Greer, Pam. 1994. "Aboriginal Women and Domestic Violence in NSW." Pp. 64–78 in *Women, Male Violence and the Law,* edited by Julie Stubbs. Sydney: Institute of Criminology.

Hopkins, C. Quince and Mary P. Koss. 2005. "Incorporating Feminist Theory and Insights into a Restorative Justice Response to Sex Offenses." *Violence Against Women* 11:693–723.

Hopkins, C. Quince, Mary P. Koss, and Karen J. Bachar. 2004. "Applying Restorative Justice to Ongoing Intimate Violence: Problems and Possibilities." *St. Louis University Public Law Review* 23:289–311.

Hudson, Barbara. 2003. "Victims and Offenders." Pp. 177–194 in *Restorative Justice and Criminal Justice: Competing or Reconcilable Paradigms?* edited by Andrew von Hirsch, Julian Roberts, and Anthony Bottoms. Oxford, UK: Hart Publishing.

———. 2006. "Beyond White Man's Justice: Race, Gender and Justice in Late Modernity." *Theoretical Criminology* 10:29–48.

Incite!. 2003. *Incite! Women of Color Against Violence Community Accountability Principles/Concerns/Strategies/Models Working Document.* March 5. Retrieved February 26, 2009 (http://www.incite-national.org/index.php? s=93).

Jülich, Shirley. 2006. "Views of Justice Among Survivors of Historical Child Sexual Abuse: Implications for Restorative Justice in New Zealand." *Theoretical Criminology* 10:125–138.

Justice Options for Women (Who Are Victims of Violence). 2006. *Justice Options for Women: Phase 4. Designing a PEI Domestic Violence Treatment Option Court Process.* Charlottetown, PEI, Canada. Retrieved March 30, 2007 (http://www.isn.net/~tha/justiceoptions/Feb_2006_project_update.pdf).

Kelly, Loretta. 2002. "Using Restorative Justice Principles to Address Family Violence in Aboriginal Communities." Pp. 206–222 in *Restorative Justice and Family Violence,* edited by Heather Strang and John Braithwaite. Cambridge, UK: Cambridge University Press.

Kurki, Leena. 2003. "Evaluating Restorative Justice Practices." Pp. 291–314 in *Restorative Justice and Criminal Justice: Competing or Reconcilable Paradigms?* edited by Andrew von Hirsch, Julian Roberts, and Anthony Bottoms. Oxford, UK: Hart Publishing.

LaRoque, Emma. 1997. "Re-examining Culturally Appropriate Models in Criminal Justice Applications." Pp. 75–96 in *Aboriginal and Treaty Rights in Canada: Essays on Law, Equity and Respect for Difference,* edited by Michael Asch. Vancouver: University of British Columbia Press.

Lawrie, Rowena and Winsome Matthews. 2002. "Holistic Community Justice: A Proposed Response to Family Violence in Aboriginal Communities." *The University of New South Wales Law Journal* 25: 228–232.

Lund, Kirsten and Julie Devon Dodd. 2002. *Justice Options for Women Who Are Victims of Violence Final Report.* Retrieved March 30, 2007 (http://www.isn.net/~tha/justiceoptions/finalreport.pdf).

Marchetti, Elena and Kathleen Daly. 2004. "Indigenous Courts and Justice Practices in Australia." *Trends and Issues in Crime and Criminal Justice* No. 277. Canberra: Australian Institute of Criminology.

McGillivray Anne and Brenda Comaskey. 1999. *Black Eyes All of the Time: Intimate Violence, Aboriginal Women and the Justice System.* Toronto:University of Toronto Press.

McNamara, Luke. 2000. "The Locus of Decision-Making Authority in Circle Sentencing: The Significance of Criteria and Guidelines." *Windsor Yearbook of Access to Justice* 18: 60–114.

Memmott, Paul, Catherine Chambers, Carroll Go-Sam, and Linda Thomson. 2006. "Good Practice in Indigenous Family Violence Prevention—Designing and Evaluating Successful Programs." Issues Paper: 11 Australian Domestic &

Family Violence Clearinghouse. Retrieved March 30, 2007 (http://www.austdvclearinghouse.unsw.edu.au/Word%20Files/Issues_Paper_11.doc).

Miers, David. 2007. "The International Development of Restorative Justice." Pp. 447–467 in *Handbook of Restorative Justice,* edited by Gerry Johnstone and Daniel W. Van Ness. Cullompton, Devon, UK: Willan.

Ministry of Justice (Canada). 2003. *Final Report of the Ad Hoc Federal-Provincial-Territorial Working Group Reviewing Spousal Abuse Policies and Legislation.* Prepared for Federal-Provincial-Territorial Ministers Responsible for Justice. Retrieved March 30, 2007 (http://www.justice.gc.ca/en/ps/fm/reports/spousal.html#15ii).

Ministry of Justice (NZ). 2004. *Principles of Best Practice for Restorative Justice Processes in riminal Cases.* Retrieved March 11, 2007 (http://www.justice.govt.nz/restorative-justice/partb.html).

Nahanee, Teressa. 1992. "Dancing with a Gorilla: Aboriginal Women, Justice and the Charter." Paper prepared for the Royal Commission on Aboriginal Peoples, Canada. On file with the author.

Nancarrow, Heather. 2006. "In Search of Justice for Domestic and Family Violence: Indigenous and Non-Indigenous Australian Women's Perspectives." *Theoretical Criminology* 10:87–106.

Native Women's Association of Canada. 2008. *Aboriginal Women in the Canadian Criminal Justice System: A Policy Paper.* Retrieved 1 October 2008 (http://www.nwac-hq.org/en/documents/AboriginalWomenintheCanadianJusticeSystem.pdf).

Nightingale, Marg. 1994. *Just-Us and Aboriginal Women.* Report prepared for the Aboriginal Justice Directorate, Department of Justice, Canada.

Parker, Wendy. 2004. *Restorative Justice and Family Violence: An Overview of the Literature.* Wellington, NZ: Ministry of Justice.

Pennell, Joan and Gale Burford. 2002. "Feminist Praxis: Making Family Group Conferencing Work." Pp. 108–127 in *Restorative Justice and Family Violence,* edited by Heather Strang and John Braithwaite. Melbourne: Cambridge University Press.

Pennell, Joan and Stephanie Francis. 2005. "Safety Conferencing: Toward a Coordinated and Inclusive Response to Safeguard Women and Children." *Violence Against Women* 11:666–692.

Potas, Ivan, Jane Smart, Georgia Brignell, Brendan Thomas, and Rowena Lawrie. 2003. *Circle Sentencing in New South Wales: A Review and Evaluation.* Sydney: Judicial Commission of New South Wales. Retrieved March 30, 2007 (http://www.lawlink.nsw.gov.au/ajac.nsf/pages/reports).

Pranis, Kay. 2002. "Restorative Values and Family Violence." Pp. 23–41 in *Restorative Justice and Family Violence,* edited by Heather Strang and John Braithwaite. Cambridge, UK: Cambridge University Press.

————. 2007. "Restorative Values." Pp. 59–74 in *Handbook of Restorative Justice,* edited by Gerry Johnstone and Daniel W. Van Ness. Cullompton, Devon, UK: Willan.

Provincial Association of Transition Houses Saskatchewan (Canada). 2000. *Restorative Justice: Is it Justice for Battered Women? Report on the April 2000 Conference.* Retrieved March 30, 2007 (http://www.abusehelplines.org/restorative_justice_121006.pdf).

Presser, Lois and Christopher Lowenkamp. 1999. "Restorative Justice and Offender Screening." *Journal of Criminal Justice* 27:333–343.

Razack, Sherene. 1994. "What Is To Be Gained by Looking White People in the Eye? Culture, Race, and Gender in Cases of Sexual Violence." *Signs* 19:894–923.

Refuge (UK). 2003. *Refuge Response to Restorative Justice—Government Consultation.* Retrieved March 30, 2007 (http://www.refuge.org.uk/cms_content_refuge/attachments/policyAndResearch/RestorativeJustice.pdf).

Roberts, Tim. 1995. *Evaluation of the Victim Offender Mediation Project, Langley B.C. Final Report.* Ottawa: Solicitor General Canada. Copy on file with the author.

Roche, Declan. 2003. *Accountability in Restorative Justice.* Oxford UK: Oxford University Press.

Rubin, Pamela. 2003. *Restorative Justice in Nova Scotia: Women's Experience and Recommendations for Positive Policy Development and Implementation, Report and Recommendations.* Retrieved March 30, 2007 (http://www.nawl.ca/ns/en/documents/Pub_Brief_NSRestorativeJustice03_en.pdf).

Sherman, Lawrence W. and Heather Strang. 2007. "Restorative Justice: The Evidence." Retrieved March 30, 2007 (http://www.smith-institute.org.uk/pdfs/RJ_full_report.pdf).

Smith, Andrea. 2005. "Book Review: Restorative Justice and Family Violence." *Violence Against Women* 11:724:730.

Social Services Research and Information Unit. 2003. *The Dove Project: The Basingstoke Domestic Violence Family Group Conference Project. Phase I (Pilot): January 2001 to December 2002.* Portsmouth, UK: University of Portsmouth. Retrieved March 30, 2007 (http://www.hants.gov.uk/daybreakfgc/Main_ReportPortsmouth.pdf).

Stewart, Wendy, Audrey Huntley, and Fay Blaney. 2001. *The Implications of Restorative Justice for Aboriginal Women and Children Survivors of Violence: A Comparative Overview of Five Communities in British Columbia.* Vancouver, British Columbia: Aboriginal Women's Action Network. Retrieved March 30, 2007 (http://epe.lac-bac.gc.ca/100/206/301/law_ commission_of_canada-ef/2006–12 06/www.lcc.gc.ca/research_project/01_aboriginal_1-en.asp).

Strang, Heather. 2002. *Repair or Revenge: Victims and Restorative Justice.* Oxford, UK: Clarendon Press.

Strang, Heather, Lawrence Sherman, Caroline Angel, Daniel Woods, Sarah Bennett, Dorothy Newbury-Birch, and Nova Inkpen. 2006. "Victim Evaluations of Face-to-Face Restorative Justice Conferences: A Quasi-Experimental Analysis." *Journal of Social Issues* 62:281–302.

Stubbs, Julie. 2002. "Domestic Violence and Women's Safety: Feminist Challenges to Restorative Justice." Pp. 42–61 in *Restorative Justice and Family Violence,* edited by Heather Strang and John Braithwaite. Cambridge, UK: Cambridge University Press.

———. 2004. "Restorative Justice, Domestic Violence and Family Violence." *Australian Domestic & Family Violence Clearinghouse, Issues Paper* No. 9. Retrieved March 30, 2007 (http://www.austdvclearinghouse.unsw.edu.au/PDF%20files/Issues_Paper_9.pdf).

———. 2007. "Beyond Apology? Domestic Violence and Critical Questions for Restorative Justice." *Criminology and Criminal Justice* 7:169–187.

Tauri, Juan. 1999. "Explaining Recent Innovations in New Zealand's Criminal Justice System: Empowering Maori or Biculturalising the State." *Australian and New Zealand Journal of Criminology* 32:153–167.

Umbreit, Mark 1990. "Victim-Offender Mediation with Violent Offenders: Implications for Modification of the VORP Model." Pp. 337–351 in *The*

Victimology Handbook: Research Findings, Treatment, and Public Policy, edited by Emilio Viano. New York: Garland Publishing.

Umbriet, Mark, Jean Greenwood, Claudia Fercello, and Jenni Umbreit. 2000. *National Survey of Victim-Offender Mediation Programs in the United States.* St. Paul, MN: Center for Restorative Justice & Peacemaking, School of Social Work, University of Minnesota.

Van Ness, Daniel W. 2007. " Prisons and Restorative Justice." Pp. 312–324 in *Handbook of Restorative Justice,* edited by Gerry Johnstone and Daniel W. Van Ness. Cullompton, Devon, UK: Willan Publishing.

Van Ness, Daniel and Mara Schiff. 2001. "Satisfaction Guaranteed? The Meaning of Satisfaction in Restorative Justice." Pp. 47–62 in *Restorative Community Justice: Repairing Harm and Transforming Communities,* edited by Gordon Bazemore and Mara Schiff. Cincinnati, OH: Anderson Publishing.

Wemmers, Jo-Anne. 2002. "Restorative Justice for Victims of Crime: A Victim Oriented Approach to Restorative Justice." *International Review of Victimology* 9:43–59.

Wemmers, Jo-Anne and Marisa Canuto. 2002. *Victims' Experiences with, Expectations and Perceptions of Restorative Justice: A Critical Review of the Literature.* Ottawa: Department of Justice Canada, Policy Centre for Victim Issues. Retrieved March 30, 2007 (http://Canada.justice.gc.ca/en/ps/rs/rep/rr01–9.pdf).

Women's Aid (UK). 2003. *Women's Aid Consultation Response to Restorative Justice—The Government's Strategy.* Retrieved March 30, 2007 (http://www.womensaid.org.uk/page.asp?section=00010001000900030004005).

6

RESTORATIVE JUSTICE FOR DOMESTIC AND FAMILY VIOLENCE

Hopes and Fears of Indigenous and Non-Indigenous Australian Women

HEATHER NANCARROW

The origins of this chapter lie in my experience of working in the field of domestic and family violence prevention for over 25 years in Australia, and my growing concern that mainstream domestic and family violence policy and programs seem to differentially benefit Indigenous[1] and non-Indigenous women. For approximately 11 years, I worked in community-based women's services and activism, followed by work in government policy and the administration of Queensland's domestic violence legislation. In both the community and government roles, I observed that Indigenous and non-Indigenous women often differed on key strategies aimed at responding to domestic and family violence. Indigenous women called for different models of service delivery, such as a "safe house" for a brief stay at times of crisis, before returning to their partners, rather than the high-security women's refuges,[2] where mostly non-Indigenous women sought high-level security to hide from a pursuing partner and emergency accommodation as a means to end a violent relationship. They also called for an analysis of "family violence," rather than "domestic violence" to better reflect their lived experiences; these women also call for a consideration of alternatives to the formal criminal justice system to

123

address family violence, whereas non-Indigenous women call for increased criminalization of domestic violence.

The way in which Indigenous and non-Indigenous women differ on key justice strategies for ending domestic and family violence are starkly revealed in the results of two Queensland task force investigations, conducted at the same time. One of these investigations was conducted entirely by Indigenous women (the Aboriginal and Torres Strait Islander Women's Task Force on Violence [2000]), which I will refer to as the "Indigenous women's task force," and it recommended that restorative justice (RJ) must be considered as an alternative to the formal criminal justice system. The other was conducted almost entirely by non-Indigenous women (Taskforce on Women and the Criminal Code [2000]), which I will refer to as the "non-Indigenous women's task force," and it recommended that RJ must never be used as an alternative to the formal criminal justice system. These opposing recommendations arise from fundamental differences in the way the two groups of women perceive the role of the state versus the role of community in responding to domestic violence (Nancarrow 2006).

Drawing on the literature, my experience in the field, and my research about these disparate positions (Nancarrow 2003), this chapter explores the hopes and fears of Indigenous and non-Indigenous Australian women concerning justice responses to domestic and family violence, and it seeks to explain the incongruence in the views of the two groups. This exploration is from the perspective of a non-Indigenous woman coming to grips with the limitations of mainstream feminist analyses for understanding and responding to Indigenous Australian family violence. In many respects, it is a critique of my own practice in the prevention of domestic violence from a mainstream feminist perspective; therefore, an overview of this perspective, followed by critiques of it, begins the discussion. This is followed by discussion of Indigenous women's relationship to the state and to the mainstream feminist movement, and their perspectives on family violence, which leads into the discussion of my research.

A BRIEF OVERVIEW OF DOMESTIC AND FAMILY VIOLENCE IN AUSTRALIA

In Australia, as elsewhere, the term "domestic violence" emerged from, and became synonymous with, men's abuse of their female intimate partners. The terms "domestic violence" and "intimate partner violence" are often used interchangeably, and in some Australian jurisdictions, the term "family violence" is also used in reference to domestic violence and violence involving other family members. However, the meaning of "family violence," as used by Indigenous Australians, is different again, as will be discussed later. Mainstream feminists' primary concerns remain focused on spousal domestic violence, and the inclusion of violence within a broader range of family relationships is seen as a watering down of the gender analysis of domestic violence.

Domestic violence is prevalent in Australia and has serious consequences. In their research for the Australian component of the International Violence Against Women Survey (IVAWS),[3] Mouzos and Makkai (2004) found that more than one-third of women who had a current or former intimate partner reported experiencing violence at some time in their life, whereas 4% had experienced intimate partner violence in the previous 12 months. The Women's Safety Australia survey (Australian Bureau of Statistics 1996) found that domestic violence accounted for 47% of all male violence against women, and that 4.6% of Australian women aged 18 years and over had experienced some form of violence perpetrated on them by a male with whom they had a current or past intimate partner relationship. These experiences included assault (including sexual assault) or threatened assault, emotional abuse, and being stalked. The Personal Safety Survey (Australian Bureau of Statistics 2006), a study of men's and women's experiences of all violence, confirmed that women are overwhelmingly the victims, and men the perpetrators, of violence perpetrated by a current or former intimate partner. Of the 1,731,100 Australians who had experienced intimate partner violence since the age of 15 years, 75% ($n = 1,295,600$) were women. Like other quantitative studies comparing men's and women's experiences of intimate partner violence (such as Headey, Scott, and de Vaus 1999; Statistics Canada 2000; and Straus, Gelles, and Steinmetz 1981), the Personal Safety Survey does not discuss the context or effects of the violence. Dobash and colleagues (1992), James (1999), and others argue that while women do commit violence against their male partners, the motivation, frequency, severity, and outcomes of women's violence is not the same as those associated with men's violence toward their female partners.

Various attempts have been made to estimate or measure the prevalence of Indigenous family violence within a number of Australian jurisdictions (see for example, Bolger 1991 and Ferrante et al. 1996). The term "family violence" is generally preferred by Indigenous communities to "... encapsulate not only the extended nature of Indigenous families, but also the context of a range of violence forms occurring frequently between kinspeople in Indigenous communities" (Memmott et al. 2001:1). It includes spouse abuse, abuse between others with kinship relations, and child abuse. Family violence perpetrators and victims may be individuals or groups. Therefore, "domestic violence" and "Indigenous family violence" are intersecting but different phenomena.

There is agreement in the literature that "the incidence of violence in Indigenous communities and among Indigenous people is disproportionately high in comparison to the rates of the same types of violence in the Australian population as a whole" (Memmott et al. 2001:6). Memmott and colleagues (2001) also find evidence that the "rates of violence are increasing and the types of violence are worsening in some Indigenous communities and regions" (p. 6).

Table 6.1 Comparison of Indigenous and Non-Indigenous Women's Experiences of Violence

| | Experiences of violence in the previous 12 months | | Experiences of violence in their lifetime | |
	Indigenous women	Non-Indigenous women	Indigenous women	Non-Indigenous women
Physical violence	20	7	66	48
Sexual violence	12	4	32	34
Any violence	25	10	71	57

The 2002 Australian component of the IVAWS is the only national survey on violence against women in Australia that has enabled some analysis of the violence experienced by Indigenous Australian women.[4] In line with other research, Mouzos and Makkai (2004) found that Indigenous women experienced more violence than their non-Indigenous counterparts (except for sexual violence), whether this was measured over the past 12 months or during their life time. Table 6.1, below, represents their results.

Using data from the National Homicide Monitoring Program, for the period 1 July 1989 to 30 June 2000, Mouzos (2001) reports that, although Aboriginal and Torres Strait Islander peoples are only about 2% of the Australian population, they were 15.1% of all the homicide victims (where cultural identity was known) and 15.7% of the homicide offenders (again, where cultural identity was known). The majority (61%) of homicides in which the victim was Indigenous involved family members; 38% involved intimate partners and 23% involved other family members. By comparison, this is nearly double the 33% of non-Indigenous homicide victims killed by an intimate partner or other family member.

MAINSTREAM FEMINIST PERSPECTIVES ON DOMESTIC VIOLENCE

Serious attention to domestic violence in Australia began in the early to mid 1970s and, as elsewhere, emerged from an international radical feminist movement. Within radical feminist theory, domestic violence is understood as a consequence of patriarchal power and the assertion of "male privilege" within the family through various tactics of "power and control" (Pence and Paymar 1986). Feminist activism drew attention to the prevalence and impact of domestic violence and eventually led to the establishment of public policy, consequently founded on mainstream feminist analyses.

By the end of the 1980s, most Australian jurisdictions had undertaken an investigation into the nature and extent of spousal domestic violence within their jurisdictions and, consequently, developed public policy, awareness programs, support services, and civil domestic violence legislation. By virtue of the civil law status of protection orders,[5] the allegations set out in an application for such an order must be proved "on the balance of probabilities," to be true. A breach of a condition of a protection order, regardless of the nature of the breach, is a criminal offence attracting the possibility of a term in prison and/or a substantial fine. Unlike previous civil laws designed to protect individuals from abusive behavior, the civil domestic violence laws provide for unprecedented police powers to detain a person in custody, in certain circumstances, for a specific period of time, without a charge. Courts have the power, again in certain circumstances, to make interim orders without a hearing and in the absence of the accused. These are somewhat extraordinary provisions for civil law, but they reflect the extraordinary circumstances and risks associated with spousal domestic violence.

Advocacy for Stronger Criminal Justice Sanctions

Despite these extraordinary police powers, feminist critiques of civil responses to domestic violence (Douglas and Godden 2003; Scutt 1990) assert that civil law responses collude with perpetrators of domestic violence by trivializing, minimizing, and "decriminalizing" domestic violence. Such critiques are part of a broader feminist agenda to shift domestic violence from the private to the public realm. As Schneider (2000) explains:

> Privacy ... plays a particularly pernicious role in supporting, encouraging, and legitimizing violence against women ... The state actively permits this violence by protecting the privileges and prerogatives of the batterer and failing to protect the battered women, and by prosecuting battered women for homicide when they act to protect themselves. (p. 92)

Within feminist theory, domestic violence is both a cause and a consequence of inequality between men and women, and women will continue to be oppressed with impunity until the state is held accountable for the protection of women, by holding men accountable for their violence against women. Therefore, advocacy for stronger criminal justice sanctions against violence is advocacy for equality between men and women.

Seeking increased public attention to domestic violence, and frustrated by police inaction, feminist activism has led to the establishment of integrated criminal justice system responses, many involving mandatory or "pro-arrest" and "no-drop" prosecution policies aimed at eliminating or reducing discretionary powers of criminal justice system agents to ensure domestic violence matters get to court. These initiatives were given impetus by the Minneapolis Domestic Violence Experiment (Sherman and Berk 1984a), which showed arrest to be a specific deterrent of domestic violence, with subsequent assault, attempted assault, and damage to property reduced by nearly 50% (Sherman and Berk 1984b). Although subsequent research (Coker 2001; Fagan 1996; Hirschel and Buzawa 2002; Sherman et al. 1992; Smith 2000) has highlighted the variable effects and unintended negative consequences of pro-arrest policies for victims of violence, many jurisdictions of the United States and, more recently, two jurisdictions in Australia have adopted formal pro-arrest and no-drop prosecution policies for domestic violence. The Family Violence Intervention Program (FVIP) in the Australian Capital Territory (ACT) was Australia's first such coordinated criminal justice system response with increased application of criminal law provisions through a pro-arrest approach (Holder and Mayo 2003). The Tasmanian Government has also adopted a criminal justice strategy with a "pro-arrest policy . . . which requires police to pro-actively gather evidence and where sufficient evidence exists, proceed to prosecution . . . and proceedings would continue, regardless of the wishes of the victim to the contrary" (Tasmanian Government 2003:27).

Critiques of Restorative Justice

In addition to concerns about civil laws trivializing domestic violence, feminist critiques of informal justice, particularly mediation (Astor 1991, 1994), gained strength in the early 1990s. At that time, mediation was increasingly being used as a strategy to divert child custody and divorce-related property settlement cases, including those cases involving domestic violence, from the Family Court. Key concerns about the mediation process related primarily to the imbalance of power between the victim and perpetrator of abuse and the mediator's inability to effectively balance this power. Consequently, fears were held for the safety of women during and after mediation and for their ability to achieve their desired outcomes. Subsequent critiques of a wider range of RJ practices also center on and expand these concerns. Coker (1999) groups the range of problems of RJ for cases of domestic violence under three headings: (1) the "coercion problem," involving "forced participation in informal adjudicatory processes . . . and coercive tactics [by the perpetrator] in these processes" (p. 14); (2) the "cheap justice problem," referring to the tendency to "overemphasize the value of an offender apology" (pp. 14–15); and (3) the "normative problem," referring to "the ideology of mediator and norm neutrality" (p. 88) and the interplay between unspoken, informal rules that affect participant behavior and orient the process toward future rather than past behavior. In regard to the problem of "cheap justice" Busch (2002) and Stubbs (2007) add that apology is frequently used by those who perpetrate domestic violence as a mechanism to reinstate control over their partner. Braithwaite and Daly (1994), Busch (2002), and Stubbs (2002) also highlight additional problems with the "norms" operating in a RJ process. They point out that the prevailing "norm" in a RJ process might reinforce, rather than sanction, the violent behavior, because domestic violence is not universally condemned and it is "the norms of the micro-community, the conference participants" (Stubbs 2002:3) that will prevail.

International Critiques of Mainstream Feminist Reform Efforts

Expanding on her concerns about the differential effects of pro-arrest policies, Coker (2002) says that feminists' activism around making domestic violence a public problem is based on "an incomplete analysis of the relationship between battered women and the state" (p. 132), with the risk of reinforcing state control of women. Coker (2001) also draws attention to the unlikely alliance between feminists and conservative governments, pointing out the appeal to conservative governments of increased criminal justice responses compared to the fundamental structural changes that would reduce women's vulnerability to domestic violence by facilitating their economic and social independence. Similarly, Martin (1998) refers to conservative forces' appropriation of the feminist legal reform agenda as "the dark irony at the core of feminist legal reform" (p. 155), arguing that feminist-inspired criminal justice reforms simply reinforce the status quo and do nothing to improve real equality and security for women.

A similar but wider set of concerns have been expressed through black feminist thought, represented in the works of bell hooks (1981, 1984, 1989), Patricia Hill Collins (1986, 1990), and Angela Harris (2000), for example. Their key concern is "gender essentialism," the source of which, says Harris is the "voice that claims to speak for all . . . (and) . . . in feminist legal theory . . . it is mostly white, straight, and socioeconomically privileged people who claim to speak for us all" (p. 263). Critiquing Catharine MacKinnon's (1987) "dominance theory," Harris (2000) demonstrates how essentialism operates to "bracket race as . . . a separate and distinct discourse" (p. 265), effectively removing black women from gender discourse and "meaning that white women now stand as the epitome of Woman" (p. 265). Along with Crenshaw (1989, 1991) and others, these African American feminist scholars brought to attention the dimensions of gender, race, and class as intersecting systems of oppression in women's lives. Crenshaw (1991) applied this intersectional analysis to domestic violence and rape, considering:

How the experiences of women of color are frequently the
product of intersecting patterns of racism and sexism, and how
these experiences tend not to be represented within the discourse
of either feminism or antiracism . . . the interests and experiences
of women of color are frequently marginalized within both
(pp. 1243–1244).

INDIGENOUS AUSTRALIAN WOMEN'S RELATIONSHIP TO THE STATE AND TO THE NON-INDIGENOUS WOMEN'S MOVEMENT

The mainstream feminist movement's struggle for liberation from male oppression has been paralleled by Indigenous women's (and men's) struggle for liberation from systemic discrimination and state oppression, a struggle that continues to this day in the form of the "reconciliation process." Huggins, a founder and leader of the "reconciliation" movement in Australia describes the movement as encompassing three things: " . . . recognition, justice and healing . . . (a)t its core . . . a liberation movement" (Huggins 2007).

Since colonization, Indigenous Australians have been subjected to various government policies aimed at achieving control, initially over land and then over Indigenous people, ostensibly for the benefit of Indigenous people themselves. Table 6.2 provides a brief overview of developments in the Australian women's liberation struggle, compared with the Indigenous Australian liberation struggles. It highlights the women's liberation movement's struggle with men's oppression while Indigenous people (men and women) continued to struggle with state oppression and their disparate perceptions of the role of the state, through the criminal justice system, in their respective liberation struggles.

Indigenous Australians continue to be over-represented in the criminal justice system, including in prison. This is despite the 339 recommendations of the Royal Commission into Aboriginal Deaths in Custody (Johnston 1991), which aimed to address systemic discrimination and reduce the rate of Indigenous incarceration by using prison only as a last resort. Analyzing prison population data for the decade from 1991 to 2001, Wijesekere (2001) finds that Indigenous people were eight times more likely than non-Indigenous people to be imprisoned in 1991 (when the report was released), and that the "over-representation ratio has increased each year since 1991 . . . . From 1998 to 2001 this ratio began to fluctuate around 9.6, which was still higher than that recorded in 1991" (p. 6). Further, the Aboriginal and Torres Strait Islander Social Justice Commissioner (2002) reports that in the 10-year period between 1991 and 2001, the national rate of Indigenous women's incarceration increased by 255.8%; for the June 2002 quarter, Indigenous women were overrepresented at 19.6 times the rate for non-Indigenous women. Much of this over-representation of Indigenous people in the criminal justice system can be attributed to minor offences, such as public drunkenness and other public disorder offences, covering a range of behaviors including offensive language (often directed at police), urinating in public, and vagrancy. As observed by Cunneen (2001) " . . . it is the poverty and homelessness of Aboriginal people which is being criminalized" (2001:97), an observation recently reinforced by research on the impact of the criminal justice system on people living in poverty in Queensland (Walsh 2007).

Table 6.2 Australia's Women's Liberation and Indigenous Liberation Struggles

Women's Liberation Struggles		*Indigenous Liberation Struggles*
Early 1900s	*Commonwealth Franchise Act 1902*, which gave *most* women the right to vote	Aboriginal natives (men and women) of Australia, Africa, Asia, and the Pacific Islands (except New Zealand) excluded from *Commonwealth Franchise Act* Policy of "dispersal" from traditional lands (resulting in Aboriginal Australian diaspora and widespread slaughter of Aboriginal people)
1960s	Consciousness-raising groups to expose and remedy patriarchal oppression	Right to vote in Commonwealth elections (1962; 1965 for Queensland) Aboriginal "protection" policy, accompanied by "segregation" of half-caste children; segregation later gave way to "assimilation" policy, with expectations that Aborigines would adopt European culture People's movement to change the Constitution to effectively give Indigenous Australians citizenship; achieved in 1967 referendum
1970s	Establishment of women's shelters; radical feminist "separatist" movement (women-only spaces; no men/male adolescents)	Assimilation policy continues, including removal of "half-caste" children (who have become known as the "stolen generation")
1980s–1990s	Civil domestic violence laws with unprecedented police powers Advocacy for increased criminal justice sanctions, including mandatory/ pro-arrest policies, for domestic violence	Royal Commission into Aboriginal Deaths in Custody Continued over-representation of Aboriginal and Torres Strait Islander people in criminal justice system
1990s–early 2000s	Integrated criminal justice system responses to domestic and family violence, with pro-arrest policies, established in two jurisdictions	Indigenous Australians 9.6 times more likely than non-Indigenous Australians to be imprisoned

The current relationship between Indigenous Australians and the state is perhaps best characterized by the fear and cynicism felt by many Indigenous people when, in June 2007, the Australian Government called a "state of emergency" to deal with Indigenous family violence, specifically child sexual abuse. Purportedly in response to the report

"Ampe Akelyernemane Meke Mekarle: Little Children Are Sacred" (Board of Inquiry into Protection of Aboriginal Children from Sexual Abuse 2007),[6] the Government's emergency plan utilizes the resources of the armed services and includes increasing the number of police in designated communities, banning alcohol and pornography, enforcing school attendance by withholding a proportion of welfare payments for absenteeism, and checking the health status (including sexual victimization) of all Aboriginal children under 16 years of age. Initially, these health checks were to be compulsory, but this was reverted to "strongly encouraged." More controversially, the plan also includes scrapping the permit system that enables Aboriginal people to control access to their lands, and acquiring Aboriginal townships, prescribed by the Australian Government, through 5-year leases. There is no basis for these extraordinary measures in the Little Children Are Sacred report, nor any other research report on Indigenous family violence. Indeed, the lack of involvement of affected Indigenous communities in the development and implementation of the emergency plan is antithetical to that report's recommendations and the recommendations of numerous other reports, including those commissioned by the Federal Government itself.[7] The Combined Aboriginal Organisations of the Northern Territory have produced an alternative plan to address family violence (including sexual abuse of children), which includes some of the features of the Government plan, but rejects the acquisition of 5-year leases over Aboriginal townships and the Government's plan to scrap the permit system as nothing more than a "land-grab."

Comparing the mainstream women's liberation movement with the Indigenous Australian people's liberation movement brings into clearer focus the lack of equity between Indigenous and non-Indigenous women and their different relationships to the state. That is not to say that the two groups of women do not share the experience of male oppression, particularly male violence, nor does it say that the two groups of women do not support each others' campaigns for liberation; indeed, many examples of such mutual support do exist. However, the context in which gender-based oppression occurs and the utility of various methods of redress are not shared.

INDIGENOUS AUSTRALIAN WOMEN'S PERSPECTIVES ON FAMILY VIOLENCE

Indigenous Australian women have been speaking out about violence within their families, as well as violence upon their communities, at least since the mid-1980s (see, for example, Daylight and Johnson 1986, Queensland Domestic Violence Taskforce 1988). They have largely preferred the term "family violence," a concept overlapping with the mainstream notion of "spousal domestic violence" but including a much broader range of family, kin, and community relationships and a wider range of abusive behaviors (see, for example, Aboriginal and Torres Strait Islander Women's Task Force on Violence 2000; Blagg 2000; Department for Women 2001; Memmott et al. 2001; Mow 1992; and Southside Domestic Violence Action Group 1994) and situations in which both victims and offenders may be, for example, within the same clan groups (Memmott et al. 2001). Consistently, Aboriginal and Torres Strait Islander women have called for "holistic" responses to family violence, meaning "responsive to all—men, women, children ..." (Department for Women 2001:22) and encompassing:

> A knowledge and understanding of the broader social context in which people live, such as alcohol abuse, unemployment, housing, lack of transport and its relationship to family violence, and physical, emotional, mental and spiritual aspects of individuals. (Department for Women 2001:26)

Indigenous Australian Women's Critiques of Mainstream Feminist Reform Efforts

Aboriginal scholars in Australia, including Patricia Grimshaw (1981), Larissa Behrendt (1993), Melissa Lucashenko (1994, 1997), Jackie Huggins (1995, 1998), and Aileen Moreton-Robinson (2000) have similarly critiqued the mainstream feminist perspective within the context of gender and race relations in Australia. Applying an analysis of gender essentialism to the experiences of Aboriginal Australian women, Behrendt (1993) challenges the mainstream feminist representation of power struggles between men and women, which relegates black men to a subset of all men, and black women to a subset of all women. For Behrendt, the experience of differential economic, social, and political power is more accurately represented as a struggle between white Australia, with white women being subordinate to white men, and black Australia, with black women being subordinate to black men.

Grimshaw (1981), Huggins (1995, 1998), Lucashenko (1994, 1997), and Moreton-Robinson (2000) have also challenged the essentialist position inherent in mainstream feminist approaches to addressing inequality. They strongly contend that "our oppressions are not interchangeable" (Lucashenko 1994:21), and they call for racial oppression—and in the case of Grimshaw, class oppression—to be brought to the fore. They draw attention to the interactions of class, race, and gender in shaping individual experience, which may include simultaneously experiencing privilege and oppression. Hence, Indigenous men, particularly, can simultaneously be victims of violence (at least, but not only in terms of the oppressive state and the dominant culture) and perpetrators of violence against women (and others).

Huggins (1995) finds parallels between the mainstream feminist movement's invitation to Aboriginal women to join its struggles against male oppression and doctrines of integration and assimilation that divided Aboriginal families:

> Many Aboriginal women view their incorporation into the white feminist movement with contempt and suspicion and as being equivalent to the old, patronising governmental doctrines of integration and assimilation. (p. 78)

Central to this contention is that non-Indigenous women have failed to acknowledge the state's oppression of Indigenous men and women through strategies that aim to divide and conquer them. For Indigenous women, it is the state, rather than their men, that represents the greatest threat to safety, well-being, and self-determination.

Theoretical Perspectives on Family Violence

Such holistic responses draw attention to the limitations of mainstream feminist theory for understanding Indigenous family violence and call for theoretical frameworks that locate the abuse within a context of alienation and broader social disadvantage. Insights from ecological theory and conflict theory seem particularly relevant, although they were developed mainly with city environments in mind; here, I mainly have rural and remote communities in mind. These theories conceptualize crime as a product of normal people suffering cultural conflict, social disorganization, and social reorganization (Einstadter and Henry 1995). That is not to say that individuals have no agency in perpetrating domestic and family violence; but, as Coker (1999) says "women are often aware of the oppressive structures (such as institutionalized racism) operating in her partner's life and while this doesn't excuse the abuse, it can act as an inhibitor for women to seek support from the same societal structures" (p. 72). Borrowing from Alan Jenkins' (1990) model, based on a theory of restraint, these oppressive structures also restrain perpetrators from stopping their violence. This broader theoretical framework provided the foundation for my research on the disparate views of the Indigenous and non-Indigenous women on the utility of RJ for domestic and family violence.

RESEARCH METHODS

While drawing on broader theoretical frameworks for the analysis, I adopted a "feminist research practice" approach (Kelly 1988:6) to better understand how the Indigenous and non-Indigenous women's task force reports arrived at such divergent positions about RJ and domestic and family violence. The reflexivity within this approach, the ability to draw on my experience as a woman and a worker in the field of domestic and family violence prevention, and acknowledgment of power and control dynamics in the research process were all very pertinent. To accommodate this feminist approach, I designed a qualitative research plan that involved semi-structured interviews with key women. The flexibility of the semi-structured interviews enabled increased visibility of women's subjective experience and increased involvement of research participants in the research process, two key elements of feminist research practice (Neuman 2000). I also adopted a constructionist approach that accepts that "interviewers and interviewees are always actively engaged in constructing meaning" (Silverman 2001:87) and recognizes situated knowledge (i.e., the diverse and constructed experience of women), which was critical for the cross-cultural context of the research, as was the "active interviewing" (Holstein and Gubrium 1997) process I employed. Active interviewing enables a description of *how* discussion is situated and how *what* is being said relates to the experience and lives of the people being interviewed; it enables the researcher to:

> Acknowledge and capitalize upon interviewers' and respondents' constitutive contributions to the production of interview data . . . attending to the interview process and its products in ways . . . more sensitive to the social construction of knowledge. (1997:114)

In the Indigenous/non-Indigenous research relationship, language and culturally based concepts can provide a particular challenge to the researcher who may be struggling to comprehend the "what" and have difficulty attending to the "how" of the process. I audiotaped the interviews so that I was able to more fully engage, visually and aurally, with the women and our immediate environment. I found this was particularly important when interviewing the Indigenous women. Nonverbal communication, mine and theirs, was critical in generating and guiding discussion because it provided clues about the degree to which questions were understood, when the point had been made, or if there was a need for further discussion.

From a range of in-depth interview strategies that also accommodate a feminist/constructionist approach to research (Minichiello et al. 1990), two were particularly relevant to my research: the use of a themed interview guide rather than a highly structured schedule of questions to be asked dispassionately, and story telling. The Indigenous women, particularly, conveyed their key messages through stories. The focus on themes rather than a rigid, sequential question-and-answer style ensured that the research process could be relatively free-flowing and inclusive of important contextual information that might not otherwise have arisen. A more detailed discussion of the research method is available in Nancarrow (2006).

Sample

Selection

The total number of women interviewed was 20, comprised of 10 Indigenous women and 10 non-Indigenous women. The divergent positions of the Indigenous women's task force and the non-Indigenous women's task force on restorative justice were central to the research endeavor, so the participant sample was drawn primarily from the membership of each task force. Altogether, I approached 22 women to invite their participation; two Indigenous women declined. The final sample included half the members of the Indigenous women's task force (excluding myself) and nearly a third (30%) of the core membership of the Indigenous women's task force. To round out the sample, I also included Indigenous and non-Indigenous women who work with victims of domestic and family violence, but who were not members of either task force. The interviews were conducted in 2002.

I made initial contact with the women by telephone and followed with a Participant Information Package for those who were interested. The initial contact and the Participant Information Package briefly outlined the current international debate about the utility of RJ as a response to domestic violence, and how this debate was reflected in the results of the two Queensland task force investigations. I explained that I was undertaking research to better understand how and why women think differently about RJ practices in relation to domestic and family violence.

Sample selection also included consideration of the geographic locations of the members of each task force. I wanted to replicate that geographic distribution, because location was likely to be a significant factor in the women's perspectives. All of the non-Indigenous women were from large urban centers, and all but one were located relatively close to or within the State's capital city. The Indigenous women were drawn from urban, rural, and remote communities throughout the State.

Demographics

Analyzing the interview material, I saw that the Indigenous women were, on average, older and had less formal education than the non-Indigenous women. All of the Indigenous women disclosed that they had direct experience of family violence, either personally or within their family, whereas none of the non-Indigenous women disclosed such experience and most of them said their exposure to domestic violence was through their work.

KEY FINDINGS

Meanings

As expected, reflecting on the literature and my experience in the field, the non-Indigenous women consistently referred to *domestic violence* as being violence perpetrated by men on their female intimate partners and, being based on power and control dynamics, was fundamentally different from violence in nonspousal relationships. Equally expected, the Indigenous women defined *family violence* as covering a wide range of forms of abuse and as involving a wide range of kinship relations, including children. Two of them stated that Indigenous women had consciously decided to use the term "family violence," as the term "domestic violence" was a white construct that did not represent their experience of violence involving the whole family and often the broader community. In keeping with these perspectives, most of the non-Indigenous women had victims in mind, whereas most of the Indigenous women had both victims and offenders in mind when thinking about justice responses to domestic and family violence.

Similarly, my expectations of Indigenous and non-Indigenous women's views on the meanings of the criminal justice system and RJ were largely realized. Generally, the Indigenous and non-Indigenous women had a shared understanding of the "criminal justice system." However, Indigenous women were more likely than the non-Indigenous women to include the civil domestic violence protection order system within the realm of the criminal justice system, particularly because of the police powers (in relation to implementation and enforcement) within the domestic violence laws. The views of the two groups of women on the meaning of RJ were more disparate, with Indigenous women having a wider set of practices in mind than the non-Indigenous women. Indigenous women saw RJ as including mediation involving family members, outstations where elders guide people to achieve a sense of belonging and self-worth, families supporting people to stop the violence, and community/family meetings. The Indigenous women commonly saw RJ an alternative to the current criminal justice system, and one that allowed an element of self-determination for Indigenous people. Indicative of this concept is Arlene's[8] statement:

> It [restorative justice] could be part of empowering ourselves . . . taking on board our own problems and looking for solutions . . . given that we are not nuclear family people [and] how we operate within our extended family . . . given expectations on us by the rest of our mob and . . . my expectations of them.

Non-Indigenous women, however, had a relatively narrow set of practices in mind when thinking of RJ and tended to conflate RJ with mediation, one of several such practices.

Views on the Appropriateness of Each Justice Model

The Criminal Justice System

The Indigenous women were overwhelmingly negative about the criminal justice system as a response to family violence and none of them preferred it as a justice model for responding to domestic and family violence. The following comments are indicative of their views:

> We need to be holistic about substance abuse, racism and offending . . . we need to deal with this together . . . [we] don't want further separation. We need healing for the *whole* family.

The Indigenous women had three specific concerns about the appropriateness of the criminal justice system: (1) that it is irrelevant to Indigenous people's lives and contexts; (2) that it escalates violence against women and children, and perpetuates violence against men; and (3) that it separates families, without enabling a resolution of the broader context that contributed to the violence. The sense of irrelevance was explained in terms of a lack of cultural competence; the belief that Indigenous people must be involved in the implementation of the criminal justice system, such as Indigenous magistrates. It was also seen as irrelevant because of a lack of meaning. In Dulcie's words, "... being judged by white law is irrelevant, black lore means more." Several Indigenous women raised serious concerns about the role of the criminal justice system itself perpetrating violence and escalating others' violence against women (through increased violence by the initial perpetrator and retaliatory violence by his kinship relations). The third category of concerns held by the Indigenous women involves two recurring themes in Indigenous discourse: objections to forced separation of Indigenous families by white authority and calls for holistic responses that address contextual factors (such as substance abuse and racism) and enable the involvement of the extended family in resolving the matter to their satisfaction. Speaking about the spousal homicide of her husband's sister, Anna explained that her husband's family and the family of the man who killed his sister live in the same island community and have no way of moving beyond the trauma of the murder because there was no "healing" process in the criminal justice system. Anna said:

> She was stabbed, and no-one gave any support to my husband, his brother and sisters or the parents ... They went to court ... to hear the sentencing, but they lost a sister, there was no process ... nothing to bring them together to talk about (what) happened.

In spite of these concerns with the criminal justice system, several of the Indigenous women thought it had a role for "some cases ... because of the seriousness," consistently including homicide, rape, and sexual assault of children by adults, and for cases where the "Murri way ... doesn't work" in the first instance. Reflecting on the complex and competing needs of women having to choose between self-protection and loyalty to their men, several of the Indigenous women emphasized the need for women to be able to decide whether or not to involve police and the formal criminal justice system.

For all but two of the non-Indigenous women, the criminal justice system was seen to be the most appropriate response to domestic and family violence. Central to this view was the notion of the criminal justice system as representative of community views and values. In Madeline's words it "acts in the public interest when individuals don't want to proceed with cases." However, some of the women also expressed some concerns about the appropriateness of the criminal justice system. For example, Blanca said, "It's not always appropriate ... It depends on what the victim wants" and Judith, who thought the criminal justice system was neither appropriate nor effective, said, "there is a tendency to blame the victim . . . It doesn't address victims' needs."

Restorative Justice

Seven of the ten Indigenous women strongly felt that RJ was an appropriate justice response to domestic and family violence. Their reasons were embedded in their concept of what constitutes a RJ response: involving the whole family, use of "black lore," and, for Selena, " . . . elders teaching them [offenders] things." Chrissie said:

> Because of what's happened in history, we want to . . . hold on to our culture . . . to be able to respond to family violence, we need to look deeper [to] underlying factors . . . and [restorative justice] might be the mechanism that at least gets things started.

Others saw it as appropriate because it was responsive to "what the woman wants [which is] usually to stay with the man and get the violence to stop." Anna, Bonita, and Winnie saw RJ as a preventative measure and an opportunity for communities to take control when there is evidence of violence at an early stage. They thought that RJ might be able to prevent violence by letting women know about their rights, and the perpetrators about their responsibilities, in terms of the law; looking at the family as a whole (i.e., recognizing the effects of the violence on their children); and emphasizing "respect for culture and for each other, for mothers (wives) and children." Two of the Indigenous women were reluctant to fully support RJ because they "don't know much about how it operates . . . can only imagine what (it) might be," while a third clearly preferred a model that would be a combination of the criminal justice system and RJ practices.

Although all of the non-Indigenous women were wary of RJ, only two were vehemently opposed and most saw that there were some cases, or circumstances, of domestic and family violence that would benefit from both systems playing complementary roles. Here, the non-Indigenous women were distinguishing between cases of spousal domestic violence and nonspousal family violence, including "Indigenous family violence." The distinction centered on perceived differences in the power and control dynamics at work and on the view that partners or ex-partners who had come together through choice could extricate themselves from the relationship, whereas in other family relationships the ties were seen as inextricable. Their major concerns about using RJ for cases of spousal domestic violence were that women's safety would be compromised; that they may not be able to make genuinely informed decisions about participating in a RJ process, nor negotiate what they really want; and that the chance existed that the process would trivialize domestic violence and not send a strong enough message that it is wrong.

Key Justice Objectives

Each of the women participating in the research was given a list of eight justice objectives and asked to identify the three most important objectives, in order of priority. Using a point system to score the results, I was able to identify the priorities for each group (for further details see Nancarrow, 2006). Indigenous and non-Indigenous women agreed that "stopping violence" was the top priority for a justice response to domestic and family violence, and both groups listed "support for women" in their top three priorities. The non-Indigenous women also listed in their top three priorities the need to "hold men accountable" for their violence, while this was not a priority for the Indigenous women. They placed the importance of "sending a message to the community that violence is wrong" and "restoring relationships" as their equal third priorities. Analysis of the views about the effectiveness of each justice model for achieving these priority objectives yields both expected and unexpected results.

Perceived Effectiveness of Each Model for Key Justice Objectives

As expected, the two groups of women strongly disagreed about the effectiveness of each justice model in stopping violence, their shared number-one priority. Consistent with their views on the appropriateness of the criminal justice system and RJ for domestic and family violence cases, the Indigenous women believed that RJ could be effective in stopping violence and that the criminal justice system was not effective, and the non-Indigenous women held the opposite view. Both groups saw the criminal justice system as ineffective in supporting women by validating their stories and agreed that RJ could be effective. They also agreed that the criminal justice system is effective in "holding men accountable," but the Indigenous women also saw that RJ could be effective in achieving this objective.

The results were the same for sending a message to the community that violence is wrong, with the Indigenous women seeing that both models could be effective, and the non-Indigenous women seeing that only the criminal justice system could be effective. Although the non-Indigenous women challenged the notion of "restoring relationships" as being a justice objective, they agreed with the Indigenous women that only RJ could be effective in achieving this outcome.

DISCUSSION

Indigenous women are "torn between the self-evident oppression they share with indigenous men ... and the unacceptability of those men's violent sexist behaviours toward their families" (Lucashenko 1997:156). They see the criminal justice system, including the civil protection order system, as, at best, irrelevant and ineffective and, at worst, as a tool of oppression that continues to perpetrate violence on Indigenous Australians and separate Indigenous people from their families and communities. Their antipathy toward the criminal justice system reflects a continuing history of its use as a means of dividing and controlling Indigenous people. Recalling the centuries of oppressive government policies, enforced through the agents of the criminal justice system, and in response to the current "invasion" of the Northern Territory by the Federal Government to address child sexual abuse, Aboriginal women and children have fled some communities and taken refuge in the desert, for fear their children will be taken away by the government. Also evident in this development in the Northern Territory is the unlikely alliance between feminists and conservative governments (Coker 2001) in seeking increased criminal justice sanctions, purportedly to address violence, but also as a means of control—the "dark irony at the core of feminist legal reform" (Martin 1998), wherein the increased policing of family violence within Northern Territory communities is doing nothing to advance real equality and security for Indigenous women and their children. The "state of emergency" plan does not, for example, address systemic, overt, or covert racism, nor does it include funding to address critical housing needs, long-term health services, detoxification units, or poverty, although the extensive literature on Indigenous family violence consistently calls for holistic responses to the broader context of "dispossession, cultural fragmentation and marginalisation [which] have contributed to . . . high unemployment, poor health, low educational attainment and poverty [that] have become endemic in Indigenous lives" (Aboriginal and Torres Strait Islander Women's Task Force 2000:x). Indigenous communities are sceptical about the government's motives in taking over 5-year leases on 60 Northern Territory communities and scrapping the permit system that enables communities to control who enters their land. Some Indigenous women are seeing the promise of addressing family violence as the Australian government's "Trojan horse."[9]

In addition to these kinds of concerns about the criminal justice system, my research identified the relevance of the Indigenous women's preference for RJ to the complex, non-nuclear, relational systems operating in Indigenous communities. That is, individuals' actions must be in the interests of the extended family and broader community, and the extended family and broader community must act in the interests of the individual. This is consistent with the value that Indigenous people place on *reciprocity*, a principle associated with the concept of mutual obligation to achieve equal access to resources and quality of life, and to the value placed on collective identity as a strategy for survival and protection.[10] These principles sit more comfortably with justice strategies that involve the community, rather than the criminal justice system. Also, and apart from stopping the violence, the Indigenous women were largely focused on rehabilitation of the offender and restoring relationships between the offender and the victim, and the offender and the broader community.

However, the Indigenous women's preferences for RJ practices were contingent on the inclusion of elements they envisaged as part of a RJ process, including a role for elders in restoring cultural values, elements of self-determination, and the ability to address underlying factors in the process. As discussed in Daly and Nancarrow (Chapter 5 in this volume) and in the critiques of Cunneen (1997) and Kelly (2002), current RJ practices would not meet these criteria. The Indigenous women's preference for RJ was also contingent upon the availability of the criminal justice system as a back-up for more serious cases.

In contrast, the non-Indigenous women embraced the criminal justice system, also because of what it represents rather than what it actually delivers. Their major concerns with RJ included that women may be coerced into participating in such a process, yet the mainstream feminist advocacy for increased criminalization includes removing decision-making from individual women and placing it in the hands of criminal justice agents. Apart from the goal of stopping violence, they were primarily focused on holding men accountable for their violence. The non-Indigenous women thought that only the criminal justice system could achieve this, even though, as Catherine said, the adversarial criminal justice system "encourages men to avoid acknowledging guilt"; it facilitates men denying, minimizing, and blaming others for their violence, while guilt is accepted in the RJ process. The non-Indigenous women also saw the potential for RJ to complement the criminal justice system although, for them, the criminal justice system must be the principal response. Their support for some kind of RJ process was also generally limited to cases involving nonspousal domestic violence, in which they perceived different dynamics operating that eliminated the kinds of risks found in spousal domestic violence.

CONCLUSION

Indigenous women are at greater risk of domestic and family violence, including intimate partner and family homicide, than are non-Indigenous women, so they have the most to gain from strategies that effectively end the violence. They argue for holistic, community-based responses that address the context of disadvantage and systemic racism in which domestic and family violence occurs, and they see that the state, embodied in the criminal justice system, is a major contributor to this context. While for the last 40 years mainstream feminists have been engaged in a campaign against male oppression and for state-enforced equality between men and women, Indigenous women (and men) have been focused on their continued struggle against state oppression and inequality between Indigenous and non-Indigenous Australians. In effect, Indigenous women see that the state must also be held accountable for its contribution to the perpetration of violence against women. Indigenous women see that a role exists for the criminal justice system in serious cases of family violence, but generally the decision to involve the criminal justice system should be left to individual women. For them, community involvement in dispensing justice does not represent privatizing of crime; it represents an alternative public realm, which has more meaning and is safer than the state's involvement in dispensing justice for Indigenous people. On the other hand, non-Indigenous women argue for individual perpetrators of domestic violence to be held accountable by the state, through the criminal justice system, as a matter of public interest. They recognize the problems with the state and its criminal justice system, but persist with it as the preferred justice response because of its symbolic power. The two groups of women agree that stopping violence is the top priority for a justice response to domestic and family violence, but they are opposed in their views on the justice model best able to achieve that objective. For the non-Indigenous women, only the criminal justice system can achieve an end to domestic violence, whereas for the Indigenous women the criminal justice system results in more, not less violence.

Indigenous women want justice strategies that empower and unite Indigenous communities, rather than divide them, as the criminal justice system has done for so long. They place equal emphasis on achieving gender and racial equality. Still, the Indigenous women see that the criminal justice system is necessary for the most serious cases. Non-Indigenous women, who are far less likely than Indigenous women to distinguish between more and less seriousness of violence, want to reform the criminal justice system in ways that will achieve gender equality.

Current models of RJ do not meet the criteria necessary to fulfill the hopes of Indigenous women in addressing the underlying factors associated with domestic and family violence. However, Indigenous women have clearly articulated that their experiences of violence, and their justice needs and objectives, are largely different from those of non-Indigenous women. Care must be taken when pursuing mainstream feminist advocacy for increased criminalization and opposition to RJ processes to avoid compromising the interests and safety of Indigenous women. Although current RJ models fall far short of the Indigenous women's vision, it represents hope for a justice response that will protect them from both state and male violence.

ACKNOWLEDGMENTS

I wish to acknowledge and express my gratitude to the women who participated in my research, particularly the Indigenous women, recognizing that Indigenous people have been researched extensively on the topic of family violence in recent years. I wish to thank Kathy Daly for funding from her Australian Research Council Grant to transcribe the 20 interview tapes; my former employer, the Department of Families, for study leave; and Jackie Huggins, James Ptacek, Michelle Bradford, Kass Fenton, Annie Webster, and Karen Woodley for comments on early drafts.

NOTES

1. Indigenous Australians are comprised, broadly, of two groups: Aboriginal people (a collective term for many different precolonial nations) and Torres Strait Islanders, who are of Melanesian origin and traditionally inhabit the tip of Cape York and the islands between there and Papua New Guinea. While it is preferable to distinguish between these distinct cultural groups, they have been amalgamated as "Indigenous" by successive state and federal governments for administrative purposes, and data sets generally also amalgamate the two groups because of relatively small numbers appearing in data collection (particularly Torres Strait Islanders), which is also true for my research discussed here.

2. Women's refuges in metropolitan areas, where I worked, had secret locations, but secret locations were simply not feasible in many rural and regional areas.

3. The International Violence Against Women Survey is coordinated by the European Institute for Crime Prevention and Control. This body is affiliated with the United Nations and operates within the framework of the UN Crime Prevention and Criminal Justice Programme.

4. Mouzos and Makkai note that the estimates for Aboriginal and Torres Strait Islander women should be "viewed with caution ... [although] ... the results of the IVAWS reinforce findings from previous research" (2004:30).

5. The name of the court orders issued under the civil domestic violence legislation varies from one jurisdiction to another. In Queensland, the orders are called "protection orders." Orders generally include standard conditions requiring that the abusive person desist from the abuse, as well as other conditions, such as not contacting the aggrieved, specific to the circumstances.

6. The report was commissioned by and presented to the Northern Territory Government just 8 weeks before the Federal Government announced it would intervene with an emergency response.

7. The "Partnerships Against Domestic Violence" initiative, a collaboration between the commonwealth, state and territory governments of Australia, commissioned several reports on effective interventions for Indigenous family violence. These, and various state-initiated reports such as the *Aboriginal and Torres Strait Islander Women's Task Force on Violence Report* (2000) and *Putting the Picture Together* (Gordon, Hallahan, and Henry 2002) consistently advocate Indigenous leadership in the design, development, and implementation of initiatives aimed at addressing family violence.

8. Pseudonyms are used to protect the identity of the women who participated in the research.

9. Pat Turner, speaking at Sister's Inside Conference, Darwin, 29 June 2007.

10. For further details of these values, see "Values and Ethics: Guidelines on Ethical Matters in Aboriginal and Torres Strait Islander Health Research" (National Health and Medical Research Council 2003).

REFERENCES

Aboriginal and Torres Strait Islander Social Justice Commissioner. 2002. *Social Justice Report*. Canberra: Human Rights and Equal Opportunity Commission.

Aboriginal and Torres Strait Islander Women's Task Force on Violence. 2000. *Aboriginal and Torres Strait Islander Women's Task Force on Violence Report*. Brisbane: Queensland Government Department of Aboriginal and Torres Strait Islander Policy and Development.

Astor, Hilary. 1991. *Position Paper on Mediation*. Canberra: National Committee on Violence Against Women. Office of the Status of Women.

———. 1994. "Swimming Against the Tide: Keeping Violent Men Out of Mediation." Pp. 147–173 in *Women, Male Violence and the Law*, edited by Julie Stubbs. Sydney: Institute of Criminology.

Australian Bureau of Statistics. 1996. *Women's Safety Australia*. Canberra: ABS and the Office for the Status of Women.

———. 2006. *Personal Safety Survey, Australia*. ABS Catalogue N0.4906.0. Canberra: Commonwealth of Australia.

Behrendt, Larissa. 1993. "Aboriginal Women and the White Lies of the Feminist Movement: Implications for Aboriginal Women in Rights Discourse." *Australian Feminist Law Journal* 1:27–44.

Blagg, Harry. 2000. *Crisis Intervention in Aboriginal Family Violence: Summary Report*. Partnerships Against Domestic Violence. Canberra: Commonwealth of Australia.

Board of Inquiry into the Protection of Aboriginal Children from Sexual Abuse. 2007. *Ampe Akelyernemane Meke Mekarle: Little Children Are Sacred*. Northern Territory Government. Retrieved February 28, 2009 (http://www.nt.gov.au/dcm/inquirysaac/pdf/bipacsa_final_report.pdf).

Bolger, Audrey. 1991. *Aboriginal Women and Violence: A Report for the Criminology Research Council and the Northern Territory Commissioner of Police*. Darwin: Australian National University, North Australia Research Unit.

Braithwaite, John and Kathleen Daly. 1994. "Masculinities, Violence and Communitarian Control." Pp. 189–213 in *Just Boys Doing Business?*, edited by Tim Newburn and Elizabeth A. Stanko. New York: Routledge.

Busch, Ruth. 2002. "Domestic Violence and Restorative Justice Initiatives: Who Pays If We Get It Wrong?" Pp. 223–248 in *Restorative Justice and Family Violence*, edited by Heather Strang and John Braithwaite. Cambridge, UK: Cambridge University Press.

Coker, Donna. 1999. "Enhancing Autonomy for Battered Women: Lessons From Navajo Peacemaking." *UCLA Law Review* 47:1–111.

———. 2001. "Crime Control and Feminist law Reform in Domestic Violence Law: A Critical Review." *Buffalo Criminal Law Review* 4:801–860.

———. 2002. "Transformative Justice: Anti-Subordination Practices in Cases of Domestic Violence." Pp. 128–152 in Restorative *Justice and Family Violence*, edited by Heather Strang and John Braithwaite. Cambridge, UK: Cambridge University Press.

Collins, Patricia Hill. 1986. "Learning from the Outsider Within: The Sociological Significance of Black Feminist Thought." *Social Problems* 33:14–32.

————. 1990. *Black Feminist Thought: Knowledge, Consciousness, and the Politics of Empowerment.* New York: Routledge, Chapman, and Hall.

Crenshaw, Kimberlé. 1989. "Demarginalising the Intersection of Race and Sex: A Black Feminist Critique of Antidiscrimination Doctrine, Feminist Theory and Antiracist Politics." *University of Chicago Legal Forum:*139–167.

————. 1991. "Mapping the Margins: Intersectionality, Identity Politics, and Violence Against Women of Color." *Stanford Law Review* 43:1241–1299.

Cunneen, Chris. 1997. "Community Conferencing and the Fiction of Indigenous Control." *Australian and New Zealand Journal of Criminology* 30 (3): 292–311.

————. 2001. *Conflict, Politics and Crime Aboriginal Communities and the Police.* Sydney: Allen & Unwin.

Daylight, Phyllis and Mary Johnstone. 1986. *Women's Business: Report: Report of the Aboriginal Women's Task Force.* Department of the Prime Minister and Cabinet, Office of the Status of Women. Canberra: Australian Government Publishing Service.

Department for Women. 2001. *Community Solutions to Aboriginal Family Violence: Final Report and Model of Best Practice 1999–2000.* Partnerships Against Domestic Violence. Commonwealth of Australia. Retrieved February 28, 2009 (http://www.aic.gov.au/topics/indigenous/interventions/prevention/fv.html).

Dobash, Russell, Rebecca Dobash, Margo Wilson, and Martin Daly. 1992. "The Myth of Sexual Symmetry in Marital Violence." *Social Problems,* 39:71–91.

Douglas, Heather and Lee Godden. 2003. "The Decriminalisation of Domestic Violence: Examining the Interaction between the Criminal Law and Domestic Violence." *Criminal Law Journal* 27:23–43.

Einstadter, Werner and Stuart Henry. 1995. *Criminological Theory: An Analysis of its Underlying Assumptions.* New York: Harcourt Brace College Publishers.

Fagan, Jeffrey. 1996. "The Criminalization of Domestic Violence: Promises and Limits." Presentation at the *1995 Conference on Criminal Justice Research and Evaluation.* Washington DC: National Institute of Justice, U.S. Department of Justice.

Ferrante, Anna, Frank Morgan, David Indermaur, and Richard Harding. 1996. *Measuring the Extent of Domestic Violence.* Sydney: Hawkins Press.

Gordon, Sue, Kay Hallahan, and Darrell Henry. 2002. *Putting the Picture Together: Inquiry into Response by Government Agencies to Complaints of Family Violence and Child Abuse in Aboriginal Communities.* Perth, Australia: Department of Premier and Cabinet, Western Australia.

Grimshaw, Patricia. 1981. "Aboriginal Women: A Study of Culture Contact." Pp. 86–94 in *Australian Women: Feminist Perspectives,* edited by Norma Grieve and Patricia Grimshaw. Oxford, UK: Oxford University Press.

Harris, Angela. 2000. "Race and Essentialism in Feminist Legal Theory." Pp. 261–275 in *Critical Race Theory: The Cutting Edge,* edited by Richard Delgado. Philadelphia: Temple University Press.

Headey, Bruce, Dorothy Scott, and David de Vaus. 1999. "Domestic Violence in Australia: Are Men and Women Equally Violent?" *Australian Social Monitor* 2:57–63.

Hirschel, David and Eve Buzawa. 2002. "Understanding the Context of Dual Arrest with Directions for Future Research." *Violence Against Women* 8:1449–1473.

Holder, Robyn and Nicole Mayo. 2003. "What Do Women Want? Prosecuting Family Violence in the ACT." *Current Issues in Criminal Justice* 15:5–25.

Holstein, James and Jaber Gubrium. 1997. "Active Interviewing." Pp. 140–161 in *Qualitative Research: Theory, Method and Practice,* edited by David Silverman. London: Sage Publications.

hooks, bell. 1981. *Ain't I a Woman? Black Women and Feminism.* Boston: South End Press.

———. 1984. *Feminist Theory: From Margin to Center.* Boston: South End Press.

———. 1989. *Talking Back: Thinking Feminist, Thinking Black.* Boston: South End Press.

Huggins, Jackie. 1995. "A Contemporary View of Aboriginal Women's Relationship to the White Women's Movement." Pp. 70–79 in *Australian Women: Contemporary Feminist Thought,* edited by Norma Grieve and Ailsa Burns. Oxford, UK: Oxford University Press.

———. 1998. *Sister Girl.* Brisbane: University of Queensland Press.

———. 2007. "Vote Lit the Way to Untapped Goodness." *The Australian,* May 23. Retrieved February 28, 2009 (http://theaustralian.news.com.au/story/0,20867,21777733–7583,00.html).

James, Kerrie. 1999. "Truth or Fiction: Men as Victims of Domestic Violence?" Pp. 153–162 in *Challenging Silence: Innovative Responses to Sexual and Domestic Violence,* edited by Jan Breckenbridge and Lesley Laing. Sydney: Allen & Unwin.

Jenkins, Alan. 1990. *Invitations to Responsibility.* Adelaide: Dulwich Centre Publications.

Johnston, Elliot. 1991. *Royal Commission into Aboriginal Deaths in Custody: National Report,* Vol. 1–5. Australian Government Publishing Service, Canberra. Retrieved February 28, 2009 (http://www.austlii.edu.au/au/other/IndigLRes/rciadic).

Kelly, Liz. 1988. *Surviving Sexual Violence.* Minneapolis: University of Minnesota Press.

Kelly, Loretta. 2002. "Using Restorative Justice Principles to Address Family Violence in Aboriginal Communities." Pp. 206–222 in *Restorative Justice and Family Violence,* edited by Heather Strang and John Braithwaite. Cambridge, UK: Cambridge University Press.

Lucashenko, Melissa. 1994. "No Other Truth?: Aboriginal Women and Australian Feminism." *Social Alternatives* 12:21–24.

———. 1997. "Violence Against Indigenous Women: Public and Private Dimensions." Pp. 147–158 in *Women's Encounters with Violence: Australian Experiences,* edited by Sandy Cook and Judith Besant. Thousand Oaks, CA: Sage.

MacKinnon, Catharine. 1987. *Feminism Unmodified: Discourses on Life and Law.* Cambridge, MA: Harvard University Press.

Martin, Dianne. 1998. "Retribution Revisited: A Reconsideration of Feminist Criminal Law Reform Strategies." *Osgoode Hall Law Journal* 36:151–188.

Memmott, Paul, Rachael Stacy, Catherine Chambers, and Catherine Keys. 2001. *Violence in Indigenous Communities: Full Report.* National Crime Prevention. Canberra: Attorney-General's Department.

Minichiello, Victor, Rosalie Aroni, Eric Timewell, and Loris Alexander. 1990. *In-Depth Interviewing: Researching People.* Melbourne: La Trobe University/Longman Cheshire.

Moreton-Robinson, Aileen. 2000. *Talkin' Up to the White Woman: Indigenous Women and Feminism*. St. Lucia, Australia: University of Queensland Press.

Mouzos, Jenny. 2001. "Indigenous and Non-Indigenous Homicides in Australia: A Comparative Analysis." *Trends & Issues in Crime and Criminal Justice No. 210*. Australian Institute of Criminology, Canberra. Retrieved May 3, 2009 (http://www.aic.gov.au/publications/tandi/ti210.pdf).

Mouzos, Jenny and Toni Makkai. 2004. *Women's Experiences of Male Violence: Findings from the Australian Component of the International Violence Against Women Survey (IVAWS)*. Canberra: Australian Institute of Criminology.

Mow, Karen. 1992. *Tjunparni: Family Violence In Indigenous Australia*. Canberra: Aboriginal and Torres Strait Islander Commission.

Nancarrow, Heather. 2003. "In Search of Justice in Domestic and Family Violence," MA (Hons) dissertation, Griffith University, Queensland. Retrieved February 28, 2009 (http://www.noviolence.com.au).

———. 2006. "In Search of Justice for Domestic and Family Violence: Indigenous and non-Indigenous Australian Women's Perspectives." *Theoretical Criminology* 10:87–106.

National Health and Medical Research Council. 2003. *Values and Ethics: Guidelines for Ethical Conduct in Aboriginal and Torres Strait Islander Health Research*. Canberra: National Health and Medical Research Council, Commonwealth of Australia. Retrieved February 23, 2009 (http://www.nhmrc.gov.au/publications/synopses/e52syn.htm).

Neuman, W. Lawrence. 2000. *Social Research Methods: Qualitative and Quantitative Approaches (4e)*. Sydney: Allyn and Bacon.

Pence, Ellen and Michael Paymar. 1986. *Power and Control: Tactics of Men Who Batter*. Duluth, MN: Minnesota Program Development.

Queensland Domestic Violence Taskforce Report. 1988. *Beyond These Walls*. Brisbane: Queensland Government.

Schneider, Elizabeth. 2000. *Battered Women and Feminist Lawmaking*. New Haven, CT: Yale University Press.

Scutt, Jocelynne. 1990. *Women and the Law: Commentary and Materials*. Sydney: Law Book Company.

Sherman, Lawrence and Richard Berk. 1984a. "The Minneapolis Domestic Violence Experiment." *Police Foundation Reports,* April 1984.

———. 1984b. "The Specific Deterrent Effects of Arrest for Domestic Assault." *American Sociological Review* 49:261–272.

Sherman, Lawrence, Douglas Smith, Janell Schmidt, and Dennis Rogan. 1992. "Crime, Punishment and a Stake in Conformity: Legal and Informal Control of Domestic Violence." *American Sociological Review* 57:680–690.

Silverman, David. 2001. *Interpreting Qualitative Data (2e)*. London: Sage.

Smith, Alisa. 2000. "It's My Decision, Isn't It? A Research Note on Battered Women's Perceptions of Mandatory Intervention Laws." *Violence Against Women* 12:1384–1402.

Southside Domestic Violence Action Group. 1994. Challenging the Legal System's Response to Domestic Violence Conference Report. March 23–26, Brisbane.

Statistics Canada. 2000. *Family Violence in Canada: A Statistical Profile*. Toronto: Canadian Centre for Justice Studies.

Straus, Murray, Richard Gelles, and Suzanne Steinmetz. 1981. *Behind Closed Doors: Violence in the American Family*. New York: Anchor Books.

Stubbs, Julie. 2002. "Domestic Violence and Women's Safety: Feminist Challenges to Restorative Justice." Pp. 42–61 in *Restorative Justice and Family Violence,* edited by Heather Strang and John Braithwaite. Cambridge, UK: Cambridge University Press.

———. 2007. "Beyond Apology? Domestic Violence and Critical Questions for Restorative Justice." *Criminology and Criminal Justice: An International Journal* 7:169–187.

Taskforce on Women and the Criminal Code. 2000. *Report of the Taskforce on Women and the Criminal Code.* Brisbane: Office of Women's Policy, Queensland Government.

Tasmanian Government. 2003. *Safe at Home: A Criminal Justice Framework for Responding to Family Violence in Tasmania.* Hobart, Australia: Department of Justice and Industrial Relations Options Paper.

Walsh, Tamara. 2007. *No Vagrancy: An Examination of the Impact of the Criminal Justice System on People Living in Poverty in Queensland.* Brisbane: University of Queensland.

Wijesekere, Gaminiratne. 2001. "Incarceration of Indigenous and Non-Indigenous Adults: 1991–2001: Trends and Differentials." Paper presented at 11th Biennial Conference of the Australian Population Association, 2–4 October. University of New South Wales, Sydney. Retrieved June 30, 2007 (http://www.apa.org.au/upload/2002–1C_Wijesekere.pdf).

7

RESTORATIVE JUSTICE AND YOUTH VIOLENCE TOWARD PARENTS

KATHLEEN DALY & HEATHER NANCARROW

Consider this case of Carolyn and Des:[1]

One afternoon in September 2001, Des (16 years old) came home drunk. His mother Carolyn (35 years old) told him that he had received a phone call about a job. He went to change his clothes, but had trouble getting his belt on. He got aggravated, started punching the walls, and then smashed a hole in the wall. He went to the kitchen and walked toward Carolyn, yelling at her and calling her names, before pushing her in the chest with both hands. Carolyn ran to the phone to call the police, but Des ripped it out of the wall. He went to another room and pulled another phone out of the wall. Carolyn tried to leave the house, but Des grabbed and pushed her against the wall, repeatedly yelling at her "you're not leaving the house. I'll fucking kill you." Carolyn was scared that he would hurt her, although she didn't think he would kill her. He picked up a knife from a kitchen drawer, she started to cry, and she said that "this seemed to make Des more aggressive and violent towards me." Des then slammed the knife into the breakfast bar, just missing Carolyn's hand. The knife hit with such force that its point was bent and the laminate and wood were damaged.

Carolyn ran from the house and called the police. A police officer came about an hour and a half later, took her statement, and searched for Des. After finding Des, he took him to the police station, where he was interviewed and charged with assault. That evening, he made "full

150

and frank admissions" to the police about pushing his mother, slamming the knife near her fingers, and threatening to kill her. The police report says that Des was "remorseful for what he had done" and was "affected by alcohol and did not know exactly why he had gone off." In her police statement, Carolyn said that "this has been going on for the past 18 months, and I believe that [Des] needs some sort of help from the authorities." She didn't want her son to be in her house that night.

This offence occurred in a suburb of Adelaide, South Australia, a jurisdiction that has used restorative justice (RJ) conferences as a diversion from court for youth crime since February 1994. About a week after the incident, Des's case was referred by the police to a conference.

Several questions arise from this case. If you were Carolyn, what police and court action would you take? Des is your son, and you do not want him criminalized unduly, but you need to do something to control his violence, especially when he drinks. How do you view your options, and is youth conferencing viable?

It is crucial to situate current debates on the appropriateness of RJ for partner, sexual, or family violence with a clear sense of what women like Carolyn face. Her son's assault shares elements of partner (or ex-partner) violence, but not fully. Hers is one of three cases of sons assaulting mothers that were finalized by a conference in the second half of 2001 in Adelaide, South Australia. We analyze the three cases, describing the contexts of the violence, and what happened before, during, and after a conference. We relate the findings to the literatures on youth violence toward parents, and feminist and victim advocates' concerns that a standard RJ conference cannot adequately address the unique qualities of these cases.

RESEARCH LITERATURE AND DEBATES

Gender and Power in Youth–Parent Violence

Reviewing the quantitative literature, Cottrell and Monk (2004) find that 9–14% of parents are "at some point physically assaulted by their adolescent children" (p. 1072), and the rate can be as high as 29% for sole-mother families (Livingston 1985). Mothers or stepmothers are the more frequent victims, and males the more frequent offenders. Abusive youth are likely to have been sexually or physically abused by their parents or have witnessed partner violence[2] (Cottrell and Monk 2004:1073).

Cottrell and Monk's (2004) synthesis of two Canadian qualitative studies finds that, although abuse by male youth "was influenced by the role modelling of masculine stereotypes that promote the use of power and control in relationships," violence by female youth was "a paradoxical response used to create distance from the 'feminine ideals' that were often ascribed to them" (p. 1081). They attribute the gendered dynamics of youth violence toward parents to several factors. Male youth learn that it is acceptable to control and dominate women, and female youth use violence against their mothers to distance themselves from what they see as weak and powerless women. Fathers are seen by children as powerful and intimidating, and thus, not appropriate targets; also, because mothers and stepmothers are more likely than fathers to be sole heads of families, they are more accessible targets.

Cottrell and Monk (2004:1081) also find that whereas "stronger youth use intimidation and control tactics against parents, less powerful youth cause injury as a means to establish power." Parents who are excessively controlling *or* permissive are at greater risk of youth abuse. For controlling parents, youth violence reflects an increasing struggle for a sense of power; for permissive parents, youth learn that their violence is effective in coercing parents into compliance. The authors see evidence of a "cycle of violence" in these cases, similar to that first identified by Lenore Walker (1979) for partner violence. They note, for example, that many youth "described . . . having strong feelings of remorse for their actions but recalled that they instead projected intense anger toward their parents to compensate for this feeling of emotional vulnerability" (pp. 1085–1086).

A key question is the degree to which feminist conceptual frameworks for partner violence apply to youth violence toward parents. There is some evidence that they do, as studies by Eckstein (2004), Gallagher (2004), Bobic (2004), and Cottrell and Monk (2004) show.[3]

Eckstein's (2004) findings on youth–parent violence show striking similarities to the "tactics of control" that have been identified in partner violence. Pence and Paymar (1986) conceptualize these tactics with a "power and control wheel," which depicts a range of nonphysical strategies, including verbal and psychological abuse, threats, and intimidation on the wheel's spokes. The rim of the wheel, holding it all together, has tactics of physical and sexual assault. Nonphysical strategies may be all that is required to achieve the desired control and domination because an ever-present threat of actual physical and sexual assault exists. Such tactics of control are evident in Eckstein's (2004) study (although she does not make this link herself). She finds that "the ability to implement emotional abuse is often a consequence of a previous physical abuse episode . . . [that is,] . . . the fear of physical abuse is a powerful form of emotional abuse" (p. 10). Eckstein concludes that the experience of abuse results in "a new type of parental role, one that includes a loss of power" (p. 10). This evolves over time from parents' attempts to avoid an escalation of conflict and abuse to a gradual ineffectiveness in disciplinary measures, and finally, to acceptance of abuse as normal behavior. Parents sometimes regain power only when their child turns 18, and they are no longer legally required to provide for the youth.

Drawing on his research and that of others, Gallagher (2004:5) points out that in "almost all clinical studies, . . . police records of assaults, . . . and records of intervention orders taken out against children," the recurring finding is of gendered violence: males are the primary offenders, and females (mothers) are more likely victims than males (fathers). This pattern occurs for several reasons; among them, he suggests that "mothers have far more often been past victims of spouse abuse than fathers, [and] common attitudes allow males (even juveniles) to feel superior to women."

Parents who are victimized by their children may not want criminal justice intervention, nor do they want to end the relationship with their child. There is a "veil of denial" (Gallagher 2004:11, citing Harbin and Madden, 1979) surrounding the behavior. Bobic (2004:10) says that abused parents "distance themselves from one another or isolate themselves from family and friends for fear of the family secret being revealed." Cottrell and Monk (2004) attribute the maintenance of secrecy to parental denial and self-blame, parental concerns about the negative impact on their children of reporting the behavior, and parental fear about the negative impact on themselves for reporting the behavior, including fears of an escalation of abuse after disclosure. These circumstances—isolation, denial, and fears of what will happen if the behavior is reported to authorities—are similar to those that inhibit women from reporting partner violence.

Thus, we see some similarities in the dynamics of partner violence and youth violence to parents. However, gendered theories of male violence against women alone do not tell the whole story. In fact, youth violence may reflect an even more complex set of family dynamics and pose more quandaries for justice than partner violence. This is because, as Downey (1997:76) suggests, youth violence may be the tip of a more systemic family violence iceberg, which includes partner abuse, child abuse, and parental abuse "that may be co-occurring or occurring over time." Further, Downey says that youth violence toward parents disrupts a taken-for-granted understanding of power in family violence. "Adolescents do not fit the typical conception of a perpetrator (who is physically and socially more resourced) and parents do not fit the idea of the physically and socially vulnerable victim" (p. 77).

Downey's main interest is in how to respond to violence "in the therapy room" (p. 77). But how, one wonders, should it be handled in the "justice room"? This is not straightforward because, as Downey suggests, violence in families is often *recursive:* it is "mutually shaping," not linear or a "cause–effect relationship" (p. 76). This poses problems for justice in that responsibility for violent acts may be diffused. We may find, for example, that male adolescents are both perpetrators and victims of parental violence (i.e., they assault mothers, but have been or are being assaulted by their fathers), and complex cycles of violence may generate collusion between fathers and sons against partners or mothers. Responsibility for a male youth's violence toward his mother may be shifted away from him and toward his father; at the same time, he may join with his father in denying and minimizing the violence. It is difficult to imagine how these highly complex gendered and intergenerational violence dynamics can be addressed in a justice practice alone. Downey suggests the need to hold two apparently mutually antagonistic views together: a recognition of the "complexity and uncertainty" that arises from seeing violence as recursive, and a strong feminist position that "advocates for the rights of women and children to be safe from the violence of men" (p. 72). Unless such a feminist perspective is present, the danger exists that justice practices in responding to youth–parental violence may create a *recursive trap* for victims. In section C, we consider this point further.

Feminist Debates on the Appropriateness of Restorative Justice for Partner, Sexual, or Family Violence

Many types of RJ practices exist, but they normally entail meetings between an offender, victim, and their supporters (along with others) after an offender has admitted to committing an offence. Such practices may be used as diversion from court, as actions taken in parallel with court practices (as in pre-sentence advice), and at the post-sentence stage. In the language of RJ, the aims are to hold offenders accountable for their behavior, to right the wrong, and to "repair the harm" caused by crime.

Critiques of Restorative Justice

Feminist scholars, such as Busch (2002), Coker (1999, 2002), Lewis and colleagues (2001), and Stubbs (2002, 2004, 2007), along with victim advocates, have serious reservations about the appropriateness of RJ for partner, sexual, and family violence. (Their critiques are largely concerned with partner violence, which may be less relevant to sexual violence; see Daly and Curtis-Fawley 2006.) The thrust of this criticism is twofold: most RJ advocates do not have in mind the unique elements of partner violence, and many of the valued components of RJ (e.g., an apology) may not be at all suitable for these cases.

Partner violence differs from other offending because it is ongoing, not one discrete incident. For these reasons, Stubbs (2002) argues that a control-based theoretical analysis is required to understand partner violence dynamics. Such an analysis recognizes the ongoing nature of partner violence, the coercive (although subtle) tactics used, and how the violence reflects and reproduces gender-based inequalities.

Among the valued components of RJ are an informal, dialogic process, which uses community norms to censure offenders and emphasizes the positive effects of apologies. Each of these may, in fact, serve to revictimize victims of partner violence. An informal process may permit an offender to exert power over the victim through subtle forms of intimidation, and community members may not universally oppose partner violence or may blame victims. Partner violence perpetrators are typically adept at making apparently sincere apologies for their violence, and victims may be willing to accept and forgive, wanting to believe that the violence will end. However, without effective intervention, the violence often continues in a cyclic fashion (Walker 1979), with apology and forgiveness following episodes of violence.

Potential Benefits of Restorative Justice

Braithwaite and Daly (1994), Daly (2002, 2006), Daly and Curtis-Fawley (2006), Hudson (1998, 2002), Koss (2000), Koss and colleagues (2004), Morris (2002), Pennell and Burford (2002), and Pennell and Anderson (2005), among others, identify some potential benefits of RJ in these cases. These include the opportunity for victims to voice their story and be heard, to validate their account of what happened, to receive acknowledgment that they are not to blame for the violence, and to participate in decision making about the case. Because offenders are supposed to take responsibility for the offence (at least ideally), victims' accounts may be validated and a group-based censure of the violence can take place. The process is more flexible and informal; thus, it may be less threatening and more responsive to victims' needs. It may also address violence between those who want to continue the relationship or to repair it, if this is a goal.

Linking Youth Violence to Feminist Debates on Restorative Justice

The literature on youth–parent violence is focused mainly on counting, explaining, and devising therapeutic interventions for it, whereas feminist debates are focused on explaining and identifying appropriate justice responses to adult men's violence toward women. The two sets of literature are not well articulated, although we see points of overlap. Specifically, the dynamics of youth–parent and partner violence are similar in the tactics of control used, the ongoing cyclic nature of the violence (violence, apology, and forgiveness), the denial and shame associated with the violence, and its highly gendered qualities. At the same time, the recursive nature of violence is more evident in youth–parent violence.

In a systemic family violence context, the dynamics of sons beating mothers may also include fathers abusing sons and partners (or ex-partners), sons attempting to retaliate for their father's violence, and mothers whose boyfriends attempt to exert control over their sons. Several family members are thus both victims and offenders. In these contexts, mothers may be even more compromised and marginalized as "real victims" of their son's violence, and they may be blamed (or blame themselves) for it. How a woman understands her son's violence and how the justice system constructs and responds to it raise questions of a diffusion of responsibility in these cases that is less evident in partner violence cases. Unless feminist voices participate in the conference (or other legal) process, these dynamics set in motion a "recursive trap" for victims, one in which women blame themselves for, or in some cases are immobilized by, their son's violence.

IN-DEPTH STUDY METHODS

This study is part of a program of research on the race and gender politics of new justice practices (see published and ongoing work at www.griffith. edu.au/school/ccj/kdaly.html). The study centers on victims' experiences of gendered and sexualized violence, and their views on and experiences with the youth justice conference process and its aftermath. The research time frame was six months, July to December 2001, and the site was Adelaide, South Australia. Readers should consult a detailed technical report that describes the conceptual framework, research methods, and research instruments (Daly et al. 2007). During the research period, six family violence[4] conferences were held: three were of sons assaulting mothers; two of sons assaulting fathers; and one of a daughter assaulting her mother. The three cases analyzed here draw on police reports, criminal history data, and interviews with the three different Youth Justice Coordinators (YJCs) who organized and ran the conferences and victim.[5] While acknowledging the limits of the study, it is the first to examine family violence in a routine youth justice conference practice.[6]

THREE CASE STUDIES

As anticipated from the literature, in all cases, the youth's assault was not isolated, but part of an ongoing pattern of violence. In all cases, the mother had separated from a spouse, who was violent toward her and the son; in one case, the mother subsequently had a boyfriend who was violent toward her and the son. All the women had experienced a loss of power as parents, and all sought police intervention to remove their sons from the household.

Case #1, Carolyn and Des: Assault, Threats with a Knife, and Threats to Kill

Carolyn's case was presented at the beginning of the chapter. She was a sole parent, having separated from Des's father some years ago. She had a nervous breakdown, but the file is not clear on when this occurred. She is employed as a nurse on a casual basis, and her primary social support is her mother. According to the YJC, the assault was "not an isolated event," although it was "by far the most serious. . . . There's been a pattern of damage to the house in the past."

The Aftermath of the Assault

Des was interviewed by the police several hours after his arrest, charged with assault, and then released. Among the release conditions, he was to attend an anger management and alcohol program, and not drink or be around friends who are drinking. Because Carolyn did not want him back in the house that night, the police arranged for alternative overnight accommodation. Des was supposed to move to his father's house; however, although his father agreed to take him, Des refused to go and returned to live with Carolyn. The YJC described the father–son relationship as "broken down," with the father having "younger children from a new relationship." The YJC described Carolyn as "one of these people, who is not always easy to talk to.... Conversations are a bit jumpy...." As we shall see, this YJC was not entirely sympathetic toward Carolyn.

Leading up to the Conference

In the preconference period, the YJC had one 10- to 15-minute telephone conversation with Des, and two telephone conversations with Carolyn; the first, for about 1 hour and 30 minutes, and the second for about 10 to 15 minutes. In his first conversation with Carolyn, the YJC learned that no further physical violence had occurred in the pre-conference period. However, less than a week before the conference, Des stole five of Carolyn's CDs and pawned them. In addition, she noticed that the key to the house side gate was missing, and she thought that Des was letting his friends in. Carolyn was eager to have Des removed from the house, and she asked the YJC about having him placed in foster care. She was also interested in how Des might gain employment training.

The YJC was concerned that Carolyn would see the conference as "only part of the whole general broken down relationship between her and her son.... She's not going to focus...on the actual incident, as serious as it was...." He described her as "exasperated...[there's] almost a resignation that she's just got to wear the problem until [Des] is 18 and leaves home." The YJC agreed with the arresting officer's observation that Carolyn did not want to help herself, saying "she's defeated by the problem—like a complainer rather than an activist."

Carolyn was a nominal support for Des, but she was also a victim, the YJC saying that "this mum will be wearing the exasperated victim hat well and truly." Compared to other parents with whom the YJC was familiar, Carolyn seemed less able to move on from a victim status. The YJC sought another support person for Des, but when he suggested Des's father, both Carolyn and Des said it would not work because the conference "would just get bogged down in their warfare." The YJC thought that Carolyn needed a support person, and after some prompting, Carolyn nominated her mother, Mary.

When asked if Des was taking responsibility for the offence, the YJC said "for a male...I couldn't have asked more of him [although] he could have said, 'look I'm really sorry for what I've done....'" The YJC detected no signs of victim-blaming by Des before the conference although he suspected it would occur during the conference. Specifically, he thought that Des would blame his violence on alcohol and Carolyn's "negative tone." The YJC believed that Carolyn would "not feel threatened" at the conference, and he saw no reason to be concerned for her safety. Reflecting a recursive view of violence, but with little feminist insight, the YJC noted "an interesting dynamic in this case and a lot of domestic violence cases":

> The men themselves are victims too . . . He may well be the victim of his own dad's aggression and mistreatment, and he's probably feeling a victim of his own social circumstances, frustration at not doing very well at school, not moving into work . . . not enjoying the economic success.

The YJC thought that a desirable conference outcome would be to require Des to "make a pledge that he will not use violence against his mum," and if this were "hang[ing] over him, . . . combined with some positive stuff like [employment counseling]," there would be hope for his future.

At the Conference

The conference lasted for about 1 hour and 45 minutes. Present were Des, Carolyn, and her mother Mary, along with the YJC and a police officer. It began with the YJC's explaining the reason for and purpose of the conference, followed by the police officer reading the offence report. Des was then invited to tell his story. He struggled in telling it, unable to remember why "he exploded," but then Carolyn jumped in, saying that he was frustrated about not being able to get his belt on. During the conference, the YJC focused on ways to ensure Carolyn's safety and to help Des find work. He wanted Des to see how serious the knife incident was, and he spent considerable time exploring the potential danger.

Apology and the Agreement

It was agreed that Des would apologize to his mother in private in the coming week, rather than at the conference. In addition to the verbal apology, other elements in the six-month agreement included Des's staying away from his mother's house, not damaging it or allowing anyone to enter it, not threatening or harming her, and making an effort to find a job. Although the YJC felt he had worked hard to include specific elements in the agreement, he perceived that Carolyn did not appreciate his efforts. "Her final sentiment was, 'I don't believe he'll follow through.'" As it turns out, Carolyn was right, but at the time, the YJC's allegiance was with Des. "He was more responsive to my way of running the conference. I was a lot happier with the way it was going with him than with the victim."

Conference Dynamics

Des initially seemed unaffected by Carolyn's story, but when prompted, he agreed that he felt bad about having hurt her. When asked if there was external validation of Carolyn, the YJC said "I thought we did lots of validation, and I thought that Des . . . was not running away from that." But yet, the YJC recalled, "that didn't seem to have any effect on her at all.

There was no show of response from her." The YJC saw no evidence that Des attempted to exercise control or intimidate Carolyn. Overall, he judged the conference as having no restorativeness between Carolyn and Des, although connections were made between Mary and Des. Mary saw Des as a good person who was acting out of boredom and who needed a job.

The YJC described Carolyn's demeanor as "bubbling away with animosity, . . . prickly, . . . at the end of her tether, and wanting practical solutions." His earlier suspicion that Carolyn's "dynamics might be feeding the problem" was, in his mind, "confirmed." He said he "felt almost uncomfortable in there with mum. . . . I thought: Is mum pissed off with me or is she pissed off with the process? My impression in the end was she was probably pissed off with the kid mostly."

Some time was spent discussing Des's theft and pawning of his mother's CDs. Carolyn's focus was "on those things every bit as much as on the violent stuff." She was dissatisfied with the police response to Des's having breached the conditions of his preconference bond, and the YJC believed that this was all "part of mum's cynicism about change." Our reading of the file suggests that Carolyn had good reasons to be cynical, but that she sought confirmation of her legal rights and saw them as a lever of power. For example, at the conference, she asked the police officer what her rights were if Des came home drunk, "banging on the doors and wanting to get in." She wanted to know if this would be interpreted as a risk of violence to her. She had asked a second officer the same question when she gave her statement concerning Des's theft of her CDs.

The YJC acknowledged that he had a closer bond to Des, and he made several negative comments about Carolyn during the interview. Although he could not pinpoint the sources ("whether it's abuse in her childhood, abuse from the marriage, . . . bitterness from the marriage break-up . . ."), he believed that "Des is wrapped up and tarred with the same brush." This comment exemplifies Downey's (1997) concern that responsibility for violence can be diffused in youth violence cases, although this YJC went further, suggesting that Carolyn's personality and "cold" affect motivated Des's violence:

> She comes across as a very hard person. . . . I think her son felt sadder about the situation between them than [she] did. . . . She's a very damaged person. . . . It's not normal for people to be like that. . . .

After the Conference

Although the YJC had been critical of Carolyn's "cynicism about whether the process would be of any use to her," she had every reason to be cynical. About five weeks after the conference, she supplied a detailed typewritten statement to the YJC, at his request. She said that Des came home at about midnight, drunk, was "verbally abusive" to her, "loud, very angry, and could not be reasoned with." He threw a dish and food around, telling

Carolyn to ring the police on three occasions. He said that by the time the police arrived, "the house would be totally trashed and he would be gone." She didn't "retaliate or challenge" his behavior, fearing that it "would escalate into violence." She rang Des's father, and they agreed that Des should move into his house. However, Des could not be found. Carolyn also reported that since the conference Des broke into her house at least four times; food and some items of her clothing were taken, and she suspects that several of his friends had been there. Des made no further efforts to get a job after his first appointment with the counselor. Since he broke the conditions of the conference agreement, Carolyn asked that "prompt action be taken."

Immediately upon receiving Carolyn's statement, the YJC issued paperwork to breach Des, referring the case back to the police late in 2001. The record shows that the police referred the case to court, but it was dismissed nearly a year later, in October 2002. From then to December 2004, there is no record of official offending on the police file.

Case #2, Anna and Tom: Assault with a Broom Handle

At mid-day in June 2001, Anna was at home when she heard distressed shouts from her daughter, Tina (10 years old). Anna rushed to see what was happening and saw her son, Tom (14 years old), pushing Tina into the couch where she was lying. Anna intervened and an argument with Tom ensued, resulting in Anna being struck by a broom handle. Afraid for her safety, Anna fled the house and called the police to meet her at a local shop. When they arrived, she was reluctant to proceed and declined to make a statement against Tom. She was visibly upset, and the police noted a red mark on her upper arm, consistent with having been hit by an object. Anna said she wanted the police to accompany her home and to speak with Tom about the assault, but she did not want to make a formal complaint.

The police escorted Anna to her home, and they spoke to a woman who knew about problems in the household, but had not witnessed the assault. Several hours later the police arrested Tom. They described Anna as a "hostile witness who will not support police proceedings in this matter," and noted "there is a history of family violence at this address . . . that could only be resolved by police intervention."[7]

At the time of the assault, Anna (47 years old) had been separated from her husband (and Tom's father), Ernst, for about 18 months. The two were engaged in a complicated and bitter settlement in the family court, which involved a lot of money and property. Ernst is a violent man, who beats Tom; Anna thought that if Tom had to live with Ernst, he would appreciate her more. Anna also wanted to demonstrate that she was protective of her daughter Tina. Anna believed that Ernst was sexually abusing Tina and that he was trying to take Tina away from her.

The Aftermath of the Assault

After Tom's arrest, he was interviewed by police in the presence of his father and charged with assault. He was released on police bond and went to live with his father. Soon after, however, he rang Anna very distressed because "he'd had a very hard time with his dad" and wanted to move back. Anna "thought he'd had enough" and acceded to his request, although she still wanted him to live with Ernst.

Leading up to the Conference

The YJC had two conversations with Anna before the conference, one of which lasted for an hour and a half. Anna described a long history of violence by Ernst, which both children had witnessed. Anna believed that Tom was treating her in the same way because he saw her take Ernst's violence rather than defend herself, and thus she saw herself as partly responsible for Tom's behavior. Her comment exemplifies the "recursive trap" for victims. Anna also reported that Tom's arrest had not stopped the violence. According to the YJC, "he was still hitting her . . . had always hit her," and Anna was "very ambiguous in the description of her son and her husband. It is one context for her: it just rolls back and forth in her mind, and she can't differentiate." Anna has a history of "mental instability" and is concerned that others, including the police, label her as crazy.

Anna had a dual role in the conference: as victim and as Tom's supporter. The YJC did not invite Ernst to the conference because, among other reasons, he had taken out a restraining order against Anna. The YJC described Anna as a victim of Tom's assault and "a much wider picture as well," and she viewed Tom as "very manipulative, egotistical, and indulged." He had many problems in school because, according to the YJC, "he thinks he's better than everyone else . . . a sort of condescending, a pompous boy. . . . " He has been excluded from school many times and has not attended for nearly two years.

In setting up the conference, the YJC had only a very brief phone conversation with Tom. She noted that he "wasn't very interested" in the conference, he ". . . didn't very easily take responsibility, and he said he was coming . . . because his mum made him." Anna, on the other hand, had high hopes for what the conference could do for Tom. She was looking for an "organized way" to sit down and talk with Tom and was fully committed to the conference, so long as Ernst was not there. In the YJC's words, "she wanted him to see more clearly what he was doing, she wanted him to change, and she wanted it to be miraculous, . . . and she really wanted to have a chance to talk with him, without feeling alone because she can't do it alone." When asked about concerns for Anna's safety at the conference, the YJC replied, "no more than anywhere else; she was unsafe everywhere."

At the Conference

The conference was held about two months after the assault. Only Tom and Anna attended. They arrived late, and Anna was flustered. They, together with the YJC and police officer, sat around a small table. Tom sat in the back of the room, while Anna sat diagonally from him, near the door. The conference went for about an hour and a half.

Tom said he was "tricked" into attending the conference: his mother told him they were going shopping, but instead they came to the conference. Despite this, he agreed to continue with it. Anna started talking about the broader context of violence with Ernst, the YJC recalling that "she found it much easier to talk about her husband and his pattern of behaviour towards her...." As a result, the YJC thought that Anna was "excusing" Tom's behavior, "she was giving him an out." Although the YJC tried to bring her back to Tom's assault, Anna "found it hard to talk about that one incident." To Anna, the "real" offender was Ernst, and the "real" victim was Tina. The YJC put it this way:

> She talks about her own victimization through the experience of her daughter . . . [She is] under emotional pressure that has pushed her right over the edge . . . [S]he's very scared about everything. Her world's disintegrating, and she is the victim of a huge amount of violence.

Tom agreed with the police report, saying "that's exactly what happened," but he then blamed his sister for provoking him. Tom took no responsibility for the assault, and he saw himself more as a victim. His solution was to leave home and live independently. He talked a lot about having to be dependent on his mother for transport and how she would not give him enough money. He refused to discuss anything about the "disagreements" between his parents.

Apology and the Agreement

Although Tom apologized to his mother when he wanted to move back with her, no apology was made at the conference, and the YJC did not push for it. Tom said he regretted what he had done, but his regret had more to do with the fact that he had to live with his father. Although Anna had called the police many times before, this was the "first time she had actually pressed for something to happen, for him to be taken away." By her actions, she hoped that Tom would "know that was the consequence: either he'd get locked up or his dad would have him. That was the punishment she wanted." The conference outcome was minimal: Tom was to make an appointment to see a counselor about job training and employment. This occurred, despite the YJC's acknowledging the deep problems within the family: "they need family counselling [and] haven't had any."

Conference Dynamics

Tom was extremely defiant and brash during the conference. He was actively involved in the process, but not in a positive way. The YJC observed that he was "very dismissive and blank about what she [Anna] said.... He seemed to enjoy being there.... He has quite a lot of interest in seeing his mother emotional.... Anna cried through the whole thing. She was crying when they arrived."

The police officer emphasized the seriousness of the offence to Tom, pointing out the consequences of being in the juvenile justice system, and this, the YJC believed, was a form of external validation for Anna. However, at times, the officer's remarks about family life were highly ill-suited to the reality of violence for this family.

The YJC often had to intervene in Anna's minimization of Tom's abuse. This was because

> The victim is also not a victim.... She considers herself a perpetrator of violence towards her son, [which has] has caused him to rebel. Or the victim of her husband, therefore he [Ernst] is the real offender in all of this.

When asked if any revictimization elements occurred in the conference (e.g., victim distress, minimization of the harm, the youth not fully admitting to the offence), the YJC said "well, yes, all that happened." She continued, "it happened partly because she [Anna] let it happen, ... and it's what has always happened." However, the YJC added, "I just didn't let it happen.... I did challenge every one of those things ... and for once they were challenged...."

Tom was extremely rude to Anna, although this seemed typical of their relationship. When asked if he tried to coerce Anna through any kind of subtle control or intimidation strategies, the YJC said, "no, she's too mad ... too beyond it, to notice that.... Her mind is very fluid, and she can honestly talk non-stop herself, as long as you'll listen, and it's all very dark, dark stuff."

After the Conference

The police record suggests that about three months after the conference, in September, Tom was charged with property damage, but in a town more than four hours' drive from Adelaide. Some time later, Anna called the YJC to report that Tom had trashed her friend's house in Adelaide and may have assaulted her. She wanted Tom out of the house and sought information on referrals from the YJC; but when given some leads, she seemed to reject them all.

On reflection, the YJC believed that the case was "far more appropriate to have gone to conference than court," but much depended on how Anna would deal with any subsequent abuse, and "the conference hasn't resolved that at all." This was "a classic, classic case" of family violence, with entrenched patterns "that can't be broken down in one meeting." The conference "was far more about them showing who they were, than changing." Indeed, the YJC noted that the conference seemed to be "an interlude in the middle of their day," reporting that "at the end of the conference, Tom said, 'Now can we go shopping?' and Anna said 'Yes,' so they were off shopping."

The YJC's characterizations of Tom as "totally empty, an empty little person," "not a good boy," and "a very dangerous boy," were born out in his criminal history. Three years after the conference, he was sentenced to serve eight months in detention for a violent offence committed the previous year. During the three-year period, he was in and out of court for assault and property and driving offences committed on over a dozen different occasions.

Case #3, Sheila and Mitch: Assault and Strangling

Sheila, age 45, arrived home from a pizza shop, where she works. She then ordered a pizza from the same shop, and had it for dinner with her son, Mitch (age 15). When they were finished, Sheila announced that she was going to take the leftovers to her friend, Bevan. Mitch got "very mad" about this, and just as Sheila was about to walk out the door, he said, "You're not going." She said, "I am going," and as she proceeded to walk out the door, Mitch "snapped." The police report continues:

> He grabbed her around the throat and punched her in the head. He was strangling her and holding her against the wall near the front door.... He held her there for a few seconds ... released her and then said "Get the [expletive] out and don't [expletive] come back."

After separating from her husband, Greg, some years ago,[8] Sheila began to see Bevan, whose house is around the corner from hers. Bevan is a "chronic alcoholic" and violent toward Mitch and Sheila. Her failure to protect Mitch from Bevan, coupled with Bevan's violence toward Sheila, led to police and child protection intervention on many occasions. Although Mitch had been verbally abusive to Sheila many times, this was the first time, she said, that he became seriously physical and that she sought to have him arrested. Sheila and Greg attribute Mitch's violence to a "chemical imbalance" for which he takes medication. The YJC took a different view: "Mitch grew up in the house" with a violent father who beat his wife. Mitch "saw dad's behaviour, learnt from it, then when Dad left, Mitch took over." Added to this is Bevan's presence in Sheila's life. According to the YJC, Mitch "hates Bevan ... [When] everything goes wrong for Mitch, Bevan's behind it." He is very jealous of Bevan.

The Aftermath of the Assault

Immediately after the assault, Sheila fled to Bevan's house; from there, she rang the police. A couple of hours later, the police arrived, had a short conversation with Mitch, and arrested him. Sheila watched as they drove Mitch away. He was interviewed by the police and made full admissions to grabbing his mother around the neck and holding her against the wall. He said he wanted to frighten her into staying at home instead of going to Bevan's because, in his view, she was always going to Bevan's house and did not spend enough time with him. He was charged and placed in the police cells for some time before his father picked him up.

The police file suggests that Sheila initially did not want the police to divert the case from court to conference. However, after speaking to the police some time later, she was grateful that it meant that Mitch did not have to go to court and potentially receive a criminal record. Sheila said there had been no physical injuries or bruising from the assault, and she had not experienced stress-related effects such as sleeplessness, fear of being alone, or nightmares.

Leading up to the Conference

From his phone conversation, the YJC described Sheila as sounding "pathetic, washed out . . . looking over her shoulder to see who is listening, . . . but at the same time accepting that stuff." The YJC said that Bevan is very controlling of Sheila; he (the YJC) recounted that when he rang Sheila, Bevan picked up the phone first, passed it along to Sheila, and then listened in on the conversation in another room.

Sheila was ambivalent about participating in the conference, vacillating between being very positive one day, and then negative and unsure the next. She said many times that she was fearful of going to the conference if Greg was going to be there because of his level of "agro." The YJC thought that Sheila's ambivalence might also have been caused by things that Bevan was saying. When asked if she wanted to Bevan to be at the conference, Sheila quickly said "no." Mitch's supporter was Greg, his father, whom the YJC described as "a supporter in the true sense because he is downplaying it totally. . . . I'm not sure how supportive he will be of a true consequence. . . . He's more an advocate for dropping it." The YJC was concerned about Sheila's emotional safety at the conference; when he discussed his concerns with Sheila, she confirmed that she was far more fearful of Greg than Mitch. The YJC reassured her that a police officer would be present, and that no one would be allowed to harass her. Sheila's support person was a teacher at Mitch's school, who knew her and Mitch well.

In his conversations with Sheila before the conference, the YJC said she was intensely angry toward Mitch: his abusive behavior had gone too far, and she had to throw him out of the house. While Sheila did not have any specific outcomes in mind for the conference, the YJC felt that it was more about punishment for Mitch than anything else: "what she wants is Mitch to have a bit of a shake-up, to say it's not on." The YJC said it was important to have an authoritative police officer, along with a male YJC, at the conference because of the gendered nature of the abuse and the history of Greg's violence toward Sheila.

The day before the conference was scheduled, Greg and Mitch turned up to attend, a day early. Their attitudes caused considerable concern to the YJC. They tried to convince him to hold the conference then, arguing that it wasn't necessary to have Sheila present, that she would just get off track ("Give her a chance, she'll just talk about her problems") and dominate the proceedings. Greg said something else that disturbed the YJC. "He said, 'Look I saw her two days after this, and she didn't have a mark on her, and I can tell you she's not one that doesn't bruise easy. . . ' . . . I thought umm, thanks for that." When the YJC told them that Sheila was fearful of coming to the conference, they "were laughing hysterically at that, thinking why would she be scared?" Mitch did not take any responsibility for the violence, and his father "was feeding it a fair bit." From their point of view, there was nothing wrong with them; rather, the problem was Bevan.

The YJC took Mitch aside twice (once with his father present), warning him about his attitude: if he acted like that during the conference, it could be terminated and he would have to go to court. The YJC spent some time showing Mitch and Greg the security set-up in the conference room, including the duress alarm, which if activated, would have a sheriff on the scene immediately. He did this "more as a deterrent than anything else."

On the day of the conference, before it started, the YJC spoke with the police officer about a plan of action should Greg or Mitch say or do anything inappropriate or threatening. They agreed that on a signal from the YJC, the police officer would jump in and give Greg or Mitch (or both) a verbal warning for a public order offence. The YJC had a sheriff in the hallway, visible to Greg and Mitch as they walked in. Not only they, but also Sheila knew there was a duress alarm in the room. Also, it was planned in advance that Sheila and her support person would be excused from the conference after the agreement was reached but before it had been written up, so they could leave safely.

At the Conference

Compared to the previous day, Mitch's and Greg's attitude had improved. At the start of the conference, however, Mitch said he was angry because his mother was never home for him and was always with Bevan. Initially, he was reluctant to talk about the offence, but was encouraged by the YJC and the police officer. Before Mitch finished telling his story, Sheila jumped in, saying that she understood his feelings. She took some responsibility for Mitch's actions by saying that perhaps she did spend more time with Bevan than she should. This had a positive effect on Mitch, who shifted his orientation by taking responsibility for his behavior and acknowledging that his attack would have hurt her. Sheila said that it wasn't the assault that hurt her, but seeing him being dragged away by the police, and she "had done that." She had cried the whole night after that, and this seemed to "cut into the quick" for Mitch. He seemed to genuinely understand and be moved by what he had done to her. Mitch did not expect his mother to understand his feelings, but when she did, he was more willing to take responsibility. According to the YJC, "even his tone of voice changed from that point on; it became more conversational rather than defensive."

When interviewed, Sheila said that Mitch was truthful at the conference. She was surprised, but proud of him, when he admitted "he went really overboard ... because it takes a lot of guts to do that." She believed that he was remorseful when he said he was sorry, and she trusted his word, saying that he went "straight to the point" and didn't minimize its seriousness. She did not feel she was blamed for the offence, although she felt she contributed to it, saying "he did wrong, I did wrong," a comment that exemplifies the "recursive trap" for victims. She attempted to explain her culpability by saying she "was in the wrong place at the wrong time."

Apology and the Agreement

It took a long time for Mitch to apologize to Sheila, and initially he directed his apology to the YJC, who then asked him to apologize to Sheila directly. He did this, saying "I'm really sorry for what I did to you, and that you had to get the police to drag me away." Neither the police officer nor the YJC was convinced of the sincerity of his apology, or that Mitch really understood what he was apologizing for, so it was agreed that he would write an apology letter to Sheila. Other elements of the agreement were to attend a youth agency with the aim of discussing participation in an anger management program (this cannot be mandated); to make contact with a counselor, with the aim of returning to school or seeking job training; and not to be in Sheila's house for six months, although phone contact was all right. Greg was the supervisor.

Sheila thought that the agreement was fair, but that only the YJC and police officer were involved in deciding it. She thought it very likely that Mitch would comply with all the elements and that the police officer had explained well the consequences of not complying. Compared to the YJC and police officer, Sheila was far more positive about Mitch, saying he took full responsibility for the offence and was "really sorry."

Conference Dynamics

The YJC reported that as Greg and Mitch entered the conference room, they "gave the glare of death" toward Sheila, but this changed during the conference. In the introduction phase, the YJC warned against any disrespect and intimidation, emphasizing that the conference could be terminated as a result.

According to the YJC, "Once mum had ... accepted some of the responsibility," so did Mitch. But, the YJC believed, it was a "contingent responsibility.... He would never get to 'fully [responsible]' by himself."

Although Mitch's initial defiance dissipated, Greg attempted to undermine Sheila. He made comments such as "I don't want to say anything nasty about you, but the police I spoke to all said Mitch was looking for a mother.... If you'd spend more time with the kids...." The YJC said that he and the police officer had to pull Greg off that tangent, and at one point Mitch turned to his dad and told him to "shut up." The YJC viewed Greg's behavior as attempted intimidation, controlling, and offence minimizing, but this was checked and challenged by him and the police officer.

According to the YJC, Sheila was extremely anxious and fearful during the conference ("she'd compressed two or three tissues into a solid block by the end of the conference"), and it was very hard for her to hear Greg denying the assault had happened. Although the YJC viewed these and other remarks by Greg as potentially distressful to Sheila, he believed that she was not revictimized because she "was quite strong throughout." She seemed to have prepared herself for Greg's comments and was able to ignore them and remain calm. Sheila did not recall any negative experiences at the conference, although she left the conference, feeling "relieved... that it was over."

Throughout the conference Sheila referred to herself as the "weaker parent," implying that this contributed to Mitch's abuse, and that Greg was the "stronger parent." This was reframed by the YJC as Mitch being the "more powerful child" and Greg having strategies to exert power over Mitch. There was external validation of Sheila by the police officer, who said that abusing a family member was extremely serious, "the worst of the worst," and by Mitch, who acknowledged that his mother was scared and he was wrong to have assaulted her. The benefit of the conference, in Sheila's words, was that "we all sat down and talked like people, without any swearing or cursing or blaming. We talked like civilized people.... We got to the whole incident and worked it all out." The benefits for Mitch were "help[ing] him with his anger...and to put things in perspective." After the conference, Sheila felt more positive toward Mitch, although she continues to feel "wary" and a "little frightened."

After the Conference

When Sheila was interviewed two weeks after the conference, she described Bevan as her "ex-friend" because he had hit her the day after the conference. She had known him for 10 years, and he had never hit her before, she said; but it seemed that he had "put 10 years into one hit and that was it." She called the police, and Bevan was charged with assault.

Sheila was impressed with Mitch's letter of apology, saying it made her feel "teary." She did not think he would assault her again because "he learnt his lesson." Overall, she was satisfied with the conference, emphasizing that it saved Mitch from getting a criminal record and ruining his employment prospects. She recommended conferences to victims in her circumstances because "that way the child would be protected and the parents would be protected." Police records show that Mitch has not been subject to police or court action for three years since the conference.

CONCLUSION

Sons assaulting mothers share some elements with partner violence, but their dynamics can be more complex. Mothers have an ambivalent relationship to their sons' offending and toward their role in seeking justice: they are not only victims, but also they are expected to be their sons' supporters. They blame themselves for their sons' behavior, and at times, they blame their ex-partners, who have been abusive toward them and their sons. They explain and excuse their sons' behavior as emulating their fathers' violence. In all cases, although the women have separated from their partners, the ongoing and often fraught relationships between the male youth and their fathers, or, in one instance, a pending family court case, can compromise a woman's ability to take an independent stance and move forward. The recursive quality of the violence sets up the potential for a "recursive trap" for victims, in which the responsibility for violence is diffused, women partly blame themselves for it, and sons adopt a victim status, which allows them to minimize and excuse their behavior. In addition to the well-known "cycle of violence" in partner violence, these cases have an intergenerational recursive dimension. The complex character of these cases is recognized in the therapeutic literature, but how can or should it be recognized in justice practices?

In all cases, the incident was one of many the women had experienced over the years at the hands of their sons, ex-partners, or both. In all cases, the women invoked legal authority as a mechanism of punishing their abusive sons; this meant not only removing them from their house, but wanting them to live with their fathers. After trying other measures, the women's calls to the police to have their sons arrested seemed the only way to take a stand against their sons' behavior and to live with a sense of safety in their homes. In two cases (Des and Tom), we know that the women's efforts were not successful because their sons did not comply with the agreement. Over the long term, one youth (Tom) persisted in offending that came to police and court attention.

Two mothers were described as nonstop talkers, and the third, as cold and distant. All three were presented as a bit strange, mad, or pathetic, and viewed by the YJCs as damaged in some way. Two had clear signs of trauma: a nervous breakdown (Carolyn) and mental instability (Anna). The YJCs varied in their assessment of the women's personality: two saw the women's outlook as caused by years of abuse (cases #2 and #3), but a third often blamed the woman (case #1).

The conference dynamics show a complex interaction of each woman's interests and capacities to find common ground with her son (or not) and the son's readiness to change his behavior. In case #1, Carolyn was not interested in repairing the relationship with her son: she was fed up with him and saw little hope that he would take a more mature and responsible path. Des was not ready to change, and the conference did little to shift his attitude toward his mother or to change his behavior in the short term. No common ground was established between mother and son. In case #2, Anna felt that she and her husband were responsible for Tom's violence, and this served to excuse his behavior. Anna wanted the conference to be "miraculous," a moment when she could confront Tom "without feeling alone." Tom was not ready to act any differently than before: he remained callous, dismissive, and unaffected by his mother's feelings and concerns. The conference largely recapitulated ongoing dynamics of violence between mother and son, even as the YJC attempted to intervene and challenge the instances of revictimization. In case #3, Sheila wanted to "shake up" her son, but she had not yet given up on him. She was effective in breaking through Mitch's defences by saying that perhaps she spent too much time with Bevan, which resulted in Mitch's acting more positively toward her. The common ground established between them was contingent on her taking some blame for the offence. Compared to the two other cases, case #3 stood out in the degree to which the YJC set in motion (and needed to set in motion) a security plan and, working with the police officer, continually checked and "pulled up" Mitch, and even more so, his father for their inappropriate comments. It was fortunate that the two turned up a day early for the conference because it was not until then that the YJC fully appreciated their negative and victim-blaming attitudes and potential for violence.

Several key points emerge. First, the dynamics of youth–parent violence (in particular, son–mother violence), although somewhat similar to partner violence, have added problems. They demonstrate vividly how ongoing violence between intimates and family members differs from "incident-based" violence, and why the standard conference model (and indeed, the standard police or court model) is poorly equipped and resourced to address the violence. All three cases required more than a legal or police response: the assaults were a symptom of a longer story about a wider set of conflicts in gender, family, and intimate relations. That is why, in all the cases, the women wanted to tell the longer story and found it difficult to focus on one incident alone.

Second, with respect to resources for victims, feminist and victim advocates argue that these should be part of case outcomes. Ideally, in all three cases, the victims would have been aided by professional counseling and support, and the offenders would have been aided by a targeted, sustained therapeutic intervention to address adolescent male violence toward family members (designed along the lines of a similar program in Adelaide, for youth sexual violence). None of these elements was part of the agreement. The reason is threefold: legislation guiding youth conferencing in South Australia, the role of YJCs in following-up cases, and the lack of a sustained therapeutic program for youth violence toward family members. The Young Offenders Act 1993 states that conference can only devise outcomes for the young person; no outcomes can be directed to victims or any other adult in the conference. The YJCs do not case manage; rather, their role is to monitor outcomes and, when necessary, breach a youth for noncompliance. The principal resource available to youth is counseling for training, employment, or anger management. Although a conference outcome cannot direct resources to victims, YJCs do engage with victims, offering support service information for self-referral.

Third, because of their complexity, these cases required more time and work by the YJCs in setting up the conference appropriately; talking and listening to victims, offenders, and their supporters; and putting in place security and safety measures for victims. In addition, a coordinator may continue to be a lifeline of information and support after the conference is over (as in case #2). These cases call for a sophisticated understanding of the dynamics of partner and family violence, and the need to ensure that facilitators are competent and well-trained in handling them. They require considerable professional time and resources to prepare, conduct, and monitor post-conference (see, e.g., Pennell and Anderson's [2005] "best practice" model for child welfare cases). Such time and resources were not available to the Adelaide Family Conference Team, nor, more generally, are they available in family violence cases in any criminal court jurisdiction.

Fourth, the cases show that informal processes can revictimize when offenders (or their supporters) do not take responsibility for the violence, minimize the harm, or cause distress to victims. However, the YJCs and police officers intervened to check and challenge inappropriate behaviors and attitudes, emphasizing norms of nonviolence and respect for others. All the YJCs said the case was appropriate for a conference. For Des (case #1), the YJC said "we've underscored how dangerous things were, and we have a plan that will meet family needs for him to move." For Tom (case #2), the YJC said that while "the conference hasn't resolved" the deep family problems, the agreement set in motion a way for Tom to find another place to live. For Mitch (case #3), the YJC believed the conference addressed the "general conflict between mum and son" and emphasized the need for respect. Had the case gone to court, "he would have walked away laughing at the system because it meant nothing."

The cases invite reflection on whether *any justice practice* can address longstanding and deep-seated conflicts in families, which require sustained social work and psychological intervention. A justice practice—whether RJ or standard courthouse justice—cannot do this work alone. As a routine criminal justice practice in South Australia, with few resources or supports, the most a conference can achieve is to reimage appropriate relations of respect and nonviolence, and to check and challenge pro-violence and victim-blaming behaviors. Ultimately, the criminal justice challenge for youth–parent violence is how to address the recursive qualities of violence in families in which both parents and children are or have been abused by family members or intimates, while at the same time addressing the wrong of the immediate offence.

ACKNOWLEDGMENTS

We thank the members of the South Australian Family Conference Team, the South Australian Police, and the South Australian Courts Administration Authority for their assistance and support in conducting this research, as well as Sarah Curtis-Fawley and Brigitte Bouhours for their research assistance. The research was funded by grants from the Australian Research Council and the Australian-American Fulbright Association.

NOTES

1. All names used are pseudonyms.
2. By "partner violence" we refer to violence between adult intimates, who may or may not be living with each other or legally married.
3. As this paper goes to press, we note that two quite recent and relevant papers analyzing adolescent violence toward parents in Australia have been published: Stewart and colleagues (2007) and Howard and Rottman (2008).
4. We use the term "family violence" as an umbrella concept, which includes partner, adolescent–parent, sibling, and adult–parent (elder) violence. The term is used by Australian Indigenous women to refer to an even wider set of social relations and violence.
5. Of the three victims, one agreed to be interviewed (case #3), one did not (case #1), and one was in the "retrospective sample" group, which was not contacted for an interview (case #2) (see Daly et al. 2007).
6. Three studies have investigated (or are investigating) RJ, but both are (or were) pilot projects, with a dedicated focus on conferences in cases of sexual or family violence (Pennell and Burford 2002; Koss et al. 2004; Social Services and Research Information Unit 2003). Pennell and Anderson (2005) analyze conferences in child welfare social work cases, some of which involve domestic violence.
7. It is not possible to reconcile these earlier statements by the police with the YJC's subsequent account, described below, that Anna wanted the police to arrest Tom.
8. It is uncertain how long ago they separated; the likely range is four to seven years.

REFERENCES

Bobic, Natasha. 2004. *Adolescent Violence Towards Parents.* Sydney: Australian Domestic and Family Violence Clearinghouse. Retrieved February 28, 2009 (http://www.adfvc.unsw.edu.au/PDF%20files/adolescent_violence.pdf).

Braithwaite, John and Kathleen Daly. 1994. "Masculinities, Violence and Communitarian Control." Pp. 189–213 in *Just Boys Doing Business?*, edited by Tim Newburn and Elizabeth A. Stanko. New York: Routledge.

Busch, Ruth. 2002. "Domestic Violence and Restorative Justice Initiatives: Who Pays If We Get It Wrong?" Pp. 223–248 in *Restorative Justice and Family Violence*, edited by Heather Strang and John Braithwaite. Melbourne: Cambridge University Press.

Coker, Donna. 1999. "Enhancing Autonomy for Battered Women: Lessons from Navajo Peacemaking." *UCLA Law Review* 47:1–111.

————. 2002. "Transformative Justice: Anti-Subordination Practices in Cases of Domestic Violence." Pp. 128–152 in *Restorative Justice and Family Violence,* edited by Heather Strang and John Braithwaite. Melbourne: Cambridge University Press.

Cottrell, Barbara and Peter Monk. 2004. "Adolescent-to-Parent Abuse: A Qualitative Overview of Common Themes." *Journal of Family Issues* 25:1072–1095.

Daly, Kathleen. 2002. "Sexual Assault and Restorative Justice." Pp. 62–88 in *Restorative Justice and Family Violence,* edited by Heather Strang and John Braithwaite. Melbourne: Cambridge University Press.

————. 2006. "Restorative Justice and Sexual Assault: An Archival Study of Court and Conference Cases." *British Journal of Criminology* 46: 334–356.

Daly, Kathleen and Sarah Curtis-Fawley. 2006. "Restorative Justice for Victims of Sexual Assault." Pp. 230–265 in *Gender and Crime: Patterns of Victimization and Offending,* edited by K. Heimer and C. Kruttschnitt. New York: New York University Press.

Daly, Kathleen, Brigitte Bouhours, and Sarah Curtis-Fawley. 2007. *South Australia Juvenile Justice and Criminal Justice (SAJJ-CJ) Research on Conferencing and Sentencing Technical Report No. 4: In-Depth Study of Sexual Assault and Family Violence Cases.* Brisbane: School of Criminology and Criminal Justice, Griffith University.

Downey, Laurel. 1997. "Adolescent Violence: A Systemic and Feminist Perspective." *Australian and New Zealand Journal of Family Therapy* 8:70–79.

Eckstein, Nancy. 2004. "Emergent Issues in Families Experiencing Adolescent-to-Parent Abuse." *Western Journal of Communication* 68:365–388.

Gallagher, Eddie. 2004. "Parents Victimised by Their Children." *Australian and New Zealand Journal of Family Therapy* 25:1–12.

Harbin, Henry and Denis Madden. 1979. "Battered Parents: A New Syndrome." *American Journal of Psychiatry* 136:1288–1291.

Howard, Jo and Naomi Rottem. 2008. *It All Starts At Home: Male Adolescent Violence to Mothers.* St. Kilda, Victoria, Australia: Inner South Community Health Service.

Hudson, Barbara. 1998. "Restorative Justice: The Challenge of Sexual and Racial Violence." *Journal of Law and Society* 25:237–256.

————. 2002. "Restorative Justice and Gendered Violence: Diversion or Effective Justice?" *British Journal of Criminology* 42:616–634.

Koss, Mary. 2000. "Blame, Shame, and Community: Justice Responses to Violence against Women." *American Psychologist* 55:1332–1343.

Koss, Mary, Karen Bachar, C. Quince Hopkins, and Carolyn Carlson. 2004. "Expanding a Community's Justice Response to Sex Crimes through Advocacy, Prosecutorial, and Public Health Collaboration." *Journal of Interpersonal Violence* 19:1435–1463.

Lewis, Ruth, Rebecca Dobash, Russell Dobash, and Kate Cavanagh. 2001. "Law's Progressive Potential: The Value of Engagement for the Law for Domestic Violence." *Social and Legal Studies* 10:105–130.

Livingston, Larry. 1985. *Children's Violence to Single Mothers.* Urbana: University of Illinois.

Morris, Allison. 2002. "Critiquing the Critics: A Brief Response to Critics of Restorative Justice." *British Journal of Criminology* 42:596–615.

Pence, Ellen and Michael Paymar. 1986. *Power and Control: Tactics of Men Who Batter*. Duluth: Minnesota Program Development.

Pennell, Joan and Gary Anderson, eds. 2005. *Widening the Circle: The Practice and Evaluation of Family Group Conferencing with Children, Youths, and Their Families*. Washington DC: National Association of Social Workers.

Pennell, Joan and Gale Burford. 2002. "Feminist Praxis: Making Family Group Conferencing Work." Pp. 108–127 in *Restorative Justice and Family Violence*, edited by Heather Strang and John Braithwaite. Melbourne: Cambridge University Press.

Stewart, Michelle, Ailsa Burns, and Rosemary Leonard. 2007. "Dark Side of the Mothering Role: Abuse of Mothers by Adolescent and Adult Children." *Sex Roles* 56:183–191.

Stubbs, Julie. 2002. "Domestic Violence and Women's Safety: Feminist Challenges to Restorative Justice." Pp. 42–61 in *Restorative Justice and Family Violence*, edited by Heather Strang and John Braithwaite. Melbourne: Cambridge University Press.

———. 2004. *Restorative Justice, Domestic Violence and Family Violence* (Issues Paper 9). Sydney: Australian Domestic and Family Violence Clearinghouse. Retrieved February 28, 2009 (http://www.austdvclearinghouse.unsw.edu. au/ PDF%20files/Issues_Paper_9.pdf).

———. 2007. "Beyond Apology? Domestic Violence and Critical Questions for Restorative Justice." *Criminology and Criminal Justice: An International Journal* 7:169–187.

Walker, Lenore. 1979. *The Battered Woman*. New York: Harper & Row.

III

FROM CRITIQUE TO NEW POSSIBILITIES

Innovative Feminist Projects

8

OPENING CONVERSATIONS ACROSS CULTURAL, GENDER, AND GENERATIONAL DIVIDES

Family and Community Engagement to Stop Violence Against Women and Children

JOAN PENNELL & MIMI KIM

Institutions, communities, and families target victims along the divides of culture, gender, and generation. Although these divides are used as justifications for committing violations and enforcing acquiescence, they also offer opportunities for stopping violence. The rationales encompass large social groupings, and thus point beyond the narrow definitions of domestic violence as that committed by one intimate partner against another and of child maltreatment as that committed by parents against their children. Such definitions fail to grasp the intersections of victimization and lead to criminal justice sanctions and human service interventions that fracture people's lives. Nevertheless, these fractures can create openings for conversations that engage people's hopes and abilities to work together for peace and social justice.

We start from the premise that identities divide people and at the same time mobilize them to push for social change. Our own distinct identities have prompted convergences and divergences in our perspectives on

177

antiviolence work. We are both uneasy about the reliance of domestic violence organizations and child welfare services on legal remedies to protect women and children; and both of us are committed to identifying ways to engage culturally based groups—the family and community—in stopping family violence. We use the term "family violence" to refer to violations that cut across generations and gender within family groups, that is, the immediate family members, their relatives, and other close connections.

To effect these family and community engagements, Mimi is seeking "creative interventions" outside the state (Kim 2006) while Joan is seeking to "widen the circle" of informal and formal supports (Pennell and Anderson 2005). Mimi's creative interventions serve as alternatives to law enforcement, the courts, and prisons while Joan's widening the circle seeks to elevate the leadership of the family and its community while still exerting legal leverages to safeguard children and adults within the home.

Widening the circle and creative interventions are theories of change, each with its strategies for stopping family violence. Joan's theory, based on research in Canada (Pennell and Burford 1994) and the United States (Pennell and Anderson 2005), identifies four main strategies, or what she refers to as "pathways," for engaging family and community in supporting and protecting child and adult family members. These pathways are "family leadership" that centralizes the role of the family in making and carrying out plans, "inclusive planning" that involves different sides of the family in the process, "cultural safety" that fosters a context in which family members can tap into their traditions in reaching resolutions, and "community partnerships" that encourage local collaborations in which each party retains its distinct functions while seeking to achieve shared goals (Pennell 2004, 2006b).

Mimi's theory of creative interventions is part of a broader set of theories and strategies variously known as community accountability, community-based responses to violence, transformative justice, and restorative justice (RJ). Embedded within a social justice sector connecting progressive strands of the antiviolence, antiracist, and anti-homophobic movements, as well as those challenging the prison–industrial complex, creative interventions describes one effort within a larger movement to create solutions to interpersonal and family violence that do not engage criminal legal remedies. Using community organizing strategies, this approach looks toward the building of collective responses, mapping of allies, and use of resources available and familiar to those affected by violence to construct remedies from within the family or community.

Both authors' approaches are aligned with RJ aspirations of bringing to bear the caring and knowledge of those harmed, those who committed the harm, and the wider community in order to build trust, heal the trauma, and create the conditions for peace (Pranis, Stuart, and Wedge 2003). Many proponents of RJ do not see this approach as a replacement for the legal system but instead as a means of engaging and empowering communities with recourse to the law to safeguard human rights as needed (Braithwaite 2001; Zehr 2002). At the same time, they recognize the constant tension of aligning with state systems: Governments provide funds to services and access to people charged with offenses and at the same time limit the goals and shape the processes of organizations seeking to effect RJ (Sullivan and Tifft 2006).

In the spirit of opening conversations to address identity-laden violence, we acknowledge starting places, identify both/and positions, and seek to displace our own thinking to move toward new possibilities. Joan discusses ways in which child welfare is seeking to respond more flexibly to children and their families in addressing violence, and Mimi offers an example of a creative intervention to stop family violence in an immigrant family. Both emphasize the centrality of families and their communities in making and carrying out plans. All of this is placed within the context of national trends in child welfare, domestic violence, and immigration.

STARTING PLACES

As an American of predominantly Western European descent, Joan has the privilege that comes to those whose ancestors were early white settlers in the Colonies. At the same time, her understanding is shaped by her Quaker faith in the peace testimony, social activism to include people of diverse backgrounds, and traditions of reaching decisions through a "unity of spirit." Her participation in peace, civil rights, and feminist movements has guided her commitments, and her work with families, groups, and communities has influenced her approaches. Fresh from her graduate education in social work, she became a child protection worker and quickly found that the families with whom she worked experienced high levels of trauma from domestic violence, racism/ethnocentrism, and poverty. To counter violence within the home, she helped to establish the first shelter for abused women and children in the Canadian province of Newfoundland and Labrador. In groups with battered women, she repeatedly heard fears about leaving the safety and support of the shelter. Later in Manitoba (Canada), she co-facilitated a support group for First Nation abused women within the framework of the Medicine Wheel (Perrault, Hudson, and Pennell 1996) and learned about drawing upon cultural practices to promote nonviolence and equality. These series of experiences made her receptive to testing the model of family group conferencing that was promoted by Indigenous people in Aotearoa New Zealand for child welfare and youth justice (Hassall 1996; Love 2000). A trial demonstration of family group conferencing with family violence situations was conducted in three culturally and geographically diverse communities in Newfoundland and Labrador with positive results in safeguarding children and their mothers among Inuit, Francophone, and Anglophone families (Pennell and Burford 2000). On her return to the United States, she continued her work in family group conferencing and then family-centered meetings within child welfare and public schools in North Carolina and found both black and white families receptive to the approach (Pennell 2008b). Initially, Joan did not view her work as part of RJ because this language is infrequently referenced in child welfare and domestic violence settings. Overtime, she has come to identify with RJ, which she defines as peacemaking within and around the places called "home" (Pennell 2006a). Congruent with her Quaker traditions, she recognizes that people need to experience not only physical, sexual, and emotional safety but also cultural and spiritual safety to realize an enduring sense of peace in how they lead their lives.

Mimi's experience has been as a domestic violence advocate and community educator in immigrant anti-violence organizations, primarily within Asian immigrant communities, which have held an ambivalent relationship with state institutions. As a second-generation American of Korean heritage, Mimi is keenly aware that for immigrant survivors of violence, systems of state intervention, including the criminal justice and child welfare systems, are often perceived equally as a source of harm as of assistance. Moreover, for lesbian, gay, bisexual, and transgender people within these communities, few would consider state systems to be a viable source for help if facing intimate violence. While seeking improvements or reforms within state systems, Mimi also understands that immigrants, including those in same-gender or gender-variant relationships, who are experiencing intimate violence may be as interested in avoiding state systems as they are in getting help. Despite improved relationships with some state agencies or some personnel within these agencies, "seeking safety" often involves complex engagement with restraining order procedures, child custody processes, police reports, mandated reporting forms, and so on. As an advocate, Mimi spends as much energy minimizing harm from these systems as maximizing their benefits. She recognizes parallels with RJ concerns, but currently describes her strategies as aligned with those falling under the terms of transformative justice or community accountability. For Mimi, the term "community accountability" concerns building the capacity of community members to reach out to and support survivors and to hold perpetrators accountable for their actions (Kim 2005; see also Chapter 9 in this volume). Her preference for more pragmatic language to describe a still emerging set of principles and practices tends toward descriptions that stress reliance on communities. Alternatively, many social justice activists and advocates are turning to the term "transformative justice" (Generation Five 2007) to describe non-state interventions to violence that challenge larger oppressive structural conditions, including violence perpetrated by the state. Although these various terms are often interchangeable, Mimi values diverse characterizations reflecting diverse practices to counter tendencies to prematurely homogenize a vibrant field of alternative approaches to violence intervention. Both Joan and Mimi's positions on redressing family violence reflect trends across the United States.

We turn next to developments in child protection and domestic violence and focus on their impact for immigrant families.

NATIONAL TRENDS

During the 1980s and 1990s, the application of legal interventions to the maltreatment of children, intimate partner violence, and immigration rose. As governments reduced their social supports to families and reporting of child abuse and neglect increased, the net for child protection widened. With limited resources and escalating referrals, child welfare became increasingly restricted to forensic investigations and child removal from homes rather than supporting families in caring for their children (Kamerman and Kahn 1997). At the same time, domestic violence agencies came to rely even more on the criminal justice system, despite their distrust of the police and the courts and their concerns about zero-tolerance policies leading to the dual arrest of couples (Martin 1997; Pleck 1987). The convergence of both child protection and domestic violence programs on legal remedies heightened tensions between the two services. The greater involvement of law enforcement in domestic violence identified to the state the huge number of children exposed to violence in the home. In attempting to protect children from this harm, public child welfare was mandated to remove children simply on the grounds of witnessing the violence. Such an across-the-board approach failed to assess the actual impact on children and, thus, in many instances, compounded both the mothers' victimization and their children's traumatization (Edleson 2004).

For their part, child welfare systems identified the limitations of a child-rescue strategy that undermined rather than strengthened families (Walton, Sandau-Beckler, and Mannes 2001), disproportionately led to placement of children of color in foster homes and institutions (Roberts 2002), and raised case loads among an increasingly disgruntled and unstable workforce (U.S. General Accounting Office [GAO] 2003). Moreover, states faced financial penalties from federal reviews if they continued to fail to involve families in service planning (U.S. Department of Health and Human Services [DHHS] 2004). As a result, states began adopting differential response systems in which high-risk situations are placed on a forensic investigation track, while a family assessment track is reserved for those cases in which public child welfare must intervene, but without the same level of police and court involvement. This reform has not appeared to endanger children's safety (Waldfogel 2008). Along with this dual-track system, states have increased their use of various types of meetings to engage family and community in making and carrying out plans (Nixon, Burford, and Quinn 2005).

This has opened up some space for less adversarial and more restorative processes for children and their families. Studies in the United States and other countries report that, using such approaches, families are mobilized in support of their young relatives (Falck 2008), families' sense of cohesion increases (Walton, McKenzie, and Connolly 2005), their relations improve with workers (Kemp 2007) and school (U.S. Department of Health and Human Services [US DHHS] 2007), reliance on formal proceedings declines (Morris 2007; Walker 2005), and services at the time of the conference are accessed more readily (Weigensberg, Barth, and Guo 2008). Most significantly, these family meetings are keeping children and young persons connected to their families and culture, whether by placing siblings together, reunifying them with their families, or putting them in kin rather than nonrelative foster care (Kieley and Bussey 2001; Titcomb and LeCroy 2005; University of Washington 2007). Maintaining these connections appears to go hand in hand with enhancing the safety of children (Sawyer and Lohrbach 2008) or with no or limited impact on their safety (Edwards and Tinworth 2006; Sundell and Vinnerljung 2004). The beneficial effects seem to be particularly pronounced for Hispanic and African American families as compared with white, non-Hispanic families (Texas Department of Family and Protective Services 2006). Although these are positive developments, children whose parents are new to the country, undocumented, or both encounter additional challenges.

Beginning in the 1980s, increasingly harsh political conditions for immigrants added another set of factors for immigrants experiencing domestic violence (Fitzpatrick 1997). Immigrants were faced with concerns regarding their immigration status. Strict rulings passed under President Clinton and augmented post-9/11 raised fears of detention and deportation even for those with the protection of citizenship. Although some advocates, such as those in San Francisco, were at one time relatively comfortable assuring domestic violence survivors that arrest would not lead to deportation, this was no longer true. Regular sweeps of county jails could result in deportation for undocumented people. Deportation for immigrants convicted of felony charges dramatically increased the potential consequences for those engaging the criminal justice system.

Advocates, frequently themselves survivors of some form of intimate partner violence, faced the dilemma of weighing the potential benefits against potential harms. Their task was often to serve as an interpreter of these risks and benefits to frightened clients. And, in the case of suspected child abuse, they often found themselves reluctant but mandated reporters to a system they, themselves, did not trust. On the surface, antiviolence advocates engaged in what has been called the "coordinated community response" (Pence and Shepard 1999); that is, coordination of the nonprofit, antiviolence sector with state systems including the criminal justice system, child protective services, and the public welfare system. For immigrants, Immigration and Customs Enforcement (ICE), formerly known as Immigration and Naturalization Services (INS), could be significant state actors. In reality, advocates employed complex negotiations with these systems and their own organizational policies and procedures to provide options of most benefit to their clients.

The relationships of antiviolence organizations serving immigrant communities and child protective services were complex and uneven. Informal discussions with advocates around the country revealed an array of strategies, some organizational and others individual. While critiques of or ambivalence toward child protective services might be quite common, public discussion of strategies to avoid or negotiate involvement with this state institution were often silenced because of fears of criminal charges, loss of credentials, or other unknown threats by state agencies or other authorities. In fact, the fears and coping strategies surrounding these fears very much paralleled strategies engaged in by women seeking help but avoiding unwanted control by institutions perceived to be powerful and arbitrary.[2]

Within some organizations, advocates developed close ties to local child protective services agencies and might even use the threat of child removal to motivate women to take action to leave abusers or seek assistance. Other antiviolence organizations remained ambivalent about the benefits of child protective services, and constructed internal policies and procedures that mitigated the impact of their status as mandated reporters. For example, crisis-call policies might ask advocates to inform callers that they are required to report suspected child abuse, to provide callers with the option of concealing information regarding child abuse or be better prepared for managing the impact of an investigation by child protective services. Acting outside of their service's mandates, many advocates hid their knowledge of child abuse to avoid reporting. A surprising number of advocates were unaware that they fell under mandated reporter status and did not report through ignorance of this legal requirement.

Given these uneasy and often conflicting relationships among state institutions, domestic-violence organizations, and immigrant alliances, we now examine examples of practice within frameworks of "widening the circle" and "creative interventions."

BOTH/AND POSITIONS

The family group meetings with which Joan is involved take place with the authorization of state agencies, whereas the creative interventions that Mimi is studying are under community auspices. As our examples demonstrate, these use overlapping but different strategies for stopping family violence. Unlike much of the discourse in domestic violence circles, both emphasize the helpful role of the family. Joan refers to the meetings as "family-centered" forums in which family members and their informal networks are integral to decision making, without relinquishing state resources and protections (Pennell 2007). Mimi refers to Asian and Pacific Islander communities as benefiting from "family-style" interventions that acknowledge the familial commitments of the survivors and reflect the long-term caring and cultural ties between the women and their advocates (Kim 2002:5). Such practices as referring to professional advocates by more familial terms such as "auntie" or "sister" and blurred professional–client boundaries emphasizing shared cultural understandings—and often shared community spaces— tend to characterize antiviolence organizations operating in Asian and Pacific Islander communities. In Joan's meetings, child maltreatment has already been established by the protective authorities, and as a result, the question is not if it occurred but instead how to address it. Conversely, Mimi's interventions seek to remain outside the state system and are thus more amenable to addressing violence between adult partners than against a minor in a legal context requiring reports of suspected child abuse and neglect (Kim 2002).

Joan has found that family members and their service providers view the meetings as advancing the leadership of the families, including in situations of family violence (Pennell and Anderson 2005). Building a context of cultural safety in which family groups can speak in their own language and access their traditional practices goes hand in hand with increasing physical and emotional safety at meetings (Pennell 2004). Notably, inviting different sides of the family to the meetings promotes stronger systems of evaluating and monitoring the outcomes and more timely approvals of plans by child protection (Pennell 2006b). Having both survivors and perpetrators at the same meetings, however, raises concerns regarding safety before, during, and after the meetings. For this reason, focus groups were conducted in North Carolina with domestic violence advocates, abused women, and shelter staff to inquire about safety concerns and safety strategies at family meetings (Pennell and Francis 2005). Building upon this earlier work, interviews and focus groups were held with North Carolinian child protection workers and meeting facilitators, who reported that referrals commonly pertain to family violence, and a number of steps are being taken to enhance the safety of participants (Pennell 2007).

These steps include consulting with the survivor on whom to invite; checking if a protective order is in place and respecting its stipulations; if necessary and permissible, having the offender join the meeting by telephone, or holding separate or staggered meetings; negotiating ground rules for the meetings; checking with the family on where and when to hold the meeting; notifying police to be on stand by; strategically using breaks to ease tensions; inviting support persons, domestic violence advocates, or therapists to attend; having a second facilitator; and providing copies of the plan to all participants while ensuring that safety measures for the survivors are kept confidential (Pennell 2007). A meeting facilitator observed, "Social workers are not warmed to [the meetings], but the families like the process" and "the family becomes proactive after the meeting and says 'the next time it happens, call me before it gets too serious.'" The safety steps demonstrate concerted efforts by some child protective programs to widen the circle and engage family and community as safely and effectively as possible in the planning process, and these efforts elicit positive responses from families. At the same time, the numerous steps required demonstrate how much effort must go into organizing such planning forums under state sponsorship and the unease of many workers and their agencies with their liability if participants become violent or if the plans fail to protect the children.

Locating creative interventions in situations of family violence is more problematic, in large part because of the previously discussed mandatory reporting of child maltreatment in the United States. Mimi's example, described next, demonstrates both the effectiveness of a creative intervention and its covert nature when the subject is an immigrant family. Case 1 is constructed from interviews that Mimi has held with various domestic violence advocates describing the complex factors and considerations that come into play when working with immigrant communities experiencing family violence.

Case 1

A middle-aged women with two children called an immigrant agency for help. She had been beaten brutally by her husband for almost 20 years. Her concern, however, was not for her own safety. Like many women, she believed that her role was to endure her husband's violence for the sake of her marriage and the well-being of her children. She finally called for help because her son, despondent after years of humiliation and abuse from her husband, had retreated into a deep depression. She feared that he was suicidal.

This woman revealed years of extreme violence by her husband but worried about her son's happiness and survival. Her son, no longer a minor, was not subject to mandated reporting requirements. However, the woman also talked about a daughter, still in her pre-teen years, whose behavior indicated signs of possible sexual abuse by the father. Although the woman did not witness direct abuse, she saw how her daughter became violent in her presence when her father touched her in any way. This woman showed much more concern for the welfare of her son than her daughter, but when allowed the opportunity to discuss more of the details of the lives of her children, the possibility of her daughter's sexual abuse was revealed.

In relaying this story, the advocate, as a mandated reporter, shared that her suspicion of child sexual abuse required her to call child protective services. But she also discussed her reluctance. If she had identified her role as a mandated reporter, she was certain that this woman would have retreated from her. Previous to this call, the woman had not revealed details of her life with anyone. The advocate did not want to raise any reason for distrust that would inhibit the woman from sharing important information with her.

In addition, the woman and her family were undocumented. The family's undocumented status is significant in several ways. First, their status prevented them from seeking help for fear that they would be discovered and deported. The woman's attempt to reach out was a significant step for her. Reports to legal authorities could have closed the door to her openness to further help. Second, reporting abuse to child protective services exposed the father to criminal charges, thereby threatening his status. The woman needed to weigh the cost of possible exposure of the entire family to Immigration and Customs Enforcement and deportation when considering any options. Likewise, the advocate considered these possibilities when balancing her legal mandate to report to child protective services against the potential negative consequences of deportation for the father and the whole family.

In considering the option of not reporting despite this legal requirement, the advocate decided that the best way to protect the daughter was to strengthen the capacity of the mother to provide protection. Ceding this authority to child protective services would likely diminish the protective powers of the mother and withdraw her trust in the advocate, thereby eliminating the possibility for the advocate to act on behalf of the daughter. Although child protective services is meant to protect children, experience with this agency showed that its involvement was much more likely to result in the withdrawal of the family as a means to protect the perpetrator of violence.

The woman and her son decided together that their best option was to send the son back to the home country. She was going to accompany him to make sure he settled into a comfortable situation and reduced his depression. She was less concerned about the welfare of the daughter, whom she was going to leave with the father. The advocate convinced her of her duty to protect her daughter and reminded her of the fears that the woman had herself raised. The woman agreed that taking both her son and daughter to the home country was a better option.

Although this creative intervention occurred without state intervention, it was shaped throughout by such a possibility. We turn now to examining how praxis displaces our logics on stopping family violence.

DISPLACING THINKING THROUGH FEMINIST PRAXIS

Every theory of change has its own logic and thus elevates one strategy over others. Joan's concept of widening the circle is based on a feminist praxis (Pennell and Burford 2002). She starts from the position that the entrapment and abuse of women within the privacy of the home were challenged by women's leadership in advocating for reforms. This, in turn, led to efforts to invoke state sanctions against men who batter, but also to penalties against abused mothers and the removal of their children. Out of this conundrum came appeals for a coordinated response that joined the efforts of government and community organizations. None of these, though, included the family as full partners. Thus was formed the desire to widen the circle to include familial and cultural networks. Not surprisingly, much of this push came from Indigenous people based on their cultural traditions (Bushie 1997; Glode and Wien 2006; McCaslin 2005; Rangihau 1986; Strega and Carrière 2009).

Joan welcomes Mimi's creative interventions that point out the limitations of operating in partnership with state institutions. She respects that Mimi's understanding is grounded in the experiences of Asian and Pacific Islander families, especially in the context of the increasing control and expulsions by Immigration and Customs Enforcement. Her creative interventions thus serve to challenge Joan's articulation of widening the circle, which assumes the inclusion of criminal legal and child welfare systems within that circle. Rather, Mimi poses the question: In what circumstances would it be best to constrict the perimeter of the circle and exclude state agencies? Nonetheless, children and abusive men remain problematic in Mimi's creative interventions (Kim 2005): How can these interventions ensure the protection of children while helping them learn to stand up for themselves? And in working for change, how can these meetings include abusive men without further endangering the women and children?

For her part, Mimi has benefited greatly from Joan's extensive experience in engaging families, violence intervention organizations, and the child welfare system in her "widening the circle" approach to family violence. She appreciates that Joan's collaborations with the criminal legal and child welfare systems have afforded a breadth and depth of on-the-ground RJ practice that has greatly increased the knowledge of how to build a family's capacity to transform violence. While questioning the reliance on state systems, Mimi nevertheless values the years of practice and documentation surrounding an approach that centers the leadership of families and builds upon a fundamental belief that families harmed by violence are able to construct viable solutions. She views her ongoing dialogue and collaboration with Joan as a rich resource for families and communities engaged in building alternative interventions to violence.

In reaching the limits of their own logics, Joan and Mimi both reference cultural traditions. Mimi appeals to the importance of extended family and community leaders in playing a critical role in defining and maintaining community norms (Kim 2002:17). Joan proposes creating a context of cultural safety in family meetings, so that participants can access traditional ways to resolve issues, such as family elders transmitting cultural practices so that the family group members can develop competency in their own culture. Given the heterosexist assumptions of so many cultural groups, both creative interventions and widening the circle struggle to address same-sex unions. Given such cultural biases, Mimi and Joan emphasize the importance of upholding human rights to safeguard adult and child survivors.

Nevertheless, displacing logics serves to draw attention to other strategies. Widening the circle can mean intervening creatively to change norms and practices in child welfare. This may take the form of embedding domestic violence advocates within social services to advise staff, or including youth and adults who have experienced family-centered meetings as part of the training team for child welfare workers (Pennell 2008a). Widening the circle may mean creatively engaging men who batter in being responsible fathers (cf. Edleson and Williams 2007). The links between child maltreatment, animal cruelty, and domestic violence are well established (Randour 2008). Still, some men may more readily identify the impact of their violence on their children and animals before they can do so for their intimate partners. The family-centered meetings can be a means of determining if a fathering program is a suitable option and if so, how to ensure a coordinated response that safeguards all family members while the men participate in such a program. For still other men, empathy may be better developed through animal-assisted interventions that build a sense of connections. These are strategies yet to be tested. Multiplying the possibilities continues the conversation across cultural, gender, and generational divides while maintaining a steadfast commitment to engaging families and communities in stopping the violence.

ACKNOWLEDGMENTS

Joan Pennell wishes to acknowledge the dedicated staff of the North Carolina Family-Centered Meetings Project and funding by the North Carolina Division of Social Services and North Carolina Department of Public Instruction. Mimi Kim thanks fellow colleagues at Creative Interventions, Incite! Women of Color Against Violence, Asian Women's Shelter, Shimtuh, Narika, Generation Five, Critical Resistance, and DataCenter.

REFERENCES

Braithwaite, John. 2001. *Restorative Justice and Responsive Regulation*. New York: Oxford University Press.

Bushie, Berma. 1997. "A Personal Journey." In *The Four Circles of Hollow Water*. Hull, Quebec: Aboriginal Peoples Collection, Aboriginal Corrections Policy Unit, Supply and Services Canada, JS5–1/15–1997E.

Edleson, Jeffrey L. 2004. "Should Childhood Exposure to Adult Domestic Violence Be Defined as Child Maltreatment Under the Law?" Pp. 8–29 in *Protecting Children from Domestic Violence: Strategies for Community Intervention,* edited by Peter G. Jaffe, Linda L. Baker, and Alison J. Cunningham. New York: Guilford Press.

Edleson, Jeffrey L. and Oliver J. Williams, eds. 2007. *Parenting by Men Who Batter: New Directions for Assessment and Intervention*. New York: Oxford University Press.

Edwards, Myles and Kathleen Tinworth (with Gale Burford and Joan Pennell). 2006. *Family Team Meeting (FTM) Process, Outcome, and Impact Evaluation: Phase II Report*. Englewood, CO: American Humane Association.

Falck, Sturla. 2008. *Do Family Group Conferences Lead to a Better Situation for the Children Involved?* Oslo, Norway: NOVA (Norwegian Social Research). Ministry of Education and Research.

Fitzpatrick, Joan. 1997. "The Gender Dimensions of U.S. Immigration Policy." *Yale Journal of Law and Feminism* 9: 23–49.

Generation Five. 2007. *Toward Transformative Justice: A Liberatory Approach to Child Sexual Abuse and Other Forms of Intimate and Community. Violence.* San Francisco: Author.

Glode, Joan and Fred Wien. 2006. *Evaluating the Family Group Conferencing Approach in a First Nations Context: Some Initial Findings.* Halifax, NS: Mi'kmaq Family and Children's Services and School of Social Work, Dalhousie University.

Hassall, Ian. 1996. "Origin and Development of Family Group Conferences." Pp. 17–36 in *Family Group Conferences: Perspectives on Policy and Practice,* edited by Joe Hudson, Allison Morris, Gabrielle Maxwell, and Burt Galaway. Monsey, NY: Willow Tree Press.

Kamerman, Sheila B. and Alfred J. Kahn, eds. 1997. *Children and Their Families in Big Cities: Strategies for Service Reform.* New York: Columbia University Press.

Kemp, Tony. 2007. *Family Welfare Conferences—The Wexford Experience: An Evaluation of Barnardos Family Welfare Conference Project.* Ballincollig, County Cork, Republic of Ireland: Nucleus.

Kiely, Patricia and Kay Bussey. 2001. *Family Group Conferencing: A Longitudinal Evaluation.* Sydney: Macquarie University.

Kim, Mimi. 2002. *Innovative Strategies to Address Domestic Violence in Asian and Pacific Islander Communities: Examining Themes, Models and Interventions.* San Francisco, CA: Asian & Pacific Islander Institute on Domestic Violence.

———. 2005. *The Community Engagement Continuum: Outreach, Mobilization, Organizing and Accountability to Address Violence Against Women in Asian and Pacific Islander Communities.* San Francisco, CA: Asian & Pacific Islander Institute on Domestic Violence.

———. 2006. "Alternative Interventions to Violence: Creative Interventions." *International Journal of Narrative Therapy and Community Work* No. 4: 45–52.

Love, Catherine. 2000. "Family Group Conferencing: Cultural Origins, Sharing, and Appropriation—A Maori Reflection." Pp. 15–30 in *Family Group Conferencing: New Directions in Community-Centered Child & Family Practice,* edited by Gale Burford and Joe Hudson. New York: Aldine de Gruyter.

Martin, Margaret E. 1997. "Policy Promise: Community Policing and Domestic Violence Victims Satisfaction." *Policing: An International Journal of Police Strategies & Management* 20: 519–31.

McCaslin, Wanda D., ed. 2005. *Justice as Healing: Indigenous Ways.* St. Paul, MN: Living Justice Press.

Morris, Kate. 2007. *Camden FGC Service: An Evaluation of Service Use and Outcomes.* Edgbaston, Birmingham, UK: University of Birmingham, Institute of Applied Social Studies.

Nixon, Paul and Gale Burford and Andrew Quinn (with Josh Edelbaum). 2005. *A Survey of International Practices, Policy & Research on Family Group Conferencing and Related Practices.* Retrieved August 26, 2006 (http://www.americanhumane.org/site/DocServer/FGDM_www_survey.pdf?docID=2841).

Pence, Ellen L. and Melanie L. Shepard. 1999. "An Introduction: Developing a Coordinated Community Response." Pp. 3–23 in *Coordinating Community*

Responses to Domestic Violence: Lessons from Duluth and Beyond, edited by
Melanie F. Shepard and Ellen Pence. Thousand Oaks, CA: Sage.

Pennell, Joan. 2004. "Family Group Conferencing in Child Welfare: Responsive and
Regulatory Interfaces." *Journal of Sociology and Social Welfare* 31:117–135.

———. 2006a. "Culture, Safety, and Family Violence: Restorative Justice as
Peacemaking." Pp. 81–93 in *New Frontiers in Restorative Justice: A
Reviewed Selection of Conference Papers,* edited by Warwick Tie, Shirley
Jülich, and Vicky Walters. Auckland, NZ: Massey University, Center for
Justice and Peace Development, School of Social and Cultural Studies.

———. 2006b. "Stopping Domestic Violence or Protecting Children?
Contributions from Restorative Justice." Pp. 286–298 in *Handbook of
Restorative Justice: A Global Perspective,* edited by Dennis Sullivan and Larry
Tifft. New York: Routledge.

——— (with Amy Coppedge, Jenny King, and Cherie Spehar). 2007. *North
Carolina Family-Centered Meetings Project: Annual Report to the North
Carolina Division of Social Services, Fiscal Year 2006–2007.* Raleigh, NC:
North Carolina State University, Department of Social Work, North
Carolina Family-Centered Meetings Project.

——— (with Amy Coppedge and Jenny King). 2008a. *North Carolina Family-
Centered Meetings Project: Annual Report to the North Carolina Division of
Social Services, Fiscal Year 2007–2008: Summary and Projections.* Raleigh, NC:
North Carolina State University, Center for Family & Community
Engagement. Retrieved February 28, 2009 (http://www.cfface.org/dss/
documents/07–08DSSAR_SumProj_9–12–08jp.pdf).

——— (with Kara Allen-Eckard, Susan Gasman, Raymond Kirk, Marianne Latz,
Billy Poindexter, and Anne Wakefield). 2008b. *School-based Child and Family
Teams Project: Summary Report to the North Carolina Department of Public
Instruction, Fiscal Years 2006–2007 and 2007- 2008.* Raleigh, NC: North
Carolina State University, Center for Family & Community Engagement.
Retrieved February 28, 2009 (http://www.cfface.org/dpi/documents/06–
08DPIAR_2YrSummaryReport_8–28–08jp.pdf).

Pennell, Joan and Gary Anderson, eds. 2005. *Widening the Circle: The Practice and
Evaluation of Family Group Conferencing with Children, Youths, and Their
Families.* Washington, DC: NASW Press.

Pennell, Joan and Gale Burford. 1994. "Widening the Circle: The Family Group
Decision Making Project." *Journal of Child & Youth Care* 9(1):1–12.

———. 2000. "Family Group Decision Making: Protecting Children and
Women." *Child Welfare* 79:131–158.

———. 2002. "Feminist Praxis, Making Family Group Conferencing Work."
Pp. 108–127 in *Restorative Justice and Family Violence: New Ideas and
Learning from the Past,* edited by Heather Strang and John Braithwaite.
Cambridge, UK: Cambridge University Press.

Pennell, Joan and Stephanie Francis. 2005. "Safety Conferencing: Toward a
Coordinated and Inclusive Response to Safeguard Women and Children."
Violence Against Women 11:666–692.

Perrault, Sharon, Betsy Hudson, and Joan Pennell. 1996. "Having a Balance."
Pp. 24–32 in *Community Research as Empowerment: Feminist Links,
Postmodern Interruptions,* by Janice L. Ristock and Joan Pennell. Toronto:
Oxford University Press.

Pleck, Elizabeth. 1987. *Domestic Tyranny: The Making of Social Policy Against Family Violence from Colonial Times to the Present.* New York: Oxford University Press.

Pranis, Kay, Barry Stuart, and Mark Wedge. 2003. *Peacemaking Circles: From Crime to Community.* St. Paul, MN: Living Justice Press.

Randour, Mary Lou (with Howard Davidson). 2008. *A Common Bond: Maltreated Children and Animals in the Home: Guidelines for Practice and Policy.* Englewood, CO: American Humane Association.

Rangihau, John. 1986. *Pau-te-Ata-tu (Daybreak): Report of the Ministerial Advisory Committee on a Maori Perspective for the Department of Social Welfare.* Wellington, NZ: Department of Social Welfare, Government Printing Office.

Roberts, Dorothy. 2002. *Shattered Bonds: The Color of Child Welfare.* New York: Basic Books.

Sawyer, Robert Q and Susan Lohrbach. 2008. *Olmsted County Child and Family Services: Family Involvement Strategies.* Rochester, MN: Olmsted Country Child & Family Services.

Strega, Susan and Jeannine Carrière, eds. 2009. *Walking This Path Together: Anti-Racist and Anti-Oppressive Child Welfare Practice.* Black Point, Nova Scotia: Fernwood.

Sullivan, Dennis and Larry Tifft. 2006. "Introduction: The Healing Dimension of Restorative Justice: A One-World Body." Pp. 1–16 in *Handbook of Restorative Justice: A Global Perspective,* edited by Dennis Sullivan and Larry Tifft. New York: Routledge.

Sundell, Knut and Bo Vinnerljung. 2004. "Outcomes of Family Group Conferencing in Sweden: A 3-Year Follow-Up." *Child Abuse & Neglect* 28:267–287.

Texas Department of Family and Protective Services. 2006, October. *Family Group Decision-Making: Final Evaluation.* Retrieved December 27, 2006 (http://www.dfps.state.tx.us/Documents/about/pdf/2006–10–09_ FGDM_ Evaluation.pdf).

Titcomb, Allison and Craig LeCroy. 2005. "Outcomes of Arizona's Family Group Decision Making Program." *Protecting Children* 19:47–53.

United States Department of Health and Human Services (US DHHS), Administration for Children and Families, Administration on Children, Youth, and Families, Children's Bureau. 2004. *General Findings from the Fedral Child and Family Services Review.* Updated September 9, 2004. Retrieved February 28, 2009 (http://www.acf.hhs.gov/programs/cb/ cwmonitoring/results/genfindings04/index.htm).

———. 2007, June 25. *Final Report: North Carolina Child and Family Services Review.* Retrieved April 27, 2008 (http://www.ncdhhs.gov/dss/stats/docs/ NC%20CFSR%202007%20Final%20 Report.pdf).

United States General Accounting Office (US GAO). 2003. *Child Welfare: HHS Could Play a Greater Role in Helping Child Welfare Agencies Recruit and Retain Staff.* Washington, DC: US GAO.

University of Washington, School of Social Work, Northwest Institute for Children and Families and Catalyst for Kids. 2007. *Finding Our Roots: Family Group Conferencing in Washington.* Seattle, WA: Author.

Waldfogel, Jane. 2008. "The Future of Child Protection Revisited." Pp. 235–241 in *Child Welfare Research: Advances for Practice and Policy,* edited by Duncan Lindsey and Aron Shlonsky. New York: Oxford University Press.

Walker, Lorenn. 2005. "A Cohort Study of 'Ohana Conferencing in Child Abuse and Neglect Cases." *Protecting Children* 19:36–46.

Walton, Elaine, M. McKenzie, and Marie Connolly. 2005. "Private Family Time: The Heart of Family Group Conferencing." *Protecting Children* 19:17–24.

Walton, Elaine, Patricia Sandau-Beckler, and Marc Mannes, eds. 2001. *Balancing Family-Centered Services and Child Well-Being: Exploring Issues in Policy, Practice, Theory, and Research.* New York: Columbia University Press.

Weigensberg, Elizabeth C., Richard P. Barth, and Shenyang Guo. 2008. "Family Group Decision Making: A Propensity Score Analysis to Evaluate Child and Family Services at Baseline and After 36-months." *Children and Youth Services Review* 31:383–390.

Zehr, Howard. 2002. *The Little Book of Restorative Justice.* Intercourse, PA: Good Books.

9

ALTERNATIVE INTERVENTIONS TO INTIMATE VIOLENCE
Defining Political and Pragmatic Challenges

Mimi Kim

We live in a town, but many of my husband's whanau (extended family) live in the valley where he grew up, about 40 kilometers away. My husband and his brother are renowned for a number of things—one being how they extend the life of their cars and vans using highly technical items like string and wire—another for how they share these vehicles for a variety of tasks such as moving furniture or transporting relatives, building materials, tractor parts, rongoa (traditional herbal medicines), eels, vegetables, dogs, and pigs (dead or alive). They are renowned for being people of the people, the ones to call on in times of trouble and death, the ones who will solve the problem and make the plan. They travel to and from town, to the coast to dive for seafood, to endless meetings, to visit whanau—along the many kilometers of dirt roads in and around the valley, through flood or dust depending on the season, in those patched up, beat up, prized cars.

There are a number of things to know about the valley—one is that the last 33 children in the world of their hapu ririki (small subtribe) to grow up and be educated on their own lands go to school here, despite government efforts to close the school. Another is that the valley is known to outsiders and insiders as "patu wahine"—literally meaning "to beat women," and this is not said as a joke. The mountain for this valley is named as the doorway spirits pass through on their way to their final departure from this life. This valley is also the valley where my husband and his siblings were beaten at school for speaking their first language. It is the valley their mother sent them to so they would be safe from their father—back to her people. It is where they milked cows, pulled a plow, fed pigs but often went hungry, and were stock whipped, beaten, and worse.

My brother-in-law still lives in the valley, in a group of houses next to the school. So it's no surprise that one of our cars would be parked by these houses—right by where the children play. Perhaps also not a surprise that while playing that time old international game of rock throwing our eight-year-old nephew shattered the back window of the car. If I'd been listening, I probably would have heard the "oh" and "ah" of the other children that accompanied the sound of glass breaking from town, and if I'd been really tuned in I would have heard the rapid, frightened heartbeat of "that boy" as well.

His mother is my husband's cousin—and she was on the phone to us right away. She was anxious to assure us "that boy" would get it when his father came home. His father is a big man, with a pig hunter's hands who hoists his pigs onto a meat hook unaided. He is man of movement and action, not a man for talking. Those hands would carry all the force of proving that he was a man who knew how to keep his children in their place. Beating "that boy" would be his way of telling us that he had also learned his own childhood lessons well.

So, before he got home we burned up the phone lines—sister to sister, cousin to cousin, brother-in-law to sister-in-law, wife to husband, brother to brother. This was because my husband and his brother know that some lessons you are taught as a child should not be passed on. The sound of calloused hand on tender flesh, the whimpers of watching sisters, the smell of your own fear, the taste of your own blood and sweat as you lie in the dust—useless, useless, better not born. This is a curriculum like no other. A set of lessons destined to repeat unless you are granted the grace of insight and choose to embrace new learning.

So, when the father of "that boy" came home and heard the story of the window, "that boy" was protected by our combined aroha (love) and good humor, by the presence of a senior uncle, by invitations to decide how to get the window fixed in the shortest time for the least money. Once again phone calls were exchanged, with an agreement being made on appropriate restitution. How a barrel of diesel turns into a car window is a story for another time.

Next time my husband drove into the valley it was to pick up the car, and "that boy" was an anxious witness to his arrival. My husband also has very big hands, hands that belong to a man who has spent most of his life outdoors. These were the hands that reached out to "that boy" to hug, not hurt.

A lot of bad things still happen in the valley, but more and more they are being named and resisted. Many adults who learned their early lessons there will never return. For tangata whenua (people of the land) this is profound loss—our first identifiers on meeting are not our own names but those of our mountains, rivers, hapu (subtribe), and iwi (tribe). To be totally separate from these is a dislocation of spirit for the already wounded. This is only a small story that took place in an unknown valley, not marked on many maps. When these small stories are told and repeated so our lives join and connect,

when we choose to embrace new learning and use our "bigness" to heal not hurt, then we are growing grace and wisdom on the earth.
—He Korero Iti (A Small Story) submitted to The StoryTelling &
Organizing Project, a project of Creative Interventions, by
Di Grennell, Whangarei, Aotearoa-New Zealand.

Creative Interventions was established in Oakland, California in 2004 as a resource center to create and promote community-based interventions to intimate and interpersonal violence, in alignment with the liberatory goals of the social justice movement. The motivations for this endeavor stem from multiple concerns spanning from political to pragmatic, each pointing toward an approach to violence intervention that, for now, this organization refers to as "community-based interventions to violence." Although Creative Interventions is grounded in the needs and experiences of communities of color and immigrant and lesbian, gay, bisexual, transgender (queer) communities, the implications of its work transcend the specificity of these oppressed communities and are intended to challenge prevailing conventions within the antiviolence and social justice movements.

At the heart of Creative Interventions is the deeply held belief that our approach to violence intervention must be guided by the knowledge held by everyday people, carried out by those closest to and most impacted by violence, and situated in the very spaces and places where violence occurs—within our homes, neighborhoods, and communities. Looking straight into the face of violence perpetrated upon those we love, live with, raise, and grow old with provides an opportunity for us to disentangle ourselves from the madness that guides our world today and free ourselves to come together as co-creators of a future closer to that which so many of us dream.

We live at a time when communities face unprecedented rates of dislocation and devastation. Domestic violence, sexual abuse, child abuse, and other forms of intimate and interpersonal violence result from community conditions of increasing economic, social, and environmental degradation and contribute to their deterioration. We yearn for community while deeply distrusting those very people with whom we live and work. We look for community and often find only scattered remains. Thus we have created a system outside of community—in shelters, advocacy centers, child welfare systems, foster care homes, prisons—to protect us from violence, complete with a qualified set of experts to manage our way toward that mirage called safety.

Community education and publicity campaigns reach out to communities, heightening awareness about intimate violence and asking us to take a stand. However, community education merely informs us how to recognize violence, how to provide emotional support to survivors of violence, and where to call to "end violence." This end to violence is to be found in a program that may not speak our language, a restraining order that may ask us to leave someone whom we do not wish to leave, a lawyer who may be able to process our divorce for a cost we cannot afford, or the police who may decide to arrest the perpetrator of violence or who may even end up arresting us.

The community-based interventions approach turns back to community, not expecting a healthy, thriving, cooperative set of family members, friends, neighbors, or congregation members, but rather an incomplete and imperfect collection of individuals connected in some way to a situation of intimate violence that we assume at least some are motivated to end. Whether defined by family ties, geography, identity, workplace, religion, or merely by convenience or happenstance, many of us remain connected to others in ways that form the basis for concern and collective action.

The community-based intervention model is fundamentally an organizing model. It seizes upon the opportunities offered by violence, rather than succumbing to its disintegrating effects. It shifts attention and resources back toward those directly impacted by violence, beyond individual survivors and perpetrators, to engage circles of friends, families, and communities. Through the process of coming together to address violence, identify the problem, map allies, create common goals, and coordinate a plan of action and response, communities in their various formations can create a new set of norms, practices, and relationships to not only end violence but to build community health.

What models of violence intervention can we create to support caring and motivated individuals to come together and take effective action to end violence, replacing it with a shared commitment to safety and healing? How can we provide adequate information, skills-building, and accessible resources to strengthen these systems enough to be effective in sustaining the necessary long-term strategies? How can we learn from these strategies and share successes with other communities, thus expanding our collective capacity to end violence?

Communities already have a lot to tell us. The StoryTelling & Organizing Project of Creative Interventions, in collaboration with DataCenter, Generation Five, and individuals and organizations across the country, is collecting stories from everyday people who have already come together to try to end violence. These stories such as *He Korero Iti* (A Small Story) that introduces this chapter excavate the wisdom embedded in otherwise neglected and forgotten community memory to inspire and inform us on the creative and courageous efforts of everyday people.

The antiviolence movement in the United States and across the globe offers many lessons about the ways in which survivors transform victimization into a sense of power, about the complexity and persistence of patterns of abuse, and about how some perpetrators have changed their own behaviors so that they can enjoy relationships based upon respect and equality rather than power and control.

We begin with this partnership among grassroots communities, the antiviolence movement, and the broader social justice movement to build toward an alternative response to intimate violence. And we take advantage of the structure and resources of an organization committed to long-term social change to transform these lessons and experiences into accessible community resources. In this way, we contribute to ongoing efforts to build a new set of community-based knowledge and practices that may some day become as familiar as violence is today.

POLITICAL AND PROGRAMMATIC LINEAGE

Creative Interventions is just one among a growing community of individuals and organizations working toward alternative social justice responses to intimate and interpersonal violence. Although the Creative Interventions project is based on practical, down-to-earth models of community-based interventions to violence that can be carried out by individuals, organizations, and community institutions, this work is situated within a broader context of emerging conceptual and political frameworks. A landscape of alternative interventions to violence is developing throughout various sectors of the social justice movement. Constantly shifting, evolving, and renaming itself, this landscape currently includes such formations as "transformative justice" as articulated by Generation Five (Generation Five 2007) and Critical Resistance in the United States, and a broad movement of organizations and individuals throughout Canada, Australia, and New Zealand-Aotearoa (Second Maori Taskforce on Whanau Violence 2004). "Harm free zones" constitute a set of principles and practices developed by a coalition of New York community-based social justice organizations challenging state, intimate, and community violence (Harm Free Zone [n.d.]). The more general term "community accountability," is used by Incite! Women of Color Against Violence (Incite! 2003, 2005, 2006) and other social justice organizations (Communities Against Rape & Abuse [CARA] 2008; Kim 2002, 2005, 2006) to describe a wider array of practices challenging interpersonal violence and other forms of violence outside of the context of the state.

Although those working within the sphere of restorative justice (RJ) have engaged many similar concerns (Coker 1999, 2002; Pennell and Anderson 2005; Pennell and Burford 2002; Pranis 2002; Strang and Braithwaite 2002), antiviolence advocates and social justice activists have been largely removed from such discussions and practices. Indeed, many of the alternative frameworks have developed, in part, as a response to the perceived limitations of RJ concepts and practices (Generation Five 2007; Second Maori Taskforce on Whanau Violence 2004; Smith 2005). This book offers a much needed opportunity for dialogue across these terrains.

Creative Interventions also draws upon the concrete programmatic advances of many sister organizations in the movement led by women of color, immigrant, and/or queer women. These include Communities

Against Rape and Abuse (CARA 2008) and Northwest Network of Bi, Trans, Lesbian and Gay Survivors of Abuse in Seattle (Incite! 2003; Smith 2005); Institute for Family Services in Somerset, New Jersey (Almeida, Dolan-Del Vecchio, and Parker 1999; Almeida and Durkin 1999); Audre Lorde Project and Sista II Sista in Brooklyn (Incite! 2003; Smith 2005); Freedom, Inc. in Madison, Wisconsin (Kim 2005); Caminar Latino in Atlanta (Perilla, Lavizzo, and Ibanez 2007; Perilla and Perez 2002); and Sharon Spencer's Men's Program and Ke Ala Lokahi in Hawaii (Kim 2005). Despite the marginalized or invisible status of many of these achievements, the resulting experiences and innovations hold wisdom for the diversity of oppressed classes and communities that constitute the majority of the U.S. population.

Although these frameworks and programs have arisen as positive advances in struggles to address and end violence in its many forms in alignment with a broader social justice vision, they are also a response to the limitations of the conventional antiviolence movement. In this chapter, I outline how the "binary logic" of the conventional antiviolence model aligns with individualistic and state-based remedies. I follow with the alternative vision of intersectionality and the radical challenges represented by Incite! Women of Color Against Violence, Critical Resistance, and other organizations challenging interpersonal and state violence. I end with some observations based upon the early experiences of Creative Interventions and posit current successes and contradictions presented in a community-based intervention approach to intimate and interpersonal violence.

THE BINARY LOGIC OF THE CONVENTIONAL FEMINIST MODEL

The prevailing feminist model of violence intervention follows a familiar coherence and logic. The dominant ideology within our culture and sub-cultures, whether within a white middle-class suburb of Cleveland, a Korean immigrant community in Los Angeles, or an African American neighborhood in Baltimore, remains decidedly patriarchal. Men's lives are valued over women's; male-defined values determine dominant societal and subculture values; violence or the threat of violence continues to be the way in which these values are maintained and enforced. Denial, mini-mizing, and victim-blaming in the face of all forms of intimate violence remain rampant even in the most politically progressive communities. Those whose sexual orientation or gender identity fail to conform to the conventional appearances or practices of heterosexual masculinity and femininity face invisibility, marginalization, and endangerment not only within abusive intimate relationships but throughout the spaces and insti-tutions of everyday life. They likewise fall out of the very conceptualization of patriarchy and the liberatory framework of conventional feminism.

To counter these ideological and institutional patterns of patriarchy, the antiviolence movement has embraced the division of gender and turned it on its head, thus privileging the voices and perspectives of women. Championing those women who have suffered physical, sexual, emotional, and economic violence at the hands of men and the demands of patriarchy, it has designated such forms of intimate violence as "gender-based." Domestic violence, sexual assault, sexual harassment, and child sexual abuse—formerly private, invisible, unnamed, and unchallenged matters— have risen to the forefront of public discussion and policy, although with contradictory results.

Safety and protection for women and girls have become paramount principles in the face of what has been experienced as an overarching pattern of physical, sexual, economic, and emotional violence at all levels of society. Gender-based violence is not only perpetrated by abusive family members, intimate partners, and other individuals. It is maintained, supported, or encouraged by a community that often colludes with violence and by a state that often responds with actions and policies paralleling or further contributing to the harms inflicted by more intimate perpetrators.

In an effort to challenge the denial, minimizing, and victim-blaming expressed by male perpetrators of violence and reinforced by colluding community members, the antiviolence movement has held a strong us– them position based upon the divisions of gender. "We" as women are the victims or survivors of intimate violence or the advocates for survivors of violence. "They" are male perpetrators of gender-based violence or those who collude with the abuses of patriarchy. The framework for our understanding of gender-based violence is thus situated within an assumption of a conventionally gendered and heterosexually defined context. Although we may contend that violence results from unequal power dynamics embedded within these structures and categories, we often fail to question the categories themselves.

The antiviolence movement has long been criticized for its universalist categories of women, which silently presume white, heterosexual, middle-class, Christian, able-bodied, U.S.-born, English-speaking characteristics. Despite some colorization within the antiviolence movement, today's leadership, prevailing program designs, and policies remain largely driven and defined by this same constituency.

Patriarchal, white-supremacist, heterosexist notions of gender further define victims deserving protection as those who conform to this idealized norm (Kanuha 1996). Those deviating from this norm face reduced access to the institutions of protection and are even subject to persecution by these same systems (Richie 1996; Ritchie 2006; Smith 2005). Behind the bureaucratic language of "underserved" or "under-represented" communities lies the complex system of attitudes, procedures, policies, and laws that constitute the institutionalized systems of oppression that we more familiarly name as racism, sexism, classism, ableism, and so on.

Within the antiviolence social service sector, lack of access manifests itself in many different forms. In many communities, lack of access means complete unavailability of services. "Lack of access" can also be embedded in program practices and policies, such as screening processes designed to exclude "difficult/nonconforming" clients. Women who do not speak English are still denied shelter because they cannot participate in their support groups; undocumented women are still told that funding does not permit them access to services; women racially profiled as drug users are still routinely screened with tyrannical scrutiny; persons who fall outside the conventional definitions of sexual orientation or gender identity are often left with no options whatsoever or vulnerable to further dangers of homophobia or transphobia within those spaces meant to deliver safety.

THE ANTIVIOLENCE MOVEMENT AND THE STATE

For many sectors of the antiviolence movement, the involvement of the state as an active agent in violence intervention and prevention follows an evolutionary process initiated by antiviolence advocates challenging the state's policies and practices of collusion with perpetrators of intimate violence. In the struggle to get state systems to "take violence against women seriously," advocates and activists have pushed for local, state, and federal legislation supporting the increased criminalization of acts of domestic violence and sexual assault. Changes in legislation have been accompanied by antiviolence advocate participation in police and judicial trainings, in an effort to "sensitize" these state agents to the issues facing survivors of violence and to their responsibility in enforcing laws meant to enhance protection for survivors of violence and increase penalties for perpetrators.

This reformist strategy has resulted in increasing collaboration between the antiviolence sector and the state. Advocacy led to legislative and procedural gains, followed by partnerships between advocates and the state as these changes were negotiated and implemented into practice. Relative successes, particularly within the domestic violence arena, have resulted in what may be regarded as concrete benefits for this sector, such as inclusion of domestic violence advocates in police review teams or state advisory panels and significant funding increases throughout the 1980s and 1990s.

The passage of the Violence Against Women Act (VAWA) of 1994 represents a watershed moment for the antiviolence movement. This first federal legislation decrying violence against women remedied many of the measures that had devastated the lives of immigrant women following passage of the Immigration Fraud and Marriage Amendments of 1986 (Schor 2000). VAWA 1994 mandated a national domestic violence hotline and established the Office of Violence Against Women, thus opening significant funding and advocacy opportunities for antiviolence programs. Under the auspices of the Clinton administration, advocates struggling many years for the passage of these provisions were finally able to get the Act passed as an attachment to the Violent Crime Control and Law Enforcement Act of 1994 (Crime Act), an example of pragmatism or opportunism that took the breath away from many who were struck by the political and practical implications of this compromise.

The increasing coordination between the criminal legal system and Immigration and Customs Enforcement (ICE), formerly known as the Immigration and Naturalization Service (INS), presents further implications for violence intervention strategies that engage the state (Ritchie 2006). For example, felony conviction on domestic violence charges of noncitizen perpetrators can now result in deportation. Current practices allowing ICE "sweeps" of local jails for undocumented persons can also lead to deportation even if that person is never actually convicted of any criminal offense. While advocates could once reassure survivors of violence with some confidence that calling the police would not lead to deportation, this is no longer the case.

The child welfare system poses similar threats, particularly to communities of color, which face disproportionate rates of child removal. Recently, concerns have risen throughout the antiviolence movement due to increasingly punitive measures against mothers experiencing domestic violence, such as charges of "failure to protect" against mothers remaining in violent relationships (Enos 2003; Generation Five 2007).

Many mothers face a complex web of threats—fears of harm to themselves and their children by abusive intimate partners, distrust of social services or state remedies, and threats that any action or lack thereof could expose them to accusations of "failure to protect" their children. For parents involved in same-gender or gender-variant relationships, the real and perceived threats of child removal are heightened by discriminatory attitudes, policies, and laws limiting the rights of parenthood for queer people. Immigrant women face further fears of ICE scrutiny and the risk of detention and deportation—their own, their partner's, and/or their children's—often compounded by repeated threats by abusive partners that seeking help will lead to the possibility of permanent separation from children.

THE PRIMACY OF SAFETY IN THE ANTIVIOLENCE MOVEMENT

In many ways, the conventional binary logic of the feminist antiviolence model supports this historic reliance upon the state. The response to the culture of patriarchal violence and danger has been increasingly focused on a concern for safety. Safety has been defined as a state achieved through securing individualized safety from the harm of the individual perpetrator. Physical safety is best met by physical distance from the perpetrator, thereby requiring temporary if not permanent separation (through leaving the relationship and/or separation of the perpetrator from physical access to the survivor of violence).

Thus, the use of civil and criminal restraining orders, the most commonly applied criminal legal tool in situations of domestic violence, attains safety largely through mandated physical separation of the survivor from the perpetrator of violence, a requirement often surprising to women who simply wanted a safeguard from the act of violence, not necessarily from the person perpetrating the violence.

Because intimate violence is often characterized by a pattern of many overt and covert acts of power and control and not simply a single act of violence, the maintenance of safety through a persistent state of separation from the person exhibiting this pattern of behavior offers an easily under-stood if not achievable goal. Many women experiencing domestic violence seek assistance from antiviolence programs with the goal of leaving an abusive relationship. But many women do not choose to leave, or only choose this option after all other possibilities have been exhausted or refused.

Those working in the antiviolence movement understand the power of the notion of safety for persons whose most intimate sense of safety has been ruptured or for those who have never experienced its possibility. Physical separation from an identified perpetrator of violence offers a seemingly controllable context in which safety can be achieved. Thus, safety is reduced to the level of the individual's physical body or perhaps expanded to include those of involved children. It follows that if we find ways to maintain and sustain the individual woman or the woman and children separate from the perpetrator of violence, then they can achieve safety.

ACCOUNTABILITY AND ITS VOID

The perpetrator of violence stands on the other side of this situation. Insofar as we have identified the perpetrator to be male or, as we often say, "95% of all intimate violence is men perpetrating against women," our model of violence intervention still overlays the gender bias of victim/perpetrator. Our primary concern for women who conform to acceptable notions of femininity and are hence "deserving" victims can be stated as safety and increased choices. However, our position concerning men and/or perpetrators of violence falls into a complex of emotions and opinions resulting in few definable principles or strategies. Many refuse to discuss "what about the men?" because we rightly contend that this parallels the caretaking role of women in society. Crossing this line makes us susceptible to putting more energy and care into the well-being of those who violate us than into the safety and well-being of affected women and children. Others point to the countless experiences and studies finding that the possibility of changing violent behavior in men is questionable at best.

Currently, the antiviolence movement has adopted a common lan-guage of *accountability*, a term covering a range of meaning vastly diver-gent and rarely specified. Coming to terms with what we mean by accountability demands that we explore our concerns for men and/or perpetrators beyond our political and emotional comfort zones. This exploration leads us into dangerous territories: on one hand, it may reveal sympathies for men and/or perpetrators of intimate violence that slide us perilously close to collusion. On the other, it may reveal hopelessness about the possibilities of change, leading us to question the real possibility of safety. Ultimately, we face untenable fears of our own complicity in and/or vulnerability to violence.

The antiviolence movement demands accountability but, in actuality, expects none. The understandable skepticism resulting from countless stories of manipulation, disappointments, and lies by abusers claiming remorse and promises to change have ossified into a mantra of impossibility. Indeed, many of us fail to imagine what accountability would even mean. No wonder that we are left with a void readily filled by the state and its one-dimensional response to the demands of violence. Despite our growing recognition of the political and material problems embedded in the criminal legal response, our answering machines still tell women in crisis to call 911 in case of emergency. We still instruct women—whether undocumented immigrants, queer, transgender, fearful of the police due to targeted brutality, or otherwise unwilling to subject themselves or their abusers to this system—to call the police.

PROTECTIONISM AND STATE PARTNERSHIP WITHIN THE ANTIVIOLENCE MOVEMENT

This coupling of the unquestioned primacy of safety with the void of accountability gives rise to a paternalistic protectionism within the antiviolence movement, in partnership with the state as the overarching defender of safety. Our narrow focus on safety as an individual, physical separation from danger has led to the belief that safety is best achieved through survivors leaving the abusive relationship or situation of violence. The ability and power to engage with abusers has been ceded to the state. The many women who do not want such outcomes are left with few alternative options.

Rather than expanding options for women, the antiviolence movement has endorsed a narrowing vision of safety supported throughout the interweaving systems of counseling centers, shelters, hotlines, and legal advocacy programs. What has become known as the "coordinated community response" (Pence and Shepard 1999) has promoted and legitimized the partnership between antiviolence programs and the state, a partnership strengthened by the "embedded" placement of many advocates within criminal legal settings. Many antiviolence programs have increased capacity due to expanded funding under the Office of Violence Against Women following VAWA, a source of funding that has promoted such activities as enhanced arrest policies, narrowing definitions of intimate violence language to coincide with criminal codes, and the recent proliferation of Family Justice Centers that have attempted to physically and procedurally centralize domestic violence–related services under criminal legal leadership.

The antiviolence movement has unwittingly colluded with the state's law-and-order agenda by allowing the state to categorize certain activities and people as threats to liberty and to control them through the mechanisms of protection and punishment. Thus, reliance on the state to protect women from the patriarchal violence of "dangerous" men can be compared to U.S. military policy that uses invasion and occupation to protect the rights of women in Afghanistan and Iraq against the tyranny of Islamic patriarchy (Razack 2004). How is it that so many segments of the feminist movement have fallen for such unquestioned support of policing and militarization as a solution to gender oppression and gender-based violence?

THE PROMISE AND CHALLENGES OF INTERSECTIONALITY

Despite efforts to maintain the prevailing feminist model of violence intervention, the intersection of women of color, immigrant, and queer people struggling to end violence against women in all of its forms has challenged the once-dominant white, middle-class, Christian, heterosexual, and able-bodied leadership and assumptions of the antiviolence movement. Intersectionality is now publicly recognized as an alternative paradigm contesting the simple primacy of gender and promoting the perspectives and agendas of marginalized communities (Crenshaw 1994; Sokoloff and Dupont 2005).

In practice, intersectionality has meant that women of color, including queer and gender-variant people, have increasingly created independent institutional spaces that support complex identities, analyses, and responses to intimate, state-initiated, and other forms of violence. During the 1980s and 1990s, much of this activity was focused on the creation of "language accessible and culturally competent" programs and institutions targeted to the needs of specific communities characterized by race, ethnicity, language, sexual orientation, gender identity, and disability. Many of these programs were constructed in the likeness of the conventional model of violence intervention, with variations based on accommodations to culture, language, accessible community resources, and geographic specificity.

The inclusive framework of intersectionality has too often been limited by a myopic interpretation and implementation. The concept is often employed to make room for one or two additional categories of oppression, depending upon which best fits one's interests or experience. It often names and privileges certain categories while dismissing or excluding others. Hence, persons championing the rights and perspectives of women of color may fail to include immigrant or disabled women or persons whose sexuality or gender identity falls beyond the boundaries of comprehension or concern.

The increasing visibility of transgender and gender-variant persons presents a set of challenges and opportunities to the conceptualization of intersectionality among those opposing gender oppression. The questioning of woman-only spaces, gendered language, and our very definitions of women (and men) demands that we expand our notions of patriarchy and our views of liberation. It also asks us to broaden our understanding and practice of intersectionality to include the realities of gender-variant persons and the differences marked by race, class, immigrant status, ability/disability, and so on.

INCITE! AND CRITICAL RESISTANCE: DEFINING A NEW TERRITORY FOR LIBERATORY ALTERNATIVES

The founding of Incite! Women of Color Against Violence in 2000 with the Color of Violence Conference in Santa Cruz represented a critical opportunity for women of color with a radical agenda to organize nationally. Originally representing women of color with a history of participation and leadership in the antiviolence movement, the co-founders of Incite! created an institutional space from which to address interpersonal and state violence, as well as the intersection of all systems of oppression including those based on race, class, sexual orientation, gender identity, ability/disability, and age. Critical Resistance, founded at the Critical Resistance: Beyond the Prison-Industrial Complex conference in Berkeley in 1998, represents the coalescence of a national and international organizing force challenging the prison-industrial complex. These two organizations formed powerful new institutional spaces from which to push for an alternative social justice agenda.

Together, these two organizations came together to define the territory historically dividing the strands of the broader social justice movement represented by the antiviolence movement and the anti-prison-industrial complex movement. The Incite! Critical Resistance Statement (Incite!/ Critical Resistance 2005) names areas of challenge represented by each movement while committing to a common vision and future collaborative strategies.

Although concerns regarding "overreliance on the criminal legal system" have gained attention among an increasing sector of the antiviolence movement (Dasgupta 2003), Incite! and other advocates and activists have moved beyond the language of "overreliance" to challenge the very notion of the state as a viable partner in the struggle against violence against women and children (Generation Five 2007; Harm Free Zone [n.d.]; Incite! 2003, 2006; Ritchie 2006; Smith 2005).

These movements also challenge the primacy of individual safety, noting that, for oppressed people, the possibility of individual safety is a myth or luxury afforded to the privileged few. The goal, rather, is liberation; and this goal can only be achieved through a collective struggle toward the radical transformation of the material conditions contributing to violence on all of its levels.

ALTERNATIVE COMMUNITY-BASED VIOLENCE INTERVENTION STRATEGIES

Despite growing concerns over current antiviolence interventions to domestic violence, sexual assault, and other forms of intimate and inter-personal violence, the development of concrete, on-the-ground alternative approaches and programs remains remarkably sparse in comparison to the demand for such measures. National conversations and conferences have increasingly called for new strategies, but have produced limited developments.

Although RJ responses have engaged the issues of intimate violence in limited instances, the few programs in North America, Australia, and New Zealand-Aoetearoa still remain the most documented strategies of alternative interventions to intimate violence (Coker 1999, 2002; Paulin et al. 2005; Pennell and Anderson 2005; Pennell and Burford 2002; Pranis 2002; Strang and Braithwaite 2002). Distrust of RJ measures among antiviolence advocates, the dominance of legal theorists and practitioners in discussions and implementation of RJ activities, and negative reports among antiviolence advocates witnessing the lack of power analysis and safety mechanisms within RJ have limited meaningful discussion and engagement between antiviolence advocates and proponents of RJ (Coker 1999, 2002; Smith 2005; Stubbs 1997, 2002).

Furthermore, RJ practices have primarily been initiated by the state or practiced in close coordination with the state (Generation Five 2007, Smith 2005). While they do represent alternatives to the conventional criminal legal response, they are generally diversionary practices still held within a criminal legal context. State control limits participation to those who are already within the criminal legal system, determines procedural constraints and allowable outcomes of such practices, and excludes mean-ingful engagement by those challenging the viability of state intervention.

THE COMMUNITY-BASED INTERVENTION MODEL: CREATIVE INTERVENTIONS

Creative Interventions enters this relatively unexplored territory with a deliberate set of strategies aimed toward bridging the gap between critique and new possibilities, grassroots community needs and programmatic response, and the safety concerns of the antiviolence movement versus the liberatory aims of the broader social justice movement.

Based upon initial discussions among the former Community Accountability Task Force of Incite! (Incite! 2003, 2005) and an early draft model co-created with Generation Five, Creative Interventions has begun some preliminary explorations in concrete situations of intimate and interpersonal violence, with a primary focus on communities of color, including immigrant and queer communities. Several individuals and groups, particularly from the social justice movement, have come forward seeking alternative responses to their situations of violence.

Following these early explorations, Creative Interventions initiated the Community-Based Interventions Project. This demonstration project seeks to develop, pilot test, evaluate, document, and distribute a replicable comprehensive alternative community-based approach to violence intervention. This approach is aimed toward expanding the capacity of oppressed communities to end and prevent violence by equipping its most accessible resources—family, friends, neighbors, co-workers, and others toward whom persons in need first turn—with the model and tools to effectively intervene. This focus on the front lines of intimate and family violence raises the possibility of intervention at early stages of abuse, offers more accessible and sustainable resources, and builds intervention and prevention strategies into the very spaces and places where violence occurs—homes, streets, and communities.

The current phase of the Community-Based Interventions Project features a collaborative project led by Creative Interventions along with Asian immigrant domestic violence organizations based in the San Francisco Bay Area. These organizations include Shimtuh, a domestic violence and sexual assault advocacy organization serving the Korean community; Narika, a South Asian domestic violence advocacy organization; and Asian Women's Shelter, which is a pan-Asian domestic violence shelter with an interest in developing alternative strategies for the Asian Pacific Islander queer community and Mien community. It should be no surprise that interest in a community-based model is particularly keen within immigrant communities since they are distrustful of criminal legal systems, oriented toward problem-solving approaches actively engaging intimate networks, and interested in solutions that hold the possibility of keeping families and community intact.

Creative Interventions defines community-based intervention to violence as "any intervention to intimate violence that primarily involves community or collective solutions and/or engages the perpetrator without involving the state." Central characteristics of the model distinguish it from most currently available options. Rather than relying upon social service organizations as the primary site for violence intervention, the model offers an alternative facilitated space for participants to create an intervention to violence that is carried out within their own home or community space.

Another significant characteristic of this approach is that the model engages anyone interested in exploring further action toward violence intervention, including allies such as friends and family. It is not dependent upon the initial engagement by the survivor, as are most conventional antiviolence services. It does not necessarily rely upon the knowledge or consent of the primary survivor. Leadership (or at least buy-in) of the primary survivor may be a desired goal of the particular intervention using this approach, but, in general, is not a presumed prerequisite to initiation or implementation.

Unlike most conventional antiviolence approaches, this alternative model does not presume safety to be the ultimate goal of violence intervention. Rather, Creative Interventions offers space for the articulation of a more nuanced individual and collectively oriented set of goals often held by survivors and community members (Davies, Lyon, and Monti-Catania 1998). Key components of this model are (1) articulating individual goals; (2) making transparent the tensions that exist between individual goals, often according to the power and affiliation relationships of respective players in situations of violence; and (3) constructing a consensus within the collective involved in the intervention.

This organizing model recognizes anyone able and motivated to come forward to initiate a possible intervention as a potential leader and entry point to a given situation of intimate violence. From this starting point, the initial participant or participants are engaged in an organizing strategy that facilitates a process that encourages clarification of the situation of abuse, maps the parties involved, identifies common goals, prepares safety plans, and creates and implements viable strategies for ending violence or promoting repair and healing. At each point, the possibility for further collective engagement is explored. Who else can help? What role can they play? Do they want to come into this facilitated space? Or, do the participants want help preparing themselves to facilitate team-building on their own, within their own community space?

Another feature is the possibility for engagement with the perpetrator of violence or the person doing harm. While this is by no means a necessary component of the model and is only approached with great care, it is considered a possible option. The community-based model assumes that people within the survivor's intimate network may already be engaged with the perpetrator. Some may hold particular influence or connection. Some may also wield a meaningful threat. As RJ practices show, meaningful engagement of the perpetrator through the authority of the community and a connection of care can hold more promise for long-term and sustainable change than the transfer of this authority to the criminal legal system (Pranis 2002).

What this model offers for the survivor of violence is a greater access to options than those conventionally available. What does she value? What are her goals? In what ways can she take leadership in attaining these goals? How can she organize her intimate network and other accessible resources to help her attain these goals or initiate others to take this role? If engagement with the perpetrator is a possibility, who can participate? Is this strategy feasible?

It also builds upon the capacity of those resources most accessible and meaningful to survivors of violence. While intimate networks have often failed to provide adequate support to survivors or effective interventions to reduce harm, these networks hold the most knowledge about those involved in violence. Such networks include those whose attitudes and actions may carry the most meaning, and those who face the greatest risks when violence continues unabated or unaddressed. Meaningful collective action toward positive change holds transformative potential not only for individual survivors or perpetrators of violence but for all of those involved in creating healthy solutions—or who at least come together to imagine their possibility.

While we share information regarding safety and explore critical questions regarding safety and safety planning, this model does not presume that immediate safety is a goal. The space to explore and co-create more meaningful goals allows for more creative strategies and actions more aligned with the broader principle of self-determination at the level of the individual and community.

A concrete example from one of the collaborative Asian immigrant organizations illustrates how this model offers access to a different array of options and displaces immediate physical safety as a necessary primary concern.

Case 1

A young immigrant woman came to one of the collaborative organizations seeking assistance. She had gone to a party with her former employer, the owner of a bar. That evening, he attempted to rape her. She struggled free and was able to get away. However, the experience was clearly traumatizing. The woman had decided that she wanted to confront this man. She talked to the advocate about her plan to enter the bar and confront her assailant, convinced that her sense of violation and indignity could only be met by this bold move.

The advocate, moved by the courage of this woman, responded by offering to go into the bar with her, a strategy ultimately challenged by the advocate's team of co-workers. This offer went beyond the usual practices of this organization and much beyond what most antiviolence organizations would recommend. Interested in further exploring this woman's request, the organization invoked the model of the community-based intervention and its role as a facilitator for further exploration rather than as an advocate accompanying her on this mission or imploring her to give up this idea for reasons of safety.

The staff team discussed what a facilitated community-based intervention would look like in this situation. The advocate met again with this young woman. This time, she helped her explore her goals in confronting this man. Could her goals be met in other ways? Upon further exploration, it became clear that her goal was direct confrontation. She was open to discussing safety plans and to role-play this action, but she was not willing to give up her primary goal.

The advocate role-played possible scenarios based upon her knowledge of the dynamics of sexual assault. She presented possible dangers as well as responses of victim-blaming, denial, threats, and violence. She helped the woman explore who else in her intimate network might be willing to help.

The role-play brought up many situations that this woman had not considered.
It helped her to clarify a safer plan that still met her goals.

The woman could not identify anybody within her community to help out
when this plan was first discussed. The exploration did, however, raise possi-
bilities as she prepared on her own. She talked to a friend who agreed to stay
close to her phone in case any crisis occurred. She called her assailant and asked
him to meet her at a restaurant. In preparation for the meeting, she talked to
the wait person at the restaurant and asked him to keep a close watch on the
situation in case anything happened. It is notable that she ended up engaging
another community member to participate in her plan.

The woman ended up meeting with her assailant, and confronted him by
naming his action and her outrage. He admitted his guilt and apologized
without further incident. She called the organization following this confron-
tation with great appreciation, relief, and a sense of closure.

This case illustrates the basic principle of this model: the critical role of
helping the survivor identify her own goals and create a plan of action to
meet these goals. It also highlights the importance of exploring a collective
response and the opportunity that this opens for a different set of options
resulting from the involvement of other people. It also offers one example
of engagement with the perpetrator and the transformative power of this
possibility for the survivor.

Of course, this example begs further questions. We do know that the
survivor took back her sense of agency and power through this intervention. We can reasonably assume that the healing that this experience
allowed was more immediate and powerful than a more conventional
individual counseling approach or engagement with the state. We do not
know if or how this man was changed by this experience. Did this prevent
further assaults? Did this simply inform more successful strategies for
future assaults? Did he find that apologies could relieve him of more painful
consequences, including the possibility of criminal legal engagement?

The "facilitated community-based intervention model" represents the
organization's central contribution to alternative interventions to intimate
and interpersonal violence. If communities fail to provide concrete solutions to individual situations of violence, then conventional social service
and criminal legal remedies will remain the only viable option. The development of effective intervention responses involving individual situations
of violence, however, are linked to strategies addressing those wider circles
of community that violence impacts.

Effective and sustainable interventions rely upon the involvement of
intimate networks that include friends and family, as well as broader community supports. The development of specific education, tools, and curriculum targeted to intimate network members is a critical component to the
overall community-based intervention model.

The long-term vision for the development of this intervention
approach includes the development and involvement of broad levels

of community leadership as agents of community accountability. Programmatically, the training of informal and formal community leaders as intervention facilitators, community allies, and community leaders promoting violence intervention and prevention are important components to the expansion and sustainability of this model. Further work on creative supports aimed at deeper and more sustainable change for perpetrators of violence is also being explored.

CONTRADICTIONS AND CHALLENGES FACING COMMUNITY-BASED INTERVENTIONS TO VIOLENCE

Early experience with the model has also raised areas of contradiction and challenge. Collective involvement opens up the arena of public disclosure, defying the usual antiviolence practices of confidentiality as well as community practices of secrecy surrounding intimate violence. Public disclosure for survivors still raises the possibility of shame and victim-blaming. Public disclosure for perpetrators suggests public shaming as punishment rather than as a restorative measure or as an attempt to destigmatize violence. Most communities are not yet prepared to perceive and carry out public disclosure without succumbing to the level of rumors, gossip, victim-blaming, or persecution.

Another tension exists between survivor-centered principles and notions of the collective good. The recognition of the community as a victim of violence, as well as an important actor in ending violence competes with the primacy of the individual survivor supported by the survivor-centered tenet of the antiviolence movement. While I contend earlier that the protectionism of the antiviolence movement and its partnership with the state actually subverts this very principle, the community-based intervention approach also challenges survivor-centeredness. At best, this model allows for a negotiated process in which the individual interests of the survivor and her allies (who have their individual and collective interests) can reach consensus about shared vision and goals. It also acknowledges the wide impact of violence, not only on individual survivors but on the broader community, and supports the involvement of this wider network to coordinate more effective and sustainable solutions to violence. In practice, we have witnessed how the sentiments of the survivor can come into active conflict with those of her allies or how allies may feel pressured to comply with actions with which they disagree.

A related contradiction occurs between transformation and collusion. In the desire for a more reparative and holistic model for violence intervention, it would be easy to advocate for resolutions that offer excuses to perpetrators and that pressure survivors to accept processes or outcomes for the sake of the public perception of resolution and closure. Many criticisms of RJ warn of such tendencies (Coker 1999; 2002; Smith 2005; Stubbs 1997, 2002). My own work in community conflicts reveals how easy it is to push for premature closure out of compassion, weariness, and a host of other conflicting emotions and agendas. Political demands for alternative interventions to violence that are more "transformative" open ample opportunities for community processes that provide excuses for violence.

On the other side of this tendency is the replacement of state punishments with our own parallel forms of retributive community justice. Community banning, firing from jobs, persistent public shaming and persecution of perpetrators, unclear and arbitrary consequences to unspecified demands, and physical violence are all tactics that have been employed in the name of community accountability. Are such tactics ever justified? In what situations?

Clearly, the accountability void discussed earlier in this chapter has not yet been filled by those seeking alternative interventions to violence. The tendencies either for punishment or easy excuses are unacceptable if we are looking for solutions that are truly transformative to survivors, perpetrators, and communities. Unfortunately, it appears that we tend to choose one option over another depending upon who has power, who we like, who we pity, who appears most accommodating, and a myriad of other subjective factors.

As we create and test these alternative models, Creative Interventions also faces the contradictions of creating a community-based response from within the boundaries of a formal organizational structure. On the one hand, this structure allows for the consolidation of resources including funding, collaborative staffing, outreach capacity, and more, thus increasing the possibility of reaching the goal of creating lasting documented public resources to support community-based alternatives. On the other hand, we constantly ask ourselves whether the models and approaches we create will ultimately come to rely upon the kinds of institutional resources afforded to formal organizations.

One of our most significant measures of success will be the ability for these models, tools, and approaches to be adopted effectively and safely (enough) by the least-resourced and least-formally organized communities. The collection of stories deriving from grassroots communities through The StoryTelling & Organizing Project, the constant testing of practices within diverse organizations and communities, and an attempt to maintain the least organizational infrastructure necessary to create the greatest desired outcomes are some of the intentional practices driving this project.

PROMISING DIRECTIONS: A TRIBUTE
TO MANY PATHWAYS

The exploration of accountability and principled and effective processes for accountability is an area requiring much more resources and research. Developments in other antiviolence programs offer promising conceptualizations and practices for accountability within a more transformative framework. The work of Alan Jenkins (Jenkins 1990; Jenkins, Hall, and Joy 2003) and the narrative therapy theorists and practitioners affiliated with the Dulwich Centre in Adelaide, Australia (Dulwich Centre 2003) have developed language and processes "inviting responsibility," as opposed to using more conventional authoritarian or behaviorist models found in "batterer treatment" programs. Rhea Almeida and the Cultural Context Model of the Institute for Family Services in Somerset, New Jersey promote active discussion and analysis of systems of oppression and individual acts and attitudes that collude with these systems. Their model also values change through collective engagement using group work and the inclusion of community allies to support accountability and transparency. Stith, Rosen, McCollum, and Thomsen (2004) have developed and evaluated programs for couples experiencing domestic violence. In response to more conventional contraindications against such work, they have developed an innovative group model for couples that specifically addresses domestic violence. Pennell and Burford (Pennell and Anderson, 2005; Pennell and Burford 2002) developed RJ practices that build upon the expertise and motivations of family members closest to and most impacted by intimate violence, being careful to include even the most problematic members in developing collective solutions that are workable for that family after they leave the office.

New models for addressing accountability specifically rooted in communities of color address the parallels between colonization, state-based violence, and gender-based violence. Freedom, Inc. in Madison, Wisconsin organizes with Hmong youth, prioritizing an analysis of gender-based violence within the context of war, immigration, poverty, racism, and state-based violence (Kim 2005). Caminar Latino has developed an explicitly "liberation" social change model that integrates women's, men's, and children's violence intervention programming and challenges gender- and generationally-separated conventions (Perilla, Lavizzo, and Ibanez 2007; Perilla and Perez 2002).

The Ke Ala Lokahi (Turning Point) program in Hilo, Hawaii has created a batterer's treatment program based upon indigenous Hawaiian cosmology and an analogy between the destructive legacy of colonization on the Hawaiian people with the devastating impact of domestic violence (Kim 2005). *Whanau* (family) violence intervention models among the Maori in New Zealand/Aotearoa have similarly posited a violence intervention framework that centers collective Maori values, recognizes colonization as the source of and historical context giving rise to the increase in family violence, and challenges Western state-based approaches that rely upon the punishment and criminalization of the Maori people (Second Maori Taskforce on Whanau Violence 2004). The Just Therapy Team operating out of The Family Centre in Wellington, New Zealand/Aotearoa share a unique collaborative program model challenging *pakeha* (white) domination and colonization within a multiracial organizational setting. The result has been an evolving set of holistic approaches to sexual and family violence intervention that build upon Indigenous cultural values and practices grounded within Maori, Samoan, and *pakeha* communities, respectively (Waldegrave et al. 2003).

Each of these models and programs has developed through the search for solutions to intimate violence that do not replicate the individualism, separation, and dislocation inherent in conventional remedies, but rather build new visions and practices for collective and community change. Each has faced and continues to face challenges from those championing conventional violence intervention approaches. And each has offered invaluable insights and inspiration to the work of Creative Interventions.

CONCLUSION

Our collective work in creating a new approach to violence intervention is just beginning and, at the same time, follows trajectories that go as far back as violence, itself. Currently, many of us have refined our critique of the prevailing intervention model and must now challenge ourselves to take the risks necessary to shift our assumptions and defy our dogmas so that we can realize new possibilities. I believe that the answer lies deep within our own selves and our communities. If we learn to trust and build upon this wisdom, we will be able to create models that harness the creativity and reparative energy of those most motivated for change.

ACKNOWLEDGMENTS

I wish to thank the board and advisors of Creative Interventions: Crystal Baik, Trishala Deb, Staci Haines, Isabel Kang, Kalei Valli Kanuha, Helen Kim, Susun Kim, Thao Le, Sujin Lee, Catie Magee, Ann Rhee Menzie, Susan Murray, Sue Osthoff, Joan Pennell, Julia Perilla, Beth Richie, Poroshat Shekarloo, and Kabzuag Vaj; sisters at Incite! Women of Color Against Violence; Generation Five, with special appreciation to Sara Kershnar; courageous collaborators at Shimtuh, Asian Women's Shelter, Narika, and DataCenter; Critical Resistance-Oakland with special thanks to Rachel Herzing, Serena Huang, and Nat Smith; and the many other friends and colleagues who have helped to support this project.

REFERENCES

Almeida, Rhea, Ken Dolan-Del Vecchio, and Lynn Parker. 1999. "Foundation Concepts for Social Justice Based Therapy: Critical Consciousness, Accountability, and Empowerment." *Violence Against Women* 5:654–683.

Almeida, Rhea and Tracy Durkin. 1999. "The Cultural Context Model: Therapy for Couples with Domestic Violence." *Journal of Marital and Family Therapy*. 25:169–176.

Coker, Donna. 1999. "Enhancing Autonomy for Battered Women: Lessons from Navajo Peacemaking." *University of California Los Angeles Law Review* 47:42–50.

————. 2002. "Anti-Subordination Processes in Domestic Violence." Pp. 128–152 in *Restorative Justice and Family Violence,* edited by Heather Strang and John Braithwaite. Cambridge, UK: Cambridge University Press.

Communities Against Rape & Abuse (CARA). 2008. "About Us." Seattle, WA: CARA. Retrieved February 26, 2009 (http://www.cara-seattle.org).

Crenshaw, Kimberlé Williams. 1994. "Mapping the Margins: Intersectionality, Identity Politics, and Violence Against Women of Color. Pp. 93–118 in *The Public Nature of Private Violence,* edited by Martha Albertson Fineman and Roxanne Mykitiuk. New York: Routledge.

Dasgupta, Shamita Das. (2003). *Safety and Justice for All: Examining the Relationship Between the Women's Anti-Violence Movement and the Criminal Legal System.* New York: Ms. Foundation. Retrieved February 26, 2009 (www.ms.foundation.org/user-assets/PDF/Program/safety_justice.pdf).

Davies, Jill, Eleanor Lyon, and Diane Monti-Catania. 1998. *Safety Planning with Battered Women: Complex Lives/Difficult Choices.* Thousand Oaks, CA: Sage.

Dulwich Centre. 2003. *Responding to Violence: A Collection of Papers Relating to Child Sexual Abuse and Violence in Intimate Relationships.* Adelaide: Dulwich Centre Publications.

Enos, V. Pualani. 2003. *Learning from the Experiences of Battered Immigrant, Refugee and Indigenous Women Involved with Child Protective Services to Inform a Dialogue Among Domestic Violence Activists and Advocates.* San Francisco: Asian & Pacific Islander Institute on Domestic Violence.

Generation Five. 2007. *Toward Transformative Justice: A Liberatory Approach to Child Sexual Abuse and Other Forms of Intimate and Community Violence.* San Francisco: Generation Five.

Harm Free Zone Collective. (n.d.). *Building Harm Free Zones: An Organizing Booklet.* New York: Harm Free Zone Collective.

Incite! 2003. *Incite! Women of Color Against Violence Community Accountability Principles/Concerns/Strategies/Models Working Document.* March 5. Retrieved February 26, 2009 (http://www.incite-national.org/index.php?s=93).

————. 2005. *Gender, Oppression, Abuse, Violence: Community Accountability Within the People of Color Progressive Movement.* July. Retrieved February 26, 2009 (http://www.incite-national.org/index.php?s=94).

————. ed. 2006. *Color of Violence: The INCITE! Anthology.* Boston: South End Press.

Incite!/Critical Resistance. 2005. "Gender Violence and the Prison Industrial Complex: Interpersonal and State Violence against Women of Color," with an Introduction by Julia Sudbury. Pp. 102–114 in *Domestic Violence at the Margins: Readings in Race, Class, Gender & Culture,* edited by Natalie J. Sokoloff with Christina Pratt. Piscataway, NJ: Rutgers University.

Jenkins, Alan. 1990. *Invitations to Responsibility: The Therapeutic Engagement of Men Who Are Violent and Abusive.* Adelaide: Dulwich Centre Publications.

————, Rob Hall, and Maxine Joy. 2003. "Forgiveness and Child Sexual Abuse: A Matrix of Meanings." Pp. 35–70 in *Responding to Violence: A Collection of Papers Relating to Child Sexual Abuse and Violence in Intimate Relationships.* Adelaide: Dulwich Centre Productions.

Kanuha, Valli. 1996. "Domestic Violence, Racism, and the Battered Women's Movement." Pp. 34–50 in *Future Interventions with Battered Women and*

Their Families, edited by Jeffrey L. Edleson and Zvi C. Eisikovits. Thousand Oaks, CA: Sage.

Kim, Mimi. 2002. *Innovative Strategies to Address Domestic Violence in Asian and Pacific Islander Communities: Examining Themes, Models and Interventions.* San Francisco: Asian & Pacific Islander Institute on Domestic Violence.

————. 2005. *The Community Engagement Continuum: Outreach, Mobilization, Organizing and Accountability to Address Violence Against Women in Asian and Pacific Islander Communities.* San Francisco: Asian & Pacific Islander Institute on Domestic Violence.

————. 2006. "Alternative Interventions to Violence: Creative Interventions." *International Journal of Narrative Therapy and Community Work* 4:45–52.

Paulin, Judy, Venezia Kingi, Tautari Huirama, and Barb Lash. 2005. *The Rotorua Second Chance Community-Managed Restorative Justice Programme: An Evaluation.* Wellington, NZ: Ministry of Justice.

Pence, Ellen L. and Melanie F. Shepard. 1999. "An Introduction: Developing a Coordinated Community Response." Pp. 3–23 in *Coordinating Community Responses to Domestic Violence: Lessons from Duluth and Beyond,* edited by Melanie F. Shepard and Ellen Pence. Thousand Oaks, CA: Sage.

Pennell, Joan and Gary Anderson, eds. 2005. *Widening the Circle: The Practice and Evaluation of Family Group Conferencing with Children, Youths, and Their Families.* Washington, DC: NASW Press.

———— and Gale Burford. 2002. "Feminist Praxis, Making Family Group Conferencing Work." Pp. 108–127 in *Restorative Justice and Family Violence: New Ideas and Learning from the Past,* edited by Heather Strang and John Braithwaite. Cambridge, UK: Cambridge University Press.

Perilla, Julia, Evelyn Lavizzo, and Gladys Ibanez. 2007. "Towards a Community Psychology of Liberation: Domestic Violence Intervention as a Tool for Social Change." Pp. 291–312 in *Advancing Social Justice Through Clinical Practice,* edited by Etiony Aldarondo. Mahwah, NJ: Lawrence Earlbum Associates.

Perilla, Julia and Felipe Perez. 2002. "A Program for Immigrant Latino Men Who Batter Within the Context of a Comprehensive Family Intervention." Pp. (11–1)–(11–31) in *Programs for Men Who Batter: Intervention and Prevention Strategies in a Diverse Society,* edited by Etiony Aldarondo and Fernando Mederos. Kingston, NJ: Civic Research Institute.

Pranis, Kay 2002. "Restorative Values and Confronting Family Violence." Pp. 23–41 in *Restorative Justice and Family Violence,* edited by Heather Strang and John Braithwaite. Cambridge, UK: Cambridge University Press.

Razack, Sherene H. 2004. "Imperilled Muslim Women, Dangerous Muslim Men and Civilised Europeans: Legal and Social Responses to Forced Marriage." *Feminist Legal Studies* 12:239–174.

Richie, Beth E. 1996. *Compelled to Crime: The Gender Entrapment of Battered, Black Women.* New York: Routledge & Kegan Paul.

Ritchie, Andrea J. 2006. "Law Enforcement Violence Against Women of Color." Pp. 138–156 in *Color of Violence: The INCITE! Anthology,* edited by the Incite! Collective. Cambridge, MA: South End Press.

Schor, Elizabeth. 2000. "Domestic Abuse and Alien Women in Immigration Law: Response and Responsibility." *Cornell Journal of Law and Public Policy* 9:697–713.

Second Maori Taskforce on Whanau Violence. 2004. *Transforming Whanau Violence—A Conceptual Framework.* Wellington, NZ: Ministry of Maori Affairs.

Sokoloff, Natalie and Ida Dupont. 2005. "Domestic Violence at the Intersections of Race, Class, and Gender: Challenges and Contributions to Understanding Violence Against Marginalized Women in Diverse Communities." *Violence Against Women* 11:38–64.

Smith, Andrea. 2005. *Conquest: Sexual Violence and American Indian Genocide.* Boston: South End Press.

Stith, Sandra, Karen Rosen, Eric McCollum, and Cynthia Thomsen. 2004. "Treating Intimate Partner Violence within Intact Couple Relationships: Outcomes of Multi-Couple Versus Individual Couple Therapy." *Journal of Marital Therapy* 30:305–318.O

Strang, Heather and John Braithwaite, eds. 2002. *Restorative Justice and Family Violence.* Cambridge, UK: Cambridge University Press.

Stubbs, Julie. 1997. "Shame, Defiance and Violence Against Women: A Critical Analysis of 'Communitarian Conferencing.'" Pp. 109–126 in *Women's Encounters with Violence: Australian Experiences,* edited by Sandy Cook and Judith Bessant. Thousand Oaks, CA: Sage.

———. 2002. "Domestic Violence and Women's Safety: Feminist Challenges to Restorative Justice." Pp. 42–61 in *Restorative Justice and Family Violence,* edited by Heather Strang and John Braithwaite. Cambridge, UK: Cambridge University Press.

Waldegrave, Charles, Kiwi Tamesese, Flora Tuhaka, and Warihi Campbell. 2003. *Just Therapy: A Journey. A Collection of Papers from the Just Therapy Team, New Zealand.* Adelaide: Dulwich Centre.

10

RESTORATIVE JUSTICE FOR ACQUAINTANCE RAPE AND MISDEMEANOR SEX CRIMES

MARY P. KOSS

Empirical evidence suggests that restorative justice (RJ) programs are typically viewed as satisfying and empowering to crime victims (Umbreit et al. 2005). However, examination of program enrollment statistics reveals very few sexual assault cases and some programs specifically exclude these crimes either by policy or practice. Within jurisprudence scholarship, the consensus is that restorative methods must be approached cautiously in cases of intimate crimes against women (Cameron 2006; Curtis-Fawley and Daly 2005; Daly and Stubbs 2006, 2007; Hudson 1998). Service providers and advocates, when knowledgeable about RJ believe that there are appropriate uses for these methods but have concerns, especially about their application to sexual assault (Achilles 2004; Mika et al. 2002; Nancarrow 2006; Strang 2004). Because few RJ programs are specifically designed for sexual assault, little experience exists that can inform ongoing scholarly discussion and community practice.

This chapter focuses on a pioneering effort undertaken by a collaboration of law enforcement, prosecution, sexual assault advocates, and public health prevention specialists in Pima County, Arizona. Beginning in 2001, this group undertook the implementation and outcome evaluation of RESTORE (Responsibility and Equity for Sexual Transgressions Offering a Restorative Experience) a RJ pilot program for selected sex crimes involving adults, specifically excluding rape and other sexual assaults within relationships where domestic violence had occurred. We collectively agreed upon a mission, which was "to facilitate a victim-centered, community-driven resolution of selected individual sex crimes that creates and carries out a plan for accountability, healing, and public safety" (RESTORE 2006:i). From the vantage point of public health, RESTORE is secondary prevention. It is initiated after an offense has been perpetrated and someone has already been intentionally psychologically and/or physically injured. Within the secondary level, RESTORE represents *targeted* prevention because it involves individuals who by virtue of previous offending are at elevated risk of perpetrating future crimes and those harmed by their acts are more vulnerable than others to revictimization. RESTORE was funded by the U.S. Centers for Disease Control and Prevention to develop, implement, and evaluate a secondary-level, targeted prevention program designed to reduce perpetration. However, it will become clear throughout this chapter that, consistent with the values of the RESTORE team and of the RJ community generally, the commitment of the program was to well-serve all constituents—direct and indirect victims, perpetrators, and the community-at-large and to avoid subordinating the needs and welfare of those intentionally injured to those responsible for the harm.[1]

This chapter begins with a definition of terms. There follows a conceptual discussion of the range of concerns that confronted our team in designing the RESTORE program. This includes our proposed activities to create a viable alternative where existing criminal justice practices have been identified as less than satisfying or effective, and our strategies to proactively avoid RJ methods that could themselves be damaging if applied without accommodation to the sexual assault context. Following the conceptual discussion, the activities that comprised each of the program's four stages are reviewed. The chapter concludes by reinforcing existing cautions for proponents of RJ to be cognizant of the unique features of sexual crime before rushing to launch programs, and it acknowledges some innovative programs that have debuted since RESTORE was launched. The chapter ends with a request that readers carefully consider the extent to which the RESTORE program design demonstrates that carefully reasoned, safe, and respectful alternatives can be offered for sexual assault if we collaborate, consult, and listen to the needs of our constituencies. Case vignettes, enrollment statistics, process evaluation, qualitative and quantitative outcome data, and lessons learned from the demonstration are excluded due to space limitations. This information will be made available in subsequent papers.

DEFINITION OF KEY TERMS

Because RESTORE was a collaboration of public health, community sexual assault service providers, and the criminal justice system, it was important to create agreed-upon terminology. The term *survivor/victim* (SV) was selected to retain the empowerment conveyed by the word *survivor* and the outrage implied by the word *victim*. The term *responsible person* (RP) was created to label the individual who perpetrated unlawful, unwanted sexual activity instead of words such as "perpetrator" or "offender." The goal was to identify a wrongdoer without implying that an arrest has been made or charges issued, and to draw a contrast reflective of restorative philosophy. Entry into the program required that the RP acknowledge *responsibility,* which was defined as agreeing that the act happened. There might or might not have been a guilty plea entered, and the individual may have failed to agree that his/her act was a sex crime. Cognitive understanding was expected to progress over the time enrolled in the program (for an overview of forgiveness, see Armour and Umbreit 2006). *Rape* was defined as unwanted oral, anal, or vaginal penetration against consent through force, threat of force, or when incapacitated. At the urging of law enforcement, RESTORE also addressed noncontact sex crimes such as indecent exposure, public masturbation, and voyeurism. The term s*exual assault* is used consistent with Arizona Revised Statutes to reference the range of sex crimes up to and including rape. In legal terms, RESTORE cases included selected misdemeanor and felony sexual assaults. *Selected* means that not all reported sexual assaults were eligible for referral to RESTORE, and the exclusion criteria are discussed later in the chapter.

The definition of *restorative justice* used in this chapter follows Umbreit and his colleagues and references a philosophy that expands traditional views of victimization to include harm done to families, friends, and the community, and that specifies the RP's responsibility for harm as well as his/her obligation to repair the negative impacts of their acts to the extent possible (Umbreit et al. 2005). Restorative options that have been intended at least in part to meet victim needs include sharing circles, victim-offender dialogue, victim impact panels, community reparation boards, circles of support, sentencing circles, conferencing, and restorative discipline in educational settings (Johnstone and Van Ness 2007; Umbreit et al. 2005; for a discussion of these approaches in the context of sexual violence, see Koss and Achilles 2008).

The starting point for the design of the RESTORE Program was the conference model. Restorative conferencing may be convened at various points in the justice process, including pre- or post-charging, with or without entering a plea of guilty or nonguilty. In the standard conferencing model, which is used most commonly in cases of juvenile crime, victims might or might not attend a face-to-face meeting that includes the offender and family members. Conferencing typically is pursued regardless of the victim's preference to remain in the criminal justice system or attend the conference. Police officers often facilitate the conference, although social service providers may also serve in this capacity. The meetings are held as soon after the crime as possible, precluding much preparation of the parties to come together. A script is frequently used to conduct the meetings, which are often held in a police station, especially when the program is a law enforcement initiative. The agenda includes the offender's description of his/her acts, the impact statement by the victim, and the development of a redress plan. Afterward, there might or might not be an appearance before a judge to finalize the redress plan. Thereafter, significant variance exists in the extent to which completion of the reparations and rehabilitation requirements are monitored and fulfilled.

Despite what could be considered suboptimal elements in the standard model *vis a vis* the victim, satisfaction rating from conference participants on consent, preparation, and safety typically exceed those of conventional justice. Some evidence documents modest impact on reoffending among juvenile offenders (Latimer, Dowden, and Muise 2005; Poulson 2003; Sherman et al. 2005), including those who have committed sex crimes (Daly 2003, 2006).

THE CONCEPTUAL PLAN FOR RESTORE

The cautions that have been expressed about RJ for sexual violence stem from several sources. First, sexual assault has some unique features compared to other crimes, including intense shame, stigma, and emotionality. Scientific literature has established that even after taking into account personal history and social characteristics that could explain symptom severity, sexual assault still provokes more serious psychological distress than other crimes (Breslau et al. 1998). Sexual assault elicits more fear for personal safety than other crimes (Gordon and Riger 1989). Fear of rape is the most powerful predictor of women's general fear of crime and, once victimized, fear of the offender and of reoffense is aggravated. Because most rape victims know their perpetrator and the act is an intimate bodily invasion, sexual violence is a more severe violation of personal trust than other crimes such as burglary even though both transgress the boundaries of private, personal spaces.

The post-crime response to sexual assault is similar in many ways to other crimes (Orth and Maercker 2004, 2006). Yet there are important differences in the reactions to survivor/victims by criminal justice personnel, friends, family, and the community-at-large. Well-documented, widely held myths and attitudes cast rape victims as partially responsible for being assaulted and thus undeserving of the sympathy and response that would be accorded a "legitimate" victim (Campbell 2005; 2006; Campbell et al.1999; Jordan 2004; Monroe et al. 2005). SVs share the attitudes of the general public, believing that they are culpable and this self-blame is reinforced by the reactions they receive. Self-blame is the single most important determinant of the severity of post-rape distress and the length of recovery (Koss and Figueredo 2004a, 2004b).

In the aftermath of sexual assault and other crimes of intimate violence, SVs have two major categories of needs—*survival needs* and *justice needs*. Survival needs include safety; physical health; economic issues such as housing and employment, education, or retraining; and immigration problems (Koss 2006; Seidman and Vickers 2005). Justice needs involve an innate motivation to right wrongs. According to SVs, satisfying their justice needs rests on the extent to which they (1) contribute input into key decisions and remain informed about their case, (2) receive response with minimal delay, (3) tell their story without interruption by adversarial and sometimes hostile questioning, (4) receive validation, (5) shape a resolution that meets their material and emotional needs, and (6) feel safe (Herman 2005; Mika et al. 2002; Nancarrow 2006; Strang 2004).

After rape, SVs frequently do not experience the criminal justice system as meeting these needs. A review of empirical evidence suggests that offenders are infrequently held accountable for unlawful sexual acts due to significant case attrition at reporting, investigation, charging, and trial stages of the justice process (Koss 2000, 2006; Koss and Achilles 2008; Koss, Bachar, and Hopkins 2003; Koss et al. 2004). Second, retraumatization of SVs by medical and criminal justice system personnel is widespread, despite gains in training. Satisfaction with existing justice avenues is low in typical sexual assault cases; the exceptions are some survivors of stranger rapes. The consensus is that, despite improved training and criminal justice reforms over the last 30 years, SV satisfaction has not improved and rape remains the "least reported, least indicted, and least convicted non-property felony in America" (Seidman and Vickers 2005:472; see also Frazier and Haney 1996; Orth and Maecker 2004; Walker and Louw 2007).

Although there is great enthusiasm for RJ in many countries, careful and well-reasoned analyses raise concerns that these methods could create new risks and potential harms for SVs of intimate crime (e.g., Hopkins and Koss 2004; Hopkins, Koss, and Bachar 2004; Stubbs 2002). When our collaboration in Pima County, Arizona resolved to develop a restorative option for selected sex crimes, we recognized that our planning must acknowledge the unique features of sexual assault, consider how alternative justice practices might improve SV experiences in documented areas of dissatisfaction, involve responsible persons without violating their constitutional or statutory rights, and anticipate and minimize potential risks of restorative methods.[2]

Tables 10.1 and 10.2 organize the conceptual phase of program development. Table 10.1 is our analysis from the SV's perspective, and Table 10.2 from the RP's perspective. The content of the tables was developed through collaborative information gathering and idea generation, a review of the professional literature, and consultation with key players. This included national and international RJ experts, as well as local police, prosecutors, defense attorneys, indigent defense providers, civil attorneys, victim service providers, and sex offender therapists.

The concerns summarized in the left-hand column of Table 10.1 include features that have been dissatisfying to SVs, such as feeling blamed, disrespected, unsupported, and left out. This table also identifies ways that restorative methods might be unhelpful, such as feeling unsafe, coerced, silenced, reabused, or pressured to forgive. The middle column of the table identifies a feature that would be included in the design of RESTORE in response to each concern.

Some program features in the middle column are no different from standard conferencing models, such as involving family and friends, using an agenda to govern speaking order, employing trained facilitators, having conference rules, and meeting in a safe location. Other features were added

Table 10.1 Conceptual Overview of RESTORE from the Survivor/Victim (SV) Perspective

Concern	RESTORE Program Design	Potential Impact
Self-blame exacerbated by adversarial process	SV is a wronged party; responsible person (RP) must acknowledge responsibility	Less secondary victimization
Myths and blame even by family and friends	Involve and work with family and friends	Perceived social support
Space for SV to voice impact directly or indirectly to the RP	Encourage SV to express feelings; provide opportunity to meet face-to-face if desired	Impact statement created and delivered
Coercion to participate	Offer RESTORE to SV first	Signed informed consent
Insufficient attention to SV safety	Limit access to victim; monitoring of the offender	Perceived safety; reports of unauthorized contact
Compliance with offender's constitutional rights emphasized more than provision of victim's rights	Arrange pro-bono legal advice and implement victim's rights throughout SV participation and RP follow-up and monitoring	Perceptions that procedures were fair
Promised counseling and psychological services unavailable or inaccessible	Staff program with human service professionals with close ties to service providers	Referrals made; perceptions that staff were supportive
Vulnerability to reabuse	Use trained facilitators and enforce conference guidelines prohibiting hostile, blaming, or profane language	Rules of conference observed as verified by observation
Limitations on ability to speak and to be heard	Agenda governs speaking opportunities; SV prepares what to say in advance; others speak for SV if desired	SV approves agenda
Violation of confidentiality	All attendees sign confidentiality contract	Confidentiality contract signed
Limits on SV input by judicial discretion and mandatory sentencing guidelines	Use SV input to shape redress and rehabilitation	Redress plan signed by SV
SV validation; RPs are advised to maintain innocence even after conviction	Create process to receive responsible person's reflection on his/her transgression	Letter of Reflection delivered to SV
Pressure to forgive	RP apology at program exit with no expectation of forgiveness	SV is notified of exit meeting
Avoidance of criminal justice	Disseminate availability of options and effects of RESTORE	Public media campaigns and press

to address the unique demands of sexual assault. These include offering RESTORE to the SV first, and giving her/him control over whether the case is processed through an alternative to criminal or civil justice; limiting the RP's access to the SV; monitoring the RP for an extended period; arranging pro-bono legal consultation for the SV; using human service providers to deliver program elements; finalizing the conference agenda based on SV input; providing the SV with options for degrees of participation in the conference; presenting the SV with an apology only at the RP's program completion; offering the option to receive the apology in person or by letter; and communicating no expectation for response to the apology.

The right-hand column of Table 10.1 specifies the types of information needed to monitor the components of the program. Assuming that these indicators confirmed that the program was delivered as designed, RESTORE's impact on SVs would be seen in the extent to which they feel in control of decisions, supported, informed and prepared, safe, validated, able to access services, emotionally stable or less emotionally distressed compared to at program entry, and satisfied with the fairness of the conference process and the redress plan. It would be ideal to follow-up SVs during a longer term, but the pilot demonstration was funded to measure prevention of the RP's reoffending and not prevention of future SV victimization. Other important outcomes for the SV include a reduction of vulnerability, continued safety, satisfaction with fulfillment of the reparations, and perceptions of the post-conference program activities involving the RP.

The concerns summarized in the left-hand column of Table 10.2 are similar to those in Table 10.1, but they address the RP's perspective. Notice that, in contrast to Table 10.1, scant reference is made to existing criminal justice process in Table 10.2. The reason is that low levels of reporting, investigation, charging, and guilty findings exact little accountability across the spectrum of sexual assaults. Thus, from a RP's perspective, the system is currently acceptable in subjecting them to no long-term consequences except for the small minority who are selected to receive the full force of law. Generally, these are repeat offenders, with crimes involving injuries, harm to children, or assaults on strangers. None of these crimes was eligible for participation in RESTORE. Thus, the issues comprising Table 10.2 almost exclusively reference concerns that restorative methods could be ineffective or even counterproductive for RPs. These concerns include low motivation to participate, increased legal exposure, retaliatory aggression elicited by excessive shaming, superficial participation, and inefficacious therapeutic interventions.

The middle column of the table outlines features included in RESTORE in response to each concern. Some of the program features in the middle column are typical of standard conferencing models, such as conducting training of personnel, building support for restorative methods within the criminal justice system that houses or partners with

Table 10.2 Conceptual Overview of RESTORE from the Responsible Person (RP) Perspective

Concern	RESTORE Program Design	Potential Impact
Attrition rates at all levels of system are too high	Cultivate and "train" law enforcement and prosecutors to change norms and practice	Increased percentage of reported sexual assaults that pass each stage of criminal justice processing
Merit in referred cases must be vetted	Receive referrals through the police and prosecutors following usual practice; work collaboratively to identify appropriate cases	Viable numbers of program participants referred
Motivation of RP to participate may be low	Exclude a sexual assault criminal record, vulnerability to jail time, and mandatory registration from possible consequences; work collaboratively with defense counsel	High participation rate among eligible cases, with benefit of advice from defense counsel
Liability to both criminal and civil process	Encompass resolution into one process with a defined endpoint; exclude subsequent civil action if program is completed	High program completion rate
Self-incrimination	No record of proceedings	Conference protocol followed; judicial orders obtained
Counterproductive shaming	Limit number of SVs and attendees; prepare them for participation in conference	Process perceived as fair
Insincere and superficial apologies	Deliver Letter of Responsibility to victim at program completion	Apology rated as sincere
Agreement for reparations may not be fulfilled or program rules not followed	Center redress plan on providing reparation directly to the victim	RP completes all elements of redress plan
Insufficient rehabilitation	Tailor redress plan rehabilitation components to the deficits of the RP that reduce risk factors for offending	No reoffending
Exclusion from support and bonds with the non–sex offender community	Involve a community board to meet with RP throughout participation	Community board meetings with RP occur according to schedule

the conferencing program, and using a process that limits referrals to meritorious cases that would otherwise be subject to standard criminal justice. Other features respond to the unique demands of sexual assault. They include creating trade-offs in forms of accountability to increase willingness to meaningfully engage in RJ, addressing the multiple forms of legal exposure confronting an adult accused of a sex crime, implementing a range of constitutional rights (e.g., against double jeopardy and self-incrimination), limiting shaming to that inherent in having family and friends know the details of the sex offense committed, creating a process to maximize cognitive readiness to understand the transgression and make a sincere apology, tailoring rehabilitation to the causes of sex offending in each individual case, monitoring RPs for compliance, keeping concerned parties (including prosecutors, defense attorneys, and SVs) aware of the RP's progress, and destigmatizing and providing support for the RP, to increase his/her identification with the law-abiding as opposed to the deviant sex-offending population.

The right-hand column of Table 10.1 specified how evaluators would document that the components of the program were delivered as designed. A faithful application of the program was expected to reduce reoffending, deliver a process perceived as fair, result in a redress plan perceived as equitable and proportional to the offense, and communicate respect for the RP while setting clear limits.

RESTORE PROGRAM PROCESS

A phrase commonly heard in RJ is that "the devil is in the details." Figure 10.1 summarizes the specific steps that were involved in carrying out the RESTORE Program. It is intended as a flowchart for the activities and time-ordering that comprises the four stages of the RESTORE Program from intake to exit. These activities reflect the considerable time and effort spent in transforming the concepts in Tables 10.1 and 10.2 into a functional program ready to be unrolled to the public and able to withstand the scrutiny of law enforcement, prosecution, private attorneys, therapists, specialized sexual assault service providers and advocates, potential participants, the media, and the community-at-large. Besides the idea generation and problem-solving of our staff and collaborators, we were assisted by input from 14 diverse focus groups on program design and achieving buy-in from the community. Meetings were held with victims, offenders, treatment providers, advocates, diverse ethnic groups, and GLBT activists. After the program was under way, we also discovered unanticipated gaps or problems in process and implemented new or different activities based on input from participants. For example, we did not anticipate that noncontact SVs would want the process to go forward but did not desire to be further involved. In response, we developed the use of a "Permission to Proceed" consent form and developed a corps of community volunteers to speak as surrogate victims in the conferences.

- All referrals come from the Pima County Attorney's Office (PCAO) or Tucson City Attorney's Office (TCAO). Program personnel make all contacts with the survivor/victim (SV). A telephone call script is used to introduce the **RESTORE** Program and options available. The SV is given a deadline for response only when mandated by requirements to preserve prosecution options.

- The initial meeting with the SV can take place at the **RESTORE** office or an alternate location if required and/or needed by the SV. At this meeting, the SV is given a program manual and questions are answered. Consultation with a civil attorney free of charge is offered to the SV. All documents requiring signatures are gone over carefully, and the consent form is signed along with all other documents. The SV is provided additional time to decide, if needed, with a deadline given.

- After the SV consents, **RESTORE** personnel contacts the responsible person (RP) and/or their legal counsel regarding **RESTORE** as an option. Information is sent to the RP's counsel for review prior to the initial meeting. The RP is given 10 days to respond regarding participation.

- The initial meeting with the RP takes place at the **RESTORE** office where the RP's counsel can attend. If counsel for the RP requests, this meeting can take place in their office. The RP is given a manual, and all program requirements are gone over and documents signed along with the consent form. The RP is provided additional time to decide, if needed, with a deadline given.

- Additional meetings may be scheduled with either the SV or the RP for additional information or explanation.

If RESTORE is accepted by the RP:

- The RP meets with a qualified evaluator and undergoes a psychosexual evaluation.

- If the evaluator has concerns about the appropriateness of the RP's participation in **RESTORE**, these concerns are shared with the Program. If these concerns cannot be addressed prior to conference, a team decision is made to refer the case back to PCAO or TCAO.

If RESTORE is refused by the SV or RP:

- The case will be referred back to the PCAO or TCAO for conventional prosecution.

If the psychosexual forensic evaluator approves the RP's participation in **RESTORE**, the case continues on to stage 2.

Figure 10.1   Operational Process of RESTORE

Survivor/Victim (SV) Preparation

- The SV is given various options regarding his/her participation in the conference.

- The SV and case manager meet to review:

  – Safety concerns during **RESTORE**

  – Ground rules for participation in the program

  – The format of the conference and what the SV is going to say (or read if he/she prepares an impact statement)

  – The friends and family that the SV would like to attend the conference

  – The things that the SV wants to hear from the RP or ask the RP at the conference

  – The things that might be said at the conference and what may be included in the Redress Agreement

- The SV completes short assessment.

- Subsequent meetings may be scheduled for additional preparation.

- The SV and RP do not have face-to-face contact through the program prior to the conference.

Responsible Person (RP) Preparation

- The RP and case manager meet to review:

  – Safety concerns during **RESTORE**

  – Rules concerning his/her participation in the program

  – The format of the conference and what the SV is going to say

  – Things that the RP might be asked for during the conference (like restitution)

  – The friends and family that the RP would like to attend the conference

  – The things that might be said at the conference, and what may be included in the Redress Agreement

- The RP completes several evaluation forms, including a risk assessment, and other program-related assessments.

- Subsequent meetings may be scheduled for additional preparation.

- Regardless of the SV's decisions about participation in the conference, the RP must attend the conference and have with them at least one support person.

Support Network Preparation

- Program Personnel has separate meetings with the SV and his/her friends and family attending the conference, and with the RP and his/her friends and family attending the conference.

- In both meetings, participants review the **RESTORE** process, the rules of participation, the conference format, how friends and family can support the SV or RP, and what can be said during the conference. The process of completing the Redress Agreement is explained and discussed, and any safety concerns are listened to and dealt with. Friends and family receive informed consent and complete a pre-conference survey.

- The family and friends are prepared to make their impact statement during the conference.

- Additional preparation meetings may be scheduled with either the SV or RP and their friends and family.

Figure 10.1 (continued)

- Program personnel and a facilitator conduct the conference at a secure location.

- Prior to the conference, the SV will have decided whether or not he/she wants to give his/her recollections of the incident first, or if he/she wants the RP to review his/her behavior during the incident first.

- When the RP speaks, he/she describes the incident and his/her responsibility for it. When the SV or representative speaks, he/she describes the incident and how the incident has affected him/her and his/her friends and family. The RP then summarizes what the SV has said.

- The friends and family of the SV each, in turn, say how the incident has affected them. The RP is asked to summarize how the incident has affected the SVs friends and family.

- The friends and family of the RP each, in turn, say how the incident has affected them. The RP is asked to summarize how the incident has affected his/her friends and family.

- The SV and RP discuss the terms of the Redress Agreement with input from their friends and family. The SV, RP, Program Personnel, and Facilitator sign the Redress Agreement that specifies what will be done, timeframes, and rules governing RP conduct, including those relating to victim's rights and safety.

- After the conference, all participants complete a short evaluation of their experiences. Everyone is invited to participate in sharing refreshments, giving the participants an opportunity to talk with one another. This provides another opportunity for closure and reintegration.

After the Redress Agreement is signed the SV's active participation in the program ends. The SV will be notified of the RP's progress. If the RP fails to successfully complete the program or reoffends, the SV is notified immediately.

If the RP fails to complete the program or reoffends, the case is referred back to the PCAO or TCAO for conventional prosecution.

Stage 4: Accountability and Reintegration

- For the next 12 months, Program Personnel supervise the RP while he/she completes the requirements of the Redress Agreement.

- If the SV wishes, he/she is advised every three months whether the RP is in or out of compliance with the program requirements. The SV and anyone who attended the conference can also attend any meetings of the Community Accountability and Reintegration Board (CARB) related to the RP in his/her case.

- Any financial obligations the RP committed to in the Redress Agreement are paid, including any payments to the SV. **RESTORE** is the intermediary for all financial transactions.

- Twelve months after the conference, the RP attends a final meeting with the CARB. The SV and anyone who attended the conference may be present at this meeting. The RP reads a prepared reflection and clarification letter indicating his/her progress throughout the year. This is the formal recognition of his/her reintegration back into society as a law-abiding citizen.

Figure 10.1 (continued)

The consultations also revealed areas needing elaboration that program designers were too close to recognize. Questions drawn from the focus group transcripts were condensed into more than 150 unique topics. These questions were answered and posted on the program website as "Frequently Asked Questions," where they were available to potential participants, professionals, students, and the general public (RESTORE [n.d.]). RESTORE opened its doors in March, 2003. From the start, we excluded from our scope persons under age 18, repeat offenders, sexual assaults that were part of an ongoing intimate partner violence pattern, and crimes in which the violence exceeded that required to compel unwanted sex acts.

Stage 1: Referral and Intake

Figure 10.1 conveys the steps involved in RESTORE's four stages. The first is *referral and intake*. Referral is by prosecutors. Participation is voluntary. Legal counsel is provided for victims at no cost. Felony offenders who lack resources have public defenders or a low-cost ($35) legal consultation. Informed consent is obtained in writing. Only if survivor/victims consent is the program offered to offenders. The intent of these steps is to make participation voluntary and to provide transparent, nonbiased, and concrete information on what the selection of RESTORE would entail.

Some SVs told us that they did not want a face-to-face conference. In response, we modified the program to allow victims to determine their degree of involvement, ranging from simply giving permission for RESTORE to work with the offender through full participation except being in the same room with the RP. Regardless, SVs received the Letter of Reflection written by the RP at program exit, so that they were informed of the case outcome. This process is an important avenue to inform the community about the availability of alternatives, the accountability these alternatives impose, and the impact they have in the RP's own words. Many of the SVs who gave permission to proceed were security guards who observed sex acts on their premises and were required to report to law enforcement. RESTORE handled a great many cases that occurred at Target stores because that organization is known for its state-of-the-art security system. Other SVs who did not participate in the conference were represented by someone of their choosing, or by community members matched as closely as possible on age, ethnicity, and gender.

Stage 2: Preparation

The second stage of RESTORE is *preparation*, which is typically much longer than in other conferencing models in recognition of the complex nature of sexual victimization and the commitment to avoid reabuse at all costs. Preparation involves meeting separately and individually with the SV and her/his family and friends and the RP and his/her group. The agenda for every participant who wishes to attend the conference begins with the development of their conference statement (of impact for SV, and of responsibility for RPs). This step is done in writing because RESTORE worked with many people who were less educated than average and were anxious about speaking before a group. Many initial statements of responsibility by the RP are too short, vague, and impersonal. The case manager works with RPs to increase the amount of information and emotion included. Because case managers are in possession of police reports, they know the specific details of the offense and can work with the RP not to gloss over the offense. Many RPs do not initially understand why they are in the program. For example, they do not realize it is a criminal act to have sex with a woman who is unconscious from drinking. In these cases, preliminary work is required to reach a point at which they can acknowledge their acts and eliminate those sections of their statement that shift blame to the SV.

Responsible persons are discouraged from including an apology at this stage, and there is no requirement that RPs use words such as *rapist* or *rape* to identify themselves or their acts. We disagree with programs in Australia that require these actions from juvenile sex offenders. We believe that the conference is too soon after the incident for apology to be earned or meaningful to either the RP or the survivor/victim. Some SVs want to say in their impact statement that they were raped and that the RP is a rapist. We consider this their opinion, which they should express. In contrast, we discourage *ad hominem* statements such as pervert, scumbag, or words that could be considered profanity. Following the analysis of Toni Massaro (1997), we work with SVs to avoid excessive shaming, which can be counterproductive and even potentially dangerous in the context of sexual assault. We also limit the number of SVs who speak at the conference. We learned through experience that after approximately three impact statements, RPs are overwhelmed by input that they can no longer cognitively process, and as a result their behavior may violate conference rules and become abusive.

Preparation also focuses on family members and friends. As opposed to the adversarial treatment in the criminal justice process that may trigger family rejection, RESTORE works throughout to build up the credibility and legitimacy of the SV and to assist family and friends with input on how to provide social support. For the family and friends of the RP, a critical element of preparation is to allow them to hear the statement of responsibility in advance. There is no point in shocking family members, who are already distressed by having a loved one who committed a sex crime, with further humiliating details about the offense that the RP has minimized or withheld from them.

It is also important to do preparation around the redress plan. SVs often had suggestions for what type of community service should be included in the plan, but sometimes they need to be modified somewhat, such as when work with children is suggested. It is the rare children's agency that has established opportunities for sex offenders to volunteer and in any case our staff considered it unsafe. Some RPs want to use their professional skills, such as in fundraising or accounting, to help nonprofit agencies. In many instances, that is acceptable to the SV, but in others SVs preferred that the RPs experience work that placed them in laboring roles. In a few instances, SVs want reparation that is impossible or out of proportion to what would be imposed by a court, such as a $10,000 fine. Often, the RP is receptive to the redress proposals, but needs help working out logistics, such as a payment schedule. Most commonly, the payments are not monetary compensation to the SV, but symbolic reparation such as charitable donations, payment for wellness services such as massage, and replacement of sentimental items that may have been damaged in the assault. RESTORE also had requirements for supervision and treatment that need to be explained. In some cases, RPs do not feel that they need recommended treatment; most typically, this was because they do not believe that they have a drug or alcohol problem. However, it is an important element of individualizing redress and rehabilitation that the plan is directed at the each individual's pattern of risks for sexual offending, as opposed to a generic plan wherein all offenders are referred to the same service.

The ultimate goal of preparation is to ensure that the SV is ready to go to a meeting with enough emotional control and confidence that she/he will not feel reabused by completely breaking down, that the RP is ready to stay on message and accept redress plans without resistance, and that everyone knows the ground rules in advance and the consequences of breaking them.

Stage 3: The Conference

The third stage is the *conference*. It is professionally facilitated by a trained human service provider, held in a police station, and conducted according to a detailed protocol to maximize the safety of participants prior to, during, and after the conference. For example, the RP's group arrives first and waits in a separate room. The SV group then arrives and is escorted into the conference room in the order they select (RP first or SV first). One important difference from standard conferencing models is that a conference table is used, as opposed to sitting in a circle. Survivor/victims should not have their bodies exposed to the gaze of the responsible persons, nor sit without the perceived protection of a barrier wide enough to preclude bodily contact.

The agenda order is finalized by the SV but typically begins with an offender statement describing the wrongful act. Then the primary victim impact statement is made. Afterward, the RP is asked to restate in his/her own words what he/she heard. The SV is asked to provide feedback on whether the restatement captures her intended meaning, or to reemphasize certain points until the RP can verbalize them. Then, the family and friends of the SV speak, followed by those of the RP. After each speaker, the RP again restates what he/she has heard. Finally, the preliminary redress plan developed by the victim with program consultation is presented and agreed upon by all in attendance. The redress plan in its entirety is read by the facilitator prior to being presented to the SV and RP for signature. Redress plans consist of program demands (recommended psychotherapy or other treatment, no contact, community service, weekly supervision by program staff, quarterly supervision by the community board) and SV requirements.

RESTORE allows observers to be present with prior notification and the consent of SVs, RPs, and families and friends. Those requesting attendance include prosecutors, police officers, correctional officers, defense attorneys, and additional friends and family members, beyond the limit of five who sit at the table. Justice is a public process, and these rules balance SV control with the public need for justice accountability. Most conferences terminate with the RP party leaving immediately, and the SV group remaining voluntarily in the conference room for up to an hour to discuss what they have experienced and felt.

Stage 4: Monitoring and Reintegration

Stage four is *monitoring and reintegration*. Although supervision of the RP was governed by a professional case manager, RESTORE also included a Community Accountability and Re-Integration Board (CARB) of volunteer community members. The CARB fulfils a role for both survivor/victims and responsible persons. SVs may feel shame and may be ostracized or self-isolate. The program aims to generate support for victims from their family and friends, which partially flows from the very fact that the justice system is taking the crime seriously. The SV may also attend each CARB meeting in which her/his RP appears, which offers further opportunities for CARB, as a representation of the general community, to demonstrate condemnation of the RP's acts. RESTORE must also respond to the community's insistence on credible accountability from any alternative that diverges from conventional justice. The CARB disseminates information about what RESTORE is imposing on RPs. The decision to either continue offering support to RPs to complete their plan or to terminate RP for noncompliance rests with the CARB.

The inclusion of formal supervision represents a commitment to the SV of sexual assault to not retraumatize her with promises that are not kept. The CARB also helps to protect the community. This represents a method to mobilize a broader circle of community support/control agents and to reinforce the community-involvement value of restorative approaches. Representatives of the affected community can offer suggestions and assistance to the RP. They also make decisions about when a RP poses too great a threat to community safety or has exceeded citizens' tolerance for good faith efforts to reform.

RESTORE was designed with back-up from criminal justice. RPs were either liable to prosecution if they did not fulfill all the requirements placed on them for rehabilitation and reparation (felonies), or had already entered a guilty plea (misdemeanors). Upon successful program completion, a judge dismisses the case without the possibility of refiling it. If the RP is terminated prematurely, they face sentencing pursuant to their plea or return of their case to the criminal justice system.

CONCLUSION

In addition to RESTORE, other programs have debuted recently that apply restorative responses to sexual assault, including the Copenhagen Rape Crisis Centre (Madsen 2004, 2006); the Phaphamani Rape Crisis Counseling Centre in Uitenhage, South Africa (Skelton and Batley 2006); and Project Restore-NZ operating in Aukland, New Zealand (Jülich 2003, 2006; see Jülich, Chapter 11 in this volume). The first is based on a victim–offender dialogue model, and the last two on the conferencing model used in RESTORE. None has yet disseminated specific program designs and activities, but Project Restore-NZ is modeled closely on the RESTORE program described in this chapter. Although beyond the scope of the present chapter, these new programs raise important questions about where to most productively site and partner RJ for sexual assault. None of the new programs relies exclusively on referrals from the criminal justice system, and all are based in independent community service agencies. They also have identified a wide range of unserved SVs to whom they can reach out, including adult survivors of child sexual abuse who were not able to come forward at the time of the assault, SVs whose cases have been rejected from the criminal justice system, instances in which no perpetrator was identified, and offenses involving juvenile SVs and RPs (providing the offending is not part of an already established deviant sexual arousal pattern and/or a violent offense).

This chapter has attempted to support three take-home messages. First, a strong case exists for offering SVs alternative pathways to justice and implementing justice accountability that qualifies as viable prevention of sexual assault. Second, many procedural changes from standard conferencing models are required to minimize the overt problems that advocates, Indigenous people, and policy makers have identified in initial attempts to apply restorative principles to crimes against women. Third, RESTORE places a concrete and operational approach before the scholarly and practitioner community that results from collaboration, consultation, and listening to the needs of constituents. It is a starting point on which to build. Many groups of unserved and underserved victims of sexual assault need creative thinking to open avenues for them to achieve satisfying justice.

NOTES

1. RESTORE was funded by a grant from the National Center for Injury Control and Prevention of the U.S. Centers for Disease Control and Prevention. Although the material on RESTORE procedures was prepared specifically for this chapter and the tables and figure have not been previously published, the remaining material draws on previously published papers that are listed in the reference section. These sources discuss conceptual issues and empirical research findings in greater depth and are more extensively documented with original sources.
2. Additional issues arose related to internationally recognized principles of human subject protection in research and constitutional and statutory protections that effect the conduct of RJ when it is based in or linked to the criminal justice system. RESTORE navigated these complex considerations and developed processes for compliance through extensive consultation and input from human subject protection personnel within the University of Arizona and at the federal level, including the U.S. Centers for Disease Control and Prevention and the Department of Health and Human Services. Detailed discussion of the concerns from these sources is beyond the scope of this chapter (see Reimund 2005; United Nations 2007).

REFERENCES

Achilles, Mary. 2004. "Will Restorative Justice Live Up to Its Promise to Victims?" Pp. 65–74 in *Critical Issues in Restorative Justice,* edited by Howard Zehr and Barb Toews. Monsey, NY: Criminal Justice Press and Cullompton, Devon, UK: Willan Publishing.

Armour, Marilyn Peterson and Mark S. Umbreit. 2006. "Victim Forgiveness in Restorative Justice Dialogue." *Victims and Offenders* 1:123–140.

Breslau, Naomi, Ronald C. Kessler, Howard D. Chilcoat, Lonni R. Schultz, Glenn C. Davis, and Patricia Andreski. 1998. "Trauma and Posttraumatic Stress Disorder in the Community: The 1996 Detroit Area Survey of Trauma." *Archives of General Psychiatry* 55:626–632.

Cameron, Angela. 2006. "Stopping the Violence: Canadian Feminist Debates on Restorative Justice and Intimate Violence." *Theoretical Criminology* 10:49–66.

Campbell, Rebecca. 2005. "What Really Happened? A Validation Study of Rape Survivors' Help-Seeking Experiences with the Legal and Medical Systems." *Violence and Victims* 20:55–68.

———. 2006. "Rape Survivors' Experiences with the Legal and Medical Systems: Do Rape Victim Advocates Make a Difference?" *Violence Against Women* 12:1–16.

Campbell, Rebecca, Tracy Sefl, Holly E. Barnes, Courtney E. Ahrens, Sharon M. Wasco, and Yolanda Zaragoza-Diesfeld. 1999. "Community Services for Rape Survivors: Enhancing Psychological Well-Being or Increasing Trauma?" *Journal of Consulting and Clinical Psychology* 67:847–858.

Curtis-Fawley, Sarah and Kathleen Daly. 2005. "Gendered Violence and Restorative Justice: The Views of Victim Advocates." *Violence Against Women* 11:603–638.

Daly, Kathleen. 2003. "Making Variation a Virtue: Evaluating the Potential and Limits of Restorative Justice." Pp. 23–50 in *Restorative Justice in Context: International Practice and Directions,* edited by Elmar G.M. Weitekamp and Hans-Jurgen Kerner. Cullompton, Devon, UK: Willan Publishing.

————. 2006. "Restorative Justice and Sexual Assault: An Archival Study of Court and Conference Cases." *British Journal of Criminology* 46:334–356.

Daly, Kathleen and Julie Stubbs. 2006. "Feminist Engagement with Restorative Justice." *Theoretical Criminology* 10:9–28.

————. 2007. "Feminist Theory, Feminist and Anti-Racist Politics, and Restorative Justice." Pp. 149–170 in *Handbook of Restorative Justice,* edited by Gerry Johnstone and Daniel W. Van Ness. Cullompton, Devon, UK: Willan Publishing.

Frazier, Patricia and Beth Haney. 1996. "Sexual Assault Cases in the Legal System: Police, Prosecutor, and Victim Perspectives." *Law and Human Behavior* 20:607–628.

Gordon, Margaret and Stephanie Riger. 1989. *The Female Fear.* New York: The Free Press.

Herman, Judith L. 2005. "Justice from the Victim's Perspective." *Violence Against Women* 11:571–602.

Hopkins, C. Quince and Mary P. Koss. 2005. "Incorporating Feminist Theory and Insights into a Restorative Justice Response to Sex Offenses." *Violence Against Women* 11:693–723.

Hopkins, C. Quince, Mary P. Koss, and Karen J. Bachar. 2004. "Applying Restorative Justice to Ongoing Intimate Violence: Problems and Possibilities." *St. Louis University Public Law Review* 23: 289–311.

Hudson, Barbara. 1998. "Restorative Justice: The Challenge of Sexual and Racial Violence." *Journal of Law and Society* 25:237–256.

Johnstone, Gerry and Daniel W. Van Ness, eds. 2007. *Handbook of Restorative Justice.* Cullompton Devon, UK: Willan Publishing.

Jordan, Jan. 2004. "Beyond Belief? Police, Rape and Women's Credibility." *Criminal Justice* 4:29–59.

Jülich, Shirley. 2003. "Critical Issues in Restorative Justice: Aotearoa New Zealand." *VOMA Connections* 14:5–8.

————. 2006. "Views of Justice Among Survivors of Historical Child Sexual Abuse: Implications for Restorative Justice in New Zealand." *Theoretical Criminology* 10:125–138.

Koss, Mary P. 2000. "Blame, Shame, and Community: Justice Responses to Violence Against Women." *American Psychologist* 55:1332–1343. (Published address given on the occasion of receiving the American Psychological Association Award for Distinguished Contributions to Research in Public Policy.)

————. 2006. "Restoring Rape Survivors: Justice, Advocacy, and a Call to Action." *Annals of the New York Academy of Sciences* 1087:206–234.

Koss, Mary P. and Mary Achilles. 2008. *Restorative Justice Responses to Sexual Assault.* Harrisburg, PA: VAWnet, a project of the National Resource Center on Domestic Violence/ Pennsylvania Coalition Against Domestic Violence. Retrieved February 19, 2009 (http://www.vawnet.org).

Koss, Mary P. and Aurelio José Figueredo. 2004a. "Change in Cognitive Mediators of Rape's Impact on Psychosocial Health across Two Years of Recovery." *Journal of Consulting and Clinical Psychology* 72:1063–1072.

————. 2004b. "A Cognitive Mediational Model of Rape Recovery: Cross-Validation in Longitudinal Data." *Psychology of Women Quarterly* 28:273–286.

Koss, Mary P., Karen Bachar, and C. Quince Hopkins. 2003. "Restorative Justice for Sexual Violence: Repairing Victims, Building Community, and Holding Offenders Accountable." *Annals of the New York Academy of Sciences* 989:384–396.

Koss, Mary P., Karen Bachar, C. Quince Hopkins, and Carolyn Carlson. 2004. "Expanding a Community's Justice Response to Sex Crimes Through Advocacy, Prosecutorial, and Public Health Collaboration: Introducing the RESTORE Program." *Journal of Interpersonal Violence* 19:1435–1463.

Latimer, Jeff, Craig Dowden, and Danielle Muise. 2005. "The Effectiveness of Restorative Justice Practices: A Meta-Analysis." *The Prison Journal* 85:127–144.

Massaro, Toni. 1997. "The Meanings of Shame: Implications for Legal Reform." *Psychology, Public Policy, and Law* 3:645–703.

Mika, Harry, Mary Achilles, Ellen Halbert, Howard Zehr, and Lorraine Stutzman Amstutz. 2002. *Taking Victims and Their Advocates Seriously: A Listening Project.* Akron, PA: Mennonite Central Committee. Retrieved August 16, 2007 (http://www.restorativejustice.org/resources/docs/mika).

Madsen, Karin Sten. 2004. "Mediation as a Way of Empowering Women Exposed to Sexual Coercion." *NORA: Nordic Journal of Women's Studies* 12:58–61.

———. 2006. "How Could You Do This to Me?" *Restorative Justice Online.* Retrieved August 16, 2007 (http://www.restorativejustice.org/editions/2006/july06/denmark).

Monroe, Laura M., Linda M. Kinney, Mark D. Weist, Denise Spriggs Dafeamekpor, Joyce Dantzler, and Matthew W. Reynolds. 2005. "The Experience of Sexual Assault: Findings from a Statewide Victim Needs Assessment." *Journal of Interpersonal Violence* 20:767–776.

Nancarrow, Heather. 2006. "In Search of Justice for Domestic and Family Violence: Indigenous and Non-Indigenous Australian Women's Perspectives." *Theoretical Criminology* 10:87–106.

Orth, Ulrich and Andreas Maercker. 2004. "Do Trials of Perpetrators Retraumatize Crime Victims?" *Journal of Interpersonal Violence* 19:212–227.

———. 2006. "Feelings of Revenge, Retaliation Motive, and Posttraumatic Stress Reactions in Crime Victims." *Journal of Interpersonal Violence* 21:229–243.

Poulson, Barton. 2003. "A Third Voice: A Review of Empirical Research on the Psychological Outcomes of Restorative Justice." *Utah Law Review* 167:167–203.

Reimund, Mary Ellen. 2005. "The Law and Restorative Justice: Friend or Foe? A Systemic Look at the Legal Issues in Restorative Justice." *Drake Law Review* 53: 667–692.

RESTORE. 2006. *RESTORE Overview Manual* (Revised March 9, 2006). Tucson: University of Arizona. Retrieved February 19, 2009 (http://www.restoreprogram.publichealth.arizona.edu/process/default.htm).

———. n.d. "Questions." Tucson, AZ: University of Arizona. Retrieved February 19, 2009 (www.restoreprogram.publichealth.arizona.edu).

Seidman, Ilene and Susan Vickers. 2005. "The Second Wave: An Agenda for the Next Thirty Years of Rape Law Reform." *Suffolk University Law Review* 38:467–491.

Sherman, Lawrence W., Heather Strang, Caroline Angel, Daniel Woods, Meredith Rossner, Geoffrey C. Barnes, Sarah Bennett, and Nova Inkpen. 2005. "Effects of Face-to-Face Restorative Justice on Victims of Crime in Four Randomized, Controlled Trials." *Journal of Experimental Criminology* 1:367–395.

Skelton, Anne and Mike Batley. 2006. *Charting Progress, Mapping the Future: Restorative Justice in South Africa*. Pretoria, South Africa: Institute for Security Studies. Retrieved August 16, 2007 (http://www.iss.co.za/index.php?link_id=3&slink_id=2920&link_type=12&slink_type=12&tmpl_id=3).

Strang, Heather. 2004. "Is Restorative Justice Imposing Its Agenda on Victims?" Pp. 96–105 in *Critical Issues in Restorative Justice*, edited by Howard Zehr and Barb Toews. Monsey, NY: Criminal Justice Press and Cullompton, Devon, UK: Willan Publishing.

Stubbs, Julie. 2002. "Domestic Violence and Women's Safety: Feminist Challenges to Restorative Justice." Pp. 42–61 in *Restorative Justice and Family Violence*, edited by Heather Strang and John Braithwaite. Cambridge, UK: Cambridge University Press.

Umbreit, Mark S, Betty Vos, Robert B. Coates, and Elizabeth Lightfoot. 2005. "Restorative Justice in the Twenty-first Century: A Social Movement Full of Opportunities and Pitfalls." *Marquette Law Review* 89:251–304.

United Nations. 2007. *Handbook on Restorative Justice Programmes*. New York: United Nations Publications.

Walker, Stephen P. and Dap A. Louw. 2007. "The Court for Sexual Offences: Perceptions of the Professionals Involved." *International Journal of Law and Psychiatry* 30:136–146.

11

RESTORATIVE JUSTICE AND GENDERED VIOLENCE IN NEW ZEALAND
A Glimmer of Hope

SHIRLEY JÜLICH

A report released in 2006 on the status of women in New Zealand[1] found that women here are subjected to intolerable levels of violence (Ministry of Women's Affairs 2006). Victim advocacy groups would not disagree, but their information indicates that women are reluctant to report violence, in particular sexual violence, to investigative authorities. This is not surprising given the outcome of recent high-profile court cases addressing historical gang rape allegations. The first plaintiff alleged that between 1985 and 1986 she had been raped and sexually abused, as an 18-year-old, by three men, then police officers in their mid 20s to early 30s (Dewes 2006). Judicial suppression orders were applied, so that previous rape convictions for two of the defendants were withheld from the jury, but notably not the history of the alleged victim.

The trial, her word against theirs, played out in the media and peoples' homes throughout New Zealand. Private and intimate details were made very public, to the extent that some critics noted that the alleged victim's character was more important in the court hearings than the characters of the accused (Martin 2006a). Subsequently, the jury's "not guilty" verdict prompted demonstrations and street marches by women's groups throughout the country and debate as to what should and should not be

239

included as evidence. When some, but not all, of the judicial suppression orders were lifted after the trial, it became public knowledge that the accused, who had maintained throughout the trial that their relationship with the plaintiff was consensual, were "... still [to] face historic sexual allegations from a second woman" (Martin 2006a:3).

The three men returned to the court room in 2007 to face further allegations by a second woman (who was 16 at the time of the alleged offense) that were very similar to the previous trial in 2006; again, the histories of the three defendants were withheld from the jury. On completion of this trial, in which a "not guilty" verdict also was returned, all judicial suppression orders were lifted, including those from the previous trial. The public, including jury members, learned that two of the defendants, no longer police officers, were currently serving sentences for previous, unrelated rape convictions. The third, a police officer of high rank, hoping to return to work now that he had been acquitted, was not only the subject of a new sex inquiry but also was subject to "unresolved 'employment issues' " and allegations of sexually inappropriate behavior in the workplace (Cook 2007).

In fairness, it should be stressed that these court cases were managed in a way that was procedurally correct and in accordance with New Zealand legislation. However, it could be argued that these cases came close to undermining the credibility of the criminal justice system in New Zealand, at least from the perspective of rape victims. Even though the two juries had returned "not guilty" pleas, public opinion did not seem to agree. Two commentators in particular seemed to encapsulate the general mood of the country, in particular its women. Jan Jordan, an academic researcher and criminologist, commented that a "not guilty" verdict "doesn't necessarily mean that they are innocent, it means that there is not enough evidence to persuade this jury to convict them" (TVNZ 2007). The New Zealand Prime Minister, Helen Clark, said "there have to be issues around the common interpretation of consent when three adult policeman are engaging in group sex with a mixed-up 16-year-old girl" (Coddington 2007, para. 9).

In addition to highlighting issues such as abuse of power and the police culture at the time of the alleged rapes, these cases have emphasized the difficulties women encounter as they seek redress in the criminal justice system, irrespective of the defendant's position in society. Indeed, there have been calls for "... judges, criminal lawyers, prosecutors and most importantly [victims] to get around a table ... and come up with something better" (Martin 2006b:D2).

Advocates of restorative justice (RJ) would argue that there is a better way, and that RJ could provide victims and offenders the privacy and the safety to address sexual abuse and rape. I cannot help but wonder what the outcomes might have been if the alleged victims and the three defendants of the cases outlined here had been offered restorative conferences instead of trials. It is, therefore, relevant and timely to ask the following questions: In cases where an abuse of power has occurred, such as with sexual violence, does RJ have the potential to overcome the shortcomings of traditional justice systems and provide victims with a sense of justice? What do victims of sexual assault say about RJ? Can RJ address violence that is power-based and reflective of entrenched societal attitudes and beliefs?

I will explore these questions by discussing research I conducted on how adult survivors of child sexual abuse perceive justice. The idea of RJ had appealed to me as a researcher, and I wondered if survivors would feel the same. Survivors of child sexual abuse share similarities with rape victims, in that victimization typically occurs within a context of abuse of power, offenders and victims are often known to each other within a family or social system, and abuse is frequently reflective of entrenched societal attitudes and beliefs (Stubbs 2002). Accordingly, the sexual abuse of children has been included by some commentators under the broader umbrella of gendered and sexualized violence (Hudson 2002) or gendered harm (Daly 2002). It is, therefore, possible that the opinions of adult survivors of child sexual abuse in relation to RJ could be similar to those of rape victims.

Although little appears to have changed in the criminal justice system for victims of gendered violence, the same might not be true of RJ. This chapter critiques three fundamental principles of RJ: the involvement of victims, the negotiation of a community response, and the transfer of power to the community. This will be followed by a discussion outlining how Project Restore-NZ, a new project in New Zealand, is attempting to address these issues as it aims to deliver a sense of justice to victims of gendered violence. The chapter concludes with a discussion of three practice issues that are particularly relevant to gendered violence: neutrality, impartiality, and confidentiality.

THE INVOLVEMENT OF VICTIMS[2]

To investigate how victims perceive justice, I conducted research with a group of adult survivors of child sexual abuse. This group included 18 women and three men, of whom four women and three men had reported sexual abuse to the police. I gathered information in a variety of ways, including participant observation in self-help and community groups, unstructured interviews with adult survivors and key community informants, a case study that involved observation of regular counseling sessions between a survivor and a registered counselor over a one-year period, and focus groups convened for the purpose of writing a report on aspects of justice, which was subsequently submitted to the New Zealand government. The majority of the interviews with survivors (18 women and three men) took place between 1995 and 1997, when RJ was beginning to emerge for use with adult offenders in New Zealand. At the end of each interview, I described RJ as it was at that time[3]: a voluntary process similar to the family group conference of the New Zealand Youth Justice system.

I briefly outlined the underlying philosophies and principles of RJ and the various processes RJ uses.[4]

When I asked survivors what would provide them with a sense of justice, they described processes that could be identified as RJ. But when I described RJ to them, they did not think it would encourage them to report the victimization they had been subjected to as children. They were not convinced that RJ could remain victim-centered and provide them with a sense of justice (Jülich 2001).

Adult survivors of child sexual abuse indicated that they wanted to confront the offender and be more involved in the process of justice, yet they seemed unable to see themselves utilizing RJ to achieve this (Jülich 2001). An underlying assumption of RJ is that victims would want to attend a restorative process in which they could confront the offender and have their say in a safe forum. Such an assumption could suggest that any pre-existing relationship was likely premised on equality. This is not the case in gendered violence. An imbalance of power exists, and it concerns critics of RJ, particularly those who discuss RJ in relation to domestic violence (Parker 2004). They recognize that RJ uses similar process techniques to those of mediation (Hooper and Busch 1996). Some women's advocates argue that because of the inherent inequality that exists between victims and offenders, the traditional adversarial process of the criminal justice system could better serve victims of domestic violence (Hooper and Busch 1996). But others have noted that the current criminal justice system is just as inadequate at equalizing power imbalances (Carbonatto 1995; McElrea 2004). Victim advocates would argue that this point was demonstrated in the recent high-profile cases outlined in the introduction of this chapter.

The dynamics of gendered violence could indicate that the pre-existing power imbalance, which enabled sexual victimization, might preclude the involvement of victims in RJ processes. Adult survivors noted that some victims might find it more acceptable to designate a person to represent them at restorative conferences (Jülich 2001). They urged that the burden of responsibility as to whether RJ would proceed should not rest solely on the victim. They suggested that RJ could proceed in some instances without the victim; the sense of justice could be achieved for absent victims through the outcomes of the process and attendance to the needs of the victim. The RESTORE Program, a feminist–restorative hybrid approach to rape in the United States (see Chapter 10), enables victims to designate a family member or friend to take their place in the restorative conference (Koss, Bachar, Hopkins, and Carlson 2004).

Adult survivors of child sexual abuse queried the role of victims in restorative conferences (Jülich 2001). Although they identified advantages for victims, offenders, and communities, they were concerned that the needs of victims to confront an offender could be exploited. Survivors indicated that RJ practitioners must be clear as to whose interests are being served: those of the victim or those of the offender. Although it could be advantageous for offenders to have the opportunity to demonstrate accountability and responsibility for their actions in the presence of their communities, this should not take place at the expense of victims.

NEGOTIATION OF A COMMUNITY RESPONSE

RJ practice emphasizes the involvement of victims, offenders, and their communities in negotiating a community response. Adult survivors of child sexual abuse queried the definition of "community" (Jülich 2001), as have other commentators. Marshall (1999) noted that it was necessary to consider what the term community might actually involve, and discussed community not only in relation to a fellowship of interest, but also in geographical terms. The distribution of resources between geographic communities is not typically equal. Some communities might not be able to provide and sustain the necessary level of commitment a RJ program would require (Marshall 1999). Indeed, not all communities have the same capacity or willingness to respond (Crawford 2000). Some families might be able to provide more resources in relation to meeting the needs of offenders and victims, whereas others might have limited ability to provide any necessary resources. It could also be argued that some communities, for example gangs and dysfunctional family systems, might tolerate higher levels of misogyny or the sexual objectification of women and children.

A restorative conference should be an opportunity for the community of interest to discuss the impacts of offending, hold offenders to account, and come to an agreement, if possible, on ways to repair the harm and put things right. The majority of victims, both child and adult, are assaulted by someone known to them (Anderson et al. 1993; Koss et al. 2004; Randall and Haskell 1995; Russell 1983). Therefore, the community of interest could be comprised of people who, for a variety of reasons, were unable to intervene in the process of victimization. Some victims of gendered violence, particularly those sexually assaulted as a child by a family member, would have no grounds to believe they could trust the "community" to do what would be right for all those involved.

If the victimization of women and children has been entrenched within the family system over several generations, it could be difficult for such communities to provide the necessary level of support to see that the agreed upon conference outcomes are carried out. Women in these family systems might be less equipped to withstand the offender's constructs of denial and other rationalizations. Conversely, some communities or family systems might have less tolerance of gendered violence and so the agreed upon conference outcomes could be more severe (Koss et al. 2004). Undeniably, it could be argued that RJ advocates are burdening a community with the responsibility of addressing such complex issues as structural inequality and misogyny in a meeting of a few hours, issues that society has been unable to resolve (Stubbs 1997).

In New Zealand, for those cases that have been referred by the courts, the agreed-upon outcomes are handed back to the courts for their consideration at sentencing. While this provides for some equality between offenders of a similar crime, The Sentencing Act 2002 requires judges to consider the outcomes of restorative conferences at sentencing. It is possible that those offenders who have participated in a restorative conference might get a lesser sentence than those who have not. However, unless there is some system that provides careful monitoring of conference outcomes, those offenders attending restorative conferences might not be fulfilling the agreed upon-outcomes of the restorative conference.

THE TRANSFER OF POWER TO THE COMMUNITY

Supporters of RJ seem to believe that a transfer of power from the state to the community is the solution to addressing increased levels of crime within our society. Political ideology tends to support this claim. Neo-liberalism, as a relatively new political ideology, with its aims of decentralization, deinstitutionalization, and devolution, was sold to the public as a means of empowering the community (Kelsey 1997). Throughout the 1980s neo-liberalist policies emerged in the United States and the United Kingdom and were adopted by New Zealand governments during the mid 1980s. Daly and Immarigeon (1998) argued that the grassroots form of social democracy, with its central aim to promote well-being, and neo-liberalism's emphasis on economic rationality, entrepreneurial activity, and empowering the consumer were congruent with the aims and objectives of RJ. Braithwaite (1996:24) noted that "some of the most savvy conservative governments in the world, [those] most imbued with the imperatives for fiscal frugality—New Zealand and Singapore—[were] early movers in embracing restorative justice." However, as Kelsey (1997:292) argued, when not properly funded—and to date it has not been—the rhetoric of neo-liberalism translated to "shifting the burden from the state to primarily women 'volunteers' who were assumed to have a limitless capacity for unpaid labor in 'the community' or the home."

Adult survivors of child sexual abuse noted this point, although not in these terms (Jülich 2001). They asked who would pay and who would be responsible for the ongoing delivery of services. They believed that the transfer of power could ultimately equate to the transfer of responsibility to women. It might be possible that women could ultimately bear not only the responsibility of ensuring the safety of vulnerable victims in the offender's network, but also be providing oversight to an offender who has returned to his community for support. Notably, Daly (2000), in her research based on youth justice conferences, found that women were not more involved than men in the supervision of conference agreements. Although this may be the case, we need to be mindful that RJ might not be able to live up to its promises regarding the ability of communities to provide redress to victims (Crawford 2000).

Adult survivors of child sexual abuse were not supportive of the transfer of power from the state to the community of interest without appropriate structures in place to protect women and victims from being further disadvantaged (Jülich 2001). However, they did not reject the principles of RJ unconditionally, as they had traditional criminal justice (Jülich 2001). They appeared skeptical that these principles could be achieved, given the complexity of historical child sexual abuse, but at the same time they acknowledged that the flexibility of RJ could enable the development of practice models that might negate their concerns.

GENDERED VIOLENCE AND RESTORATIVE JUSTICE

Gendered violence was excluded from a court-referred pilot program for RJ that was funded by the Ministry of Justice and operated in four court centers throughout New Zealand (Department for Courts 2002). Sexual offences were excluded because these attracted penalties outside of the pilot parameters, but domestic violence was deliberately excluded (Department for Courts 2002). This decision was also based on the view that such cases might not be suitable for RJ, given the power imbalance between victim and offender (McElrea 2004), a perception that is well-supported in the literature (Parker, 2004).[5] However, it should be noted that the literature tends to be speculative (Curtis-Fawley and Daly 2005) and, further, there is little information on operational programs addressing gendered violence (Parker 2004). Despite the concerns raised in the literature, some groups have implemented programs using RJ practices to address gendered violence.

The RESTORE program in the United States (Koss, Bachar, and Hopkins 2003) is using RJ to address sexual offenses that fall outside of the domestic violence context, using a joint program between the College of Public Health, University of Arizona Pima County Attorney's Office, the Tucson City Attorney's Office, and the Tucson Police Department.[6] In Copenhagen, counselors at the Centre for Victims of Sexual Assault are offering a form of mediation to victims and offenders of sexual assault as one way of empowering women to gain control over their lives (Sten Madsen 2004). Similar processes are being used to address domestic violence in Finland (Flinck and Iivari 2004) and Austria (Glaeser 2004). It is unclear if the Finnish and Austrian programs are using a conferencing model, but from their descriptions they appear to be restorative in nature. Evaluations of these four programs are yet to be published.

RJ provider groups in New Zealand have been providing restorative conferences for cases of family violence outside of the pilot program, but little is known about the processes, safeguards, and outcomes of these conferences. Counselors at Auckland Sexual Abuse Help (ASAH)[7] have supported victims of sexual assault as they pursued justice in other ways, including civil cases and face-to-face facilitated meetings that resulted in positive outcomes for victims. This informal level of support for alternatives to the criminal justice system came from counselors and victims of gendered violence outside of the RJ field, as opposed to RJ practitioners, and led to the development of a new program that has come to be known as Project Restore-NZ.

PROJECT RESTORE-NZ

Inspired by Mary Koss of the RESTORE program (Koss, Bachar, and Hopkins 2003) at a conference in April 2004, representatives of community groups came together to create Project Restore-NZ.[8] The founding members have developed a program within a New Zealand context that aims to provide a sense of justice to adult victims of gendered violence. This initiative is seated across two community groups that represent both victim and offender perspectives. The primary supporter of Project Restore-NZ is ASAH, a counseling and support provider to victims of sexual assault. The second group, the Safe Network, is an Auckland-based program for the treatment of child sexual abusers (Annan 2004). Project Restore-NZ is receiving referrals from the court system in Auckland, and is currently funded by the Ministry of Justice to develop best-practice guidelines based on their experience.

The service provided by Project Restore-NZ is underpinned by the belief that victims of sexual assault are not likely to opt for RJ unless they are confident that the community has the ability and commitment necessary to support and oversee consensual outcomes. Further, it is likely that victims will require some assurance that they are not only central to the process but also are sufficiently supported in making contributions to problem-solving and that the RJ practitioner or the community has sufficient expertise to equalize an imbalance of power.

Project Restore-NZ aims to be truly victim-centered, and as a program that is led by a victim agency, it is well positioned to protect victims from additional exploitation. This highlights the importance of having victim agencies involved in the planning and operation of RJ programs. Although the possibility of using victim substitutes at conferences has been and would be considered, the program has not used this option to date. While it might be a challenge to provide a victim-driven process without a victim present, Project Restore-NZ works with the challenges each case presents and, if it were to use victim substitutes, it would aim to develop a process that did not run the risk of becoming offender-focused. The use of victim substitutes could increase the risk of the victim's perspective being minimized or marginalized, particularly in situations in which all forms of violence are normalized.

The imbalance of power between victim and offender is mediated by including community experts—one an expert on offender issues, the other an expert on victim issues—as part of the team that works together with an

RJ facilitator. The team is responsible for meticulous preparation of all intending and potential participants in the restorative conference. The aim is to first provide sufficient information so that all participants have a realistic understanding of the process and potential outcomes and, second, to provide support for the victim at the conference. Although the victim has the final say on who will attend the conference, she is advised by the expert on victim issues. Team members regularly meet with an independent clinician, as a form of professional supervision, to discuss progress and to ascertain whether preparations or the conference itself should proceed. They meet again at the end of the restorative process to review and reflect on professional practice.

The team carefully plans the conference and selects a venue that provides private spaces both indoors and out. Conference participants are advised to set aside a whole day for the restorative conference, in an acknowledgment that a meeting of an hour or so cannot undo the harm that in some cases has taken decades to develop. Within the restorative conference, the community experts form part of the community of interest. Their roles are to challenge any constructs of denial or minimization of the offending behavior as it might occur in the conference. They also take on an educational role as they inform conference participants about issues relating to victimization or offending. Immediately after the conference, the team meets to debrief and to prepare a post-conference plan of follow-up for both victim and offender.

Project Restore-NZ plans to maintain contact with victims and offenders for as long as required while the agreed-upon conference outcomes are completed. The length of time is determined on a case-by-case basis. It should be noted that unless there is some form of court-ordered supervision in the sentence that includes the restorative conference outcomes, no legislation enacted in New Zealand can force the offender to complete these outcomes. To date, this has been left to moral obligation and informal monitoring by family members and conference facilitators. For serious crime such as gendered violence, a formal process of enforcing conference outcomes is necessary. It is important to note that if RJ provider groups accept referrals from the community outside of the court system, there is no legal obligation for alleged offenders to complete any agreed-upon conference outcomes.

Throughout the development of the program, three practice issues emerged that appear to be particularly relevant in the context of gendered violence and worthy of more investigation. In the next section I will discuss neutrality, impartiality and confidentiality from the perspective of victims.

Neutrality and Impartiality

Adult survivors of child sexual abuse queried the definitions of neutrality and impartiality and their role in RJ (Jülich 2001). They had difficulty reconciling the neutral and impartial role of a RJ practitioner in facilitating a conference for what is defined as serious crime. Yet, they indicated that a sense of fairness and equality between the victim and the offender was central to an experience of justice.

The RJ literature appears to present a confused picture in respect to the neutrality and impartiality of RJ practitioners. Marshall (1999) noted that training was essential for RJ practitioners, so that they could fulfill the role as a neutral party. Coker (1999) argued that the neutrality of the practitioner, coupled with the structural disadvantages that women have experienced, could ignore past injustices between the victim and offender. If the facilitator were to treat the victim and offender equally, the structural inequality that persists between men and women would be upheld (Coker 1999). Such practices involving victims and offenders of gendered violence will only serve to revictimize the victim. Others advocated that, although a practitioner should be a neutral third party, they accepted that a compromise of neutrality was inevitable. Bowen, Boyack, and Hooper (2000) said that practitioners should aim to be sufficiently neutral and impartial to a level that would satisfy the participants' perceptions of fairness and justice. This begs the questions of how participants' perceptions would be assessed and who would assess them. Moreover, if a facilitator were to adopt a third-party neutral stance and not challenge victim-blaming or gender-biased explanations, she would be reinforcing the offender's belief and value systems (Coker 1999). This could not be a safe environment for a victim of gendered violence.

The objectives of RJ are to generate meaningful accountability and to acknowledge the wrong that has been perpetrated against the victim (Claassen 1996; Zehr 1995). These objectives cannot be described as neutral. To achieve them, restorative conferencing attempts to empower weaker parties, so that their voices can be heard and their stories told. In so doing, practitioners use a range of interventions that support the weaker participant against the power of the more powerful participant. Restorative conferencing not only enables victims to tell their stories, but also it allows offenders to tell theirs. The experience offenders have had at maintaining elaborate rationalizations and constructs of denial could enable them to maintain their credibility with their supporters in restorative conferences. Practitioners must challenge any explanations of gendered violence that are focused on blaming the victim, or other such explanations that minimize sexual abuse. Such interventions cannot be described as neutral. Perhaps this is why Coker (1999) claimed that RJ does not ascribe to the ideal of the neutral mediator.

Boulle, Jones, and Goldblatt (1998:19) argued that it was more useful "to distinguish between neutrality in the sense of a disinterestedness and neutrality in the sense of fairness." The former explanation they defined as neutrality, the latter as impartiality. They argued that by making this distinction, the concept of neutrality could be used to describe the background of the practitioner, her expertise in the subject matter, prior knowledge of the specific circumstances, any previous relationships with the parties, and any degree of interest in the outcomes. By contrast, they described impartiality as "evenhandedness, objectivity, and fairness toward the parties during the mediation process." The challenge for RJ in relation to gendered violence is to provide an "even playing field," while at the same time treating both victim and offender fairly. The model used by the Austrian program addressing domestic violence, mentioned earlier in this chapter, abandons the concept of a *neutral* third-party mediator; instead, the role of the mediator is to provide a balance of power by protecting and supporting the victim (Glaeser 2004).

Project Restore-NZ adapted the model of restorative conferencing pioneered by the early RJ providers in New Zealand in the mid 1990s. Community experts are included in all stages of the restorative process, from pre-conference planning through to conference and follow-up. As mentioned earlier, their role is to challenge any constructs of denial and minimization of the offending behavior. While this might be treating the victim and offender differently, it aims to provide equality of outcome for the victim and enables the facilitator, who is not typically an expert on gendered violence, to focus the process more toward a perception of fairness or impartiality.

Confidentiality

Survivors of child sexual abuse questioned the notion of confidentiality in relation to disclosures arising within restorative conferences that indicated other serious offending had occurred or was occurring (Jülich 2001). What is more, other information could be shared by participants within the conference that has no bearing on the case at hand and perhaps should not be conveyed to the courts. It has been generally accepted within the RJ community of New Zealand that the proceedings of conferences remain confidential. Bowen and colleagues (2000) argued that confidentiality was a key element in establishing a safe environment in which open communication could occur between all participants. They maintained that an assurance of confidentiality facilitated truthful discussion, particularly in relation to feelings, thereby realizing the benefits of RJ. Further, the authors argued for a change in the law, so that absolute confidentiality would be assured for the content of a restorative conference, thereby ensuring that any offender who admitted to other criminal activity within a restorative conference could do so without the risk of further prosecution.

To date, no such change has been implemented, and the confidentiality of RJ conferences has not been tested in the New Zealand courts. Current practice dictates that, should other offences be admitted, or should any deadly threats be made, the facilitator would report this directly to the police. Furthermore, if a police officer is present at the conference at the time such disclosures or threats are made, he is obliged to make an arrest or initiate a police investigation.

Conference reports are the mechanisms that inform the courts and other involved parties of the discussions that took place. Given that these reports can be referred to in open court, they should be considered as public documents and, as such, disclaimers should be provided to intending participants of restorative conferences that confidentiality cannot be guaranteed. In New Zealand, it has been accepted that a conference report will include a verbatim account of some aspects of the conference. This is intended to convey the flavor of the conference and allow a judge to gain some insight as to whether the offender accepted accountability or demonstrated any remorse. Additionally, the details in a conference report provide much more information to the courts about the victim's story than has been previously provided in police reports.

Project Restore-NZ has adopted the same practice as other RJ providers in relation to reports, although some experimenting has occurred. In one instance, the traditional chronological approach of what was said in the conference was substituted by a report that outlined the main themes discussed. This particular format was accepted without comment by the courts. The victim thought it was an accurate account of the conference. However, the offender disagreed. Chronological reports have not elicited that criticism. On the other hand, Project Restore-NZ has found that a report can contain information that the prosecution or the defense could use unfairly against either the victim or the offender. Perhaps Project Restore-NZ's experience is an indication that more debate must occur within the RJ community regarding reporting.

The RESTORE program does not provide any written record of the conference itself, apart from the redress plan or agreed outcomes of the conference (Koss et al. 2004). This could provide some level of confidentiality for comments made by participants in the heat of the moment, but it could be argued that this approach is not transparent, given that justice systems claim to be open to public scrutiny. Reports go some way toward providing oversight to a process conducted in private.

CONCLUSION

I conclude this chapter by reflecting on the questions I posed earlier. Does RJ have the potential to overcome the shortcomings of traditional justice systems and provide victims with a sense of justice? Can RJ overcome the resistance to its use with violence that is power-based and reflective of entrenched societal attitudes and beliefs?

As yet, we know very little about the effectiveness of programs using RJ to address gendered violence. Support seems to be growing for such programs, as evidenced by the appearance of programs in various parts of the world. Although they may be very different, they are all using a form of RJ to address gendered violence. The differences between these programs attest to RJ's flexibility. The modifications and adaptations discussed in this chapter could be sufficient to overcome survivors' reluctance to engage with RJ. At the very least, there is a perception that RJ can overcome the shortcomings of the criminal justice system, so that victims can experience a truer sense of justice. We will not know if these programs have achieved their objective until sufficient numbers of cases have been processed, so that a reliable evaluation can be undertaken. Hopefully, in time, these programs will move the debate of whether RJ should be used to address gendered violence beyond speculation. But it is still too early to ascertain if victims can achieve a sense of justice.

RJ must develop practice models that have the ability to negate the power imbalance of gendered violence. The discussion of the fundamental principles of RJ, the involvement of victims, a negotiated community response, and the transfer of power, highlighted that some limitations remain to the potential of RJ in its current format to address gendered violence. The same was true of the discussion of practice issues, neutrality, impartiality, and confidentiality. For RJ to successfully address gendered violence, practitioners must avoid reflecting patriarchal structures within society that serve only to revictimize and further marginalize victims.

Finally, RJ must not undermine the gains of feminists in changing attitudes toward gendered violence. Any justice model, restorative or otherwise, that does not challenge offenders' distorted rationalizations is reinforcing such behavior in not only the individual but also in family systems, communities, and the broader society. Given that New Zealand has intolerable levels of violence toward women, we cannot afford to contribute to this epidemic in our society. Project Restore-NZ is in the process of developing practice models that may well address gendered violence that allow victims to experience a dignified sense of justice. As such, RJ offers a glimmer of hope to victims of gendered violence.

ACKNOWLEDGMENTS

The research discussed in this chapter was supervised by Professor Marilyn Waring of the Auckland University of Technology, previously of Massey University and Dr. Warwick Tie of Massey University. It was funded by grants from Massey University and the Auckland Medical Aid Trust. Without contributing survivors, this research would not have been possible. The author thanks Fiona Landon, restorative justice facilitator; Jennifer Annan, counsellor and restorative justice facilitator; and Islay Brown, former Court Coordinator for Restorative Justice in the Auckland District Court and currently Manager of the Restorative Justice Centre at the Auckland University of Technology for their review of this chapter.

NOTES

1. This report was released May, 2006 and was prepared by the Ministry of Women's Affairs in consultation with government departments and civil society. It is the sixth four-year report prepared as part of the reporting obligations of all

signatories of the United Nations Convention on the Elimination of all Forms of Discrimination Against Women (CEDAW).

2. I have referred to the survivors that I worked with as adult survivors or survivors. All other people who have been sexually violated as children or adults, I have referred to as victims. This is not to suggest that these people are not survivors. I have done so merely to avoid confusion. I have referred to offenders of gendered violence as offenders to highlight that this behavior is criminal activity.

3. This was based on my experience as a participant observer in Te Oritenga, the first provider group of restorative justice in Auckland.

4. This research has been described more fully elsewhere. See Jülich 2001, 2005, and 2006.

5. For a review of the literature see Parker, 2004. See also Daly and Stubbs, 2006.

6. Personal communication by e-mail on April 10, 2007 with the program's principal investigator, Professor Mary Koss.

7. Personal communication on September 24, 2005 with K. McPhillips, Clinical Manager of Auckland Sexual Abuse Help.

8. I am a co-founder of Project Restore-NZ and sit on the Executive Committee.

REFERENCES

Anderson, Jessie, Judy Martin, Paul Mullen, Sarah Romans, and Peter Herbison. 1993. "Prevalence of Childhood Sexual Abuse Experiences in a Community Sample of Women." *Journal of the American Academy of Child Adolescent Psychiatry* 32:911.

Annan, Jennifer. 2004. "Restorative Justice." July 2004. Retrieved September 25, 2004 (http://www.asah.org.nz/HelpNewsletterJuly04.pdf).

Boulle, Laurence, Judi Jones, and Virginia Goldblatt. 1998. *Mediation: Principles, Process, Practice.* Wellington, NZ: Butterworths.

Bowen, Helen, Jim Boyack, and Stephen Hooper. 2000. *The New Zealand Restorative Justice Practice Manual.* Auckland, NZ: Restorative Justice Trust.

Braithwaite, John. 1996. *Crime, Shame and Reintegration.* New York: Cambridge University Press.

Carbonatto, Helen. 1995. "Expanding Intervention Options for Spousal Abuse: The Use of Restorative Justice." *Occasional Papers in Criminology, New Series: No. 4.* Wellington, NZ: Victoria University.

Claassen, Ron. 1996. "Restorative Justice Primary Focus on People not Procedures." Retrieved September 15, 2007 (http://peace.fresno.edu/docs/rjprinc2.html).

Coddington, Deborah. 2007. "Good Cops Lost in the Race to Find Blame." *New Zealand Herald,* March 11. Retrieved March 11, 2007 (http://www.nzherald.co.nz/topic/story.cfm?c_id=240&objectid=10428171).

Coker, Donna. 1999. "Enhancing Autonomy for Battered Women." *UCLA Law Review* 1:1–111.

Cook, Stephen. 2007. "Rickards Investigated over New Sex Inquiry." *New Zealand Herald,* March 11. Retrieved March 11, 2007 (http://www.nzherald.co.nz/section/1/story.cfm?c_id=1&objectid=10428203).

Crawford, Adam. 2000. "Salient Themes Towards a Victim Perspective and the Limitations of Restorative Justice: Some Concluding Comments." Pp. 285–310 in *Integrating a Victim Perspective within Criminal Justice: International Debates,* edited by Adam Crawford and Jo Goodey. Aldershot, UK: Ashgate.

Curtis-Fawley, Sarah and Kathleen Daly. 2005. "Gendered Violence and Restorative Justice: The Views of Victim Advocates." *Violence Against Women* 11:603–638.

Daly, Kathleen. 2000. "Restorative Justice in Diverse and Unequal Societies." *Law in Context* 17:167–190.

_____. 2002. "Sexual Assault and Restorative Justice." Pp. 62–88 in *Restorative Justice and Family Violence*, edited by Heather Strang and John Braithwaite. Melbourne: Cambridge University Press.

Daly, Kathleen and Russ Immarigeon. 1998. "The Past, Present, and Future of Restorative Justice: Some Critical Reflections." *Contemporary Justice Review* 1:21–45.

Daly, Kathleen and Julie Stubbs. 2006. "Feminist Engagement with Restorative Justice." *Theoretical Criminology* 10:9–28.

Department for Courts. 2002. *Facilitator Training Manual*. Wellington, NZ: Ministry of Justice.

Dewes, Haydon. 2006. "Not Guilty on All Counts." *The Dominion Post* (Wellington, NZ), April 5, p A3.

Flinck, Aune and Juhani Iivari. 2004. "Domestic Violence in Mediation: Realistic Evaluation of a Research and Development Project (Finnish Evaluation of Social Services)." Presentation at *Restorative Justice in Europe? Where are we Heading? Conference*. Budapest, Hungary: European Forum for Victim-Offender Mediation and Restorative Justice.

Glaeser, Bernd. 2004. "Victim-Offender-Mediation in Cases of Domestic Violence." Presentation at *Restorative Justice in Europe: Where Are We Heading? Conference*. Budapest, Hungary: European Forum for Victim-Offender Mediation and Restorative Justice.

Hooper, Stephen and Ruth Busch. 1996. "Domestic Violence and Restorative Justice Initiatives: the Risks of a New Panacea." *Waikato Law Review* 4:101–30.

Hudson, Barbara. 2002. "Restorative Justice and Gendered Violence: Diversion or Effective Justice?" *British Journal of Criminology* 42:616–634.

Jülich, Shirley. 2001. "Breaking the Silence: Restorative Justice and Child Sexual Abuse." Ph.D Thesis, Social Policy, Massey University, Albany, NZ.

_____. 2005. "Stockholm Syndrome and Child Sexual Abuse." *Journal of Child Sexual Abuse* 14:107–129.

_____. 2006. "Views of Justice Among Survivors of Historical Child Sexual Abuse: Implications for Restorative Justice in New Zealand." *Theoretical Criminology* 10:125–138.

Kelsey, Jane. 1997. *The New Zealand Experiment: A World Model for Structural Adjustment?* Auckland: Auckland University Press, Bridget Williams Books.

Koss, Mary P., Karen J. Bachar, and C. Quince Hopkins. 2003. "Restorative Justice for Sexual Violence: Repairing Victims, Building Community, and Holding Offenders Accountable." *Annals New York Academy of Science* 989:384–396.

Koss, Mary P., Karen J. Bachar, C. Quince Hopkins, and Carolyn Carlson. 2004. "Expanding a Community's Justice Response to Sex Crimes Through Advocacy, Prosecutorial, and Public Health Collaboration: Introducing the RESTORE Program." *Journal of Interpersonal Violence* 19:1435–1463.

Marshall, Tony E. 1999. *Restorative Justice: An Overview*. London: Home Office, Information and Publications Group.

Martin, Yvonne. 2006a. "Her Word Against His." *The Press* (Christchurch, NZ), June 3, p. 3.

_____. 2006b. "The Rape Crisis." pp. D1–D2 in *The Press* (Christchurch, NZ), May 27, Pp. D1–D2.

McElrea, F.W.M. 2004. "Restorative Justice: New Zealand Perspectives— Strengths and Weaknesses." Paper presented at the *Third Biennial Conference of the Australian and New Zealand Association for the Treatment of Sexual Abusers Conference.* Auckland, NZ.

Ministry of Women's Affairs. 2006. "CEDAW Report: New Zealand's Sixth Report on its Implementation of the United Nations Convention on the Elimination of All Forms of Discrimination against Women." Ministry of Women's Affairs, Wellington, NZ.

Parker, Wendy. 2004. *Restorative Justice and Family Violence: An Overview of the Literature.* Wellington, NZ: Ministry of Justice.

Randall, Melanie and Lori Haskell. 1995. "Sexual Violence in Women's Lives: Findings from the Women's Safety Project, a Community-Based Survey." *Violence Against Women* 1:6–31.

Russell, Diana E. 1983. "The Incidence and Prevalence of Intrafamilial and Extrafamilial Sexual Abuse of Female Children." *Child Abuse and Neglect* 7:133–146.

Sten Madsen, Karin. 2004. "Mediation as a Way of Empowering Women Exposed to Sexual Coercion." *Nora: Nordic Journal of Women's Studies* 12:58–61.

Stubbs, Julie. 1997. "Shame, Defiance and Violence Against Women: A Critical Analysis of 'Communitarian' Conferencing." Pp. 109–126 in *Women's Encounters with Violence: Australian Experiences,* edited by Judith Bessant and Sandy Cook. Thousand Oaks, CA: Sage.

_____. 2002. "Domestic Violence and Women's Safety: Feminist Challenges to Restorative Justice." Pp. 42–61 in *Restorative Justice and Family Violence,* edited by Heather Strang and John Braithwaite. Cambridge, UK: Cambridge University Press.

TVNZ. 2007. "Not Guilty, Part 2 – Rickards Reaction." *Close Up*, March 1. Auckland: TVNZ.

Zehr, Howard. 1995. *Changing Lenses.* Scottsdale, AZ: Herald Press.

12

BEYOND RESTORATIVE JUSTICE
Radical Organizing Against Violence

ANDREA SMITH

Women of color live in the dangerous intersections of gender and race. Within the mainstream antiviolence movement in the United States, women of color who survive sexual or domestic abuse are often told that they must pit themselves against their communities—often portrayed stereotypically as violent—to begin the healing process. Communities of color, meanwhile, often advocate that women keep silent about sexual and domestic violence, in order to maintain a united front against racism. Therefore, the analysis proposed in this chapter argues for the need to adopt antiviolence strategies that are mindful of the larger structures of violence that shape the world in which we live.

Mainstream remedies for addressing sexual and domestic violence in the United States have proved inadequate for addressing the problems of gender violence in general, but particularly for addressing violence against women of color. The problem is not simply an issue of providing multi-cultural services to survivors of violence. Rather, the analysis and strategies used to counter gender violence have failed to address the fact that gender violence is not simply a tool of patriarchal control, but also serves as a tool of racism, economic oppression, and colonialism. Colonial relationships, as well as race and class relations, are themselves gendered and sexualized (Incite! 2006; Smith 2005). The issues of colonial, race, class, and gender oppression cannot be separated. Women of color do not just face quanti-tatively more issues when they suffer violence (e.g., less supportive media attention, greater language barriers, lack of support in the judicial system), but their experience is qualitatively different from that of white women. Hence, the strategies employed to address violence against women of color must take into account their particular histories and current conditions of violence. Strategies designed to combat sexual and domestic violence within communities must be linked to strategies that combat violence directed against communities, including state violence (e.g., police brutality, prisons, militarism, racism, colonialism, and economic exploitation).

As the antiviolence movement has attempted to become more "inclusive," attempts at multicultural interventions against domestic violence have unwittingly strengthened white supremacy within the antiviolence movement. All too often, inclusivity has come to mean that the generic domestic violence model, developed largely with the interests of white middle-class women in mind, should simply "add on" a multicultural component. Multicultural antiviolence curricula are often the same as those produced by mainstream groups, with merely some "cultural" designs or references added to the pre-existing model. Most domestic violence programs servicing communities of color do not have models that differ dramatically from the mainstream except for "community outreach workers" or bilingual staff. Women of color are constantly called upon to provide domestic violence service providers with "cultural sensitivity programs," in which we are supposed to explain our cultures, sometimes in 30 minutes or less. Even with longer trainings (e.g., 40 one-hour meetings), only one or two of those hours are devoted to "cultural diversity." The naïve assumption is that "the culture" of people of color is something simple, easy to understand, requires little or no substantive engagements with communities, and is homogeneous. Furthermore, those people who are marginalized *within* communities of color, such as lesbian, gay, bisexual and transgendered (LGBT) or queer people, sex workers, or addicts, are often marginalized within these "cultural" representations. Of course, many women of color in domestic violence programs have been active in expanding the notions of "cultural competency" to be more politicized, less simplistic, and less dependent on the notion of culture as a static concept. However, cultural competency, no matter how re-envisioned, is limited in its ability to create a movement that truly addresses the needs of women of color; the lives and histories of women of color call on us to radically rethink all models currently developed for addressing domestic violence.

An alternative approach to "inclusion" is to place women of color at the center of the analysis of domestic violence. What if we do not make any assumptions about what a domestic violence *program* should look like, but instead ask: What would it take *to end violence against women of color*? What would this movement look like? What if we do not presume that this movement would necessarily have anything we take for granted in the current domestic violence movement?

THE CO-OPTATION OF THE
ANTIVIOLENCE MOVEMENT

As Beth Richie notes, the co-optation of the antiviolence movement can be traced in part to the moment when the movement chose to argue that domestic violence was a "crime." The state, rather than recognized for its complicity in gender violence, became the institution promising to protect women from domestic and sexual violence (Richie 2000). As I have argued in my other work, the state is largely responsible for introducing gender violence into Indigenous communities as part of a colonial strategy that follows a logic of sexual violence (Smith 2005). The complicity of the state in perpetrating gender violence in other communities of color through slavery, prisons, and border patrol is also well documented (Bhattacharjee 2001; Davis 1981; Smith 2005).

However, rather than target the state as a perpetrator of gender violence, for many years activists in the rape crisis and domestic violence movements have promoted strengthening the criminal justice system as the primary means of reducing sexual and domestic violence. Particularly since the passage of the Violence Against Women Act (VAWA) in 1994, antiviolence centers have been able to receive a considerable amount of funding from the state, to the point where most agencies have become dependent on the state for their continued existence. Consequently, their strategies tend to be state-friendly: hire more police, give longer sentences to rapists, pass mandatory arrests laws, etc. But there is an inherent contradiction in relying upon the state to solve those problems that it is responsible for creating. The antiviolence movement has always contested the notion of home as a safe place; the notion that violence happens "out there," inflicted by the stranger in the dark alley, prevents us from recognizing that the home is, in fact, the place of greatest danger for women. However, the strategies the domestic violence movement employs to address domestic violence are actually premised on the danger coming from "out there" rather than at home. That is, reliance on the criminal justice system to address gender violence would make sense if the threat were a few crazed men whom we can lock up. But the prison system is not equipped to address a violent culture in which an overwhelming number of people batter their partners unless we are prepared to imprison millions of people. As Hopkins and Koss (2005:715) note, approaches are required to deconstruct "the systemic belief systems and norms on which gendered violence rests."

Antiviolence activists and scholars have widely critiqued the supposed efficacy of criminalization (Sokoloff 2005; Strang and Braithwaite 2002; White 2004). Unfortunately, the "remedies" pursued by the mainstream antiviolence movement have often strengthened rather than undercut state violence. While the anti–sexual/domestic violence movements have been vital in breaking the silence around violence against women and in providing critically needed services to survivors, these movements have also become increasingly professionalized in providing services. Consequently, these movements are often reluctant to address sexual and domestic violence within the larger context of institutionalized violence.

The co-optation of the antiviolence movement by the criminal justice system has far-reaching consequences that affect others in addition to the immediate victims of domestic violence. A disproportionate number of those who go to prison for domestic violence are people of color. Julie Ostrowski reports that, of those men who go to domestic violence courts in New York, only 12% are white. Half of them are unemployed, and the average income of those who are employed is $12,655 (Ostrowski 2004). However, the issue is not primarily that antiviolence advocates are supporting the prison-industrial complex by sending batterers and rapists to jail, since many antiviolence advocates simply say, "If someone is guilty of violence, should they not be in jail regardless of their racial background?" Rather, it is that when men of color are disproportionately incarcerated because of these laws (that have been passed in part through the co-optation of antiviolence rhetoric), the entire community—particularly women, who are often the community caretakers—is negatively impacted.

Furthermore, as Kimberlé Crenshaw (1991) notes, this racialization serves not just to criminalize men of color, but to codify the rapability of women of color. That is, what determines criminality is not just the race of the perpetrator, but the race of the victim (Ogletree and Sarat 2006). So, those who commit violent acts against women of color are least likely to be criminalized. This rapability of women of color under the law is continuous with the rapability of black women under slavery and native women during the colonial massacres of Indigenous peoples (Smith 2005).

RESTORATIVE JUSTICE AND COMMUNITY ACCOUNTABILITY

In critiquing the current mainstream strategies against domestic violence, the question becomes: What are the strategies that can end violence against women? Unfortunately, many of the alternatives to incarceration promoted under the restorative justice (RJ) model have not developed sufficient safety mechanisms for survivors of domestic/sexual violence. "Restorative justice" is an umbrella term describing a wide range of programs that attempt to address crime from a restorative and reconciliatory rather than a punitive framework. As opposed to the U.S. criminal justice system, which focuses solely on punishing the perpetrator and removing him (or her) from society through incarceration, RJ attempts to involve all parties (perpetrators, victims, and community members) in determining the appropriate response to a crime in an effort to restore the community to wholeness. These models have been particularly well-developed by many Native communities, especially in Canada, where the sovereign status of Native nations allows them an opportunity to develop community-based justice programs (Ross 1997; Zion and Zion 1996).In one program, for example, when a crime is reported, the working team that deals with sexual/domestic violence talks to the perpetrator and gives him the option of participating in the program. The perpetrator must first confess his guilt and then follow a healing contract, or go to jail. The perpetrator is free to decline to participate in the program and go through normal routes in the criminal justice system.

In the RJ model, everyone (victim, perpetrator, family, friends, and the working team) is involved in developing the healing contract. Everyone is also assigned an advocate through the process. Everyone also holds the perpetrator accountable to his contract. One Tlingit man noted that this approach was often more difficult than going to jail:

> First, one must deal with the shock and then the dismay on your
> neighbors' faces. One must live with the daily humiliation, and at the
> same time seek forgiveness not just from victims, but from the
> community as a whole . . . [A prison sentence] removes the offender
> from the daily accountability, and may not do anything towards
> rehabilitation, and for many may actually be an easier disposition than
> staying in the community. (Ross 1997:18)

These models seem to have much greater potential for dealing with "crime" effectively because, if we want perpetrators of violence to live in society peaceably, it makes sense to develop justice models in which the community is involved in holding them accountable. Under the current incarceration model, perpetrators are taken away from their community and are further hindered from developing ethical relationships within a community context. Rupert Ross (1997:58), an advocate for RJ models, notes that "In reality, rather than making the community a safer place, the threat of jail places the community more at risk."

The problem with these models is that they only work when the community unites in holding perpetrators accountable. However, in cases of sexual and domestic violence, the community often sides with the perpetrator rather than the victim. So, for example, in many Native American communities, these models are often pushed on domestic violence survivors, to pressure them to "reconcile" with their families and "restore" the community without sufficient concern for their personal safety (Goel 2005).

In addition, the Aboriginal Women's Action Network (AWAN) as well as Native American domestic violence advocates have critiqued the uncritical use of "traditional" forms of governance for addressing domestic violence. AWAN argues that Native communities have been pressured to adopt "circle sentencing" because it is supposed to be an Indigenous "traditional" practice. However, AWAN contends that there is no such traditional practice in their communities. Moreover, they are concerned that the process of diverting cases outside a court system can be dangerous for survivors. In one example, Bishop Hubert O'Connor (a white man) was found guilty of multiple cases of sexual abuse of Aboriginal women, but his punishment under the RJ model was to participate in a healing circle with his victims. Because his crimes were against Aboriginal women, he was able to opt for an "Aboriginal approach"—an approach, AWAN argues, that did little to provide real healing and accountability for the survivors. Angela Cameron (2006) further asserts that conflating RJ with "traditional" Native practices assumes a static and singular conception of Native societies unimpacted by colonialism. M., an Ojibwe antiviolence activist, argues that there is a tendency to romanticize and homogenize "traditional" (i.e., Native) alternatives to incarceration.[1] First, she notes that these traditional approaches might, in fact, be more harsh than incarceration. Many Native people presume that traditional modes of justice focused on conflict resolution. In fact, M. argues, penalties for societal infractions were not lenient—they entailed banishment, shaming, reparations, and sometimes death. M. notes that attempting to revise tribal codes by reincorporating traditional practices is not a simple process. It is sometimes difficult to determine what these practices were or how they could be made useful today. For example, some practices, such as banishment, would not have the same impact as today. Prior to colonization, Native communities were so close-knit and interdependent that banishment was often the equivalent of a death sentence. Today, however, Native peoples can simply leave home and join the dominant society.

We face a dilemma: On the one hand, the incarceration approach for addressing sexual/domestic violence promotes the repression of communities of color without really providing safety for survivors. On the other hand, RJ models often promote community silence and denial around issues of sexual/violence without concern for the safety of survivors of gender violence, under the rhetoric of community restoration. Thus, our challenge is to develop community-based models of accountability in which the community will actually hold the perpetrator accountable. As Judith Herman (2005:559) states: "The community support that victims so ardently desire does not presently exist. Active political organizing and advocacy are still required to create it." Unfortunately, in the discussion of ending violence, advocates often assume only two possibilities: traditional criminal justice *or* RJ. When anyone finds faults with the RJ model, it assumed that the traditional criminal justice approach is the only possible back-up strategy.

RESTORATIVE JUSTICE DEBATES AND THE STATE

What generally seems to unite both RJ advocates and critics is an inability to think outside the traditional criminal justice/social service model for addressing violence. Too many believe that RJ programs should be added as an appendage to the current criminal justice/social service model as the primary strategy for addressing violence, rather than considering how some RJ principles might be helpful in developing completely different strategies for eradicating violence.

Critics of RJ often point to the particular flaws in specific programs, such as family conferencing or face-to-face mediation. Advocates of RJ, however, generally articulate RJ in broader terms that stress community involvement in addressing crime and its aftereffects. They argue that the principles of RJ, which involve an entire community in holding perpetrators accountable, have a much greater potential to address violence effectively than does the criminal justice system acting without community input. According to Kay Pranis (2002:27): "Moral authority is ultimately more powerful in shaping behavior. Moral authority is a product of relationships. It must be grounded in some form of connection, of shared beliefs and common ground." Hence, as Joan Pennell and Gale Burford (2002) contend, the issue is not how well do current RJ programs work, but do they have the potential to work.

RJ advocates claim that their critics mistakenly assume that the traditional criminal justice system works effectively to keep women safe. For instance, Julie Stubbs (2002) defends the criminal justice system by saying many survivors seek legal intervention. But given that the antiviolence movement offers no other alternative, what does that prove? Another example is in the title of Ruth Busch's critique of RJ, "Who Pays If We Get It Wrong?," which assumes that the domestic violence movement has not *already* gotten it wrong by relying on the criminal justice system as its primary strategy for ending violence. She further states: "There are risks in discarding the court system without first establishing whether proposed alternatives are capable of providing as much protection as it presently does" (Busch 2002:226). However, as Allison Morris (2002:91) points out, while a plethora of flaws exist in current RJ programs, critics fail to show that the "criminal justice system better serves women who have experienced abuse of the hands of their partners." Similarly, Angela Cameron (2006:59) argues that RJ "without clear evidence that it is safe and effective, is gambling with the lives and safety of Canadian women." But given that there is no evidence that the criminal justice system is safe and effective, then we are also gambling with the lives of women when rely on this system as well. Rather than look at criminal justice as the "safe alternative," Beth Richie (2000) notes, we must recognize that our reliance on it is hurting women, and we should stop hurting them. Thus, the key questions to ask, says Morris (2002:90), are "What has the criminal justice system *actually* achieved for the victims of family violence? And what *might* restorative justice achieve for the victims of family violence?"

Regardless of one's stance in the RJ debate, there is often a failure to conceptualize the state, not simply as flawed in its ability to redress violence, but as a primary perpetrator of violence against women in its own right. For instance, Kay Pranis (2002:38) argues for partnering RJ programs with the state because, "Where communities are not able to act within those parameters the responsibility lies with government to protect those vulnerable to mistreatment by the community." She fails to address how the government itself mistreats communities, particularly communities of color. The state itself has failed to demonstrate any interest in protecting those most vulnerable to violence.

Because the authors generally fail to conceptualize the state as a perpetrator of violence, they often minimize the harms done to women by the criminal justice system. For example, the Right has been very successful in using antiviolence rhetoric to mobilize support for a repressive anticrime agenda that includes three-strikes legislation and get-tough-on-drugs laws. These anticrime measures make abused women more likely to find themselves in prison if they are coerced by partners to engage in illegal activity. And as mentioned previously, when men of color are disproportionately incarcerated because of laws that have been passed in part through the co-optation of antiviolence rhetoric, the entire community is negatively impacted. Thus, Kathleen Daly's dismissal of those who critique the criminal justice system because of its racism, arguing that it is only criminalizing *men* of color, and hence of no concern to *women* of color, is frighteningly short-sighted (Daly 2002:64). Her contention that we face a choice of "whether one should be compassionate to marginalized men who harm women and children they know or whether one should vindicate the women's and children's suffering" (p. 74) fails to consider that (1) the suffering of women and children of color is tied to the suffering of men of color, and (2) remaining uncritical of how antiviolence rhetoric can be co-opted to support a right-wing anticrime agenda fails to consider how this legislation disproportionately impacts all people of color trapped in the prison-industrial complex, not just men who perpetrate family violence. The tendency of many scholars to separate race from gender politics, as if there are no women of color (Cameron 2006; Cook 2006; Daly and Stubbs 2006), inhibits advocates from developing what Kimberlé Crenshaw would call an "intersectional" approach to violence. For instance, Daly and Stubbs argue that "racial . . . groups' claims commonly centre on the treatment of suspects and offenders, while feminist claims more likely centre on the treatment of victims," as if there are no feminists of color (Daly and Stubbs 2006:19). In fact, there is a significant movement of feminists of color who do organize around the intersections of state violence and interpersonal violence. This work is discussed later in this chapter.

As Donna Coker contends, zero-tolerance arrest policies and no-drop prosecution resonate with this right-wing emphasis on punishment and control and, as such, domestic violence as been transformed into a "crime control problem" (Coker 2002:133). She further notes: "The critical dilemma for feminists who seek to empower battered women is to develop strategies for controlling the criminal justice system without increasing state control of *women*" (p. 129). The way out of this dilemma, as articulated by Daly, is to develop strategies that address state and family violence simultaneously.

Daly and Stubbs (2006) do a thorough outline of the major problems with RJ models for addressing gender violence. But the underlying issue with all of these problems is that RJ frequently depends on a romanticized notion of community that will actually hold perpetrators accountable. Julie Stubbs (2002:54) outlines this problematic assumption clearly: "Making amends and restoring troubled relations in an unequal society may mean restoring unequal relations and hence reaffirming inequality." RJ strategies are more likely to be effective when community consensus confirms that an act of violence is indeed wrong. However, in cases where this consensus does not exist, RJ poses a number of risks, according to Stubbs: consensus decision making dilutes concerns about victim interests, programs lack capacity for ongoing support of victim and social control over the offender, RJ overestimates the ability to induce behavioral change, RJ advocates pressure victims to reconcile in the name of "restoration" in a manner that does not address the reality of gender oppression, and RJ is based on a mistaken assumption that all parties are equally empowered to express their needs.

This romanticization is often present in the discussion of RJ in Indigenous communities, in which RJ programs are typically described as based on "Indigenous" practices. The reality, however, is that practices such as the Navajo Peacemaking Court have been severely criticized by Native antiviolence advocates for failing to consider the patriarchal norms that have often been internalized within Native communities as a result of colonization. Also of concern is the problematic fashion in which colonial violence becomes analytically separated from gender violence in some of the analyses done by RJ advocates. For instance, Heather Strang and John Braithwaite (2002:19) argue: "There may be contexts where Indigenous families have been so disrupted by colonialism, where fears of harm in custody are sufficiently real, as to justify a prioritizing of family reconciliation and reconciliation with Elders of threats to victim safety that are not extreme." However, as Loretta Kelly (2002:207) notes: "more Aboriginal women have died from violence in their communities than all the total national Aboriginal deaths in custody."

This tendency of both RJ critics and advocates to separate gender from colonial violence fails to consider the fact that it is through gender violence that colonialism is successful. As I have argued elsewhere, sexual violence was a tool by which the bodies of Indigenous peoples become marked as inherently violable and "rapable"—and by extension, their lands and territories become marked as violable as well. Sexual violence also enables colonizers to not only destroy a nation, but to destroy its sense of being a nation. While the bodies of both Indian men and women have been marked by sexual violence, the bodies of Native women have been particularly targeted for abuse because of their capacity to reproduce the next generation that can resist colonization. To destroy a people, one must disproportionately target women for destruction; consequently, both symbolic and literal control over Native women's bodies through sexual violence is essential to the colonial project (Smith 2005). Thus, the issue is not prioritizing concerns of state violence over gender violence; rather, addressing gender violence is a critical aspect of ending state violence.

Interestingly, neither RJ advocates nor critics seem to question the role of the criminal justice system in addressing violence. According to Pranis (2002:38), "Restorative justice requires a partnership with government institutions." Daly and Stubbs (2006), Coker (2006), and others specifically argue against developing RJ models as an "alternative" to the criminal justice system. Barbara Hudson (2006:43) argues that modern liberal societies are characterized by "white male justice," and that criminal justice "cannot . . . solve problems of social inequalities and oppressions," but then does not question why we would want to continue to work within a model that is inherently patriarchal and colonial. As Native scholar Glen Coulthard (2007) argues, justice can never exist under the conditions of settler colonialism that characterize the United States, Canada, Australia, and New Zealand.

The assumption behind this insistence on working with the state is that the U.S. Government (or Canada, Australia, and New Zealand) is essentially a benevolent or neutral democratic institution that can serve peoples' interests, although they may be marred by instances of racism. Presumably, if we can simply eradicate the racism and the sexism of the state, it can then provide justice for survivors of violence. The law at least has the capability of serving the interests of even Indigenous women, women of color, and poor women through proper reform. The question then arises, however: What are we to do with the fact that, as Native scholar Luana Ross (1998:15) notes, genocide has never been against the law in the United States? On the contrary, Native genocide has been expressly sanctioned as *the law*. Certainly, Native feminist theory in particular provides critical intervention into this discourse because the United States could not exist without the genocide of Native peoples—genocide is not a mistake or aberration of U.S. democracy, it is foundational to it (Smith 2005). As Sandy Grande states:

> The United States is a nation defined by its original sin: the genocide of American Indians . . . . American Indian tribes are viewed as an inherent threat to the nation, poised to expose the great lies of U.S. democracy: that we are a nation of laws and not random power; that we are guided by reason and not faith; that we are governed by representation and not executive order; and finally, that we stand as a self-determined citizenry and not a kingdom of blood or aristocracy. . . . From the perspective of American Indians, "democracy" has been wielded with impunity as the first and most virulent weapon of mass destruction. (Grande 2004:31–32)

Thus, the nation-state, particularly the United States, is not a bastion of freedom from which ideals are being eroded through gender and racial violence—gender and racial violence represent the *fulfillment* of the ideals of U.S. democracy. Or, as Heather Nancarrow (2006:99) puts it, from the perspective of Indigenous women, "the state does not represent their interests, but embodies public violence."

The state, rather than being understood as defined through gender and racial differentiation and subordination becomes positioned as the body to recognize and protect racial and gender difference. The differences that can be recognized as subject to protection are those differences that are least threatening to the state. Thus, when "women" are protected from domestic violence, these women are not generally sex workers, drug addicted or otherwise criminalized, poor women, etc.

Furthermore, because the state actually has no interest in gender or racial justice, these laws are then often used against the people they supposedly protect. For instance, *The New York Times* recently reported that the effects of the strengthened anti–domestic violence legislation is that battered women kill their abusive partners less frequently; however, batterers do *not* kill their partners less frequently. The decline in women killing their partners is more pronounced in black than white communities (Butterfield 2000). Thus, ironically, laws passed to protect battered women are actually protecting their batterers!

So, essentially, the adoption of criminalization as the primary strategy for addressing racial/gender justice has shifted our analysis from articulating the state as partially constituted by heteropatriarchy and white supremacy to uncritically upholding the liberal multicultural state as the institution that *recognizes* and legitimizes legal and political claims based on gender and race. As Elizabeth Povinelli (2002:16) has so aptly demonstrated, the liberal state depends on a politics of multicultural recognition that includes "social difference without social consequence." As Povinelli further states:

> These state, public, and capital multicultural discourses, apparatuses, and imaginaries defuse struggles for liberation waged against the modern liberal state and recuperate these struggles as moments in which the future of the nation and its core institutions and values are ensured rather than shaken. (p. 29)

It is not a surprise, as I discuss later, that many women-of-color groups in particular are seeking strategies for ending violence that do not rely primarily on the state.

If RJ programs are always tied to the state, they may actually serve to extend the power of the criminal justice over more people, rather than fundamentally challenge the system (Behrendt 2002). Henry Blagg notes that the rhetoric around RJ can be a colonizing discourse. He is "critical of the tendency of the restorative justice movements to 'claim lineage with the dispute resolution practices of Indigenous peoples' while remaining 'on the margins of debates about the contemporary social, economic and political aspirations of living Indigenous peoples'" (2002:199). Kelly (2002), Blagg (2002), and Larissa Behrendt (2002) note that given the colonial relationship that exists between Indigenous peoples and the state, any programs that do not honor the self-determination of Indigenous peoples, including RJ programs, simply serve to further extend colonial rule. Blagg argues that Indigenous peoples require a model that does not just focus on the "one crisis" that precipitates an RJ intervention, given that Indigenous peoples live under a constant state of crises under colonialism. Consequently, "restorative justice may need to free itself from the grip of the criminal justice process, and become actively aligned with community-building, rather than just problem-fixing, strategies" (2002:203).

This tendency to assume a collaboration with the state happens because many domestic violence advocates argue that alternative models only work if they are backed by the threat of incarceration should the perpetrator not act in good faith. However, the problem with such an approach is that it can actually strengthen the criminal justice system, with all its inherent racism, rather than challenge it. Prison abolitionist Stanley Cohen (1985) argues that alternative models are typically co-opted to serve state interests, increase the net of social control, and often lose their community focus as they become professionalized. Indeed, the history of prison reform indicates time and time again that minor reform programs actually strengthen the prison system and increase the number of people who fall under its purview (Foucault 1977; Rotman 1995). For instance, women religious reformers in the 1800s advocated reforms for women prisoners being kept in the same brutal institutions as men. These reformers imagined women prisoners not as "criminal, fallen women" deserving harsh treatment, but as "sick" or "wayward" women in need of a cure or proper retraining. They fought for the establishment of sex-segregated reformatories rather than prisons to provide women the guidance they needed to fulfill their domestic roles. As a result, great numbers of women suddenly found themselves in the criminal justice system receiving domesticity training (Freedman 1981; Zedner 1995). As Luana Ross (1998) points out, the outgrowth of this ideology was that women often find themselves in prison longer than men, until they can prove they have been "cured." Simply adding RJ to the present criminal justice system is likely to further strengthen the criminal justice apparatus, particularly in communities of color that are deemed in need of restoration. In addition, a continued emphasis on simply reforming the criminal justice system takes us away from considering grassroots, political organizing strategies that have the potential to address the root causes of violence.

One reason why RJ advocates often do not seem to free themselves of this grip is because they do not consider political organizing and base-building as strategies for ending violence. Rather, they presume primarily a social service delivery model. Hence, it might be helpful to think of what a model based on political organizing might look like. What if survivors were the base of organizers rather than clients? Such an approach could both (1) challenge state violence *and* (2) build communities that would actually provide safety for survivors by challenging the sexism, homophobia, and other forms of oppression that exist within them.

ORGANIZING MODELS

A number of organizations seek to address violence from a political organizing perspective, rather than using the criminal justice or RJ model. While they do not rely on the criminal justice system, it is important to note that their approach is *not* to tell survivors that they should never call the police. They implicitly or explicitly hold a prison abolitionist perspective, but as Angela Davis (2003) demonstrates, an abolitionist project is a positive rather than a negative project. That is, rather than argue that all prisons should be dismantled tomorrow, our task is to crowd out prisons with other forms of justice-making that will eventually demonstrate both the ineffectiveness and the brutality of prisons. Similarly, these projects do not encourage survivors to engage the criminal justice system; rather, they ask "Why have we given survivors no other option *but* to engage this system?" But in seeking to develop other options, they also seek to develop new forms of governmentality based on mutual respect and interrelatedness rather than on domination, violence, and control. Many of these organizations have developed in recent years (Incite! 2006, 2007). In this section, I describe a few of these models and approaches.

Incite! Women of Color Against Violence

Incite! Women of Color Against Violence is a U.S. organization that has been working to develop community accountability models in conjunction with local organizing efforts. Through workshops and activist institutes, women of color have strategized about such models. Incite! has compiled these models and distributed them to other local groups to help them develop their own models. As groups try these models and provide feedback on what does and does not work for them, Incite! then shares this information with other women-of-color organizers. A document on Principles of Community Accountability is available on the Incite! website (2003).

These strategies further developed as Incite! built relationships with groups outside the United States. Currently, the mainstream U.S. domestic violence model is exported to other countries as *the* model for addressing violence. However, in many countries where reliance on the state is not an issue or a possibility, other organizations have developed creative strategies for addressing violence that can inform the work done in the United States. One model that was particularly informative to the work of Incite! is the model is from Brazil, the "Movement of Landless People" (known as Movimento dos Trabalhadores Rurail Sem Terra or MST). This movement is based in networks of families that claim territory that is owned privately, but is not being used. The families set up tents and fences and defend the land, which is called an "occupation." If they manage to gain control of the land, then they form a settlement in which they build houses and more permanent structures. Over the past 20 years, 300,000 families have been involved in these occupations. Families, rather than individuals, take part in this resistance. About 20 families form a nucleus, which is coordinated by one man and one woman. The nuclei are then organized into the following sectors: (1) production/cooperation/ employment, (2) education/trading; (3) education, (4) gender, (5) communication, (6) human rights, (7) health, and (8) culture. Both men and women participate in the gender sector. This sector is responsible for ensuring women are involved in all decision-making positions and are equally represented in public life. Security teams are mixed-gender, and women enforce security by carrying machetes. The gender team trains security to deal with domestic violence. Obviously, since the MST is not a legal organization and, thus, cannot utilize the state to address domestic violence, it must develop accountability structures from within.

All issues are discussed communally. As time progresses, participants report that domestic violence decreases because interpersonal relationships are communal and transparent. Also, because women engage in "physical" roles, such as being involved in security, women become less likely to be seen as "easy targets" for violence, and the women also think of themselves differently. In addition, sectors and leadership roles rotate, so that a fixed, hierarchical leadership does not develop. Hierarchical leadership tends to promote power differentials and hence abuse; this leadership model thus helps prevent the conditions of abuse from happening in the first place.

This model helped Incite! activists realize that creating strategies for ending violence is actually about creating alternative governmentalities that are not based on a nation-state model of governance. Nation-states are forms of governmentality based on domination, violence, and control. The prison-industrial complex is simply an arm of nation-state governance. So, if we want to envision a world without prisons, we must envision alternative forms of governmentality that are based on principles of mutual respect and responsibility, participatory rather than representative democracy, inclusiveness, and respect for rather than control of land and territory. Organizing must then rely on a dual strategy of what Sista II Sista (Brooklyn, New York) describes as "taking power" and "making power." That is, on one hand it is necessary to engage in oppositional politics against corporate and state power (taking power). However, if we only engage in the politics of taking power, we have a tendency to replicate the hierarchical structures in our movements. Consequently, it is also important to "make power" by creating those structures within our organizations, movements, and communities that model the world we are trying to create. Many groups in the United States often try to create separatist communities based on egalitarian ideals. However, if we "make power" without also trying to "take power," we ultimately support the political status quo by failing to dismantle structures of oppression that will undermine us.

Friends Are Reaching Out (FAR Out)

Some of the most well-developed community accountability models exist in queer communities of color, such as Friends Are Reaching Out (FAR Out) in Seattle. The premise of this model is that when people are abused, they become isolated. The domestic violence movement further isolates them through the shelter system, where they cannot tell their friends where they are. In addition, the domestic violence movement does not work with those people who could most likely hold perpetrators accountable—their friends. FAR Out's model is based on developing friendship groups that make regular commitments to stay in contact with each other. In addition, these groups develop processes to talk openly about relationships. One reason that abuse continues is that we tend to keep our sexual relationships private. By talking about them more openly, it is easier for friends to hold us accountable. In addition, if a person knows she/he is going to share the relationship dynamics openly, it is more likely that she/he will be accountable in the relationship. This model works because it is based on pre-existing friendship networks. As a result, it develops the capacity of a community to handle domestic violence.

Sista II Sista—Sisters Liberated Ground

As long-time antiviolence activist Suzanne Pharr (2004) notes, one way in which the antiviolence movement became co-opted through federal and foundation funding streams is that we started seeing survivors as clients who required services rather than as potential organizers on their own behalf. One model that focuses on organizing comes from Sista II Sista in Brooklyn, New York. This organization of young women of color addresses violence against neighborhood girls, committed both by the police and by other members of the community. Sista II Sista created a video project documenting police harassment after one girl was killed and a second was allegedly sexually assaulted and killed by the police. In addition, it has recently created a community accountability program, called "Sisters Liberated Ground," to organize its members to monitor violence in the community without relying upon the police. One of the ways it increases its base of support is by recruiting young women to attend "freedom schools" that provide political education from an integrated mind-body-spirit framework that then trains girls to become activists on their own behalf. It also started a daycare cooperative that attracts women who need daycare services, but then provides training so that they can become organizers as well.

Young Women's Empowerment Project

The Chicago-based Young Women's Empowerment Project (YWEP) is led by young women under the age of 18 who are involved in the sex trade.

They work from a harm-reduction approach, which entails working with a young woman's life conditions to help her develop strategies to keep her as safe as possible, while respecting her self-determination. Emi Koyama notes that many domestic violence advocates and shelters prescribe correct lifestyles and behaviors for women, regardless of their circumstances. If these women do not follow these prescriptions (i.e., if they are sex workers or if they are abusing drugs), then they are denied services all together. A harm-reduction approach, by contrast, does not presume how women should live, but facilitates their safety based on their current conditions.

YWEP notes that many of the young women they work with are being "trafficked" or "pimped" by family members. They want strategies to hold these perpetrators accountable. They feel that some of the "decriminalization" strategies proffered by many sex-worker organizations presume that sex workers are adults and do not consider the particular vulnerabilities faced by youth sex workers. However, in their experience, when the police are called, they never actually arrest traffickers or pimps; they simply criminalize the young women, making it more difficult for them to survive. They have concluded that criminal justice strategies are not effective in promoting the safety of their constituents. Thus, they are developing their own harm-reduction approaches for young women as they begin to create collective strategies to hold perpetrators accountable.

Communities Against Rape and Abuse

Communities Against Rape and Abuse (CARA) is a Seattle-based anti-rape organization. CARA began monitoring incidents of police brutality in Seattle. They found that the majority of police officers involved with brutality were responding to domestic violence charges in poor neighborhoods of color. As a result, CARA began organizing around the issue of prison abolition from an antiviolence perspective. At a 2002 prison abolition film festival co-sponsored with Critical Resistance, CARA outlined their philosophy in the program book:

> Any movement seeking to end violence will fail if its strategy supports and helps sustain the prison-industrial complex. Prisons, policing, the death penalty, the war on terror, and the war on drugs, all increase rape, beatings, isolation, oppression, and death. As an anti-rape organization, we cannot support the funneling of resources into the criminal justice system to punish rapists and batterers, as this does not help end violence. It only supports the same system that views incarcerations as a solution to complex social problems like rape and abuse. As survivors of rape and domestic violence, we will not let the antiviolence movement be further co-opted to support the mass criminalization of young people, the disappearance of immigrants and refugees, and the dehumanization of poor people, people of color,

and people with disabilities. We support the anti-rape movement that builds sustainable communities on a foundation of safety, support, self-determination, and accountability. (CARA 2002)

CARA has also developed an improvisational set of strategies for addressing violence that do not rely primarily on the state for community accountability. According to CARA ([n.d.]), "Our understanding of community accountability ultimately transcends the idea of simply holding an abusive community member responsible for his or her actions, but also includes the vision of the community itself." They contend that community accountability requires a "jazzy" approach—that no one model works for all context. They do, however, operate from a set of principles:

1. *Recognize the humanity of everyone involved.* They contend that a community accountability process can be confrontational, but never dehumanizing. When aggressors are dehumanized into "monsters," we fail to recognize how all peoples are capable of abusing power.
2. *Prioritize self-determination for the survivor.* Often, the needs of the survivor are minimized to promote community well-being. Often, the survivor becomes objectified as a symbol. Any plan, CARA contends, must prioritize the needs of the survivor at every step without coercing her into a plan of action she does not want to engage in.
3. *Identify a plan for safety and support for the survivor and others within the community.* The safety plan includes both physical safety for the survivor in anticipating and disrupting responses by the aggressor, but also in making sure to have a system of emotional support for not only the survivor but all those involved in the community accountability strategy.
4. *Carefully consider the potential political consequences of your actions.* CARA notes that any community accountability strategy can have unintended consequences. It is therefore necessary to consider all the "what-if" possibilities and makes contingency plans for them.
5. *Organize collectively.* Any community accountability process is difficult and requires a group of people to implement it. It cannot be done on an individual basis.
6. *Make sure everyone in the community accountability group is on the same page with their political analysis of sexual violence.* CARA argues that before any action can happen, political education and consensus-building must occur, so that people are working from a similar political analysis. Otherwise, the strategy is likely to fall apart during the implementation phase if say, some people feel that women are likely to make false accusations about rape while other reject that assumption.

7. *Be clear about what the survivor and your group wants from the aggressor in terms of accountability.* For such an accountability strategy to work, very clear and specific demands must be made from the community to the aggressor. Do you want the aggressor to go to counseling? Do you want the aggressor to leave the organization? Simply calling for "accountability" becomes a vague demand that one cannot clearly fulfill, allowing a group to degenerate into a process of just wanting the aggressor to suffer rather than allowing for the possibility that accountability can really happen.

8. *Let the aggressor know your analysis and demands.* This step is an obvious one, says CARA, but easily forgotten. It often happens that people may publicly shame the aggressor by revealing what happened, without communicating to the aggressor what you want her or him to do.

9. *Consider help from the aggressor's friends, family, and people close to him or her.* We often assume that the aggressor's friends and family will simply enable the aggressor's behavior. However, with further work, identifiable people often exist within the aggressor's circle who will also support a community accountability strategy. They are often in a better position to support accountability, particularly for the long-run.

10. *Prepare to be engaged in the process for the long haul.* Accountability is a process, not a destination. It takes time, people will probably try to thwart your efforts, and even if the aggressor engages the process, there must be long-term follow-up with her or him.

CARA has implemented its own community accountability processes numerous times and has supported other people's processes as well. In addition, it helped to develop a report for community accountability within progressive organizations (Incite! 2005).

Generation Five

Generation Five is an organization that seeks to end child sexual abuse within five generations through community action and organizing, collaboration with social services personnel, and coalition-building with other social justice movements. According to its website:

> Generation Five is an antiviolence organization that recognizes that our goal of ending child sexual abuse cannot be realized while other systems of oppression are allowed to continue. In fact, systems of oppression and child sexual abuse have an interdependent relationship: a power-over system that benefits some at the expense of others and uses violence, creates the conditions for child sexual abuse (i.e., gender inequality, class exploitation, racism, violence and threat

for difference), while in turn the prevalence of child sexual abuse fosters behaviors (obedience to authority, silence, disempowerment, shame) that prevent people from organizing effectively to work for liberation, healing and change systemic forms of violence. (Generation Five [n.d.-a])

Generation Five rejects the RJ model because it contends that this model has been co-opted by the state. It further holds that RJ models that seek to "restore" communities do not address the oppressive power structures or racism, classism, heterosexism, etc., within those communities. Instead, Generation Five proposes the model of "transformative justice," in which the goal is not simply to "restore" communities to a previous (oppressive) state, but to "transform" the oppressive structures of society, such as colonialism, patriarchy, and heterosexism, in order to build a world based on justice and nonviolence.

Generation Five argues that mandatory reporting and other child protective services approaches do not actually keep children safe. First, child protective services are used to police and surveil primarily poor communities of color rather than to ensure actual safety. When children are actually being sexually abused, the state often does not have sufficient evidence to "prove" abuse. And when abuse is proven, children are generally put into institutional or foster care settings that are as dangerous as they homes they left. They note that state intervention is often justified on the basis of "protecting children," hence the public is often not critical of the state. However, it is important to separate the interests of the state from the interests of the child. In the name of protecting the interests of children, child protective services actually protects the interests of the state in policing nonconforming families while doing little to monitor children in those families considered "respectable."

If the state is not the solution, it is critical for communities to develop active intervention strategies to keep children safe. They note that in a study conducted by the sexual abuse prevention organization Stop It NOW!, 75% of participants said they would confront someone who had been drinking and was about to drive, whereas only 9% reported that they would confront someone who was sexually abusing a child. Generation Five's work is focused on reversing this statistic to enable communities to intervene when abuse happens.

Its general principles are to:

- Promote survivor healing and agency.
- Promote offender accountability and transformation.
- Develop community response and accountability.
- Transform the community and social conditions that create and perpetuate child sexual abuse, i.e. systems of oppression, exploitation, domination, and state violence (Generation Five [n.d.-b]).

At one workshop, one such strategy was developed by elderly women in a senior housing project. The elders organized to monitor local playgrounds and other areas where children were playing. If they saw adults in engaging in abusive behavior toward children, they collectively confronted them about the abuse.

CONCLUSION

In seeking to develop strategies for ending violence that go beyond both traditional criminal justice and RJ models, many organizations recognize that ending violence requires societal transformation. Thus, any approach must be directly connected to political organizing strategies that seek to change the ways in which our society and our world is governed through domination, violence, and control. These approaches are varied, but they do share some principles:

- *First*: The work of ending violence must come from a political organizing rather than a social service model. Survivors must be seen as those who have the power to organize to end violence themselves. Healing services are critical, but they must be directly tied to political organizing. In addition, societal transformation requires that we engage in base-building—that is, not only working with activists who think like us, but recruiting people who are not already activists.
- *Second*: This work entails humility, experimentation, and sharing of stories and struggles. One of the negative impacts of the nonprofit industrial complex is that antiviolence programs often feel required to demonstrate that their programs are successful (whether or not they are) to ensure continued funding. Often, little space exists in which to share our failures because that might jeopardize funding. However, when it comes to community accountability, where groups are learning as they go, it is critical to have spaces where we simply try strategies and share what does not work, as much as we share what does work. Groups that do this do not position themselves as having the "correct" approach to ending violence, but rather as having a commitment to trying and often improvising strategies as they learn from others.
- *Third*: These groups generally understand that developing community accountability strategies that are socially transformative actually has radical implications because it shows the importance of developing alternative governing structures (both within our organizations and within the world) that are not based on violence, domination, and coercion. Thus, they must build groups that begin to model the world they want to live in now. It is difficult to tell other people in our

communities to be nonviolent if we cannot practice that in our own organization.

- *Fourth*: These groups recognize that all forms of violence are related. Any antiviolence struggle must be also part of a struggle against empire, against capital, against war, against all forms of oppression. They do not view domestic or sexual violence on a single-issue basis; they are committed to working in coalition with all social justice movements.

These models do not pretend to offer quick-fix "model programs" that work successfully all the time. Instead, they try to develop short-term strategies for protecting and supporting survivors of violence as they organize to end the societal structures that enable violence to happen in the first place. Thus, they seek not just to intervene after violence happens, but to create a world in which violence becomes unthinkable.

NOTE

1. Sources in this and the following example are from personal interviews or correspondence.

REFERENCES

Behrendt, Larissa. 2002. "Lessons from the Mediation Obsession: Ensuring that Sentencing 'Alternatives' Focus on Indigenous Self-Determination.'" Pp. 178–190 in *Restorative Justice and Family Violence*, edited by Heather Strang and John Braithwaite. Cambridge, UK: Cambridge University Press.

Bhattacharjee, Anannya. 2001. *Whose Safety? Women of Color and the Violence of Law Enforcement*. Philadelphia: American Friends Service Committee and the Committee on Women, Population, and the Environment.

Blagg, Harry. 2002. "Restorative Justice and Aboriginal Family Violence: Opening a Space for Healing." Pp. 191–205 in *Restorative Justice and Family Violence*, edited by Heather Strang and John Braithwaite. Cambridge, UK: Cambridge University Press.

Busch, Ruth. 2002. "Domestic Violence and Restorative Justice Initiatives: Who Pays If We Get It Wrong?" Pp. 223–248 in *Restorative Justice and Family Violence*, edited by Heather Strang and John Braithwaite. Cambridge, UK: Cambridge University Press.

Butterfield, Fox. 2000. "Study Shows a Racial Divide in Domestic Violence Cases." *New York Times* May 18:A16.

Cameron, Angela. 2006. "Stopping the Violence." *Theoretical Criminology* 10:49–66.

Communities Against Rape and Abuse (CARA). 2002. Critical Resistance Film Festival program book. Seattle, WA: CARA.

———, n.d. *Taking Risks: Implementing Grassroots Community Accountability Strategies*. Unpublished manuscript. Seattle, WA: CARA.

Cohen, Stanley. 1985. "Community Control: To Demystify or to Reaffirm?" Pp. 127–32 in *Abolitionism: Towards a Non-Repressive Approach to Crime,* edited by Herman Bianchi and Rene van Swaaningen. Amsterdam: Free University Press.

Coker, Donna. 2002. "Transformative Justice: Anti-Subordination Practices in Cases of Domestic Violence." Pp. 128–52 in *Restorative Justice and Family Violence,* edited by Heather Strang and John Braithwaite. Cambridge, UK: Cambridge University Press.

———. 2006. "Restorative Justice, Navajo Peacemaking and Domestic Violence." *Theoretical Criminology* 10:67–85.

Cook, Kimberly. 2006. "Doing Difference and Accountability in Restorative Justice Conferences." *Theoretical Criminology* 10:107–124.

Coulthard, Glen. 2007. "Indigenous Peoples and the 'Politics of Recognition' in Colonial Contexts." Paper presented at the Cultural Studies Now Conference, University of East London, London, England, July 22.

Crenshaw, Kimberlé Williams. 1991. "Mapping the Margins: Intersectionality, Identity Politics, and Violence Against Women of Color." *Stanford Law Review* 43:1241–1299.

Daly, Kathleen. 2002. "Sexual Assault and Restorative Justice." Pp. 62–88 in *Restorative Justice and Family Violence,* edited by Heather Strang and John Braithwaite. Cambridge, UK: Cambridge University Press.

Daly, Kathleen and Julie Stubbs. 2006. "Feminist Engagement with Restorative Justice." *Theoretical Criminology* 10:9–28.

Davis, Angela. 1981. *Women, Race, and Class.* New York: Vintage.

———. 2003. *Are Prisons Obsolete?* New York: Seven Stories Press.

Foucault, Michel. 1977. *Discipline and Punish.* New York: Vintage Books.

Freedman, Estelle. 1981. *Their Sisters' Keepers.* Ann Arbor: University of Michigan Press.

Generation Five. n.d.-a. "Politics and Principles: Our Politics." Retrieved January 8, 2008 (http://www.generationfive.org/index.asp?sec=3&pg=9).

———. n.d.-b. "Politics and Principles: Our Approach." Retrieved January 8, 2008 (http://www.generationfive.org/index.asp?sec=3&pg=48).

Goel, Rashmi. 2005. "Sita's Trousseau: Restorative Justice, Domestic Violence and South Asian Culture." *Violence Against Women* 11:639–665.

Grande, Sandy. 2004. *Red Pedagogy.* Lanham, MD: Rowman & Littlefield.

Herman, Judith. 2005. "Justice from the Victim's Perspective." *Violence Against Women* 11:571–602.

Hopkins, C. Quince and Mary Koss. 2005. "Incorporating Feminist Theory and Insights Into a Restorative Justice Response to Sex Offenses." *Violence Against Women* 11:693–723.

Hudson, Barbara. 2006. "Beyond White Man's Justice." *Theoretical Criminology* 10:29–47.

Incite!. 2003. *Incite! Women of Color Against Violence Community Accountability Principles/Concerns/Strategies/Models Working Document.* March 5. Retrieved February 26, 2009 (http://www.incite-national.org/index.php?s=93).

———. 2005. *Gender, Oppression, Abuse, Violence: Community Accountability within the People of Color Progressive Movement.* July. Retrieved February 26, 2009 (http://www.incite-national.org/index.php?s=94).

———, ed. 2006. *The Color of Violence: Violence Against Women of Color.* Cambridge, MA: South End Press.

————, ed. 2007. *The Revolution Will Not Be Funded: Beyond the Non-Profit Industria Complex.* Cambridge, MA: South End Press.

Kelly, Loretta. 2002. "Using Restorative Justice Principles to Address Family Violence in Aboriginal Communities." Pp. 206–222 in *Restorative Justice and Family Violence,* edited by Heather Strang and John Braithwaite. Cambridge, UK: Cambridge University Press.

Morris, Allison. 2002. "Children and Family Violence: Restorative Messages from New Zealand." Pp. 89–107 in *Restorative Justice and Family Violence,* edited by Heather Strang and John Braithwaite. Cambridge, UK: Cambridge University Press.

Nancarrow, Heather. 2006. "In Search of Justice for Domestic and Family Violence." *Theoretical Criminology* 10:87–106.

Ogletree Jr., Charles and Austin Sarat, eds. 2006. *From Lynching Mobs to the Killing State.* New York: New York University Press.

Ostrowski, Julie. 2004. "Race Versus Gender in the Court Room." *Africana.com.* Retrieved May 4, 2004 (http://www.africana.com/articles/daily/bw 20040504domestic.asp).

Pennell, Joan and Gale Burford. 2002. "Feminist Praxis: Making Family Group Conferencing Work." Pp. 108–127 in *Restorative Justice and Family Violence,* edited by Heather Strang and John Braithwaite. Cambridge, UK: Cambridge University Press.

Pharr, Suzanne. 2004. Plenary Address at The Revolution Will Not Be Funded conference, University of California, Santa Barbara, April 30.

Povinelli, Elizabeth. 2002. *The Cunning of Recognition.* Durham, NC: Duke University Press.

Pranis, Kay. 2002. "Restorative Values and Confronting Family Violence." Pp. 23–41 in *Restorative Justice and Family Violence,* edited by Heather Strang and John Braithwaite. Cambridge, UK: Cambridge University Press.

Richie, Beth. 2000. "Morning Plenary Session." Pp. 27–31 in *Color of Violence: Violence Against Women of Color Conference Summary.* Minneapolis, MN: Incite! Women of Color Against Violence.

Ross, Luana. 1998. *Inventing the Savage: The Social Construction of Native American Criminality.* Austin: University of Texas Press.

Ross, Rupert. 1997. *Returning to the Teachings.* London: Penguin.

Rotman, Edgardo. 1995. "The Failure of Reform." Pp. 149–77 in *The Oxford History of the Prison,* edited by Norval Morris and David Rothman. Oxford, UK: Oxford University Press.

Smith, Andrea. 2005. *Conquest: Sexual Violence and American Indian Genocide.* Cambridge, MA: South End Press.

Sokoloff, Natalie J. and Christina Pratt, eds. 2005. *Domestic Violence at the Margins: Readings on Race, Class, Gender, and Culture.* New Brunswick, NJ: Rutgers University Press.

Strang, Heather and John Braithwaite, eds. 2002. *Restorative Justice and Family Violence.* Cambridge, UK: Cambridge University Press.

Stubbs, Julie. 2002. "Domestic Violence and Women's Safety: Feminist Challenges to Restorative Justice." Pp. 42–61 in *Restorative Justice and Family Violence,* edited by Heather Strang and John Braithwaite. Cambridge, UK: Cambridge University Press.

White, Janelle. 2004. "Our Silence Will Not Protect Us: Black Women Confronting Sexual and Domestic Violence." PhD. dissertation, Department of Sociology, University of Michigan, Ann Arbor, MI.

Zedner, Lucia. 1995. "Wayward Sisters: The Prison for Women." Pp. 295–324 in *The Oxford History of the Prison,* edited by Norval Morris and David Rothman. Oxford, UK: Oxford University Press.

Zion, James, and Elsie B. Zion. 1996. "'Hazho's Sokee'—Stay Together Nicely: Domestic Violence Under Navajo Common Law." Pp. 96–113 in *Native Americans, Crime, and Justice,* edited by Marianne Nielsen and Robert Silverman. Boulder, CO: WestView Press.

IV

CONCLUSION

13

RE-IMAGINING JUSTICE FOR CRIMES OF VIOLENCE AGAINST WOMEN

JAMES PTACEK

The contributors to this book seek to expand the ways that survivors might experience justice. Each author has engaged with the problem of violence against women over a considerable period of time. The work the authors have done on violence includes community organizing, shelter and rape crisis work, legal advocacy, batterer's counseling, institutional reform, and research. Every contributor sees profound limitations to the responses of the criminal legal system. They voice concerns about how state responses have co-opted feminist activism and distorted its visions of justice. But while the authors have much in common, they illustrate that there is no unified feminist perspective on how to counteract violence against women. They assess the potential of restorative justice (RJ) differently, and they offer an array of strategies for revitalizing antiviolence work.

RETHINKING THE MEANINGS OF JUSTICE AND RESTORATION

If a common theme runs beneath all the different meanings given to "justice" and "restoration" in this collection, it is that for survivors of violence against women, a vision of justice must encompass the complex political dimensions that contribute to their silencing and isolation. Writing about practices for Indigenous women in Canada, Australia, and the United States, a number of the contributors describe cross-cutting pressures that pit community needs against personal survival needs. Violence against women is exacerbated by racism, colonialism, poverty, heterosexism, and illegal immigration status, and community responses must be crafted with an understanding of the multiple social injustices that confront survivors. A way to map these dimensions of inequality is offered in a recent article by Kathleen Daly (2008), where she speaks of an "intersectional politics of justice." She defines this as "the conflicting interests of victims and offenders, social movement groups, and individuals and collectivities in responding to crime" (p. 7). Intersectional thinking is required to address the many ways through which the complex politics of race and gender shape the experience of justice.

The ways that "restoration" is reworked by contributors further connects personal needs with broader issues of social justice. Loretta Frederick and Kristine Lizdas propose that restorative practices must be effective, redemptive, and liberating; they must break survivors out of the domination and control of offenders. Pamela Rubin reports that abused women redefined "restoration" to include meeting their needs for safety and economic assistance, and at the same time challenging systemic discrimination.

WHERE DOES JUSTICE HAPPEN? SEARCHING INSIDE AND OUTSIDE THE "JUSTICE ROOM"

These observations raise another question about the meaning of justice: If justice is, among other things, an experience, then where exactly does justice happen? In Chapter 7, Kathleen Daly and Heather Nancarrow talk about addressing family violence in the "justice room," and contrast this with how it is approached in the "therapy room," in order to distinguish the different resources and expectations each brings with it. The term "justice room" can also highlight something else—the question of where exactly justice happens. A distinction can be made between the dialogue that takes place in a restorative practice on the one hand, and the many interactions that precede and follow that encounter: the preparation, the supervision and evaluation, the relationships with informal social networks, the connections with community resources, and the offender's compliance with the agreement. Within standard RJ practices, the most powerful justice remedy lies in the victim–offender encounter in the "justice room." But for many of the contributors to this book, whether critical or supportive of RJ, great emphasis is placed on what takes place outside of the "justice room." To put it another way, in cases of violence against women, the ability of an encounter to create justice may depend upon matters that lie outside the "justice room."

Daly and Nancarrow state that the difference between the type of conferencing they studied in Australia and the models designed by Pennell lies in time and resources. In the family group conferences on youth violence against mothers, Daly and Nancarrow observe that there were limited offerings for offenders, and little available to victims in this process. If the RJ program was overmatched by the problems before it, the authors note that these issues are also poorly addressed by the existing criminal legal system. This leads Daly and Nancarrow to question whether *any* justice practice can deal effectively with such deep and complex issues of family violence.

For crimes of youth violence against mothers, intimate partner violence, child abuse, and sexual assault, the contributors sketch an image of where justice lies different from that of previous restorative models. The best way forward may be to see a justice practice as a starting point, a gateway to support, therapy, and economic resources, rather than as an endpoint. This is what Pennell emphasizes when she says that her model of family group conferencing serves as a planning forum, not as mediation, not as therapy in itself. The most powerful justice remedies in this view lie outside of the "justice room," and the goal is to mobilize them for victims and offenders.

Seen in this light, some of the most impressive aspects of the projects by Joan Pennell, Mimi Kim, Mary Koss, and Shirley Jülich lie in the painstaking community work that went into their creation, work that is essential to the fulfillment of the practices. To develop her model in Canada, Pennell and her colleague Gale Burford brought together women's organizations, child advocates, programs for offenders, justice officials, and university researchers. In her safety conferencing project in North Carolina, she involved these same kinds of organizations along with the North Carolina Coalition Against Domestic Violence and included focus group interviews with shelter residents. To create RESTORE, Koss drew upon RJ practitioners, justice officials, women's antiviolence organizations, victim advocates, therapists working with sex offenders, members of diverse ethnic groups, and lesbian, gay, bisexual, and trans-gender (LGBT) activists. Jülich describes how Project Restore-NZ was founded by community groups working with victims of sexual assault and with child sexual abusers. And Kim details the ongoing collaboration between Creative Interventions and a number of domestic violence and sexual assault programs working with Asian American and Pacific Islander communities in the San Francisco Bay area. These approaches represent ways of building the needs of survivors into the models, addressing the multiple inequalities faced by survivors, mobilizing essential resources, creating advisory boards, and making the projects accountable to their communities.

RECOMMENDATIONS FOR JUSTICE PRACTICES ADDRESSING VIOLENCE AGAINST WOMEN

Proceed with Caution: The Importance of Screening for Abuse

An understanding of the invisible, traumatic consequences of violence and abuse is essential to any work with victims and offenders (Bryant-Davis 2008; Cheon and Regehr 2006; Herman 1992). Without this background, the thoughts, feelings, and behaviors of survivors, and the impact that offenders have upon them, will be misperceived. It is also necessary to know that it is very common for child abuse and intimate partner violence to occur within the same families (Edleson 1999; Renner and Slack 2006; Zolotor et al. 2007). Thus, abuse issues should be a background consideration for all justice practices with women, youth, and families; some means of screening for abuse should always be in place; and programs should be prepared to act upon information obtained from this screening.

Screening enables programs to address safety issues, offer support, and link victims to important community resources that address legal, health, psychological, and economic needs. Without screening, it is impossible to assess the risks individuals face; it is difficult to see what problems are really present in people's lives. In a recent study, Clemants and Gross (2007) surveyed 94 community mediation programs in the United States and Canada that indicated they mediated cases involving intimate partners. Asked if they would mediate cases with a history of domestic violence, 35% of the programs said they would not; 12% said they would accept such cases; 11% stated this was the victim's choice; and 20% said they made decisions on a case-by-case basis. Leaving aside the policy differences among the programs, what was most revealing was the gap between policy and practice. The authors stated that "fewer than half of the centers employed formal screening or training for their staff and members" (p. 428). Thus, many of these programs didn't know whether they were following their own policies concerning cases of domestic violence. In Chapter 1, it was pointed out that community mediation is viewed by many as lying outside the definition of RJ. Nonetheless, this study indicates how frequently justice programs miss seeing the reality of violence against women and children, and thus miss the opportunity to do something about it.

Build Collaborations Between Advocates and Researchers

It is important that feminist activists and scholars "think big" and take leadership in creating new ways for survivors to find justice. But, given the risks and uncertainties in new approaches, activists and scholars must work together. In the United States, feminist antiviolence organizations at the national, state, and local level might consider opening conversations about new justice practices, and including in these conversations the kind of skeptics and innovators represented in this book. If antiviolence organizations sponsor and support funding for new justice projects, this will ensure that the needs of survivors are prioritized. The feminist model of advocate–researcher collaborations recommended by Edleson and Bible (2001) and Williams (2004) offers a way of bringing the insights of advocates and survivors into new antiviolence projects. This is already illustrated in the collaborative work on RJ undertaken by Curtis-Fawley and Daly (2005), Daly and Nancarrow (Chapter 7), Koss and Achilles (2008), Pennell and Francis (2005), and Ptacek and Frederick (2009).

Make New Justice Practices Accountable

The surprising lack of research on existing RJ applications to violence against women was noted in Chapter 1. Restorative and feminist/

restorative hybrids must be regarded as emerging applications that need to be evaluated for both their short- and long-term effects. There are many different ways to evaluate whether antiviolence interventions are safe, effective, and responsive to the needs of their communities, a number of which are referred to in this book. In addition to these, Pennell and Anderson (2005) give an extensive outline of how programs can evaluate the long- and short-term outcomes of family group conferencing. Mary Achilles, a victim advocate, and the RJ theorist and trainer Howard Zehr developed guidelines for assessing whether victims are truly involved in a justice practice (Achilles and Zehr 2001). More in-depth, long-term research is needed on the effects of RJ on victims and offenders generally, research that goes beyond immediate satisfaction with a justice encounter (Stubbs 2004). Herman's (2005) work on justice from the victim's perspective is instructive in this regard. Another useful direction may lie in the research by Dobash and colleagues (1999) on changes in the "quality of life" of both victims and offenders following an antiviolence intervention.

CONCLUSION

None of the contributors to this book claims that standard models of restorative practice are adequate for crimes against women, that they can be "taken off the shelf" and produce justice. Many restorative practitioners have raised cautions about this themselves (Pranis 2002; Umbreit, Vos, and Coates 2005; Zehr 2002). But many of the authors here see great potential for combining elements of RJ with feminist antiviolence approaches.

It is hoped that, when considered together, these different perspectives might inspire new thinking, new research, new ways to create justice for victims, offenders, and their communities, and new forms of social action against violence.

REFERENCES

Achilles, Mary and Howard Zehr. 2001. "Restorative Justice for Crime Victims: The Promise and the Challenge." Pp. 87–99 in *Restorative Community Justice: Repairing Harm and Transforming Communities,* edited by Gordon Bazemore and Mara Schiff. Cincinnati, OH: Anderson.
Bryant-Davis, Thema. 2008. *Thriving in the Wake of Trauma: A Multicultural Guide.* Lanham, MD: AltaMira Press.
Cheon, Aileen and Cheryl Regehr. 2006. "Restorative Models in Cases of Intimate Partner Violence: Reviewing the Evidence." *Victims and Offenders* 1:369–394.
Clemants, Elizabeth and Alan Gross. 2007. " 'Why Aren't We Screening?' A Survey Examining Domestic Violence Screening Procedures and Training Protocol in Community Mediation Centers." *Conflict Resolution Quarterly* 24:413–431.
Curtis-Fawley, Sarah and Kathleen Daly. 2005. "Gendered Violence and Restorative Justice: The Views of Victim Advocates." *Violence Against Women* 11:603–638.

Daly, Kathleen. 2008. "Seeking Justice in the 21st Century: Towards an Intersectional Politics of Justice." Pp. 3–30 in *Restorative Justice: From Theory to Practice* (Sociology of Crime, Law, and Deviance Series, Vol. 11). Amsterdam: Elsevier.

Dobash, Rebecca Emerson, Russell P. Dobash, Kate Cavanagh, and Ruth Lewis. 1999. *Changing Violent Men*. Thousand Oaks, CA: Sage.

Edleson, Jeffrey L. 1999. *The Overlap Between Child Maltreatment and Woman Abuse*. Harrisburg, PA: VAWnet, a project of the National Resource Center on Domestic Violence/Pennsylvania Coalition Against Domestic Violence. Retrieved February 16, 2009 (http://www.vawnet.org).

Edleson, Jeffrey L. and Andrea L. Bible. 2001. "Collaborating for Women's Safety: Partnerships Between Research and Practice." Pp. 73–95 in *Sourcebook on Violence Against Women*, edited by Claire Renzetti, Jeffrey L. Edleson, and Raquel K. Bergen. Thousand Oaks, CA: Sage.

Herman, Judith L. 1992. Trauma and Recovery. New York: Basic Books.

———. 2005. "Justice from the Victim's Perspective." *Violence Against Women* 11:571–602.

Koss, Mary P. and Mary Achilles. 2008. *Restorative Justice Approaches to Sexual Violence*. Harrisburg, PA: VAWnet, a project of the National Resource Center on Domestic Violence/Pennsylvania Coalition Against Domestic Violence. Retrieved February 16, 2009 (http://www.vawnet.org).

Pennell, Joan and Gary Anderson (eds.). 2005. *Widening the Circle: The Practice and Evaluation of Family Group Conferencing with Children, Youths, and Their Families*. Washington, DC: NASW Press.

Pennell, Joan and Stephanie Francis. 2005. "Safety Conferencing: Toward a Coordinated and Inclusive Response to Safeguard Women and Children." *Violence Against Women* 11:666–692.

Pranis, K. (2002). "Restorative Values and Confronting Family Violence." Pp. 23–41 in *Restorative Justice and Family Violence,* edited by Heather Strang and John Braithwaite. Cambridge, UK: Cambridge University Press.

Ptacek, James and Loretta L. Frederick. 2009. *Restorative Justice and Intimate Partner Violence*. Harrisburg, PA: VAWnet, a project of the National Resource Center on Domestic Violence/Pennsylvania Coalition Against Domestic Violence. Retrieved February 16, 2009 (http://www.vawnet.org).

Renner, Lynette M. and Kristen Shook Slack. 2006. "Intimate Partner Violence and Child Maltreatment: Understanding Intra- and Intergenerational Connections." *Child Abuse & Neglect* 30:599–617.

Stubbs, Julie. 2004. "Restorative Justice, Domestic Violence, and Family Violence." *Australian Domestic & Family Violence Clearinghouse* Issues Paper 9:1–23.

Umbreit, Mark S., Betty Vos, and Robert Coates. 2005. *Opportunities and Pitfalls Facing the Restorative Justice Movement*. Center for Restorative Justice & Peacemaking. Retrieved June 9, 2007 (http://rjp.umn.edu).

Williams, Linda M. 2004. "Researcher-Advocate Collaborations to End Violence Against Women: Toward Liberating Methodologies for Action Research." *Journal of Interpersonal Violence* 19:1350–1357.

Zehr, H. 2002. *The Little Book of Restorative Justice*. Intercourse, PA: Good Books.

Zolotor, Adam J., Adrea D. Theodore, Tamera Coyne-Beasley, and Desmond K. Runyan. 2007. "Intimate Partner Violence and Child Maltreatment: Overlapping Risk." *Brief Treatment and Crisis Intervention* 7:305–321.

INDEX